the Encyclopedia of
SMALL BUSINESS
RESOURCES

the Encyclopedia of
SMALL BUSINESS
RESOURCES

DAVID E. GUMPERT &
JEFFRY A. TIMMONS

HARPER COLOPHON BOOKS
Harper & Row, Publishers
New York, Cambridge, Philadelphia, San Francisco,
London, Mexico City, São Paulo, Sydney

This work was published in a hardcover edition by Doubleday & Company, Inc. under the title *The Insider's Guide to Small Business Resources*. It is here reprinted by arrangement.

THE ENCYCLOPEDIA OF SMALL BUSINESS RESOURCES. Copyright © 1982 by David E. Gumpert and Jeffry A. Timmons. All rights reserved. Printed in the United States of America. No part of this book may be used or reproduced in any manner whatsoever without written permission except in the case of brief quotations embodied in critical articles and reviews. For information address Harper & Row, Publishers, Inc., 10 East 53rd Street, New York, N.Y. 10022. Published simultaneously in Canada by Fitzhenry & Whiteside Limited, Toronto.

ISBN: 0-06-091111-5
LIBRARY OF CONGRESS CATALOG CARD NUMBER: 83-48350
First HARPER COLOPHON edition published 1984

84 85 86 87 88   10 9 8 7 6 5 4 3 2 1

For
Jean, Jason, and Laura
and
Jesseca and Samantha

Preface

This book started from much the same premise as many new businesses: the authors saw a need that wasn't being filled and attempted to fill it.

The need we have attempted to fill is to assemble in one place information that can enable entrepreneurs to intelligently examine their business options so as to improve their chances of success.

The book stems in large part from a seeming contradiction concerning the availability of resources for entrepreneurs; the contradiction became apparent to us in the course of our professional work in business journalism and education. On the one hand, there was an abundance of places entrepreneurs could turn to for such assistance as business training and financing. On the other hand, many entrepreneurs were unaware of these resources.

That contradiction troubled us because we know from our experience that managers of both large and small companies face endless questions requiring expert information. For instance, who can help evaluate a new business idea? What potential sources exist for financing a new manufacturing plant or expanding an existing one? Which U.S. government agencies are buying what products? How does one go about choosing a franchise or selling products overseas?

For the nation's 1,000 or so largest corporations, finding the answers to those and countless other informational questions is no problem. The executives who must answer such questions may not know the answers themselves, but they have people they can turn to for quick information. Their marketing executives can evaluate new business areas. Their investment bankers can provide ready rundowns of all potential financing sources appropriate for projects under consideration. Their Washington office representatives can keep a constant lookout for new sales opportunities to federal agencies. Their legal staffs can help evaluate franchising decisions, and their international groups can research overseas sales opportunities and report on the best possibilities.

But the individual entrepreneur has no such internal resources. Starting and operating a company is an all-encompassing task which leaves little time for a normal family life, let alone doing the reading and making the telephone calls necessary to obtain information needed to make sound business decisions.

Yet an entrepreneur who doesn't know what his or her options are is operating at a serious competitive disadvantage. It's one thing to make an incorrect decision, but quite another to make an uninformed decision. Mistakes are inevitable and a part of the learning process, but decisions made out of ignorance can be disastrous, and are avoidable.

As we noted previously, substantial resources exist to aid small businesses. Many organizations offer seminars, courses, and counseling services designed to provide management training. Billions of dollars in publicly and privately sponsored funds are available for small-business loans and investments. Special management training and financing opportunities exist for racial minorities and women who wish to start or expand businesses. Public and private agencies stand ready to help small companies exploit overseas business opportunities. The federal government is actively attempting to boost by billions of dollars the amounts of goods and services it purchases from small companies. Franchising offers exciting new business opportunities.

The primary difficulty facing entrepreneurs who attempt to use these resources is that they are literally scattered around the country. Nowhere have they been listed and described in a comprehensive and organized way.

Countless books offer advice on how to start and manage businesses. And a few books provide information on specific but relatively narrow areas of interest to entrepreneurs, such as listings of financing or venture-capital resources. But none have attempted to examine the overall informational needs of entrepreneurs and seek out the specific sources to fill those needs.

This book, in attempting to fill that void, is intended as more than a listing of sources. Within each chapter, background and assessments are offered of the subject covered. Thus, the chapter on educational resources contains an explanation of recent trends in entrepreneurial education, and the chapter on commercial financing sources attempts to explain the pros and cons of various types of financing. The idea is to explain not only what's available, but to offer insights about the quality and effectiveness of what's available.

Researching this book confirmed the existence of many more sources of potential assistance than we originally expected. Take the area of management training and assistance, for example. It turns out that several hundred colleges and universities around the country offer courses on starting and operating small businesses. Similarly, there are thousands of management consultants available to help small businesses solve financial and other business problems.

Needless to say, we spent some very busy months. Because of our professional positions, we are on the mailing lists of dozens of government and private organizations engaged in small-business assistance activities. While that helped get us started in our research, we had much more to do. We assembled hundreds of business magazine and newspaper articles for leads. With the help of several committed researchers (see acknowledgments) we followed up our leads with hundreds of telephone calls to potential small-business sources.

Because tracking down every single source of potential assistance to entrepreneurs is nearly impossible, we made an early decision to place some limits on our search. We decided to concentrate our efforts on identifying and describing those sources that fell into these three broad categories:

1. Those likeliest to be of assistance to large numbers of entrepreneurs;

2. Those likeliest to be in a position to recommend other valuable sources;

3. Those illustrative of the kinds of sources available.

The idea was to make this book a practical starting point for entrepreneurs seeking to learn their business options. With only a few exceptions, the sources we contacted were quite cooperative and many expressed interest in and encouragement for our project. Some even went beyond the call of duty and supplied leads to additional valuable sources.

Not surprisingly, we ran into some roadblocks. For instance, several management consultants whom we knew to have small-business clients requested they not be listed in this book because small businesses represented only a temporary market for them; they aspired to work with large corporations and feared that being pegged as small-business specialists would make corporations leery of them.

And several other sources, including both public and private organizations, were uncooperative in various ways. In some cases, we were unable to reach a person in a position of responsibility, despite repeated attempts. In other cases, bureaucratic regulations or perhaps just indifference prevented cooperation.

We managed to overcome most of these difficulties. When particular sources proved uncooperative, we usually obtained the information we needed from other sources. And we used some of our experiences as the basis from which to point out deficiencies in some sources.

While such experiences made our task more difficult, they also reminded us of the problems individual entrepreneurs face when they start from scratch to research their options. Thus, these experiences served to reinforce our feeling that this kind of book can serve an important function.

We feel satisfied that we accomplished our basic purpose of providing a comprehensive source guide for entrepreneurs. If it makes entrepreneurs aware of specific options they wouldn't otherwise have known about, then it is doing its job.

Acknowledgments

A book of this nature cannot happen without behind-the-scenes assistance and guidance. We were extremely fortunate to have had the help of many dedicated individuals—researchers, editorial assistants, and professionals with expertise in various small-business areas.

Researching the small-business sources which comprise the bulk of the book required endless phone calls and tedious library work. The largest single research load fell on Linda Marcellino, an MBA candidate at Northeastern University in Boston, who assembled information that made seven of the twelve chapters possible. The job consumed most of the summer and fall of 1980, sometimes to the detriment of her personal and academic lives.

Valuable research assistance was also provided by several others. Jeffrey Goodman, an MBA candidate at Northeastern University, assembled the material necessary for two chapters. Geraldine Willigan, an editorial assistant at the *Harvard Business Review,* researched one chapter, and Mary Ellen Durning, an MBA candidate at Northeastern University, helped fill in research gaps in several chapters. Cindy Shaw, a *Harvard Business Review* editorial assistant, was most helpful in assembling articles and news clippings vital for most chapters.

The bulk of the typing and manuscript preparation assistance was done by Jane Wilson, whose heroic efforts enabled us to meet our publishing deadlines. Marsha Hamilton and Leonore Gumpert provided important typing and manuscript assistance as well. We also received very worthwhile editorial inputs and advice from Wendy J. Federschneider, a freelance Boston editor, and Millicent Kindle, a manuscript editor at the *Harvard Business Review.*

A number of people who work closely with entrepreneurs were especially generous to us with their time and guidance. They included the following: Lewis Shattuck, executive director of the Smaller Business Association of New England; Stanley Pratt, president of Capital Publishing Corp. and editor and publisher of *Venture Capital Journal;* Richard America and Jerry Feigan of the Small Business Administration; Joseph P. Furber, president of the American Industrial Development Council; Samuel Beard, president of the National Development Council; James Molloy, a professor at Northeastern University; Karl Vesper, a professor at the University of Washington; Edward Shils, a professor at the University of Pennsylvania's Wharton School of Business; Donald Sexton, a professor at Baylor University's Center for Entrepreneurship; T. Lincoln Morison, a senior vice president at the First National Bank of Boston; John Brasch, a professor at the University of Nebraska; Gilbert Weinstein of the National Association of Export Management Companies; Nancy A. Rathbun, director of publications and public relations at the International Franchise Association; Martin Boehm, public relations coordinator at the International Franchise Association; Robert I. Goldman, president of Congress Financial Corp.; Gene VanArsdale, principal of VanArsdale Associates; Frank Hoy and Larry Bramblett of the University of Georgia; John Welsh, a professor at Southern Methodist University's Caruth Institute; Brian Haslett, managing director of Venture Founders Ltd. of England; and Jerry Goldstein, publisher of *In Business* magazine.

Many officials of organizations and businesses which serve small businesses were also very cooperative and helpful to us. The organizations and businesses include the Small Business Administration, the National Association of Small Business Investment Companies, the National Venture Capital Association, the National Science Foundation, and *Consultants News*. We should add a general thank you to the hundreds of other consultants, bankers, venture capitalists, trade group officials, university professors, and others who accepted our phone calls and generously gave of their time to answer our many questions.

We also owe special thanks to Kenneth R. Andrews, editor of the *Harvard Business Review,* as well as a number of the overseers of Northeastern University's College of Business Administration, including Dean David Blake, Associate Dean Thomas Moore, Professor Richard B. Higgins, and former Dean Phillip McDonald, for providing support, encouragement, and vital resources necessary to research and write this book.

Contents

xiv

Using This Book

We have attempted to make this book as easy to use as possible, given the varying needs of entrepreneurs and the varying services performed by different sources.

To assist entrepreneurs in quickly identifying sources near to them geographically, we have within the index at the end of the book sources within every state. Thus, readers can quickly determine the pages on which we describe sources for each of the fifty states.

To accommodate the frequently different needs and concerns of entrepreneurs just starting or acquiring businesses for the first time, and those operating well-established businesses, we have divided several chapters into two sections—one for start-up businesses and one for existing businesses. Not all the chapters break down that neatly, but even when they don't, we indicate within the chapters how start-up and existing businesses can best use the sources described.

Finally, to handle the problem of sources being appropriate to more than one chapter, we made heavy use of cross-references and assembled a thorough index. These approaches solve, at least partially, dilemmas such as deciding whether to include an organization for black women entrepreneurs in the chapter on sources for women or the chapter on sources for minorities. Nonetheless, we recommend that entrepreneurs whose circumstances or situation are appropriate to sources in several chapters examine all those chapters.

A New Age of Entrepreneurship?

"The role of small business in our economy is declining at an alarming rate," warned a U. S. House of Representatives subcommittee in a 1978 report entitled "Future of Small Business in America." The report, based on testimony from politicians, bureaucrats, and small-business organization representatives, added,

> As the number of small businesses in industries declines and the concentration ratios increase, the continuing viability of small firms is severely threatened . . . A decision must be made: do the American people wish to preserve the foundations upon which our nation was built or do they wish to acquiesce to the gradual spread of a system alien to the American spirit, a system of economic oligarchy?

But the entrepreneurial dream doesn't die easily. Our experience researching this book has convinced us that not only is the entrepreneurial dream a persistent one, but that it is more alive today than that 1978 report ever could have expected.

A number of important political and sociological developments occurring nearly simultaneously have given entrepreneurship a strong boost. The end result could be to make the entrepreneur a folk hero of the 1980s, akin to student activists in the 1960s and long-distance truck drivers in the 1970s.

Politically, concern about the declining growth of American productivity and an apparent deterioration of industrial innovation, compared with some European countries and Japan, has helped focus attention on small business. That is because small businesses tend to be more productive and innovative than large corporations.

The political concern has resulted in several steps designed to aid small businesses and focus attention on their problems. For instance, there have been some reductions in government regulations, which are generally acknowledged to hurt small businesses the most. Deregulation of the airline industry has already allowed a number of small airlines to compete effectively with large established carriers. Also, a reduction of the capital gains tax in 1981 to a maximum of 20 percent versus the maximum of 49 percent three years previously has encouraged more investment in small companies.

In addition, federal financing and other assistance potentially available to small businesses has grown substantially in scope. Even allowing for recent cutbacks encouraged by the Reagan administration, the federal effort will remain impressive.

Efforts to promote small-business interests are taking place at the state level as well. More than half the states now have some sort of program to provide business training, financing, or other forms of assistance to entrepreneurs; few states had such programs a decade earlier.

The political efforts seem likely to continue. The White House Conference on Small Business, which was held in early 1980, did much to focus political attention on the problems entrepreneurs face in dealing with the federal government. We relied extensively on reports prepared for the conference to provide entrepreneurs with background on federal programs to aid small businesses. Committees established by the conference to follow up on its proposals should continue focusing attention on efforts to solve small-business problems.

Sociologically as well, entrepreneurship appears to have become a steadily more attractive idea in recent years. The change in attitudes seems to stem partly from disillusionment with the conformist approaches of large corporations and partly from growing appreciation of the "small is beautiful" concept.

Thus, a *Fortune* magazine evaluation in the April 7, 1980, issue on the attitudes of 25-year-olds starting in the business world noted ". . . a significant proportion of the men are planning to leave corporate life when they are in their thirties to start their own businesses," partly because entrepreneurship allows "the freedom to control one's own destiny."

And 1960s Yippie Jerry Rubin wrote in a July 30, 1980, New York *Times* article explaining his new job as a Wall Street securities analyst in charge of identifying promising small companies,

> The challenge for American capitalism in the 80's is to bring the entrepreneurial spirit back to America. The large organizations have discouraged people's expression and ambition. America needs a revitalization of the small-business spirit.

The changing popular attitudes toward entrepreneurship have expressed themselves in a variety of developments favorable to small businesses, among them the following:

• The number of colleges and universities offering courses on starting and operating small businesses has grown to several hundred from only a handful in 1970.

• Various commercial loan sources, among them insurance and factoring companies, have committed themselves to significantly increasing the amounts they loan to small companies.

• Private venture-capital firms, an important source of investment for young companies with promising growth potential, have become more active in their financial commitments than at any time since the late 1960s.

• Sources of financing and managerial assistance for businesses owned by racial minorities have matured since the sources were started in the late 1960s and early 1970s. As a consequence, minority entrepreneurs can expect these resources to be increasingly professional and savvy.

• The number of women's organizations devoted to advancing the interests of women entrepreneurs has proliferated in recent years. Women seeking to start businesses or who already own businesses can thus turn to other women for management assistance and moral support.

• Organizations that lobby and provide various business services for small businesses in general have grown in stature and numbers during the late 1970s and early 1980s.

• Franchising has become an area of growing opportunities, both for would-be entrepreneurs and those who already own businesses. Moreover, state and federal laws have reduced fraud and other risks which once plagued franchising.

• The information sources available to entrepreneurs have increased substantially, with the start-ups in 1979 and after of several magazines devoted exclusively to the interests of would-be and existing entrepreneurs. Among these magazines are *INC.*, *Venture*, and *In Business*. And several major publications identified as catering mainly to large corporations have started special small-business columns and features. These publications include *The Wall Street Journal* and *Harvard Business Review*.

The growing attraction of entrepreneurship is reinforced by statistics, which show significant increases in recent years in the number of new businesses being started. The number of new business incorporations as recorded by Dun & Bradstreet had risen to more than 500,000 annually by 1980, from 220,000 in 1975.

There is, of course, a gloomy side to the entrepreneurship picture. Though no one knows for sure how many new small businesses succeed and fail, government and private business observers estimate that approximately three fourths of all new businesses fail within their first five years. Moreover, existence of high-level interest rates on what appears to be a permanent basis has increased the risks for small businesses, since most rely heavily on borrowed funds.

Even assuming such pessimistic estimates of small-business failures are accurate, they don't necessarily have to keep occurring at the same rate in the future. Various business observers tend to ascribe the high failure rate to inadequate managerial preparation rather than to inadequate financing. But assorted studies have suggested that entrepreneurs who have received business management training or had business operating experience do not have nearly the same dismal failure records.

The rapid expansion of resources available to train and otherwise assist entrepreneurs, then, should not only increase the number of people who aspire to become business owners, but should increase their chances of succeeding as well.

Sizable increases both in the number of new business start-ups and in their chances of success could also have significant economic repercussions. Well-publicized research carried out by David L. Birch, a professor at the Massachusetts Institute of Technology, has shown that businesses with twenty or fewer employees created nearly two thirds of all new jobs generated in the United States between 1969 and 1976. Thus, the benefits accruing both to entrepreneurs and the American economy as a whole from expanding new business activity could create a snowball effect that opens constantly expanding opportunities for entrepreneurs.

Certainly there is no dearth of opportunities for aspiring entrepreneurs. The nation's pressing need for alternative energy sources seems certain to create new business demands. The developing electronics revolution has already enabled hundreds of small businesses to start and prosper and seems likely to open additional opportunities in the future. Another kind of revolution has started in the area of microbiology, with advances in gene-splicing for the purposes of creating medicines and other valuable products; the new business opportunities will no doubt be significant. As we have already noted, more mundane areas like franchising offer a variety of opportunities for entrepreneurs. And the list goes on and on.

The chapters that follow are intended to assist entrepreneurs in understanding and using the tools available for exploiting opportunities we see developing for small businesses. Ideally, this book will be part of the new age of entrepreneurship.

the Encyclopedia of
SMALL BUSINESS
RESOURCES

CHAPTER 1

Education and Training Sources

INTRODUCTION: TEACHING SUCCESS

Are successful entrepreneurs born or made? Can the factors necessary for success in small enterprises be learned?

These questions have for years sparked hot debate in the academic community. Until recently, many academicians argued that if individuals were not born with entrepreneurial qualities or did not acquire them through an apprenticeship with the family business, little hope remained of becoming a successful entrepreneur.

While the debate continues—and may never be resolved—there is a growing feeling among small-business researchers and academics that certain aspects of entrepreneurship can be learned. Contributing to the shift in attitudes is increasingly widespread acceptance of the notion that most small businesses fail because of poor management. Inadequate management can include deficiencies in planning, controls, and accounting methods along with the inability to analyze financial statements and locate expert advice when needed. Solutions to all these problems require skills that can be learned.

Some academicians also feel they can be helpful in motivating and directing individuals with business aptitudes to exploit their talents. "A professor's role is to ignite the entrepreneurial spirit," says Albert Shapero, professor of private enterprise at Ohio State University.

Evidence of the shift in academic opinion can be seen most dramatically in the explosion during the 1970s in the availability of courses, seminars, and training programs designed to assist would-be and operating entrepreneurs. As recently as 1969, fewer than ten colleges and universities in the United States offered courses dealing with entrepreneurship, according to Karl Vesper, a professor of business administration at the University of Washington in Seattle, who has conducted surveys of such courses. By 1980, he had identified more than 200 colleges and universities offering entrepreneurship courses; their enrollments exceeded 4,000.

In addition, 485 colleges and universities involve 8,000 undergraduate students annually in the federally supported Small Business Institute Program, which allows students to add to their knowledge of small-business management techniques by assisting small-business owners in solving common business problems. More than 200 two-year community colleges offer small-business courses as well.

And dozens of other profit and nonprofit organizations offer nondegree courses, seminars, and workshops for would-be and existing entrepreneurs.

START-UP OPTIONS

Programs for would-be entrepreneurs tend to break down into two categories. The university degree programs are one category and they are mainly suited for college students interested in running their own businesses after graduation. Normal admission requirements must be met for such programs and the usual degree tuition fees apply—ranging from several hundred dollars annually at inexpensive state universities to between $4,000 and $6,000 annually at well-known private universities.

Nondegree seminars and workshops are a second category of programs that are best suited for adults who may have college degrees in nonbusiness areas. Individuals with limited business knowledge can often benefit from Small Business Administration (SBA) workshops and community college courses as well as an array of other privately sponsored programs. Such training can range in cost from nothing to several hundred dollars for short workshops. All of these options and potential sources are described in more detail later in this chapter.

Courses and seminars for would-be entrepreneurs typically consider two broad areas. First, they attempt to encourage participants to examine whether entrepreneurship is the best career for them. The instructors may point out the skills required, the risks and rewards involved, and which types of businesses are likely to be best suited for which kinds of people.

Second, the courses and seminars usually focus on important start-up skills that can be learned. These skills include the following: preparing a business plan; determining sources and amounts required for start-up capital; understanding cash-flow requirements and break-even points; analyzing business locations; and instituting credit policies.

EXISTING-BUSINESS OPTIONS

Small-business owners who have no formal business training but who are looking to improve their business skills can choose from a wide variety of nondegree courses, workshops, and seminars. Some are offered by the SBA, and a number of universities with degree programs offer nondegree night courses for business owners. Various profit and nonprofit organizations, including some which have programs for start-up entrepreneurs, offer programs for small-business owners.

The programs vary widely in cost. Government programs are free and many college night courses involve only nominal fees. But private programs can cost several hundred dollars for a weekend on up to several thousand dollars for live-in programs that last a few weeks.

The programs usually cover a wide variety of skills necessary for running ongoing businesses, including the following: obtaining financing; developing marketing strategies; delegating responsibility; setting up accounting and bookkeeping systems; evaluating data-processing needs; setting up boards of directors; avoiding labor unions; exploiting banking and investment relationships; and establishing inventory control systems.

The idea behind most of the programs is to give business owners a taste of the skills and disciplines that can aid in maximizing profits and growth. The programs are usually similar in content to those taught full-time business students, but because the programs for business owners are shorter, they can't be as thorough. An article in the November 10, 1980, *Wall Street Journal* on seminars for small-business owners noted: ". . . a few 90-minute classes provide only a nodding acquaintance with concepts that graduate business school students spend months exploring."

Evaluating programs

Most entrepreneurs find it unbearable to sit and listen to theoretical lectures and discussions about hypothetical business problems. They are doers rather than talkers, they prefer the real and practical to the theoretical and hypothetical. Actual cases, experiences, and profiles of real entrepreneurs, and examples from real start-up and existing situations best suit most entrepreneurs.

Discussion-type classes are more productive and stimulating than pure lectures. The opportunity to develop one's own business or marketing plan and have it critiqued by other entrepreneurs and expert instructors can be an invaluable exercise. Outside guest speakers with actual entrepreneurial experience or expertise in small companies add a real-world dimension to workshops and seminars. The most effective instructor teams in these programs have a variety of backgrounds and experiences in such areas as consulting, teaching, research, or venture capital. Also important is the ability to effectively lead groups through case discussions and other learning exercises.

What should entrepreneurs especially look out for and avoid in selecting programs? A number of red flags exist that can be useful warning signs for entrepreneurs attending short courses and programs. The following claims by the promoters and organizers tend to be signs of programs of questionable quality:

- "We have a battery of psychological tests which will predict whether you are an entrepreneur and whether you will succeed or fail." Such tests have not been validated and in fact may be misleading.
- "We'll package and prepare your business plan." This is a route that may save time, but it misses the point of the business plan exercise, which is to help entrepreneurs gain command of the intricacies and requirements necessary to make their ventures succeed.
- "We can raise the capital you need fast." There seems to be a gestation period in raising money; promises of quick and easy capital usually have strings attached that later often prove to be unbearable.
- "Make your fortune . . . Tremendous market waiting . . . Huge profits . . ." Be wary of such promotions. They are oversimplistic and appeal mainly to greed.
- "Our three-day course can solve all your small-business problems." We have yet to find one to have delivered on that promise.

The rest of this chapter is divided into two broad sections: sources for start-up entrepreneurs and sources for existing businesses. Within each section are listings and descriptions of seminars, workshops, and courses offered by a variety of organizations; the programs are included in the section according to the type of entrepreneur they are most suitable for.

Because hundreds of programs exist, we could not describe each one. We attempted to select those most representative of what is available and also to offer some geographic diversity. We have included several lengthy lists of colleges and universities offering degree and nondegree programs for start-up and existing small businesses.

Some sources listed in several other chapters also offer educational programs for entrepreneurs. Readers are advised to check Chapter 2, "Consultants and Management Assistance"; Chapter 4, "State and Local Government Assistance"; Chapter 8, "Assistance for Women"; and Chapter 12, "Small-Business Lobbying and Service Organizations."

SOURCES FOR START-UP ENTREPRENEURS

WORKSHOPS, SEMINARS, AND SHORT COURSES (NONDEGREE)

Nondegree programs for start-up entrepreneurs may show the widest variation in quality of all the small-business programs around, simply because so many people wish to start their own businesses. Promoters of seminars and workshops are well aware of how strong the small-business dream is, and the less reputable among them won't hesitate to exploit it with expensive and nearly worthless programs. Thus, we would especially refer start-up entrepreneurs to the material immediately preceding on evaluating programs (pp. 2–3).

Three principal sources of nondegree programs exist for start-up entrepreneurs: the U. S. Small Business Administration, private profit and nonprofit organizations, and various educational institutions. Their programs usually last from a day to several days and vary widely in cost.

Some of the programs are geared mostly to entrepreneurs who wish to open small retail and service businesses, and some are most appropriate for entrepreneurs looking to start fast-growing high-technology businesses. A few programs are directed to young entrepreneurs who want their new businesses to mesh properly with their lifestyles and life values.

Program cost doesn't seem to necessarily correlate with program value. The best approach seems to be to seek out the program that best suits one's situation, goals, and resources.

We would also advise aspiring entrepreneurs to check with their local high school, community college, or university for extension courses, and with their local Chamber of Commerce for leads on seminars and workshops dealing with starting businesses.

U. S. Small Business Administration
Assistant Administrator for Management Assistance
U. S. Small Business Administration
1441 L St., NW
Washington, DC 20416
(202) 653-6881
Information is available in more than 100 offices scattered among the nation's large- and medium-sized cities (see listing in Appendix A).

The Small Business Administration's main educational program for aspiring entrepreneurs is its Prebusiness Workshop, which lasts one day or several evenings. The workshops are geared mainly toward entrepreneurs seeking to start quite small retail and service businesses. Such participants have found the workshops quite useful.

Entrepreneurs with some business background who want to start fast-growing high-technology or other sorts of businesses requiring sophisticated financing usually shun the SBA workshops. These entrepreneurs seem to find them too primerish and basic.

The workshops attempt to impress on participants the importance of having enough money on hand to enable their businesses to survive several initial loss years. The workshops also deal in an introductory way with the essentials of borrowing funds and sound management approaches.

6

The workshops are available on a continuing basis at most local SBA offices and are free.

The Center for Entrepreneurial Management, Inc.
311 Main St.
Worcester, MA 01608
(617) 755-0770

The Center for Entrepreneurial Management (CEM) promotes entrepreneurship the way detergent and cereal makers promote their products. In addition to selling taped cassettes and various books on how to be an entrepreneur, CEM sponsors a series of traveling one- and two-day seminars on various aspects of starting businesses. Seminars in 1980 and 1981 were being offered in Boston, New York, Houston, Dallas, Los Angeles, Chicago, Philadelphia, Boca Raton, San Francisco, Atlanta, Charlotte, New Orleans, Seattle, Calgary, and Toronto, and elsewhere. Among the topics were the following:

• "How to Start, Finance, and Manage Your Own Small Business"
• "How to Raise Capital"
• "Managing an Entrepreneurial Venture"

These seminars feature as speakers entrepreneurs, venture capitalists, bankers, consultants, and academics.

Reactions to previous CEM seminars have been mixed. A *Venture* magazine article in September 1979, entitled "Where Entrepreneurs Turn for Support," said the seminars

are really a series of vague, soporific speeches—nine at one recent session. Attendees can make contacts during the lunch and coffee breaks, though, and they are encouraged to buy a variety of pamphlets, books, and tapes on everything from patents and record-keeping to finding venture capital and surviving bankruptcy.

The one-day seminars cost CEM members $195 and nonmembers $235; the two-day seminars cost CEM members $325 and nonmembers $395. Membership costs $96 annually.

Dible Management Development Seminars
Applied Management Institute, Inc.
623 Great Jones St.
Fairfield, CA 94533
(707) 422-6822

Dible Management Development Seminars consist of one-day programs on various aspects of starting businesses. The seminars were developed by Donald Dible, author of *Up Your Own Organization,* a book about starting and managing businesses. The seminars are offered on a traveling basis in collaboration with continuing-education divisions of universities in various cities. Various books and taped cassettes on entrepreneurship are offered for sale at these sessions. The seminars cost $125.

The Entrepreneurship Institute
90 E Wilson Bridge Road (Suite 247)
Worthington, OH 43805
(614) 885-0585

The Entrepreneurship Institute (TEI) is an independent, nonprofit international organization that encourages new enterprise development. It receives funding from major corporations and federal agencies.

TEI conducts intensive training conferences on starting and managing fast-growing companies. TEI says it provides starting entrepreneurs with financial, managerial, and technical contacts in each city where a training program is held.

More than fifteen entrepreneurship conferences have been held since 1976 in such cities as Dallas, Minneapolis, Columbus, Atlanta, Detroit, and Houston. The Institute keeps tabs on participants' subsequent business performances; it says the failure rate of businesses started after attending its conferences is about half the national average because many would-be entrepreneurs are discouraged by what they learn and veer away from starting businesses.

The conferences, which last two days, combine lectures, workshops, and panels. Topics for one recent two-day session included: "Are You an Entrepreneur?"; "Understanding My Market and Reaching My Customers"; "The Business Plan—How Do I Start My Business?"; "Financing My New Business"; and "How to Raise Small Amounts of Money." Instructors include entrepreneurs, consultants, academics, and others.

TEI also offers members access to business educational materials and such services as discount business equipment and car rentals. The entrepreneurship conferences cost from $195 with preregistration and $225 afterward. Annual membership in TEI is $45.

The School of Entrepreneurs
Tarrytown House Executive Conference Center
East Sunnyside Lane
Tarrytown, NY 10591
(212) WE 3-1232

The School of Entrepreneurs sponsors a two-weekend live-in program for start-up entrepreneurs, which places a heavy emphasis on psychic and lifestyle satisfaction from small businesses. One of the school's greatest assets appears to be Robert Schwartz, its director. Schwartz takes

8

an active role in the school's program, which is offered several times a year. The program is designed for people with a reasonably well-defined business concept and for people just starting businesses who wish to develop and expand them.

The program starts with self-evaluation, encounter groups, and structured tests to help participants understand their needs for achievement, affiliation, and power. The program then shifts to more practical concerns; students learn to develop business plans and present their ideas to a venture capitalist.

According to an article in the August 1978 issue of *Psychology Today,* the course is based on "the desire to make money more palatable by making business more spiritual." *Ambassador* magazine in August 1979 reported that "the sessions are free of the hucksterism, rhetoric and confrontational techniques" of other recently started entrepreneurship courses.

The two Friday-night-through-Sunday-afternoon sessions cost $500.

ENTREPRENEURSHIP DEGREE PROGRAMS AND COURSES

As the introduction to this chapter documents, entrepreneurship is a popular subject in colleges and universities, at both the undergraduate and graduate level. For high school students and undergraduates majoring in nonbusiness areas who aspire to own their own businesses, this section is of particular relevance.

At least seven colleges and universities around the country have in recent years started undergraduate and graduate programs that allow students to major or concentrate in the area of entrepreneurship. In addition, more than 200 undergraduate and graduate business schools offer one or more courses in entrepreneurship.

Not surprisingly, the degree programs and courses on entrepreneurship are usually much more inclusive than the seminars and workshops previously described. The college and university offerings allow students to read and work through a wider variety of business problems and cases than the nondegree programs. They also offer students at a relatively early age an opportunity to decide whether a career starting and operating a small business is really for them.

The material that immediately follows describes in some detail the seven undergraduate entrepreneurship programs we identified. Exhibit 1 (pp. 23–39) lists many of the colleges and universities that offer courses on starting and operating small businesses. Exhibit 2 (pp. 40–47) lists 228 two-year colleges and technical schools that offer courses on small-business start-up and management. Some of these courses are directed to owners of existing small businesses, but others are directed to entrepreneurs just getting started; readers should contact the schools nearest them to determine the exact nature of the small-business course offered.

Entrepreneurial Studies Program
Babson College
Babson Park, MA 02157
(617) 235-1200

Babson College in 1979 began an undergraduate major in Entrepreneurial Studies. Its objective is to teach students such things as understanding their own personal characteristics that affect their chances of success; evaluating new ventures; finding capital and other resources; and possibly selling or merging small businesses. Students majoring in Entrepreneurial Studies are encouraged to have a second major in either accounting, finance, management, or marketing to enable them to work for a big corporation for a few years before starting a new venture.

A student majoring in Entrepreneurial Studies must take the following four courses:

- "Fundamentals of Entrepreneurship," which considers individual traits contributing to entrepreneurial success;
- "Starting New Ventures," which teaches how to evaluate the overall viability of new ventures;
- "Financial Topics for the Entrepreneur," which focuses on raising and managing funds for new companies;
- "Entrepreneurial Field Studies," which allows students to work individually or in small groups with experienced entrepreneurs.

Courses make use of case studies, lectures, and guest speakers.

Baylor University
Center for Entrepreneurship
Waco, TX 76703
(817) 755-3766

Baylor's Center for Private Enterprise and Entrepreneurship offers both undergraduate and graduate concentrations in entrepreneurship. *Nation's Business* magazine, in a September 1980 article, referred to Baylor as a "small business oasis . . . [which] may break the barrier and offer a doctorate program in entrepreneurship."

At the undergraduate level, concentrations in entrepreneurial studies encourage dual business concentrations, such as entrepreneurship/finance or entrepreneurship/marketing. Among the entrepreneurial studies courses are "New Product Marketing," "Venture Finance," "Venture Accounting and Taxation," and "Management of Strategies of Growth." Each course requires students to work with an entrepreneur, helping prepare market analyses, cash-flow charts, and/or growth strategies. Additional courses often take the form of summers spent with an entrepreneur.

The graduate program entrepreneurship concentration includes a research-type course analyzing current topics in entrepreneurship and a course entitled "New Venture Finance," in which students develop loan packages and study financing alternatives.

Baylor also has a Professional Development Center that sponsors one-day workshops for people interested in starting small businesses. Typical workshops are "Market Analysis" and "Basic Finance and Accounting." They cost $120 each.

Duke University
Graduate School of Business
Durham, NC 27706
(919) 684-4266

Duke's Graduate Business School has a New Ventures Program that was started in 1977. The program emphasizes differences between small and large businesses. One course, "Creative Financing," covers such techniques as leveraged buyouts, capital formation, and managing businesses' growth phases.

A second course teaches the nuts and bolts of starting businesses. Students are required to present their business plan orally to a panel of financiers and entrepreneurs.

Venture magazine, in an October 1979 article, reported that 1978's program attracted forty-five students, whose projects included a "plan to start a U.S. rhesus monkey farm and a retail clothing outlet for working executive women."

The program also features successful entrepreneurs as guest speakers. J. B. Fu Qua, chairman of Fu Qua Industries, and W. Herbert Hunt of Hunt Oil were among seventeen guests who spoke to the MBA students in 1980.

Duke has been attempting to raise $500,000 as an endowment to provide no-strings financing for student entrepreneurs. With the endowment producing $50,000 a year, grants could be awarded to the most promising student projects.

Northeastern University
305 Hayden Hall
360 Huntington Ave.
Boston, MA 02115
(617) 437-3255

Northeastern offers a five-year bachelor's degree in business administration with the option to concentrate in Entrepreneurship and New Venture Management. Students can alternate a quarter on campus with a quarter working in a small enterprise so as to gain practical experience and ease the tuition burden. The concentration was started in 1973 as the first of its kind in the country. Among the courses are the following:

"New Venture Creation," which enables students to examine requirements for starting a growth-oriented enterprise. The course considers the risks, rewards, and demands of business ownership and teaches how to develop a market analysis and business plan. Outside entrepreneurs and specialists are invited to speak to classes.

"Opportunity Analysis and Seed Capital," which helps students to develop skills necessary for evaluating opportunities for starting or acquiring businesses. It also identifies sources and approaches to financing new businesses.

"Small Business Finance," which teaches students the analytical skills for financial management of small enterprises. Students learn accounting and financial tools particularly appropriate for small firms.

"Small Business Management," a traditional nuts-and-bolts course that examines the operating problems and opportunities in small firms. Cases are used to develop analytical and decision-making skills.

"Independent Study" enables students to pursue under faculty supervision projects of their choice on entrepreneurship. Past projects have included a study of family-owned enterprises; a survey of venture capitalists; and developing a business plan to start an actual business.

No major exists at the graduate level, but three courses are offered: "New Venture Creation," "Management of New Enterprises," and "Management of Smaller Enterprises." These more advanced courses focus on the skills and problems noted in the undergraduate entrepreneurship courses.

Dual concentrations are also possible, enabling students to major in Accounting and Entrepreneurship, for example. In 1980–81 over 100 undergraduates were concentrating in Entrepreneurship and New Venture Management.

Southern Methodist University
The Caruth Institute
Dallas, TX 75275
(214) 692-3326

Southern Methodist University (SMU) houses the Caruth Institute of Owner-Managed Business, which is unusual among universities offering entrepreneurship concentrations because of the diverse backgrounds and ages of students. Since the courses are open to nondegree candidates, students come from a variety of professions and range in age from sixteen to sixty, with the average being thirty-seven.

12

Caruth offers four entrepreneurial courses at both undergraduate and graduate levels. The courses have no prerequisites.

The four courses are "Qualifying a Business Idea," "Planning the New Business," "Founding and Funding the New Business," and "Managing the New or Small Business." These courses take the entrepreneurial student through each phase of business development, from conceiving and testing ideas to writing a business plan to securing financing to organizing the management structure.

Three graduate seminars are also offered. They feature different entrepreneur speakers each week. Student teams study one entrepreneur and his or her organization in depth for each meeting.

University of Pennsylvania
The Wharton School
Wharton Entrepreneurial Center
Philadelphia, PA 19104
(215) 243-4856

The Wharton School offers a wide range of courses for its entrepreneurial management major. Courses are taught by both full-time professors and industry professionals. Prerequisites for undergraduate and graduate entrepreneurship courses are completion of the basic marketing, finance, accounting, and operations management business courses. Two undergraduate courses—"Entrepreneurial Decision-Making" and "Entrepreneurship and New Venture Initiation"—focus on the start-up venture and ongoing small firm. The psychology of the entrepreneur is studied along with the risks and problems of small businesses. Decisions regarding incorporation, taxes, going public, purchasing, and cash flow are covered.

"Entrepreneurial Decision-Making in Land Development" is offered at both undergraduate and graduate levels and is taught by the case method. Other undergraduate courses involve students in the management of specific small businesses. "Mergers and Acquisitions" and "Personnel Administration" courses are also offered.

A graduate course, "Entrepreneurship and Venture Initiation" is a more thorough combination of the first two undergraduate courses and is taught by a successful entrepreneur. In 1980, the president and founder of a large Philadelphia bank taught the course. A second graduate course is entitled "Small Business Systems, a Seminar in the Creation and Management of Small Businesses."

Each semester a "Real Estate Entrepreneurship" graduate course is offered, which considers one topic in the real estate market. The fall 1980 course focused on shopping centers.

University of Southern California
The Entrepreneurship Program
School of Business Administration
Los Angeles, CA 90024
(213) 743-2451

The University of Southern California's (USC) entrepreneurship program is designed for students desiring to own a small business or planning to work within a new venture group of a large corporation. Case studies and lectures are used at both the undergraduate and graduate levels.

Undergraduate entrepreneurship courses are available only to seniors and have proven quite popular. In the fall of 1980, seventy-eight students were enrolled and fifty-four on waiting lists to get into the courses. One course, "New Venture Management," develops analytical and management skills. A second course, "Initiating New Ventures," teaches economic and market research along with strategic planning. All students are required to prepare a business plan. "Small Business Consulting" is another favorite course. Students work as unpaid consultants to individual business owners as part of the course. And finally, "Small Business Management—Design and Application of Organizational Structures and Systems" teaches students how to plan for and accommodate growth in small businesses.

The graduate program includes two basic entrepreneurship courses. One relates various business areas like marketing and finance to small-business applications, and the second requires students to prepare business plans and submit them to an advisory council made up of faculty and outside professionals for evaluation.

SOURCES FOR EXISTING SMALL BUSINESSES

Small-business owners cannot usually take the time off from running their businesses to complete two- or four-year business degree programs. Even if they could find the time, many small-business owners probably wouldn't want to, since at least some of the courses taught in such full-time programs cover territory familiar to anyone who has had practical business experience. And certainly obtaining a business degree is not initially much of an inducement for a business owner trying to solve pressing business problems.

Fortunately, owners of small businesses can choose from an array of short educational programs tailored to the needs of small-business owners or from various nondegree evening courses and seminars offered by colleges and universities. Most of the organizations that offer programs for start-up entrepreneurs also offer programs for owners of existing businesses and are covered in this section; additional organizations specialize in programs for existing-business owners. In general, the same three types of organizations that cater to start-up entrepreneurs also provide educational programs for existing-business owners: the Small Business Administration, various profit and nonprofit organizations, and colleges and universities.

And just as the programs serving start-up entrepreneurs are geared to specialized groups, so are the programs serving existing-business owners. Some programs are best suited for small retail and service businesses, while others are most appropriate for business owners seeking acquisitions, and still others are tailored to growth-oriented small businesses of certain minimum and maximum sizes.

The programs for existing-business owners vary widely in cost, from little or no cost to several thousand dollars. Quality also appears to vary widely. We advise small-business owners to attempt to check out programs they are interested in by speaking with other entrepreneurs who have attended the programs. Finally, the following programs are not all-inclusive; we suggest that business owners investigate educational programs noted in other chapters in this book and attempt to learn of additional programs by contacting nearby universities, community colleges, and Chambers of Commerce.

SEMINARS AND SHORT COURSES

U. S. Small Business Administration
Assistant Administrator for Management Assistance
U. S. Small Business Administration
1441 L St., NW
Washington, DC 20416
(202) 653-6881
Information is available in more than 100 offices scattered among the nation's large- and medium-sized cities (see listing in Appendix A).

The Small Business Administration (SBA) is the largest single provider of seminars and workshops for small-business owners; nearly 250,000 entrepreneurs each year participate in its programs.

Entrepreneurs' reactions to the programs vary widely. Some entrepreneurs find the programs quite useful, while others find them unsatisfactory. The disparity in reactions is probably partly a function of the varying quality of instructors at different SBA offices. But also a factor is the SBA's orientation to quite small retail and service businesses. Thus, owners of substantial manufacturing or fast-growing high-technology businesses frequently find SBA programs irrelevant to their particular needs.

The SBA sponsors a wide variety of classroom training sessions on any of a number of business subjects, such as selling and advertising, bookkeeping, cost control, and financial analysis. The courses are taught by professional business managers, academics, bankers, accountants, and SBA staff members. The sessions usually last one day and include fifty to one hundred participants for lectures and discussions.

The SBA also sponsors something called problem clinics, which bring together five to fifteen owners of similar businesses to examine common problems, such as credit and collections procedures. The idea behind the clinics is for business owners to help each other by providing fresh insights into solving difficult problems.

The classroom training sessions are scheduled periodically by SBA local offices, which can provide dates and locations. The problem clinics are scheduled according to the demand from individual business owners.

Best of all about SBA educational programs, they are free.

American Management Associations
135 W 50th St.
New York, NY 10020
(212) 586-8100

The American Management Associations (AMA) is one of the oldest organizations in the nation involved in management education and training. Founded in 1923, it has grown into a nationwide organization with 76,000 members. In one recent year, 85,000 business managers and owners attended 3,000 AMA courses and seminars, of which two thirds were held in New York. Regional AMA offices located in Chicago, Atlanta, Dallas, Los Angeles, New York City, San Francisco, Houston, and Washington, DC, also offer programs.

Most of the courses and seminars are directed to managers in large corporations, but a few, in such areas as finance, accounting, data processing, and supervisory skills, are appropriate for small-business owners.

The courses and seminars generally run from one to three days and, according to AMA, "More than 95% of registrants have given AMA courses impressively high ratings." The AMA, of course, could be a bit biased; a better source of feedback is a small-business owner who has attended an AMA program.

Faculty tend to be professional managers and consultants from large organizations.

The AMA makes available a free 180-page listing of all its current courses. The courses range in cost from $165 to $550.

Center for Entrepreneurial Management
311 Main St.
Worcester, MA 01608
(617) 755-0770

The Center for Entrepreneurial Management (CEM), in addition to its programs described on p. 6 for start-up entrepreneurs, has a number of seminars for owners of existing businesses. Recent titles for the traveling seminars include:

- "Managing the Closely Held Company," which considers ways to improve the management team and implement long-range planning.
- "The Role of the Board in the Smaller Company," which addresses legal responsibilities, selection, stock ownership, and other considerations for forming boards of directors in small enterprises.
- "The Affordable Small Computer System for the Smaller Company," an introduction to computer applications for small firms.
- "The Non-Union Employer: Preventive Labor Relations," which focuses on methods for avoiding unions in small companies.
- "Policies, Procedures and Techniques of Purchasing for the Small Organization," which focuses on the special problems and opportunities facing purchasing managers in small firms.

As noted in the earlier description of CEM, instructors for the seminars are drawn from a variety of business backgrounds. Appraisals of its seminars have been mixed. The seminars for owners of existing businesses last one to three days and range in cost from $195 to $695.

Country Business Services
225 Main St.
Brattleboro, VT 05301
(802) 451-4251

Country Business Services (CBS) is a business brokerage firm that specializes in helping entrepreneurs acquire small businesses. It offers educational programs and business planning services. CBS sponsors a variety of one-day seminars. One entitled "The Right Way to Buy a Small Business" considers such subjects as self-evaluation, personal net worth, choosing a business, pricing a business, the business plan, and financing a business. Other seminars are entitled "The Small Business Experience," "The Growing Role of the Computer in Small Business," and "Planning the Sale of Your Small Business."
The seminars cost $85.

Dible Management Development Seminars
Applied Management Institute, Inc.
623 Great Jones St.
Fairfield, CA 94533
(707) 422-6822

Dible Management Development Seminars are one-day seminars appropriate for small-business owners, which in the fall of 1980 covered ten subjects. The seminars are offered on a traveling basis in cities around the country. The seminars tend to be practical and on subjects of interest to managers of all-sized businesses. One seminar, for instance, entitled "Motivation Techniques for Managers and Supervisors," explores basic psychology to aid in understanding and motivating subordinates. Another seminar, entitled "Practical Negotiating Skills," considers techniques which can aid in improving negotiating abilities.

The seminars cost $125 each.

The Forum Corporation
84 State St.
Boston, MA
(617) 523-7300

The Forum Corporation is a rapidly growing small company which specializes in providing management training to small growing firms. It uses advanced computerized feedback techniques and personal assessments of participants to aid in instruction. Its three-day seminars on sales and managerial effectiveness are among the best available anywhere. They are most appropriate for owners of growing companies with annual sales of $5-10 million.

Smaller Company Management Program
Harvard Business School
Soldiers Field
Boston, MA 02163
(617) 495-6450

Launched in 1972, the Smaller Company Management Program (SCMP) is the Rolls-Royce of education programs available to owners of small firms. The program is especially designed for owners and top managers of companies with annual sales of $1-25 million. It includes three three-week units of instruction—a total of nine weeks—which are typically spread over three years to accommodate the busy schedules of entrepreneurs. Participants generally have at least ten years of small-company experience.

The program is an intense, demanding, and stimulating live-in experience tl :t relies on the traditional Harvard case method of instruction. It focuses on developing a broad array of general management skills: financial planning; marketing; motivation of key personnel; control systems; and mergers and acquisitions.

The faculty consists of tenured Harvard professors who have extensive experience consulting with small and large companies.

18

The cost of the program is $3,000 per three-week session, which includes tuition, meals, lodging, and materials.

Division of Management Education
The University of Michigan
Graduate School of Business Administration
1735 Washtenaw Ave.
Ann Arbor, MI 48109
(313) 764-1817

The University of Michigan's Division of Management Education conducts about 300 business seminars, workshops, and courses every year. Most are held in Ann Arbor, with enrollment usually limited to thirty in each course. While many of the offerings are best suited to corporate managers, a few are appropriate for small-company owners. For instance, "How to Manage a Smaller or Rapidly Growing Manufacturing Firm" is a three-day course which considers such topics as the states of business growth, designing organizational structures, and decision-making in smaller firms. The three-day courses are taught by faculty members from universities around the country and range in cost from $500 to $600.

Executive Education
The Wharton School
University of Pennsylvania
Dietrick Hall, Locust Walk
Philadelphia, PA 19104
(215) 243-7604

The Wharton School, in addition to its entrepreneurship program for degree students, offers a number of brief courses for business owners and managers. Most of the courses are geared to corporate managers, but at least one, "Fundamentals of Finance and Accounting for the Non-Financial Executive," appears appropriate for small-business owners.

The course considers such topics as analyses of financial statements, investment and budgeting decisions, and the role of accountants. It lasts three days and is offered on a traveling basis around the country. It is taught by Wharton faculty members.

The course costs $830.

UNIVERSITY CONTINUING-EDUCATION PROGRAMS

University of Alabama–Birmingham
School of Business
Birmingham, AL 35294
(205) 934-2204

The University of Alabama offers a variety of seminars, workshops, and forums for small-business owners. Its continuing-education program includes between fifteen and twenty courses each year on small-business management. Also offered are one-day seminars on business planning, financing, and developing the business plan.

Alabama has an external degree program in business designed for people who have been out of school for a while. Part of the program is devoted to small-business management and development of the business plan.

University of Colorado
Continuing Education
Boulder, CO 80304
(303) 492-5131

The University of Colorado's continuing-education program includes a Business Management Institute, which has courses for managers of all-sized businesses, rather than only small businesses. Many of the participants are small-business owners. Among the course offerings are "Accounting for Small Business," "Project Management," "Mini-Micro Computers," "Stress Management Program," "Time Management," and "Financial Planning for Non-Financial Planners."

University of Georgia
Continuing Education
Athens, GA 30603
(404) 548-1311

The University of Georgia's continuing-education program offers various small-business seminars and courses that last anywhere from half a day to nine weeks. In addition, its Small Business Development Center offers a series of courses on starting and managing small businesses; the series is offered at sixteen locations around the State. Courses include "How to Start and Manage a Small Business," "Financing the Small Business," "Credit and Collections," "Cash Flow Management," and "Tax Clinic for Small Business." All courses are taught by instructors with academic and business experience. Most courses meet twice and typically cost $15 each.

University of Indiana
Continuing Education
Bloomington, IN 47401
(812) 332-0211

The University of Indiana's continuing-education program offers several basic courses for small-business owners. Titles include "Small Business Management" and "Accounting for Small Business." The University of Indiana is also in a consortium with five other universities with executive programs and is developing an executive program for small-business owners.

> University of Washington
> College of Business Administration
> Seattle, WA 98105
> (206) 543-2100

The University of Washington's graduate program sponsors seminars and courses aimed at small-business owners. Among the courses are "Financial Planning and Control for Small Business," "Management in a Small Business," "Marketing Management for Small Firms," "Practical Management for Small Business," and "Organizational Behavior and Personnel Management in a Small Business."

Also, an Entrepreneurial Symposium is held one day each spring. It brings together investment bankers, venture capitalists, investors, attorneys, and successful entrepreneurs for lectures and discussions on small-business financing and related subjects. The symposium costs $45, and the other courses usually run eight or nine sessions each and cost in the area of $150.

> Wichita State University
> College of Business
> Wichita, KS 67208
> (316) 689-3456

Wichita State has several seminars and workshops of relevance to small-business owners. Among the offerings are two-day courses on "Management Relations and Employee Relations" and "Overview of the Economy." A one-day workshop on how small-business owners can obtain financing is also offered. The two-day courses cost $160, and the one-day course is $110.

COMMUNITY AND TWO-YEAR COLLEGES

According to a recent SBA study, 228 community colleges and two-year colleges offer courses for owners of existing small businesses. These are an important and often overlooked source of training for small-business owners. The courses are usually developed and taught by consultants, lawyers, and accountants who work with small businesses, or by small-business owners with formal business education.

The courses tend to be practical and straightforward rather than theoretical. Our survey of representative courses noted the following examples:

- Mississippi County CC: "Single-Entry Bookkeeping." Small-business owners who are perplexed by double-entry bookkeeping often find the simplicity of this system a welcome relief.
- Bee County College: "Income Tax for Small Business." The course includes explanations of allowable expenses, depreciation, and investment tax credits. Students also learn to use balance sheets and profit-and-loss statements as control devices to improve profitability.
- Tarrant County Junior College: "Small Business Management." The course exposes students to the problems of starting, operating, and evaluating small businesses. Topics covered include various forms of organization, financing, cost structure, location, sources of personnel, marketing, and competition.

The names of the 228 two-year schools are listed in Exhibit 2 on pp. 40–47.

U. S. Small Business Administration
1441 L St., NW
Washington, DC 20416

ADDITIONAL INFORMATION SOURCES

A. FOR START-UPS

Entrepreneurship and Venture Management, by Clifford M. Baumback and J. R. Mancuso. (Englewood Cliffs, NJ: Prentice-Hall, 1975)
A good book of readings on starting and operating a small business.

New Venture Creation (2nd ed.) by Jeffry A. Timmons, Leonard E. Smollen, Alexander L. M. Dingee, Jr. (Homewood, IL: Richard D. Irwin, 1977)
Probably the most widely adopted book of its kind, it is used in leading business education programs at Columbia, Duke, Indiana, MIT, Pitt, Virginia, Wharton, and others. It is a comprehensive yet practical guide for start-up entrepreneurs, covering self-assessment and goal-setting, management skills requirements, idea generation and evaluation, business plans, financing, and first-year problems. How can we not recommend it?

New Venture Strategies, by Karl Vesper. (Englewood Cliffs, NJ: Prentice-Hall, 1980)
Informative discussion of start-up approaches that have worked for others. Liberal use of actual examples and anecdotes make it readable

and worthwhile. Vesper is one of the leading gurus of entrepreneurship.

B. FOR EXISTING SMALL BUSINESSES

U. S. Small Business Administration
U. S. Small Business Administration
1441 L St., NW
Washington, DC 20416

SBA has about 300 publications covering all aspects of small-business management for a wide range of businesses. These publications present facts, figures, and techniques in readable, nontechnical form. Some of the bestsellers include:
- *Management Training.* Excellent summary of SBA's publications and materials.
- *Management Aids for Small Manufacturers.*
- *Small Marketers Aids.* Suggestions, checklists, guidelines for small retail, wholesale, and service firms.
- *Small Business Management Series* (35 vols.). Covers various businesses and problems.
- *Starting and Managing Series.* Covers various businesses.
- *Managing for Profits.* A pragmatic, how-to guide.
- *Buying and Selling a Small Business.*
- *Protecting the Small Business Cash Flow Lifeline,* January 1980, Office of Advocacy. Excellent discussion of 55 practices frequently used to cope with tight money conditions and a weak economy.

Additional non-SBA books include the following:

How to Organize and Operate a Small Business (6th ed.) by Clifford M. Baumback and Kenneth Lawyer (Englewood Cliffs, NJ: Prentice-Hall, 1979)
Probably the leading college text on the subject.

Small Business Management Fundamentals (2nd ed.) by Dan Steinhoff (New York, NY: McGraw-Hill, 1978)
Good nuts-and-bolts textbook.

Small Business Reporter (San Francisco, CA: Bank of America)
Excellent collection of reports on starting and managing specific types of businesses and their problems.

EXHIBIT 1

Colleges and Universities with Courses in Entrepreneurship, New Ventures, and Small-Business Management

ALABAMA

Auburn 36830
Auburn University

(E) Birmingham 35233
University of Alabama in
Birmingham

Florence 35630
University of North Alabama

Huntsville 35807
University of Alabama in
Huntsville

Jacksonville 36265
Jacksonville State University

Mobile 36688
University of South Alabama

Montgomery 36101
Alabama State University

Troy 36081
Troy State University

Tuscaloosa 35486
University of Alabama in
Tuscaloosa

ALASKA

Anchorage 99504
University of Alaska

Fairbanks 99701
University of Alaska–Fairbanks

ARIZONA

Flagstaff 86011
Northern Arizona University

Glendale 85306
American Graduate School of
International Management

Tempe 85281
Arizona State University

Tucson 85721
University of Arizona

ARKANSAS

Arkadelphia 71923
Henderson State University

Batesville 72501
Arkansas College

Clarksville 72830
College of the Ozarks

Conway 72032
University of Central Arkansas

Fayetteville 72701
University of Arkansas at
Fayetteville

Jonesboro 72401
Arkansas State University

Little Rock 71846
(I) University of Arkansas at
Little Rock

Magnolia 71753
University of Southern Arkansas

Monticello 71655
University of Arkansas at
Monticello

(E) Indicates courses in Entrepreneurship, New Ventures. All others have small-business management courses.
(I) Indicates Innovation Center (described in Chapter 2).

Russellville 72801
  Arkansas Polytechnical

Searcy 72143
  Harding College

CALIFORNIA

Arcata 95521
  Humboldt State University

Azusa 91702
  Azusa Pacific College

Bakersfield 93309
  California State
  College–Bakersfield

Berkeley 94720
  University of California*

Chico 95926
  California State
  University–Chico

Claremont 91711
  Claremont Men's College

Dominguez Hills 90247
  Cal State College–Dominguez
  Hills

Fresno 93710
  California State
  University–Fresno

Fullerton 92634
  Cal State University–Fullerton

Hayward 94542
  Cal State University–Hayward

Long Beach 90840
  Cal State University–Long Beach

Los Angeles
  Cal State University–Los
  Angeles 90032
  Loyola–Marymount University
  90024

University of California at Los
  Angeles 90024
  (E) University of Southern
  California 90024

Northridge 91330
  Cal State University–Northridge

Pomona 91768
  Cal State Poly–Pomona

Riverside 92521
  University of California*

Sacramento 95819
  Cal State University–Sacramento

San Bernardino 92407
  Cal State College–San
  Bernardino

San Diego
  Point Loma College 92115
  San Diego State University
  92182

San Francisco
  San Francisco State University
  94132
  University of San Francisco
  94117

San Jose
  San Jose State University 95192

San Luis Obispo 93407
  Cal Poly State University–San
  Luis Obispo

Santa Barbara
  University of California–Santa
  Barbara 93106
  Westmont College 93108

Santa Clara 95053
  University of Santa Clara*

Santa Cruz 95064
  (I) University of California

* These listed schools do not have Small Business Institutes (described in Chapter 2).

Stanford 94305
  (E) Stanford University*

Stockton 95204
  University of Pacific

Turlock 95380
  California State
  College–Stanislaus

Whittier 90607
  Whittier College

COLORADO

Alamosa 81101
  Adams State College

Boulder 80304
  University of Colorado*

Colorado Springs 80907
  University of Colorado–
  Colorado Springs

Denver
  Denver University 80210
  Metropolitan State College
  80204
  University of Denver 80208

Durango 81301
  Fort Lewis College

Fort Collins 80521
  Colorado State University

Grand Junction 81501
  Mesa College

Greeley 80631
  (E) University of Northern
  Colorado

Pueblo 81007
  University of Southern Colorado

CONNECTICUT

Bridgeport 06602
  University of Bridgeport*

Fairfield 06430
  Fairfield University*

Storrs 06268
  University of Connecticut

West Hartford 06117
  University of Hartford*

West Haven 06516
  University of New Haven

DELAWARE

Newark 19711
  University of Delaware

FLORIDA

Boca Raton 33431
  Florida Atlantic University

Coral Gables 33124
  University of Miami

Fort Lauderdale 33314
  Nova University

Jacksonville 33209
  University of North Florida

Miami 33144
  Florida International University

Orlando 32816
  The University of Central
  Florida

Pensacola 32504
  University of West Florida*

Tallahassee
  The Florida State University
  32306
  Florida A & M 32307

Tampa 33620
  University of South Florida

GEORGIA

Albany 31702
  (E) Albany State College

26

Americus 31709
  Georgia Southwestern College

Athens 30602
  (E) University of Georgia*

Atlanta
  Atlanta University 30314
  Emory University 30322
  Georgia Institute of Technology
  30332
  Georgia State University 30303

Augusta 30904
  Augusta College

Carrollton 30117
  West Georgia College

Marietta 30060
  Southern Technical Institute

Milledgeville 31061
  Georgia College

Savannah
  Armstrong State College 31406
  Savannah State College 31404

Valdosta 31601
  Valdosta State College

Hilo 96720
  University of Hawaii–Hilo

Honolulu
  Chaminade University 96816
  Hawaii Pacific College 96813
  University of Hawaii–Manoa
  96822

Maui
  Maui Community College

Boise 83707
  Boise State University

Moscow 83843
  University of Idaho

Pocatello 83201
  Idaho State University

Carbondale 62901
  Southern Illinois
  University–Carbondale

Champaign 61820
  (E) University of Illinois at
  Urbana–Champaign

Charleston 61920
  Eastern Illinois University

Chicago
  Chicago State University 60611
  De Paul University 60614
  Illinois Institute of Technology
  60616
  Roosevelt University 60605
  University of Chicago 60637
  University of Illinois–Chicago
  Circle 60680

Decatur 62521
  Millikin University

De Kalb 60115
  Northern Illinois University

Edwardsville 62025
  Southern Illinois
  University–Edwardsville

Elmhurst 60126
  Elmhurst College

Evanston 60201
  (E) Northwestern University

Jacksonville 62650
  MacMurray College

Lebanon 62254
  McKendree College

Lockport 60441
Lewis University

Macomb 61455
Western Illinois University

Normal 61761
Illinois State University

Palos Heights 60463
Trinity Christian College

Park Forest South 60466
Governor's State University*

Peoria 61606
(E) Bradley University

Quincy 62301
Quincy College

Springfield 62708
Sangamon State University

Urbana 61801
University of Illinois

INDIANA

Anderson 46011
Anderson College

Angola 46703
Tri-State University

Bloomington 47401
(E) Indiana University

Evansville
Indiana State University–
Evansville 47712
University of Evansville 47701

Fort Wayne 46805
Indiana–Purdue University

Gary 46408
Indiana University–Northwest

Goshen 46626
Goshen College

Greencastle 46135
DePauw University

Hanover 47243
Hanover College

Indianapolis
Butler University 46208
Indiana Central University 46227

Kokomo 46901
Indiana University–Kokomo

Muncie 47306
Ball State University

New Albany 47150
Indiana University–Southeast

Notre Dame
Saint Mary's College 46556
University of Notre Dame 46556

Richmond 47374
Indiana University–East

Terre Haute 47809
Indiana State University

Valparaiso 46383
Valparaiso University

West Lafayette 47907
(E) Purdue University

Whiting 46394
Calumet College

IOWA

Ames 50011
Iowa State University

Cedar Falls 50613
University of Northern Iowa

Cedar Rapids 52402
Mt. Mercy College

Davenport 52803
St. Ambrose College

Des Moines 50311
  Drake University

Dubuque 52001
  University of Dubuque

Iowa City 52242
  University of Iowa

Sioux City 51104
  Briar Cliff

KANSAS

Emporia 66801
  Emporia State University

Hays 67601
  Fort Hays State University

Lawrence 66044
  University of Kansas

Manhattan 66502
  Kansas State University

Pittsburg 66762
  Pittsburg State University

Sterling 67579
  Sterling College

Topeka 66621
  Washburn University

Wichita
  Kansas Newman College 67213
  Wichita State University 67208

KENTUCKY

Bowling Green 42101
  Western Kentucky University

Ft. Mitchell 41017
  Thomas More College

Highland Heights
  Northern Kentucky University

Lexington 40506
  University of Kentucky

Louisville 40208
  University of Louisville
  Foundation, Inc.

Morehead 40351
  Morehead State University

Richmond 40475
  Eastern Kentucky University

LOUISIANA

Baton Rouge 70803
  Louisiana State
  University–Baton Rouge

Hammond 70401
  Southeastern University

Lafayette 70501
  University of Southwestern
  Louisiana

Lake Charles 70601
  McNeese State University

Monroe 71201
  Northeast Louisiana University

Natchitoches 71457
  Northwestern State University of
  Louisiana

New Orleans
  Loyola University 70118
  (E) Tulane University 70118
  University of New Orleans
  70122
  Xavier University 70125

Pineville 71360
  Louisiana College

Ruston 71272
  Louisiana Technological
  University

Shreveport 71115
  Louisiana State University in
  Shreveport

Thibodaux 70301
  Nicholls State University

MAINE

Bangor 04401
  Husson College

Biddeford 04005
  St. Francis College

Orono 04473
  University of Maine–Orono

Portland
  (I) University of Southern
  Maine 04103
  Westbrook College 04103

Springvale 04083
  Nasson College

MARYLAND

Baltimore
  Loyola College 21210
  Morgan State University 21239
  University of Baltimore 21201

College Park 20740
  University of Maryland

Cresaptown 21502
  Frostburg State College

Salisbury 21801
  Salisbury State College

MASSACHUSETTS

Amherst 01003
  University of Massachusetts

Boston
  Boston College 02167
  (E) Northeastern University
  02115
  Suffolk University 02114
  University of Massachusetts–
  Boston 02125

Cambridge
  (E) Harvard Business School*
  02138
  Massachusetts Institute of
  Technology 02139

Lowell 01854
  University of Lowell

North Adams 01247
  North Adams State College

North Dartmouth 02747
  Southeastern Massachusetts
  University

Salem 01970
  (E) Salem State College

Springfield
  American International College
  01109
  (E) Western New England
  College 01119

Wellesley 02157
  (E) Babson College*

Worcester
  (E) Clark University 01610
  Worcester State College*
  01602

MICHIGAN

Allendale 49401
  Grand Valley State College

Ann Arbor 78109
  (E) University of Michigan*

Berrien Springs 49104
  Andrews University*

Big Rapids 49307
  Ferris State College

Detroit
  University of Detroit 48221
  (E) Wayne State University
  48202

East Lansing 48823
Michigan State University

Flint 48503
University of Michigan–Flint

Houghton 49931
Michigan Technological
University

Kalamazoo
Kalamazoo College 49003
Western Michigan University
49003

Marquette 49855
Northern Michigan University

Mount Pleasant 48858
Central Michigan University

Sault Sainte Marie 49783
Lake Superior State College

Ypsilanti 48197
Eastern Michigan University

MINNESOTA

Bemidji 56601
Bemidji State University

Duluth
St. Scholastica College 55811
University of Minnesota–Duluth
55812

Mankato 56001
Mankato State University

Moorhead 56560
Moorhead State University

Morris 56267
University of Minnesota–Morris

Northfield 55057
St. Olaf College

St. Cloud 56301
St. Cloud State University

St. Paul 55105
St. Thomas College

Waseca 56093
University of Minnesota
Technical College

Winona 55987
Winona State University

MISSISSIPPI

Cleveland 38732
Delta State University

Hattiesburg 39401
University of Southern
Mississippi

Jackson
Jackson State University 39203
Millsaps College 39202

S. Clinton 39058
Mississippi College

University 38677
The University of Mississippi

MISSOURI

Cape Girardeau 63701
Southeast Missouri State
College*

Columbia 65211
University of Missouri

Joplin 64801
Missouri Southern State College

Kansas City
Rockhurst College 64110
University of Missouri–Kansas
City 64110

Kirksville 63501
Northeast Missouri State
University

Maryville 64468
  Northwest Missouri State
  University

Rolla 65401
  University of Missouri*

St. Joseph 64507
  Missouri Western State College

St. Louis
  (E) St. Louis University 63108
  University of Missouri* 63121

Springfield 65802
  Southwest Missouri State
  University

MONTANA

Billings 59101
  Eastern Montana College

Bozeman 59715
  Montana State University

Missoula 59801
  University of Montana

NEBRASKA

Chadron 69337
  Chadron State College

Crete 68333
  Doane College

Hastings 68901
  Hastings College

Kearney 68847
  Kearney State College

Lincoln 68588
  University of Nebraska at
  Lincoln

Omaha
  Creighton University 68131
  University of Nebraska 68132

Peru 68421
  Peru State College

Wayne 68787
  Wayne State College

NEVADA

Las Vegas 89154
  University of Nevada–Las Vegas

Reno 89504
  University of Nevada–Reno

NEW HAMPSHIRE

Durham 03824
  (E) University of New
  Hampshire

Hanover 03755
  (E) Dartmouth College

Manchester 03104
  New Hampshire College

Plymouth 03264
  Plymouth State College

NEW JERSEY

Camden 08903
  (E) Rutgers University

Lincroft 07738
  Brookdale Community College

Madison 07940
  (E) Fairleigh Dickinson
  University

Mahwah 07430
  Ramapo College

Montclair 07043
  Montclair State College

Newark 07102
  New Jersey Institute of
  Technology

Pomona 08240
  Stockton State College

Trenton 08625
Trenton State College

NEW MEXICO

Albuquerque 87131
(I) University of New Mexico

Las Cruces 88001
New Mexico State University

Las Vegas 87701
New Mexico Highlands
University

Portales 88130
Eastern New Mexico University

Santa Fe 87501
College of Santa Fe

NEW YORK

Albany 12222
SUNY at Albany

Alfred 14802
Alfred University

Binghamton 13901
SUNY at Binghamton

Bronx 10458
(E) Fordham University*

Brooklyn
Brooklyn Center of Long Island
University* 11201
St. Francis College 11201

Buffalo 14208
Canisius College

Delhi 13757
SUNY Agricultural & Technical
College*

Garden City 11530
Adelphi University*

Greenvale 11548
C. W. Post Center School of
Business
Long Island University

Hamilton 13346
(I) Colgate University

Hempstead 11550
Hofstra University

Ithaca
(E) Cornell University 14850
Ithaca College* 14850

Jamaica 11439
St. John's University

Loudonville 12211
Siena College

New York
Bernard Baruch College &
Research Foundation of the City
University of New York 10010
(E) Columbia University*
10027
Pace University 10038
New York University 10023*

Old Westbury 11568
New York Institute of
Technology

Plattsburgh 12901
SUNY of Plattsburgh

Potsdam 13676
Clarkson College of Technology

Riverdale 10471
Manhattan College

Rochester
Rochester Institute of
Technology 14523
University of Rochester 14627*

St. Bonaventure 14778
St. Bonaventure University

Schenectady 12308
Union College

Syracuse 13280
Syracuse University

Utica 13502
SUNY at Utica–Rome

NORTH CAROLINA

Boone 28608
Appalachian State University

Chapel Hill 27514
University of North
Carolina–Chapel Hill

Charlotte 28213
University of North Carolina

Cullowhee 28723
Western Carolina University

Durham
North Carolina Central
University 27707
(E) Duke University 27706*

Greenville 27834
(E) East Carolina University

Raleigh 27607
North Carolina State University

Wilmington 28401
University of North
Carolina–Wilmington

Winston-Salem 27109
(E) Wake Forest University

NORTH DAKOTA

Bismarck 58501
Mary College

Fargo 58102
North Dakota State University

Grand Forks 58201
University of North Dakota

Jamestown 58401
Jamestown College

Minot 58701
Minot State College

OHIO

Ada 45810
Ohio Northern University

Akron 44325
University of Akron

Athens 45701
Ohio University

Berea 44017
Baldwin-Wallace College

Bowling Green 43402
Bowling Green State University

Cincinnati
(E) University of Cincinnati
45221
(E) Xavier University 45207

Cleveland
Case Western Reserve University
44106
(E) Cleveland State University
44115

Columbus
Capital University 43209
(E) Ohio State University 43210

Dayton
University of Dayton 45469
(E) Wright State University
45435

Defiance 43512
Defiance College

Findlay 45840
Findlay College

Hamilton 45011
(E) Miami University*

Kent 44242
(E) Kent State University*

Marietta 45750
Marietta College

New Concord 43762
Muskingum College

Oxford 45056
(E) Miami University

Painesville 44077
Garfield Senior College
(Division of Lake Erie College)

Rio Grande 45674
Rio Grande College

Springfield 45501
Wittenberg University

Toledo 43606
University of Toledo

Urbana 43078
Urbana College

Westerville 43081
Otterbein College

Wilberforce
Central State University 43584
Wilberforce University 45384

Wilmington 45177
Wilmington College

Youngstown 44555
Youngstown State University

OKLAHOMA

Ada 74820
East Central University

Durant 74701
Southeastern Oklahoma State
University

Enid 73701
Phillips University

Edmond 73034
Central State University

Lawton 73501
Cameron University

Norman 73019
(I) (E) University of Oklahoma

Oklahoma City 73111
Oklahoma Christian College

Shawnee 74801
Oklahoma Baptist University

Stillwater 74074
Oklahoma State University

Tahlequah 74464
Northeastern Oklahoma State
University

Tulsa
Oral Roberts University 74102
University of Tulsa 74104

Weatherford 73099
Southwestern Oklahoma State
University

OREGON

Corvallis 97331
Oregon State University

Eugene 97403
University of Oregon

La Grande 97850
Eastern Oregon State College

Portland
Portland State University 97207
University of Portland 97203

Newberg 97132
George Fox College

Salem 97301
Willamette University

PENNSYLVANIA

Bethlehem 18015
(E) Lehigh University

California 15419
California State College

Chester 19013
Widener College

Clarion 16214
Clarion State College*

Erie 16501
Gannon College

Gettysburg 17325
Gettysburg College

Greenville 16125
(E) Thiel College*

Indiana 15701
Indiana University of
Pennsylvania

Lewisburg 17837
Bucknell University

Middletown 17057
Penn State University–Capital
Campus

Philadelphia
(E) Drexel University 19104
La Salle College 19141
(E) Temple University 19122
(E) University of Pennsylvania
19104

Pittsburgh
(E) Carnegie Mellon University
15213
Duquesne University 15219
(E) University of Pittsburgh
15213

Scranton 18510
University of Scranton

Shippensburg 17257
Shippensburg State College

Slippery Rock 16057
Slippery Rock State College

State College 16802
Pennsylvania State University

Villanova 19085
Villanova University

West Chester 19380
West Chester State College

Wilkes-Barre
King's College 18702
Wilkes College 18703

RHODE ISLAND

Bristol 02809
Roger Williams College

Kingston 02881
University of Rhode Island

Providence 02903
Johnson & Wales College

SOUTH CAROLINA

Charleston 29409
The Citadel

Clemson 29631
(E) Clemson University

Columbia 29208
University of South Carolina*

Conway 29526
University of South Carolina

Florence 29501
Francis Marion College

Lancaster 29720
University of South Carolina*

Rock Hill 29733
Winthrop College

SOUTH DAKOTA

Aberdeen 57401
Northern State College

Madison 57042
Dakota State College

Rapid City 57701
National College of Business

Sioux Falls
Augustana College 57102
Sioux Falls College 57101

Spearfish 57783
Black Hills State College

Vermillion 57069
University of South Dakota

TENNESSEE

Athens 37303
Tennessee Wesleyan College

Chattanooga 37401
The University of Tennessee at
Chattanooga

Clarksville 37040
Austin Peay State University

Cookeville 38501
Tennessee Technological
University

Johnson City 37601
East Tennessee State University

Knoxville 37916
The University of Tennessee at
Knoxville

Martin 38237
The University of Tennessee at
Martin

Memphis
(E) Memphis State University

Murfreesboro 37130
Middle Tennessee State
University

Nashville
Tennessee State University
37203
The University of Tennessee at
Nashville 37203

TEXAS

Abilene
Abilene Christian University
79609
Hardin-Simmons University
79607

Alpine 79830
Sul Ross State University

Arlington 76019
University of Texas–Arlington

Austin
St. Edward's University 78704
(E) University of Texas at
Austin 78172

Belton 76513
Mary Hardin Baylor

Beaumont 77710
Lamar University

Brownsville 78520
Pan American University at
Brownsville

Canyon 79015
(E) West Texas State University

College Station 77834
Texas A & M University

Commerce 75428
East Texas State–Commerce

Corpus Christi 78412
Corpus Christi State University

Dallas 75275
(E) Southern Methodist
University*

Denton 76203
North Texas State University

Edinburg 78539
Pan American University

El Paso 79902
University of Texas–El Paso

Houston
Houston Baptist University
77036
Texas Southern University*
77004
University of Houston 77004
College of Business
Administration
College of Business Technology
University of Houston–Clear
Lake Campus

Huntsville 77340
Sam Houston State University

Irving 75060
University of Dallas

Kingsville 78363
Texas A & I University

Laredo 78040
Laredo State University

Lubbock
Texas Tech University 97409
Agriculture Economics
Business Administration
Home Management

Marshall 75670
Wiley College

Nacogdoches 75962
Stephen F. Austin University

Odessa 79760
University of Texas–Permian
Basin

San Angelo 76901
Angelo State University

San Antonio
St. Mary's University 78228
Trinity University 78212
University of Texas–San Antonio
78229

San Marcos 78666
Southwest Texas State University

Texarkana 75501
East Texas State–Texarkana

Tyler 75701
Texas Eastern University

Uvalde 78801
Sul Ross State University

Waco 76703
(I) (E) Baylor University

Wichita Falls 76301
Midwestern State University

UTAH

Logan 84321
Utah State University

Ogden 84403
Weber State College

Provo 84602
Brigham Young University

Salt Lake City 84112
(I) (E) University of Utah

VERMONT

Bennington 05201
Southern Vermont College

Burlington
Champlain College 05402
University of Vermont 05401

38

Castleton 05735
 Castleton State College

Johnson 05656
 Johnson State College

Northfield 05663
 Norwich University

Poultney 05764
 Green Mountain College

VIRGINIA

Blacksburg 24061
 Virginia Polytech Institute &
 State University

Charlottesville
 University of Virginia 22903
  (E) Colgate Darden Graduate
  School
  McIntire School of Commerce

Fairfax 22030
 George Mason University

Ferrum 24088
 (E) Ferrum College*

Ft. Myer 22211
 Golden Gate University

Harrisonburg 22801
 James Madison University

Lynchburg 24501
 Lynchburg College

Norfolk
 Norfolk State College 23504
 Old Dominion University 23508

Petersburg 23803
 Virginia State University

Radford 24142
 Radford College*

Richmond 23211
 Virginia Commonwealth
 University

Williamsburg 23185
 College of William & Mary

WASHINGTON

Bellingham 98225
 Western Washington State
 College*

Cheney 99004
 Eastern Washington University

College Place 99324
 Walla Walla University*

Ellensburg 98296
 Central Washington University

Lynnwood 98036
 Edmonds Community College

Olympia 98505
 Evergreen State College

Pullman 99164
 Washington State University

Seattle
 Seattle University 98122
 (E) University of Washington
 98105

Tacoma
 Pacific Lutheran University
 98447
 University of Puget Sound 98416

WASHINGTON, DC

 American University 20016
 Gallaudet College 20002
 (E) Georgetown University
 20057
 Southeastern University 20006
 University of the District of
 Columbia 20609

WEST VIRGINIA

Athens 24712
  Concord College

Bluefield 24701
  Bluefield State College

Charleston
  University of Charleston 25301
  West Virginia College of
  Graduates 25304

Elkins 26241
  Davis and Elkins College

Fairmont 26554
  Fairmont State College

Glenville 26351
  Glenville State College

Huntington 25701
  Marshall University

Institute 25112
  West Virginia State College

Morgantown 26505
  West Virginia University

West Liberty 26074
  West Liberty State College

Wheeling 26003
  Wheeling College

WISCONSIN

Eau Claire 54701
  University of Wisconsin–Eau
  Claire

Kenosha 53140
  University of
  Wisconsin–Parkside

La Crosse 54601
  University of Wisconsin

Madison 53706
  (I) University of
  Wisconsin–Madison

Milwaukee
  Marquette University 53233
  Milwaukee School of
  Engineering 53201
  University of
  Wisconsin–Milwaukee 53201

Oshkosh 54901
  University of
  Wisconsin–Oshkosh

WYOMING

Laramie 82070
  University of Wyoming

AMERICAN SAMOA

Pago Pago 96799
  American Samoa Community
  College

GUAM

Agana 96910
  University of Guam

PUERTO RICO

Hato Rey 00612
  Interamerican University

Mayaguez 00617
  University of Puerto
  Rico–Mayaguez

Ponce 00731
  Catholic University of Puerto
  Rico

Rio Piedras 00923
  University of Puerto Rico–Rio
  Piedras

VIRGIN ISLANDS

St. Thomas

EXHIBIT 2

Community and Two-Year Colleges Offering Courses
for Existing Small Businesses

ALABAMA

Alexander City 35010
  Alexander City State Junior
  College

ALASKA

Anchorage 99504
  Anchorage Community College

Nome 99762
  Northwest Community College

ARIZONA

Glendale 85301
  Glendale Community College

Kingman 86401
  Mohave Community College

Mesa 85202
  Mesa Community College

Phoenix 85004
  Rio Salado

Tucson 85709
  Pima Community College

ARKANSAS

Blytheville 72315
  Mississippi County Community
  College

Forrest City 72335
  East Arkansas Community
  College

Russellville 72801
  Arkansas Tech University

CALIFORNIA

Chula Vista 92010
  Southwestern College

Costa Mesa 92626
  Orange Coast College

Cypress 90630
  Cypress College

El Cajon 92020
  Grossmont College

Eureka 95501
  College of the Redwoods

Fountain Valley 92708
  Coastline Community College

Fresno 93741
  Fresno City College

Fullerton 92634
  Fullerton College

Gilroy 95030
  Gavilan College

Huntington Beach 92647
  Golden West College

Lancaster 93534
  Antelope Valley College

Long Beach 90806
  Long Beach City College

Los Angeles 90047
  Los Angeles City College
  Southwest College

Mission Viejo 92692
  Saddleback Community College
  District

Novato 94947
Indian Valley College

Pleasant Hill 94523
Diablo Valley College

Quincy 95971
Feather River College

Ridgecrest 93555
Cerro Coso Curriculum Proposal

Rocklin 95677
Sierra College

Sacramento 95822
Sacramento City College

San Francisco 94103
Community College Centers of
San Francisco Community
College District

San Jose 90506
Evergreen Valley College

San Pablo 94806
Contra Costa College

Santa Monica 90406
Santa Monica College

Stockton 95207
Humphreys College

Ukiah 95482
Mendocino College

Via Torrance 90506
El Camino College

Victorville 92392
Victor Valley College

COLORADO

Littleton 80120
Arapahoe Community College

Glenwood Springs 81601
Colorado Mountain College

CONNECTICUT

Danielson 06239
Quinebaug Valley Community
College

Winsted 01098
State of Connecticut
Northwestern Connecticut
Community College

DELAWARE

Wilmington 19801
Delaware Technical and
Community College

FLORIDA

Fort Myers 33907
Edison Community College

Gainesville 32601
Gainesville Junior College

Jacksonville 32205
Florida Junior College at
Jacksonville

Key West 33040
Florida Keys Community
College

Leesburg 32748
Lake-Sumter Community
College

Miami 33156
Miami-Dade Community
College

Orlando 32802
Valencia Community College

Palatka 32077
St. Johns River Community
College

Tampa 33622
Hillsborough Community
College

42

Dalton 30720
Dalton Community College

Morrow 30260
Clayton Junior College

Swainsboro 30401
Emanuel County Junior College

ILLINOIS

Belleville 62221
Belleville Area College

Carterville 62918
John A. Logan College

Champaign 61820
Parkland College

Chicago 60640
City College of Chicago
Truman College

Freeport 61032
Highland Community College

Glen Ellyn 60137
College of DuPage

Godfrey 62035
Lewis & Clark Community
College

Kankakee 60901
Kankakee Community College

Oglesby 62348
Illinois Valley Community
College

Rockford 61101
Rock Valley College

Sugar Grove 60554
Waubonsee Community College

INDIANA

Evansville 47710
Indiana Vocational Technical
College

IOWA

Iowa Falls 50126
Ellsworth Community College

Marshalltown 50158
Marshalltown Community
College

Sioux City 51104
Briar Cliff College

KANSAS

Dodge City 67801
Dodge City Community College

McPherson 67460
Central College

KENTUCKY

Louisville 40201
University of Kentucky
Jefferson Community College

Paducah 42001
Paducah Community College

MARYLAND

Baltimore County 21237
Essex Community College

Bel Air 21014
Harford Community College

Catonsville 21228
Catonsville Community College

Columbia 21044
Howard Community College

Dundalk 21222
Dundalk Community College

Largo 20870
  Prince George's Community
  College

Rockville 20850
  Montgomery College

MASSACHUSETTS

Charlestown 02129
  Bunker Hill Community College

Beverly 01915
  North Shore Community College

Boston 02116
  Fisher Junior College

Brockton 02402
  Massasoit Commι .ity College

Gardner 01440
  Mount Wachusett Community
  College

Greenfield 01301
  Greenfield Community College

Haverhill 01830
  Northern Essex Community
  College

MICHIGAN

Kalamazoo 49009
  Kalamazoo Valley Community
  College

Lansing 48901
  Lansing Community College

Livonia 48150
  Schoolcraft College

Monroe 48161
  Monroe County Community
  College

Muskegon 49442
  Muskegon Community College

Port Huron 48060
  St. Clair County Community
  College

Roscommon 48653
  Kirtland Community College

Warren 48093
  Macomb County Community
  College

MINNESOTA

Coon Rapids 55433
  Anoka Ramsey Community
  College

Crookston 56716
  University of Minnesota
  Technical College

Inver Grove Heights 55075
  Inver Hills Community College

Willmar 56201
  Willmar Community College

Worthington 56187
  Worthington Community College

MISSISSIPPI

Booneville 38829
  Northeast Mississippi Junior
  College

MISSOURI

O'Fallon 63336
  Saint Mary's College of
  O'Fallon, Inc.

Poplar Bluff 63901
  Three Rivers Community
  College

NEBRASKA

Lincoln 68506
  Southeast Community College

44

Norfolk 68701
   Northeast Technical Community
   College

Omaha 68137
   Metropolitan Technical
   Community College

NEW HAMPSHIRE

Berlin 03570
   New Hampshire Vo Tech
   College at Berlin

Nashua 03060
   New Hampshire Vo Tech
   College

NEW JERSEY

Blackwood 08012
   Camden County College

Cranford 07016
   Union City

Edison 08817
   Middlesex County College

Lincroft 07738
   Brookdale Community College

Paramus 07652
   Bergen Community College

Paterson 07505
   Passaic County Community
   College

Vineland 08360
   Cumberland County College

NEW YORK

Albany 12208
   Russell Sage College

Binghamton 13902
   Broome Community College

Bronx
   Bronx Community College of the
   City University of New York
   10453
   Eugenio Maria De Hostos
   Community College 10451
   Manhattan College 10471

Brooklyn 11201
   New York City Community
   College

Buffalo 14221
   Erie Community College

Corning 14830
   Corning Community College

Dryden 13053
   Tompkins Cortland Community
   College

Herkimer 13350
   Herkimer County Community
   College

Merrick 11566
   Five Towns College

New York
   Borough of Manhattan
   Community College 10019
   Fashion Institute of Technology
   10001

Orchard Park 14127
   Erie Community College

Sanborn 14132
   Niagara County Community
   College

Schenectady 12305
   Schenectady County College

Utica 13501
   Mohawk Valley Community
   College

NORTH CAROLINA

Clyde 28721
Haywood Technical Institute

Henderson 27536
Vance-Granville Community
College

Jacksonville 28540
Coastal Carolina Community
College

Rocky Mount 27801
Nash Technical Institute

Spindale 23160
Isothermal Community College

Whiteville 28472
Southeastern Community College

NORTH DAKOTA

Bismarck 58501
Bismarck Junior College

OHIO

Canton 44720
Stark Technical College

Cleveland 44115
Cuyahoga Community College

Mentor 44060
Lakeland Community College

Piqua 45356
Edison State Community College

Springfield 45505
Clark Technical College

Steubenville 43952
Jefferson Technical College

OKLAHOMA

El Reno 72335
El Reno Junior College

Miami 74354
Northeastern Oklahoma A & M
College

Muskogee 74401
Bacone College

Oklahoma City 73159
South Oklahoma City Junior
College

Tulsa 74119
Tulsa Junior College

OREGON

Eugene 99752
Lane Community College

PENNSYLVANIA

Bryn Mawr 19010
Harcum Junior College

Jenkintown 19046
Manor Junior College

Media 19063
Delaware County Community
College

Monaca 15061
Community College of Beaver
County

Pittsburgh 15237
Community College of Allegheny
County

Scranton 18503
Lackawanna Junior College

Williamsport 17701
Williamsport Area Community
College

SOUTH CAROLINA

Charleston 29411
Trident Technical College

46

Cheraw 29520
  Chesterfield-Marlboro Technical
  College

Pendleton 29670
  Tri-County Community College

Pine Ridge 57770
  Oglala Sioux Community College

TENNESSEE

Jackson 38301
  Jackson State Community
  College

Memphis 38134
  State Technical Institute at
  Memphis

VERMONT

Burlington 05401
  Vermont Institute of Community
  Involvement

Randolph Center 05061
  Vermont Technical College

VIRGINIA

Annandale 22003
  Northern Virginia Community
  College

Big Stone Gap 24219
  Mountain Empire Community
  College

Hampton 23668
  Hampton Institute

Middletown 22645
  Lord Fairfax Community
  College

Portsmouth 23703
  Tidewater Community College

WASHINGTON

Bremerton 98310
  Olympic College

Everett 98201
  Everett Community College

Lynnwood 98036
  Edmonds Community College

Midway 98031
  Highline Community College

Mount Vernon 98273
  Skagit Valley College

Seattle 98106
  South Seattle Community
  College

Tacoma 98493
  Fort Steilacoom Community
  College

Wenatchee 98801
  Wenatchee Valley College

Yakima 98907
  Yakima Valley Community
  College

WEST VIRGINIA

Logan 25601
  Southern West Virginia
  Community College

Wheeling 26003
  West Virginia Northern
  Community College

WISCONSIN

Eau Claire 54701
  District One Technical Institute

Fennimore 53809
  Southwest Wisconsin Vocational-
  Technical Institute

Kenosha 53140
  Gateway Technical Institute

Pewaukee 53072
  Waukesha County Technical
  Institute

Shell Lake 54871
  Wisconsin Indianhead Technical
  Institute

Wausaw 54401
  North Central Technical Institute

Wisconsin Rapids 54494
  Mid-State Technical Institute

CHAPTER 2

Consultants and Management Assistance

INTRODUCTION: JUDGING AMONG MANY OPTIONS

- You have some savings, an idea for a new business, and some relevant technical expertise and experience. But you know you need a partner who understands the marketplace better than you do. You wonder where to look beyond your circle of friends and associates for such a partner.
- Yours is a small business that you run with a checkbook and the cash in a shoebox. The business is beginning to get out of hand, you fear. You want to borrow some money, but your banker is unimpressed with the checkbook stubs and the shoebox. You want to clean up your book-keeping system and prepare some financial statements, but aren't sure how to go about it.
- Your $1 million specialty business has a limited product line and stable sales. You want to identify potential new products that might fit your existing product line, but know you need outside research assistance.

The preceding situations are fairly typical of those encountered by would-be and existing entrepreneurs. Who can these entrepreneurs turn to for help? What kind of quality can they expect in the assistance they find? And how much will it cost?

Unfortunately, there are no easy answers to these questions. Nowhere among small-business resources are the options so numerous, the quality so variable, and the costs so unpredictable as in the area of management consulting.

The number of people calling themselves management consultants is large and growing steadily. According to an article in the January 1980 issue of *Venture* magazine, there are between 35,000 and 40,000 private consultants around the country, with the number increasing by perhaps 2,000 annually. Somewhat more than half the consultants work on their own; the remainder work in firms with up to several hundred people each.

Not all consultants are hired privately, though. Government agencies —primarily the Small Business Administration—can provide consultants to work with small businesses. Some of these consultants are paid by the government and some volunteer their services. University business professors also act as consultants to small businesses, in some cases on a private basis and in some cases via federally funded programs.

Also, various private and nonprofit organizations provide management assistance to help entrepreneurs answer specific business questions or to weather financial crises. The assistance may be provided by trained consultants or by professionals such as accountants and bankers.

QUALITY AND COST FACTORS

Unfortunately, anyone can call himself or herself a consultant. Not surprisingly, there are a good number of self-promoters whose only qualification for being consultants is an interest in making lots of money.

Of course, there are also many skilled consultants who can be of invaluable assistance to small companies. The problem for entrepreneurs is to distinguish between the quacks and the legitimate consultants. As a consultant stated in a May 1980 article about small-business consulting in *INC.* magazine:

> There are unscrupulous consultants around, and others who do absolutely stupid things. Sometimes, the small businessman doesn't know what he's getting, and just gets screwed.

Avoiding the frauds isn't enough to ensure that entrepreneurs will be happy with the consultants they choose, though. Entrepreneurs must have a clear idea of what they expect consultants to accomplish. Entrepreneurs must also be able to communicate comfortably and effectively with the consultants they hire.

An article in the November–December 1977 *Harvard Business Review* by a management consultant observed:

> Management consultants are generally hired for the wrong reasons. Once hired, they are generally poorly employed and loosely supervised. The result is, more often than not, a final report that decorates an executive's bookshelf with as much usefulness as "The Life and Mores of the Pluvius Aegiptus" . . .

As if choosing consultants isn't tough enough with the problems already described, entrepreneurs face huge variations in consulting costs. At one end of the spectrum is the Small Business Administration, which provides consultants to small businesses without charge. At the other end of the spectrum are well-known consulting firms that may charge $50,000 to $100,000 for a minimal marketing or technical feasibility study. In between are consultants who will work for between $100 and $1,000 daily.

While the quality of most products at least roughly correlates with their prices, not so with consultants. The advice rendered by an SBA-sponsored consultant could prove more valuable than that offered by a high-priced consulting firm. Of course, that isn't always the case; the point is, it's difficult to judge consultants solely on the basis of the fees they charge.

NARROWING THE FIELD

As unwieldy and risky as the consulting situation might appear, there are ways of limiting the choices and minimizing the dangers. For one thing, consultants tend to have specialties. While some consultants claim expertise in all aspects of business management or with all size businesses, most will at least indicate the kinds of situations they feel most comfortable and skillful handling. Knowing the kinds of problems you want advice on, then, can help entrepreneurs quickly eliminate inappropriate consultants.

And certainly the high cost of hiring many private consultants will limit the options for most start-up businesses. Because start-up businesses tend to be financially pressed, they are usually best off trying to make use of low-cost educational programs of the sort described in the previous chapter or government-funded management assistance programs of the type described later in this chapter.

What kinds of problems can consultants be most useful in helping to solve? Certainly the types of problems vary widely between start-up situations and existing businesses.

The *start-up business* requiring help usually needs it to complete critical one-time-only tasks and decisions that can have a lasting impact on the business and its chances of success. These tasks and decisions relate to assessing business sites, evaluating lease and rental agreements, setting up record and bookkeeping systems, finding business partners, obtaining start-up capital, and formulating initial marketing plans. Obtaining sound outside advice on matters such as these can mean the difference between ultimate success and failure.

The *existing business* tends to face ongoing issues that arise as the business grows and matures; many of these issues, though, are of such a specialized nature that outside advice is helpful in resolving them. Issues that frequently arise include when and how to go about computerizing business tasks, whether to lease or buy major pieces of equipment, how to devise appropriate employee benefit and compensation plans, and whether to change inventory valuation methods. Successfully resolving these and various other issues that come up can clear the way for businesses to move on to new stages of growth.

Sometimes, of course, business owners aren't able to pinpoint the exact nature of the problem their business is having, but they feel they need an unbiased and fresh management expert to look over their businesses. Such entrepreneurs are usually well advised to try to determine the broad nature of their problem—whether it's a personnel problem or a manufacturing problem or a marketing problem—before seeking out consultants. That way they can find consultants who specialize in their area.

Once entrepreneurs make the decision to hire a consultant, they should be hard-nosed and thorough in making their choice. One approach is to identify three or more potential consultants and interview them about their expertise and approach. Those candidates the entrepreneurs feel most impressed with should be asked to prepare specific proposals for handling the entrepreneurs' situations. These candidates should also be asked for the names of other clients, who should be contacted for their assessments of the consultants.

When a business owner settles on a particular consultant, the two should work out a written agreement specifying the consultant's responsibilities and objectives along with the type and amount of compensation. Some consultants work on an hourly basis, some work on a fixed-fee basis, and some work on a retainer-fee basis.

What follows is a listing and description of important sources of consulting and management assistance. Assembling this listing was perhaps the most challenging research task we faced, simply because the choices were so numerous. Much care and attention went into selecting sources we felt to be both reputable and potentially appropriate to a broad range of small-business situations.

We did not distinguish between sources specializing in start-up and existing businesses because most of the sources, though they work mainly with existing businesses, also deal with start-up situations. Wherever possible, we have noted the emphasis of sources.

Readers are also advised to refer to several other chapters that describe sources for consulting and management assistance—Chapter 4, "State and Local Government Assistance"; Chapter 7, "Assistance for Minority Businesses"; Chapter 9, "Franchising"; Chapter 10, "Government Procurement"; Chapter 11, "Foreign Trade—Exporting"; and Chapter 12, "Small-Business Lobbying and Service Organizations."

GOVERNMENT PROGRAMS

A number of government agencies provide specialized consulting services. The U. S. Department of Commerce, for instance, provides consultants for minority entrepreneurs and for small businesses seeking to become involved in exporting. The General Services Administration provides counseling to small businesses attempting to sell goods and services to federal agencies. These and other government consulting and management assistance programs are described in other chapters as noted in the previous paragraph.

The main federal source of general management consulting services to small businesses is the U. S. Small Business Administration, via a number of programs:

U. S. Small Business Administration
Assistant Administrator for Management Assistance
U. S. Small Business Administration
1441 L St., NW
Washington, DC 20416
(202) 653-6881
Information is available in more than 100 offices scattered among the nation's large- and medium-sized cities (see listing in Appendix A).

The Small Business Administration (SBA) is the federal government's main provider of consulting and management assistance services. The SBA's services are available to any businesses which qualify as small under the agency's guidelines. (See pp. 90–91 in Chapter 3, "Federal Government Financing Sources," for a summary of the SBA's size rules.)

The SBA's consulting and management assistance services are available through the following programs:

• *Service Corps of Retired Executives* (SCORE), which is a cadre of 6,000 retired professional business managers organized by the SBA, who volunteer to consult with start-up and existing small businesses. Among the SCORE volunteers are experts in most areas of business management. The volunteers will visit individual businesses and work with business owners to attempt to resolve specific problems.

SCORE volunteers are usually experienced and, because they are volunteers, enthusiastic. But SCORE volunteers also tend to have some drawbacks. For one thing, they usually come from large company backgrounds and thus may not fully understand the different needs and problems of small businesses. Also, because they are retired, SCORE volunteers may use business methods that are outdated.

• *Active Corps of Executives* (ACE), which is a cadre of more than 2,500 practicing business managers organized by the SBA as volunteer consultants. Because ACE volunteers tend to be more specialized in their business knowledge than SCORE volunteers, ACE volunteers tend to work primarily with existing businesses. (The SBA may combine the SCORE and ACE programs.)

ACE volunteers tend also to be more up-to-date on managerial practices and government regulations than SCORE volunteers. But because they have full-time jobs, their time may be more limited. And once again, their backgrounds are primarily of a corporate variety, which can limit their ability to fully appreciate small-business problems.

• *Call Contracts Program* involves the SBA in hiring professional consultants to aid small businesses owned by racial minorities. This program is described in more detail on p. 238 of Chapter 7, "Assistance for Minority Businesses."

UNIVERSITY AND COLLEGE PROGRAMS

Many universities and colleges with business courses provide consulting and management assistance to small businesses that seek out help. Most of these consulting and management assistance programs are funded by either the Small Business Administration or the National Science Foundation. Some are funded by other agencies and a few are sponsored by the universities and colleges themselves.

The kind and quality of assistance provided under such programs vary widely. Some of the programs emphasize traditional management consulting and some are oriented to developing new products. Some of the consultants are actually business students supervised by professors, which means that the quality of the advice offered may be questionable. But some consultants are experienced business school professors.

Nearly all the programs are either free or involve nominal fees for the small businesses receiving assistance. The programs are as follows:

THE SMALL BUSINESS INSTITUTE

The Small Business Institute (SBI) program is the largest of the programs, with nearly 500 colleges and universities serving more than 8,000 small businesses annually. It is funded by the SBA and serves both as an educational tool for business students and a consulting service for small-business owners.

The SBI program permits both senior-level undergraduate and graduate business students to consult for receptive business owners for one semester. The students work under the supervision of a faculty member and an SBA official, and must present both with a final written and oral report. The students must also make final recommendations to the business owners.

Businesses are not automatically accepted for SBA assistance. They are screened by professors with an eye to ensuring that both the students and businesses will benefit. It is the job of supervising faculty members to select businesses with both reasonably straightforward problems and owners who will cooperate sufficiently with students to enable them to complete the job.

The businesses accepted usually need market research, accounting systems, inventory control, and various cost-benefit analyses. The SBIs tend to work with small retail and manufacturing businesses. Recent examples of Northeastern University's SBI projects include:

- Evaluating the market for expensive boomerangs for a boomerang manufacturing company;
- Constructing a cost-control system for a Mexican restaurant;
- Developing a business plan for a helium balloon merchant to franchise nationally.

The SBI program does not provide quick help to small businesses. The consulting is performed over one semester, which usually lasts ten to thirteen weeks. Though students are closely supervised by a faculty member and tend to be highly motivated, their lack of practical experience is usually a handicap.

Yet small-business clients appear to be pleased with the SBI program. The *Journal of Small Business Management* in August 1979 reported that over 90 percent of the clients rated the service good to excellent. Best of all, the SBI assistance is free and thus attractive to small businesses with limited cash.

Businesses need not have SBA loans to qualify for SBI assistance. The names of nearby SBIs and requests for assistance can be made at local SBA offices (a list of local SBA offices is in Appendix A). Some of the universities and colleges with SBI programs are indicated in the list in Chapter 1, "Education and Training Sources," on pp. 23–39.

SMALL BUSINESS DEVELOPMENT CENTERS

The Small Business Development Center (SBDC) program, which was started with SBA funding in 1977, is offered at eighteen universities in sixteen states (see Exhibit 1). Each SBDC is headquartered on a university campus and is designed to draw on federal, state, local, university, and private consulting and management assistance resources in the SBDC's state. They also offer seminars and workshops for small-business owners.

The specific services vary from SBDC to SBDC, though most of their efforts involve workshops and individual counseling. The expertise and experience of the consultants depend on the SBDC. The University of Maine, for instance, employs a full-time staff of professional consultants, while the University of Minnesota uses its faculty and some professional consultants; some other schools, like the University of Arkansas, use experienced graduate students.

Some SBDCs now receive funding not only from the SBA but from other agencies like the National Science Foundation and the Economic Development Administration. The amount and source of funding affect the quality and focus of SBDC efforts. So, too, do regional factors. The SBDC at Rutgers in Newark has a major program for women entrepreneurs and also concentrates on the problems of urban small businesses. This is in contrast to Maine's SBDC, which works closely with the timber industry.

Many SBDCs have no specialty and are equipped to handle most small-business problems. Feasibility studies, market studies, and financial plans are the major consulting services provided.

The SBDC program has come under some criticism, notably from the National Federation of Independent Business (NFIB), the nation's largest lobbying organization of small businesses. A survey of members showed 87 percent disapproving of the federally funded SBDC program, while 10 percent favored it. The NFIB also reported that the General Accounting Office of the federal government conducted a limited study of the effectiveness of the SBDCs and found that of the 117 clients surveyed, 56 percent said they would not have been willing to pay for the SBDC assistance, while 22 percent said they would have been willing to pay only up to $25 for the service.

Another study of SBDCs by a consulting firm found, according to an article in the December 1979 issue of *INC.* magazine, that "the concept was sound and that those who had used the centers were generally satisfied with the services they received." But the study also uncovered some problems, according to *INC.*:

> Overall objectives lacked focus, the program was underfunded, the centers were inadequately supervised by SBA, they did not provide follow-up programs, and that most of the help provided by SBDCs came from graduate students instead of faculty members.

On balance, however, we believe the SBDC program is at least worth checking out for the majority of small-business owners.

Businesses need not have an SBA loan to qualify for assistance at an SBDC. Requests for assistance may be made either through local SBA offices in those states having SBDCs or directly to the appropriate SBDC listed. In fiscal 1980 the SBDC program provided training for 16,000 entrepreneurs and counseling for another 7,000. The program is free to small-business owners. Some of the centers have regional offices elsewhere in their states.

EXHIBIT 1

Small Business Development Centers

SBDC Director
University of Maine
96 Falmouth St.
Portland, ME 04103
(207) 780-4423

SBDC Director
Rutgers University
95 Central Ave.
Newark, NJ 07102
(201) 648-5627

SBDC Director, W178 Dietrich
 Hall
The Wharton School
University of Pennsylvania
Philadelphia, PA 19104
(215) 243-4856

SBDC Director
Howard University
P.O. Box 748
Washington, DC 20059
(202) 636-7187

SBDC Director
College of Business Administration
University of South Carolina
Columbia, SC 29208
(303) 777-5118

SBDC Director
University of Georgia
Athens, GA 30602
(404) 542-5760

SBDC Director
University of West Florida
Pensacola, FL 32504
(904) 476-9500 ext. 425

SBDC Director
University of Wisconsin
One Park South St.
Madison, WI 53706
(608) 263-7794

SBDC Director
College of Business
St. Cloud State University
St. Cloud, MN 56301
(612) 255-3214

SBDC Director
University of Arkansas (P.O. Box
 3017)
1201 McAlmont
Little Rock, AR 72203
(501) 371-1971

SBDC Director
University of Missouri
8001 Natural Bridge Road (Room
 461)
St. Louis, MO 63121
(324) 553-5621

SBDC Director
University of Nebraska at Omaha
Omaha, NE 68182
(402) 554-2521

SBDC Director
Graduate School of Business
University of Utah
Salt Lake City, UT 84112
(801) 581-7458

SBDC Director
California State University
Chico, CA 95929
(916) 895-5938

SBDC Director
California State Polytechnic
  University
3801 W Temple Ave.
Pomona, CA 91768
(714) 598-4210

SBDC Director, 141 Todd Hall
College of Business & Economics
Washington State University
Pullman, WA 99164
(509) 335-1576

SBDC Director
University of Alabama
  (Birmingham)
School of Business
University Station
Birmingham, AL 35294
(205) 934-3480

SBDC Director
University of Massachusetts
School of Business Administration
(Room 205)
Amherst, MA 01003
(413) 549-4930 ext. 303

INNOVATION CENTERS AND OTHER PROGRAMS

A handful of colleges and universities have programs to assist inventors and small businesses in evaluating the potential of new products under consideration. The Innovation Centers vary somewhat in focus and approach, but generally help judge the market potential of products and find investors for products deemed promising.

The institutions offering the programs are indicated in the list of four-year colleges at the end of Chapter 1 (pp. 23–39).

OTHER PROGRAMS

In addition several other consulting and management assistance programs are offered by individual colleges and universities. Two examples are the following:

MIT Venture Clinic
MIT Alumni Center of New York
50 E 41st St.
New York, NY 10017
(212) 532-8181

The MIT Venture Clinic is just as described by its name—a place to have ideas for new businesses checked out by experts. It consists of a panel of up to thirty Massachusetts Institute of Technology graduates who are knowledgeable in the fields of marketing, banking, venture-capital securities, and management consulting. The panelists are volunteers who assemble once a month over dinner to consider presentations from initiators of one or two new ventures.

The clinic has been in existence since 1972 and is open to MIT and non-MIT entrepreneurs alike who meet two of the following three criteria: they have financial backing, a market, or a product. Entrepreneurs present their venture idea as they would to potential backers or investors, except that instead of cash, they receive hard-nosed feedback in return. The panelists provide guidance in the form of information sources for further assistance, judgments based on their own experience, and additional ideas for marketing and products. The panelists also serve as potential contacts who might themselves be able to provide assistance or else introduce entrepreneurs to others who can help.

Venture Clinic meetings are held in New York City on the fourth Tuesday of each month. The cost is $100, which includes dinner and rental expenses.

MIT Enterprise Forum
MIT Alumni Center
77 Massachusetts Ave.
Cambridge, MA 02139
(617) 253-8200

The MIT Enterprise Forum is the Cambridge version of the MIT Venture Clinic in New York. It offers young existing-company owners an opportunity to secure management and financial advice from a panel of experts consisting of Massachusetts Institute of Technology alumni entrepreneurs, venture capitalists, executives, and consultants who donate their services. Panelists vary, depending on the company under consideration.

The typical client company is a growing manufacturing company. Panelists often visit companies being evaluated and talk with their owners before formally meeting. The Enterprise Forum then helps entrepreneurs formulate a business plan. The discussion is taped and given to the company owners.

Like the Venture Clinic in New York, the Enterprise Forum convenes once a month to meet with individual company owners and assesses a fee of $100 to cover expenses. In November 1980, the Enterprise Forum conducted a one-day seminar on "Financing the Small Technical Enterprise." Representatives of financial institutions, entrepreneurs, and academics gave talks on sources of private and public financing and how to approach these sources.

PRIVATE CONSULTANTS

Entrepreneurs who choose to hire outside consultants will find that the options are seemingly endless. Potential consultants come from any number of backgrounds and charge a wide variety of fees, and of course each insists that he or she has the best approach to solving management problems. In addition, accountants can frequently serve as consultants to advise and assist in financial planning, obtaining loans, and instituting computerized services.

What we have tried to do in this section is offer entrepreneurs a wide selection of consultants with whom to at least start the search for management assistance. Of course, many competent firms aren't included for lack of space. We have organized several listings as follows:

SBA-APPROVED ACCOUNTANTS AND CONSULTANTS

The U. S. Small Business Administration hires a handful of accounting and consulting firms around the country on a part-time basis to provide various management assistance to minority entrepreneurs under its Call Contracts Program (see p. 238 of Chapter 7, "Assistance for Minorities"). The firms all have extensive experience working with start-up and existing businesses. In addition to working for the SBA, these firms also do extensive private work. Thus, entrepreneurs not eligible for participation in the Call Contracts Program can hire these firms.

The firms tend to specialize in the following areas:

• Start-up plans. Finding suppliers, locating retail and manufacturing space, obtaining marketing information, and instituting financial systems.

• Loan packaging. Deciding where to apply for loans and then completing loan applications and assembling necessary supporting documentation.

• Business plans. Helping put together plans that project marketing direction and growth for three to five years into the future.

• Turnaround situations. Working with businesses experiencing financial losses to help make them profitable.

The consulting and accounting firms in the following list were designated by the SBA in a recent year to provide assistance to minority firms on the basis of competitive bidding.

CALIFORNIA

Payne-Maxie Consultants
1510 Walnut St. (Suite E)
Berkeley, CA 94709
(415) 841-8554

COLORADO

Management Task Force
700 Broadway (Suite 1011)
Denver, CO 80203
(303) 831-1561

ILLINOIS

Thomas H. Miner and Associates, Inc.
135 S LaSalle St.
Chicago, IL 60603
(312) 236-8745

INDIANA

Fowler, Suttles and Company
(CPA)
2211 E 54th St.
Indianapolis, IN 46220
(317) 253-3481

IOWA

Dutton and Associates, P.C.
(CPA)
414 Walnut St.
Atlantic, IA 50022
(712) 243-3145

MINNESOTA

Earl F. Rasmussen & Associates
(CPA)
11000 Highway 65 NE
Blaine, MN 55434
(612) 757-5380

MISSOURI

Lawrence-Leiter and Company
427 W 12th St.
Kansas City, MO 64105
(816) 474-8340

NEW YORK

Bush & Germain (CPA)
Carrier Tower/Mony Plaza
Syracuse, NY 13202
(315) 424-1145

OHIO

Watson, Rice & Co. (CPA)
Lincoln Building (Suite 608)
Cleveland, OH 44114
(216) 696-0767

OREGON

Martech Associates, Inc.
The Bank of California Tower
(Suite 618)
Portland, OR 97205
(503) 226-4985

TENNESSEE

Camper, Henderson, and Co.
(CPA)
First Tennessee Bank Building
(Suite 1516)
Memphis, TN 38103
(901) 521-0220

TEXAS

Frank J. Leal & Associates, Inc.
(CPA)
Cypress Tower (Suite 400)
122 N Main Ave.
San Antonio, TX 78212
(512) 222-1284

Welsh, White, Wood and
Associates
5327 North Central Expressway
(Suite 200)
Dallas, TX 75205
(214) 521-5104

Innocept, Inc.
4230 L. B. J. Freeway (Suite 204)
Dallas, TX 75234
(214) 233-1067

WASHINGTON

Molitor and Grayson (CPA)
115 108th Ave., NE
Bellevue, WA 98004
(206) 455-1725

SPECIALTY CONSULTING FIRMS

One of our more ambitious projects in assembling material for this book was identifying a cross section of consulting firms with a variety of specialties known to have experience and interest in working with small businesses. Narrowing a universe of thousands down to three dozen is no easy task.

We identified candidates for our listing through a number of sources, including national associations of consultants, newspaper and magazine articles, and personal contacts. Thousands of reputable firms that justifiably could be on this list aren't included.

The information on the listed firms' specialties, noted under "Expertise/Services," was obtained through telephone interviews with the owners or principals of each firm.

Such firms can be identified by entrepreneurs in a number of different ways. The sources listed on p. 74 provide listings of consultants. Other entrepreneurs as well as accountants and bankers can frequently provide references. And the local and specialty small-business organizations listed in Chapter 12 can frequently offer specific suggestions of appropriate consultants.

Some Private Consulting Firms Responsive to Small Business

State	Years Experience	Expertise/Services
CALIFORNIA		
Earl D. Brodie and Associates 111 Sutter St. San Francisco, CA 94194 (415) 986-4834	(16)	Services independent businesses with $1 million to $30 million sales volume. Helps diagnose and solve organizational problems, such as poor management control systems. Also does much work on mergers and acquisitions, new products and sales development, as well as preparing clients for meetings with banks and regulatory committees. Serves clients worldwide.
Durkee-Sharlit Jonesboro St. Los Angeles, CA 90014 (213) 395-9973	(10)	Specializes in turnaround situations and mergers and acquisitions. The firm claims a 90 percent success rate in turning losing companies into profitable companies with at least a 40 percent pre-tax return on owners' equity. Firm works on an hourly basis and says majority of turnarounds accomplished for a total of $10,000 to $15,000.

State	Years Experience	Expertise/Services
California (contd.)		
Norris Consultants Box 16 Calabasas, CA 91302 (213) 999-4878	(7)	Operations consultants to growing firms; specializes in production and inventory control, systems and procedures, and organization.
CONNECTICUT		
Baxter, Broudy, Pompan & Starr 34–36 W Putnam Ave. Greenwich, CT 06830 (203) 869-4885	(5)	Specializes in cash management and control.
J. W. Haslett and Associates 12 McLaren Road S Darien, CT 06820 (203) 655-2204	(15)	Specializes in editorial consulting. Assists clients in communicating with their special audiences by: 1) identifying a company's editorial requirements; 2) developing the content of its publications; 3) designing the presentation and writing the text.
The Pace Consulting Group 2074 Park St. Hartford, CT 06106 (203) 525-9921	(10)	Specializes in business turnaround situations. Aids in capital restructuring and obtaining equity funding. Will assume responsibility for complete operations if desired.
Synder Associates Box 98 Essex, CT 06426 (203) 767-1122	(11)	Assists manufacturing firms to expand or reorganize their businesses by providing advice on industrial markets, new technology, new manufacturing methods, research and development, investment feasibility, license search, and joint venture management. Specializes in high-technology manufacturing industries. Serves the U.S., Europe, Japan.
ILLINOIS		
George S. May International Co. 111 S Washington St. Park Ridge, IL 60068 (312) 825-8806	(55)	This senior citizen of consulting organizations has serviced more than 5,000 small- and medium-sized businesses through its offices in Montreal, Milan, and San Francisco with a wide range of management consulting services.
INDIANA		
Shaw International, Inc. Box 375 New Albany, IN 47150 (812) 944-6751	(9)	General consulting, stressing financial management and capital formation for small businesses and entrepreneurs. Also values small businesses considering being sold. Serves the U.S.

State	Years Experience	Expertise/Services
KANSAS		
Arheson and Company 12715 High Drive Leawood, KS 66209 (913) 341-7722	(8)	Primarily works with closely held companies. Advises on turnaround situations, interim financing, mergers and acquisitions, and organizational planning. Works with start-up and existing businesses.
MAINE		
Martech, Inc. 592 Preble St. Cape Elizabeth Portland, ME 04107 (207) 799-1855	(13)	Specializes in start-ups—locating financing and helping spot early problem areas. Also does industrial marketing and other marketing research.
MASSACHUSETTS		
Advanced Management Associates 39 Old Colony Road Chestnut Hill, MA 02167 (617) 332-3141	(26)	Provides general management and financial consulting to small businesses, primarily in New England.
David T. Barry Associates 572 Washington St. Wellesley, MA 02181 (617) 235-1520	(20)	Specializes in marketing, systems, mergers, acquisitions, and management development. Worldwide.
Buckley and Co. 36 Washington St. Wellesley Hills, MA 02181 (617) 235-4592	(11)	Emphasis on small- to medium-sized manufacturing firms. General management, financial, and marketing assignments.
Executrak Systems, Inc. 470 Totten Pond Road Waltham, MA 02154 (617) 890-6170	(12)	A consulting and management strategy firm that aids small growth-oriented firms in time management, transitions, and technical areas.
Thomas A. Faulhaber 146 Mt. Vernon St. Boston, MA 02109 (617) 723-2030	(12)	Counsels small companies on acquisitions and divestitures. Works closely with management designing and executing strategies for growth and change.
Financial Management and Consulting Corporation 216 Lewis Wharf Boston, MA 02110 (617) 742-5150	(15)	Financial consulting to small- and medium-sized firms. Aids in formulating business plans and assisting in overall financial management.

64

State	Years Experience	Expertise/Services
Massachusetts (contd.)		
JDA Management Services 157 Lindell Ave. Leominster, MA 01453 (617) 537-2938	(17)	Serves rapidly growing companies that usually have 200 to 400 employees, specializing in organizational planning and development to improve operating efficiency. Also advises in turnaround situations. Serves east of Mississippi River.
Management and Marketing 176 Second Ave. Waltham, MA 02154 (617) 890-7788	(15)	Specializes in interim management of smaller companies. Also does marketing studies and general marketing consulting.
Marketing Catalysts 4 Cherry Brooks Road Weston, MA 02193 (617) 891-6331	(10)	Specializes in advising on technical marketing potential of inventions and new products.
Parker, Eldridge, Sholl and Gordon 440 Totten Pond Road Waltham, MA 02154 (617) 890-0340	(19)	Executive recruiters and compensations consultants. Serves the U.S.
University Center, Inc. 607 Boylston St. Boston, MA 02116 (617) 267-6665	(27)	Management psychologists who work with small- and medium-sized companies on selection, training, development, and retention of key employees. Also concerned with personnel operating efficiency.
MINNESOTA		
Teipel Associates, Inc. 843 S Snelling Ave. St. Paul, MN 55116 (612) 227-6625	(18)	Concentrates on concerns with $2 million to $50 million sales. Specializes in management training, accountability, compensation, and labor relations. Serves primarily the Midwest.
NEW JERSEY		
Marpet Consultants, Inc. 2 Bell Ave. Somerville, NJ 08876 (201) 526-1700	(20)	Specializes in the areas of small-business management and financial accounting. Works with start-up and existing businesses.
System Planning Associates 37 Elm St. Westfield, NJ 07090 (201) 232-3910	(15)	Serves smaller manufacturers, distributors, retailers, and service companies with advice on computer systems. Focuses on developing and implementing effective information systems and computer technology.

State	Years Experience	Expertise/Services
NEW YORK		
Joseph Auerbach 33–74 Utopia Parkway Flushing, NY 11358 (212) 463-0466	(25)	Serves small- to medium-sized manufacturing, distribution, and service businesses. Specializes in computerized systems, inventory and production control, and organization.
Don Aux Associates, Inc. 1 Lincoln Plaza New York, NY 10023 (212) 877-2115	(17)	Concentrates on organizational behavior, or the human factors to help employees better understand their goals and fellow workers. Works with independent businesses to improve their operating efficiency. Has a staff of 53 and serves primarily the Northeast.
Legge Associates 110 Allen's Creek Road Rochester, NY 14618 (716) 461-3550	(19)	Specialists in manufacturing management and facilities planning. Work on strategic planning and manufacturing control systems. Named by *Consultants News* as one of the 100 leading consultants in the U.S. today. Serves primarily the Rochester area.
Standard Research Consultants 345 Hudson St. New York, NY 10014 (212) 741-7300	(40)	Values small companies for possible sale and does financial counseling and studies on excess earnings and excess compensation. Serves the U.S.
OKLAHOMA		
Rubottom & Associates 1920 First Place Tulsa, OK 74103 (918) 584-4201	(13)	Specializes in management, financial, and systems consulting.
PENNSYLVANIA		
Problem Solvers for Industry 345 Park Ave. Chalfont, PA 18914 (215) 822-9695	(7)	Manufacturing and management problems for small- to medium-sized firms. Serves the East Coast.
RHODE ISLAND		
Guenther Associates 52 Wildwood Ave. Rumford, RI 02916 (401) 434-4559	(22)	Works with the principals of small- and medium-sized companies. General management consulting.
TEXAS		
Bain Management Consulting, Inc. 4410 W Vickery Boulevard Fort Worth, TX 76107 (817) 738-0201	(2)	Serves small- to medium-sized firms in the area of data processing. Services range from feasibility studies to management reviews of existing installations.

State	Years Experience	Expertise/Services
WISCONSIN		
Anderson-Roethle & Assoc. 811 E Wisconsin Ave. Milwaukee, WI 53202 (414) 276-0070	(17)	Primarily works with manufacturing firms in the $2 million to $20 million range, in four main areas: long-range corporate planning; marketing and sales management; organizational analysis; and mergers and acquisitions. Works nationally, but focuses on the Midwest.
Dickson Associates Box 1005 Neenah, WI 54956 (414) 725-8237	(16)	General management consulting, with emphasis on simple, understandable solutions. Also does start-up work. Serves the Midwest.

TOP 100 CONSULTING FIRMS

In 1979 *Consultants News* published a list of leading consulting firms in the United States. The firms tend to be among the country's largest consulting firms, and thus the list is somewhat biased toward large corporations, which can afford to pay the usually astronomical fees.

Nonetheless, these firms offer a wide variety of services and will work for smaller companies as well. For small companies intent on hiring a well-known and nationally established consulting firm and that aren't intimidated by high fees, this list may offer appropriate candidates.

Louis A. Allen Associates, Inc.
615 University Ave.
Palo Alto, CA 94301
(415) 322-8422

Altman & Weil, Inc.
326 W Lancaster Ave.
Ardmore, PA 19003
(215) 649-4646

Arthur Andersen & Co.
69 W Washington St.
Chicago, IL 60602
(312) 346-6262

Anderson/Roethle & Associates,
Inc.
811 E Wisconsin Ave.
Milwaukee, WI 53202
(414) 276-0070

Emory Ayers Associates, Inc.
950 Third Ave. at 57th St.
New York, NY 10022
(212) 486-1489

Bain & Co.
Faneuil Hall Marketplace
Boston, MA 02109
(617) 367-3700

Theodore Barry & Associates
1151 W Sixth St.
Los Angeles, CA 90017
(213) 481-7371

Bavier, Bulger & Goodyear, Inc.
270 Amity Rd.
New Haven, CT 06525
(203) 389-1534

Behavioral Systems Inc.
3300 Northeast Expressway
Atlanta, GA 30341
(404) 458-8251

Booz, Allen & Hamilton, Inc.
135 S LaSalle St.
Chicago, IL 60603
(312) 346-1900

The Boston Consulting Group
1 Boston Place
Boston, MA 02106
(617) 722-7901

A. Val Bradley Associates, Inc.
2950 Metro Dr.
Bloomington, MN 55420
(612) 854-6661

Cambridge Research Institute
15 Mt. Auburn St.
Cambridge, MA 02138
(617) 429-3800

Case & Co., Inc.
90 Park Ave.
New York, NY 10020
(212) 687-9010

J. P. Cavanaugh & Associates
600 Metro Bldg.
Fort Wayne, IN 46802
(219) 423-2506

Charles River Associates, Inc.
John Hancock Tower
200 Clarendon St.
Boston, MA 02116
(617) 266-0500

Cleveland Consulting Associates
25550 Chagrin Blvd.
Cleveland, OH 44122
(216) 831-0430

Cole & Associates, Inc.
(subsidiary of The Wyatt Co.)
10 Post Office Sq.
Boston, MA 02109
(617) 542-7191

Coopers & Lybrand
1251 Avenue of the Americas
New York, NY 10020
(212) 489-1100

Cresap, McCormick & Paget, Inc.
245 Park Ave.
New York, NY 10017
(212) 953-7000

Herbert W. Davis & Co.
120 Charlotte Pl.
Englewood Cliffs, NJ 07632
(201) 871-1760

Decision Sciences Corp.
814 Fox Pavilion
Jenkintown, PA 19046
(215) 887-1970

Deloitte, Haskins & Sells
1114 Avenue of the Americas
New York, NY 10036
(212) 422-9600

Drake Sheahan/Stewart Dougall,
    Inc.
330 Madison Ave.
New York, NY 10017
(212) 697-0294

The Emerson Consultants, Inc.
30 Rockefeller Plaza
New York, NY 10020
(212) 245-5738

Ernst & Ernst
1300 Union Commerce Bldg.
Cleveland, OH 44115
(216) 861-5000

Fenvessy Associates, Inc.
745 Fifth Ave.
New York, NY 10022
(212) 751-3707

Folger & Co.
214 Lewis Wharf
Boston, MA 02110
(617) 227-5900

Garr Associates, Inc.
230 Emerson Ctr.
2812 Newspring Rd., NW
Atlanta, GA 30339
(404) 434-6494

Gellman Research Associates
100 West Ave.
Jenkintown, PA 19046
(215) 884-7500

Gilbert Management Consultants
525 Lancaster Ave.
Reading, PA 19603
(215) 775-2600

Glendinning Associates
1 Glendinning Pl.
Westport, CT 06880
(203) 226-4711

P. Paul Goggi Associates
233 Broadway
New York, NY 10007
(212) 962-2662

Golightly & Co. Int'l, Inc.
1 Rockefeller Plaza
New York, NY 10020
(212) 245-0900

Gottfried Consultants Inc.
3435 Wilshire Blvd.
Los Angeles, CA 90010
(213) 387-2271

Frank K. Greisinger & Associates,
    Inc.
838 National City Bank Bldg.
Cleveland, OH 44114
(216) 241-3228

H. J. Hansen Co.
1550 Northwest Hwy.
Park Ridge, IL 60068
(312) 824-6601

Harbridge House, Inc.
11 Arlington St.
Boston, MA 02116
(617) 267-6410

Hay Associates
1845 Walnut St.
Philadelphia, PA 19103
(215) 561-7000

Robert H. Hayes & Associates, Inc.
20 N Wacker Dr.
Chicago, IL 60606
(312) 236-8600

Hendrick & Co. Inc.
395 Totten Pond Rd.
Waltham, MA 02154
(617) 890-3310

Porter Henry & Co., Inc.
103 Park Ave.
New York, NY 10017
(212) 679-8835

Nathaniel Hill & Associates, Inc.
4513 Creedmoor Rd.
Crabtree Executive Park
Raleigh, NC 27612
(919) 787-6919

William E. Hill & Co., Inc.
(subsidiary of Dun & Bradstreet)
640 Fifth Ave.
New York, NY 10019
(212) 582-5959

Ingersoll Mfg. Consultants, Inc.
(Division of Ingersoll
  Milling Machine Co.)
707 Fulton Ave.
Rockford, IL 61101
(815) 987-6110

Institutional Strategy
  Associates, Inc.
51 Brattle St.
Cambridge, MA 02138
(617) 492-7812

A. T. Kearney, Inc.
100 S Wacker Dr.
Chicago, IL 60606
(312) 782-2868

Kensington Management
  Consultants, Inc.
25 Third St.
Stamford, CT 06905
(203) 327-9860

Warren King & Associates, Inc.
20 N Wacker Dr.
Chicago, IL 60606
(312) 726-0481

Charles H. Kline & Co., Inc.
330 Passaic Ave.
Fairfield, NJ 07006
(201) 227-6262

Lester B. Knight & Associates, Inc.
549 W Randolph St.
Chicago, IL 60606
(312) 346-2100

Krall Management, Inc.
2 Radnor Corporate Ctr.
Radnor, PA 19087
(215) 687-8410

Lawrence-Leiter & Co.
427 W 12th St.
Kansas City, MO 64105
(816) 474-8340

Legge Associates, Inc.
110 Allen's Creek Rd.
Rochester, NY 14618
(716) 461-3550

Arthur D. Little, Inc.
25 Acorn Park
Cambridge, MA 02140
(617) 864-5770

LWFW, Inc.
12700 Park Central Pl.
Dallas, TX 75251
(214) 233-5561

Main, Jackson & Garfield, Inc.
535 Fifth Ave.
New York, NY 10017
(212) 867-7948

Management Analysis Center, Inc.
745 Concord Ave.
Cambridge, MA 02138
(617) 868-3042

Management Design Associates
90 Madison St.
Denver, CO 80206
(303) 320-1727

Frank B. Manley & Co.
1 Pickwick Plaza
Greenwich, CT 06830
(203) 661-6606

H. B. Maynard & Co.
(subsidiary of
  Planning Research Corp.)
2040 Ardmore Blvd.
Pittsburgh, PA 15221
(412) 351-4100

McBer & Co.
137 Newbury St.
Boston, MA 02116
(617) 261-5570

McCormick & Co.
2 Overhill Rd.
Scarsdale, NY 10583
(914) 723-5200

McKinsey & Co., Inc.
245 Park Ave.
New York, NY 10017
(212) 692-6000

MDC Systems Corp.
(owned by MDC Corp.)
1818 Market St.
Philadelphia, PA 19103
(215) 299-8213

Medicus Systems Corp.
625 N Michigan Ave.
Chicago, IL 60611
(312) 787-0915

Richard Muther & Associates, Inc.
6155 Oak St.
Kansas City, MO 64113
(816) 444-3232

MWS Consultants, Inc.
55 East Monroe St.
Chicago, IL 60603
(312) 726-8730

Robert E. Nolan Co., Inc.
90 Hopmeadow St.
Simsbury, CT 06070
(203) 658-1941

Norris Consultants, Inc.
P.O. Box 16
Calabasas, CA 91302
(213) 999-4878

Organization Resources
  Counselors, Inc.
1270 Avenue of the Americas
New York, NY 10020
(212) 765-0600

The Pace Consulting Group, Inc.
2074 Park St.
Hartford, CT 06106
(203) 236-1951

Patton Consultants, Inc.
2200 East Devon Ave.
Des Plaines, IL 60018
(312) 298-2660

Peat, Marwick, Mitchell & Co.
(Management Consulting
  Division)
345 Park Ave.
New York, NY 10022
(212) 758-9700

Price Waterhouse & Co.
(Management Advisory Srvcs)
1251 Avenue of the Americas
New York, NY 10020
(212) 489-8900

Harry J. Prior & Associates, Inc.
IBM Bldg.
Seattle, WA 98101
(206) 623-2332

Albert Ramond & Associates, Inc.
1615 Tribune Tower
Chicago, IL 60611
(312) 943-2323

Rath & Strong, Inc.
21 Worthen Rd.
Lexington, MA 02173
(617) 861-1700

Reel/Grobman & Associates
1052 W Sixth St.
Los Angeles, CA 90017
(213) 482-8084

Resource Planning Associates, Inc.
44 Brattle St.
Cambridge, MA 02138
(617) 661-1410

Runzheimer & Co., Inc.
Runzheimer Park
Rochester, WI 53167
(414) 534-3121

Kurt Salmon Associates, Inc.
350 Fifth Ave.
New York, NY 10001
(212) 564-3690

Robert H. Schaffer & Associates
401 Rockrimmon Rd.
Stamford, CT 06903
(203) 322-1604

F. R. Schwab & Associates, Inc.
645 Madison Ave.
New York, NY 10022
(212) 758-6800

Science Management Corp.
Fellowship Rd.
Moorestown, NJ 08057
(609) 235-9200

Stanton Associates, Inc.
1821 University Ave.
St. Paul, MN 55104
(612) 646-7154

Stone & Webster Management
  Consultants, Inc.
90 Broad St.
New York, NY 10004
(212) 269-4224

Summerour & Associates, Inc.
2300 Peachtree Ctr., S
Atlanta, GA 30303
(404) 577-4632

Technomic Consultants
1 N Wacker Dr.
Chicago, IL 60606
(312) 346-5901

Temple, Barker & Sloane, Inc.
15 Walnut St.
Wellesley Hills, MA 02181
(617) 237-4492

TMI Systems Corp.
1 Broadway
Cambridge, MA 02142
(617) 492-6520

Touche Ross & Co.
1633 Broadway
New York, NY 10019
(212) 489-1600

Towers, Perrin, Forster & Crosby
600 Third Ave.
New York, NY 10016
(212) 661-5080

K. W. Tunnell Co., Inc.
Valley Forge Plaza
1150 First Ave.
King of Prussia, PA 19406
(215) 337-0820

Robert M. Wald & Associates, Inc.
3540 Wilshire Blvd.
Los Angeles, CA 90010
(213) 385-3223

Roy W. Walters & Associates, Inc.
Whitney Industrial Park
Whitney Rd.
Mahwah, NJ 07430
(201) 891-3344

Emmanuel Weintraub Associates,
  Inc.
1633 Broadway
New York, NY 10019
(212) 489-7920

Werner Associates, Inc.
1450 Broadway
New York, NY 10018
(212) 730-1280

72

Worden & Risberg, Inc.
1234 Market St.
Philadelphia, PA 19107
(215) 568-4400

Arthur Young & Co.
277 Park Ave.
New York, NY 10017
(212) 922-2000

Reprinted with permission from January 1979 *Consultants News.*

OTHER MANAGEMENT ASSISTANCE FIRMS

Business Partner Search, Inc.
663 Fifth Ave.
New York, NY 10022
(212) PL 7-8557

Business Partner Search (BPS) offers three services designed to match suitable business partners. One is an Open Exchange Forum, which gathers individuals looking for partners to introduce themselves and their business aspirations. The fee for participation is $50.

BPS also offers business brokerage services through which clients are matched based on confidential dossiers they submit. In addition, BPS publishes a newsletter in which business opportunities are advertised through BPS box numbers. Both of these services are available on a sliding fee.

BPS deals with investors with a minimum of $100,000. Its matches have included art marketers, the owner of a netting company looking for younger partners, a jeweler looking for a gold buyer, and a rehearsal studio owner in need of $100,000.

Control Data Business and Technology Centers
245 E Sixth St.
St. Paul, MN 55101
(612) 292-2692

Control Data Business and Technology Centers (BTC) are intended to increase the success rate of small businesses. The BTCs provide new companies with a range of business services usually unavailable to small companies. The centers lease laboratory and office space to small businesses at competitive rates; the monthly rental fees include the opportunity to utilize a range of services at reduced costs. BTCs exist in or are planned for St. Paul, Minneapolis, Philadelphia, and Toledo.

The services include such things as a technical library along with drafting, purchasing, legal, banking, advertising, and computer services. The BTCs also offer education programs in business-related topics such as management and accounting. Other services, such as copying and a receptionist, are also available.

BTCs are geared toward technically oriented businesses. Services are available to nontenants on a fee basis.

Besides aiding small start-up businesses, BTCs are intended to generate income for Control Data Corp. and contribute to the growth of urban downtown areas.

The *Wall Street Journal* in a September 25, 1979, article profiled an entrepreneur who moved into the St. Paul BTC in May 1979 and paid $100 a month for a small office. He used the Center to find a lawyer for advice on incorporating and whether to patent his chemical-cleaning process. He also used the Center's computer to develop a business plan.

Control Data Business Resource Centers
5241 Viking Drive
Minneapolis, MN 55435
(612) 893-4200

The Business Resource Centers (BRCs) began in 1980 as a followup to Control Data's BTCs. The BRC is a walk-in clinic for small businesses. BRCs are designed to help small businesses succeed and grow through access to a wide array of financing opportunities and services most small businesses can't provide themselves, including the following:

- SBA-guaranteed loans
- Small-business loans
- Equipment financing and leasing
- Vendor financing and leasing
- Commercial financing
- Real estate financing
- Venture capital
- Vehicle leasing
- Commercial collections
- Business reviews
- Accounting services
- Tax services
- Financial planning and analysis
- Data processing
- Time-sharing applications
- Market research and related services
- Insurance coverage

BRCs also offer management training courses.

The BRCs are targeted to companies with annual sales of under $10 million. Fees for services vary but, according to a Control Data official, are competitive.

Twelve BRCs are either operating or scheduled to open in Baltimore, Los Angeles, Atlanta, Denver, Minneapolis, Dallas, Chicago, Cleveland,

Miami, Houston, San Francisco, and Charlotte (NC). Contact the Minneapolis office or a local Control Data office to determine the nearest BRC. Control Data hopes eventually to be operating 400 BRCs nationwide.

ADDITIONAL INFORMATION SOURCES

Four major associations and publications provide information and directories on management consultants:

Institute of Management Consultants
19 W 44th St.
New York, NY 10036
(212) 921-2885

Consultants News
Templeton Road
Fitzwilliam, NH 03447
(603) 585-2200

Association of Management Consultants
331 Madison Ave.
New York, NY 10017
(212) 687-2825

Association of Consulting Management Engineers, Inc.
230 Park Ave.
New York, NY 10017
(212) 697-9693

Consulting: A Complete Guide to a Profitable Career, by Robert E. Kelley (New York: Charles Scribner's Sons, 1981). Kelley is widely recognized in academic circles as an expert on consulting. He is also a fine writer.

"How to Get a Good Consultant" (*Harvard Business Review,* November–December 1977).

CHAPTER 3

Federal Government Financing Sources

INTRODUCTION: UNDERSTANDING THE BUREAUCRACY

As business lenders go, the United States Government takes what might best be described as a schizophrenic approach to potential customers. In many respects, the federal government is quite helpful. It has billions of dollars available to all sorts of small businesses, including those that commercial lenders tend to shun, such as businesses that are very new, those located in economically run-down areas, and those researching new scientific concepts and inventions.

But the federal government also has a dark side. Its loan programs are scattered among several agencies that usually know little about each other. The bureaucratic logistics involved in processing applications can cause it to take many months to make a loan decision. And loans are sometimes turned down for what seem to entrepreneurs to be trivial reasons.

It is this dark side that discourages many entrepreneurs from even trying to obtain government loans. Sponsors of the White House Conference on Small Business, which took place in January 1980, took note, in an issue paper presented to participants, of the frequently negative attitude expressed by business owners toward the government at various meetings that preceded the conference:

> A recurring theme in most of the fifty-seven field meetings and regional caucuses of the conferences among business owners was that federal programs to assist small business should be organized more effectively and delivered more efficiently. Many participants voiced the opinion that the programs were confusing, splintered, scattered, and generally inaccessible to the average small-business owner. Others pointed out that local federal officials frequently knew only about programs that existed in their own

agency, and had no awareness of complementary programs that existed elsewhere in the federal establishment.

The problem seems to be twofold: lack of centralized direction for the many assistance programs scattered through the various agencies of the federal government; and the need for more informed, effective management of program delivery at the local level.

The issue paper concluded, in part, that "The small business community is largely unaware of the available federal lending and assistance programs." It recommended

> special mechanisms and delivery systems . . . to simplify federal lending and other assistance programs to make them more attractive to small businesses and to counter the reticence within the small business community to seeking federal aid.

While the federal government seems unlikely to institute special mechanisms and delivery systems, some simplification seems likely to take place as a result of the Reagan administration's budget cutbacks. Several small-business lending agencies and programs—including the Economic Development Administration of the Commerce Department and the Business and Industry Loan Program of the Farmers Home Administration—have been curtailed sharply and could eventually be eliminated entirely.

Still and all, huge amounts of money remain available under federal programs. That and the willingness of the federal government to approve loans that commercial lenders shy away from make the federal government a potential savior to small businesses in need of financing. Thus, even entrepreneurs who are put off by the bureaucratic mumbo jumbo and red tape would do well to explore the federal alternative.

GUIDELINES FOR OBTAINING FINANCING

Entrepreneurs can improve their chances of obtaining loans under federal programs and minimize potential aggravation and frustration if they keep a few general guidelines in mind. The first, and perhaps most important, rule in dealing with the federal government is the old Boy Scout motto: *Be prepared.* Know the federal agencies' goals and prohibitions before going through the application procedures. (These goals and prohibitions are noted within the individual agency descriptions that follow in this chapter.) Also, have on hand relevant details about your business and personal finances—specifics about sales, profits, cash flow, previous loans, and other financial particulars, along with background information on all partners, including their assets and incomes. For new businesses, a complete business plan is indispensable. (For further details on information generally included in business plans, see Appendix C.)

Knowing the requirements of the agency to which you are applying and being able to come up with the requested business and personal information will minimize bureaucratic delays. The cardinal rule of any bureaucrat is to avoid easily identifiable errors—or, as bureaucrats themselves delicately phrase it, "cover your backside." The bureaucrat who reviews a loan application that violates even a minor agency rule or that is missing just a small piece of information will nearly always return the paperwork to the applicant, which means irritating and possibly costly (to you) delays.

An offshoot of the suggestion regarding advance preparation is advance application: apply for federal financing well ahead of when it is actually needed. Rick Stephan Hayes, a financial consultant on federal loans, says in his book *Business Loans:*

> if you need the money tomorrow, next week, or next month, forget about getting a government loan! You should allow at least three months for the money to get to you *after submittal.* You should also realize that the time required to gather the necessary information about your company and yourself and to prepare the loan can take up to two months.

SEVERAL FINANCING APPROACHES

Also important to bear in mind is that money under federal programs comes in a number of forms. The bulk of the money actually comes from banks, with approval by the federal government and guarantees to reimburse the banks for the bulk of the money in the event the businesses fail to repay. The government also lends money directly to businesses. The agencies that do most of the guaranteed and direct lending are the Small Business Administration (SBA), the Farmers Home Administration (FmHA) of the Agriculture Department, and the Economic Development Administration (EDA) of the Commerce Department.

Generally speaking, interest rates on loans obtained directly from the federal government are several points lower than interest on loans obtained on guaranteed loans from banks, because federal laws regulate interest rates on direct loans more tightly than on guaranteed bank loans. But the government exacts another kind of price on direct loans that can outweigh the lower interest rates: direct loans are usually more difficult to obtain because of limited congressional funding, and it takes longer to get decisions on them because of the huge application load. Those trends are likely to become more pronounced in the future because of federal government spending cutbacks.

Some federal money is made available in the form of equity investments or in that most lucrative of forms, direct grants. The federal agencies that make funds available in such ways are the Department of

Housing and Urban Development (HUD), the Department of Energy (DOE), and the National Science Foundation (NSF). The major obstacle to obtaining grants, as with any money that is given away, is that many more people are after it than there is money available.

The rest of this chapter is devoted to providing details of the specific government lending and grant programs which are of most use to small businesses. The program information is divided into two broad sections: those programs available to start-up businesses, and those available to existing businesses. The programs are listed according to what we judged to be their importance for and accessibility to entrepreneurs. Other chapters describe federal programs available primarily to special groups of entrepreneurs, including racial minorities and women, as well as programs for special purposes, including foreign trade.

The *Federal Financing Table* on p. 79 summarizes key provisions of federal financing programs.

SOURCES FOR START-UP BUSINESSES

For entrepreneurs seeking to begin their own businesses from scratch or to buy very small or relatively new existing businesses, the federal government is probably the most promising formal financing source available. It will consider loans from most kinds of businesses, including small stores or restaurants, service businesses, or manufacturing operations. Federal financing sources for start-ups include the Small Business Administration and the Department of Energy. Of these sources, the SBA offers the greatest overall hope of success. The SBA makes or guarantees between 25,000 and 30,000 loans each year, and approximately 30 percent (or between 7,500 and nearly 10,000 loans annually) go to new businesses. The Department of Energy, by contrast, makes fewer than 100 grants to investor entrepreneurs annually.

Entrepreneurs should pick the agency to which they apply carefully, based in part on the kind of business they want to start. Small retail and service operations, for instance, usually stand the best chance of obtaining funds from the SBA; but scientific and high-technology businesses are usually better off seeking loans or grants from the DOE.

Certain start-up entrepreneurs should probably avoid the federal government entirely, however, such as experienced entrepreneurs with plans to create fast-growing, high-technology businesses that require huge amounts of capital and sophisticated evaluation by lenders. Federal agencies, for the most part, do not have either the staff expertise to evaluate or the lending authority to finance adequately such projects. Entrepreneurs in this category usually get the most satisfaction from venture-capital firms. (See Chapter 6, "Venture Capital.")

FEDERAL FINANCING TABLE

Agency	Types of Businesses Aided		Types of Financing Available				Applications Only from Small Business	Preapplications Available	Job Creation Primary Criterion
	Start-ups	Existing	Direct Loans	Guaranteed Bank Loans	Grants	Investment Capital			
SBA	X	X	X	X			X		
FmHA	X	X		X				X	X
DOE	X	X		X	X	X[1]		X[1]	X
EDA		X	X	X					X
HUD		X	X		X				X
NSF		X			X	X[2]			

[1] For certain programs
[2] Through office of Small Business Innovation Research

The Small Business Administration

Office of Financing
U. S. Small Business Administration
1441 L St., NW
Washington, DC 20416
(202) 653-6570

Information and assistance are also available from more than 100 local offices scattered among the nation's large- and medium-sized cities. (For a list of local SBA offices, see Appendix A.)

The Small Business Administration (SBA) perhaps best illustrates the federal government's schizophrenic approach to small-business financing. On the positive side, its purpose is among the most noble of any federal agency. It is dedicated to preserving and encouraging America's small businesses by acting as a lender of last resort to entrepreneurs who are unable to obtain ordinary bank loans or other private financing. It has helped thousands of entrepreneurs to launch ventures and turn them into thriving businesses.

At the same time, however, the SBA tends to be viewed by entrepreneurs and the press alike as a bungling, insensitive, and inefficient agency. In a 1977 article *Fortune* magazine concluded that "an agency that started out smelling like a rose has ended up as an overgrown, pest-plagued[,] bureaucratic weed."

Part of the SBA's negative reputation stems from several well-publicized instances of fraud involving both its staff members and businesses that have obtained SBA loans. The SBA has also been accused by entrepreneurs of creating unnecessary red tape and delays in processing loan applications. In addition, the SBA is frequently thought of by entrepreneurs as catering mainly to racial minorities.

The SBA does not deny that it has problems. But it has taken a number of steps in recent years to eliminate the fraud and to streamline some of its loan processes. The agency's officials emphasize, moreover, that the bulk of its loans go to nonminorities and that its programs are open to any and all qualified entrepreneurs.

For entrepreneurs who approach the agency with some of their own capital and collateral, along with complete information about themselves, their business, and their plans for utilizing the requested financing, the SBA can be an important source of start-up financing. Traditionally, more than half the SBA's loans have been for amounts under $50,000, which suggests that many start-up and young businesses are receiving backing.

Loan Programs

The SBA until 1981 had a confusing array of about a dozen loan programs under which entrepreneurs could apply for funds. At that time, though, Congress approved the agency's request to lump all the programs into its already existing program of regular business loans—sometimes referred to by the SBA as "Section 7(a)" loans. They are available to most types of start-up and existing businesses. In going along with the SBA's proposed consolidation, though, Congress requested the SBA to continue making loans as it had previously for special purposes and for special groups, including loans for solar energy businesses, export financing, employee stock ownership plans (ESOPs), the physically handicapped, and racial minorities. Exactly how the consolidation and congressional request will work out remains to be seen.

Types, Amounts, and Terms of Loans

There are three basic types of loans that can be obtained through the SBA.

1. Direct loans are made by the agency itself, using public money. Such loans are limited to $150,000 and are available at interest rates set by the agency. These rates are approximately equal to the government's cost of borrowing money, which is usually 3 to 5 percent below the prime rate. In reality, though, such loans are frequently unavailable because of limited government funding, which is quickly used up by waiting entrepreneurs. Loans for the physically handicapped only are for 3 percent annual rates.

2. Immediate participation loans consist partly of government funds at the direct loan interest rate and partly of private money, usually supplied by banks, at higher market rates. The SBA will usually provide no more than 75 percent of immediate participation loans, with a limit of $150,000. Such loans are the least common type of SBA financing, however, partly because of the added complexity of getting both the SBA and a private lender coordinated on a single project, and partly because of limited SBA funds.

3. Guaranteed loans are funded by private lenders—usually banks— but guaranteed up to 90 percent by the SBA for loans under $100,000; loans over $100,000 can be guaranteed for between 70 percent and 90 percent. About two thirds of the nation's 15,000 banks have participated in such loans, although, in reality, only a few hundred do so on a regular basis. The SBA has encouraged this type of loan as a way of increasing the overall amount of

money loaned. Guaranteed loans account for more than 80 percent of all SBA loans. The SBA can guarantee such loans up to $500,000. Interest rates can be steep, since they approximately equal the prime rate.

While the average SBA-guaranteed loan is slightly more than $100,000, the majority of all SBA direct and guaranteed loans are under $50,000. A qualified start-up business will typically be able to borrow in the vicinity of between $10,000 and $25,000.

Repayment terms under recently enacted legislation can vary widely. Whereas the SBA has in past years required most loans to be repaid in between six to ten years, it now has the authority to extend the repayment period for most loans to twenty-five years. Such extended repayment terms, if employed by the SBA, could be a help to many small businesses by reducing the individual payments required of them and improving their cash flow. And in the cases of loans for acquiring property, terms can be extended beyond twenty-five years, also at the SBA's discretion.

The Application Procedure

Since the SBA is technically a lender of last resort, entrepreneurs must demonstrate that they are unable to procure financing elsewhere. That is accomplished by showing proof of having been rejected by two banks for their ordinary bank loans. In communities of under 200,000 people, only one bank rejection must be proved.

While most types of new or existing businesses are eligible for SBA loans or guarantees, a few are not. Businesses that are ineligible are those in the publishing industry, such as newspapers and magazines; real estate speculators; and lending or investing firms.

Entrepreneurs applying for direct or participation loans must apply directly to the SBA. Those applying for guaranteed loans may deal directly with the banks that supply the funds and have the banks handle arrangements with the SBA.

Whether application is made to the SBA or to commercial banks for an SBA guarantee, the guidelines and requirements are similar. Essentially, the SBA is primarily concerned that the loan be repaid. Therefore, it pays particular attention, in the case of start-up businesses, to the entrepreneur's background, to the amount of investment by the entrepreneurs, and to the type and amount of collateral. As might be expected, the SBA is also concerned with the viability and long-term prospects of the business.

The SBA expects that entrepreneurs starting a new business or buying an existing one will put up between one fourth and one third of the funds required. While the SBA may lend the remaining capital required to start or buy a business, it may also seek enough collateral—in the form of the entrepreneur's house, life insurance, stock, and other holdings—to secure the entire loan. Applicants must include income tax statements for the previous three years. (See pp. 104–17 for a sample SBA application.)

The SBA's decision on how much to lend or whether to lend at all is also influenced by how the agency assesses the proposed business. It bases its assessment primarily on financial and market information supplied by the applicant.

For a new business, the SBA wants a current income statement and balance sheet, along with projected income and balance sheet information looking one year ahead. Entrepreneurs buying an existing business should be prepared to supply income statements and balance sheets for the most recent three years. The SBA also wants details on how the loan will be used.

Since new businesses are unable to provide much in the way of past financial data, the SBA understandably places a heavy emphasis on the market data that applicants provide, so as to evaluate the prospects and risks of the proposal. Market data includes industry trends, financial information on competitors and the industry in general, and demographic information describing likely customers.

As noted in the introduction to this chapter, assembling the various financial and market information is a laborious and time-consuming task. Many books are devoted to the mechanics of understanding and putting together such information. The section at the end of this chapter on "Additional Information Sources" lists a few books concerned in detail with the financial and market information necessary to apply for federal loans, and the end of Chapter 1 lists other books that deal more generally with understanding financial and marketing concepts.

Once entrepreneurs have collected all the information necessary to apply for an SBA loan, how long can they expect to wait for their money or their loan rejection? Unfortunately, there is no simple or definitive answer to that question. The SBA says applicants can expect to hear about their requests two weeks after banks submit applications for guaranteed loans. Applications for direct loans may take a few weeks longer, assuming funding for such loans is available, according to the SBA.

Other accounts suggest the SBA is overly optimistic, however. A survey of Colorado banks offering SBA-guaranteed loans, which was published in the April 1979 issue of the *Journal of Small Business Management,* found that it takes an average of fifty days to process loan applications and actually disburse the money. An article on the SBA in the May 1979 issue of *Venture* magazine stated:

> Getting a guaranteed loan can take up to four months or more from the time a borrower first contacts his bank for credit. . . . Applicants might wait nine months or more for the relatively small amount of money SBA has to lend directly.

Start-up and very new businesses can expect to wait the longest for SBA loans, according to one source. "The newer the business (especially start-ups) and the larger the amount of money requested, the more time the proposal will involve," state Rick Stephan Hayes and John Cotton Howell in their book *How to Finance Your Small Business with Government Money: SBA Loans.* (For more details on this book, see "Additional Information Sources" at the end of this chapter, beginning on p. 102.)

The SBA says it is aware of entrepreneurs' complaints about long waits for loans and is trying to improve the situation by cutting red tape. One concrete step that the SBA has taken recently has been to institute a pilot program to speed action on loan guarantees by reducing or eliminating the time SBA officials spend evaluating the proposals. Under the program, the SBA essentially relies on banks' decisions as to whether or not loans should be granted and for how much. By late 1980, 250 banks were participating, and the SBA expects to add to that figure continuously in coming years. The SBA will provide a list of participating banks to entrepreneurs who request it.

One final caveat on the time required to obtain SBA loans: the survey of Colorado banks that grant SBA-guaranteed loans (published in the *Journal of Small Business Management*) noted that 65 percent of the banks blamed borrowers for delays in processing SBA loans, while only 29 percent blamed the SBA and 5 percent blamed themselves. In other words, the banks alleged that applicants had provided information that was either insufficient or inappropriate to fulfill SBA requirements.

FARMERS HOME ADMINISTRATION

Farmers Home Administration
Business and Industry Loan Program
Department of Agriculture
14th St. and Independence Ave., SW
Washington, DC 20250
(202) 447-7967

Assistance and information from FmHA are also available from approximately 1,750 offices serving every rural county. Offices are usually located in county seats.

The Department of Agriculture's Farmers Home Administration Business and Industry Loan Program is among the federal government's newest financing programs, since it dates from only the early 1970s. It is also one of the government's less secure programs, since the Reagan administration in 1981 proposed eliminating it. At the time this book went to press, the program seemed likely to survive, but with only about half the lending authority it previously had. And because it lacks the Administration's favor, it could be eliminated at some point in the not too distant future.

The FmHA is much less difficult to comprehend than the SBA, because the FmHA has essentially one business loan program (in addition to its loan programs to farmers), the rules for which are nearly the same for all businesses. The FmHA's Business and Industry (B&I) program guarantees bank loans up to 90 percent for businesses located in communities of fewer than 50,000 people, with priority given to businesses in communities of under 25,000. Loans are available for any amount to companies of any size.

The FmHA's approach differs from the SBA's in a few other important respects too. For instance, while the SBA is technically a lender of last resort, the FmHA guarantees loans that banks might make on their own. In other words, applicants do not need to demonstrate that other financing is not available. (FmHA guarantees encourage banks to make more loans than they otherwise would, because the guarantees allow banks to exceed regulatory limits on their lending authority.)

Another point of difference is that, unlike SBA loans, which are intended primarily to help strengthen individual small businesses, FmHA B&I loans are intended to contribute directly to the communities in which the businesses are located. Applicants must indicate how many jobs the loans will help create, or else must show that the financing will in some other way benefit the community—by attracting tourists, for example. The agency allows approximately $20,000 of loan value for each job created.

Thus FmHA's real objective is to back high-quality, financially sound businesses that will provide tangible and specific benefits to their communities. Entrepreneurs must keep that broad and rather unusual financing approach constantly in mind when they approach this agency.

The B&I program is available to businesses of all sizes, including start-ups. The program particularly encourages businesses designed to produce alcohol that can be used for gasohol.

Loan Terms

Unlike the SBA, FmHA does not regulate loan interest rates. Lenders can charge whatever rate borrowers will accept; rates can be fixed or variable. Borrowers must also pay FmHA a guarantee fee of 1 percent of the principal loan amount multiplied by the percentage of the FmHA guarantee.

While interest rates for FmHA loans may be higher than for SBA loans, repayment terms are more liberal. Businesses usually can take up to seven years to repay working capital loans; up to fifteen years for machinery and equipment loans; and up to thirty years for loans used to buy land, buildings, and permanent fixtures.

For start-up businesses, the FmHA likes to see owners provide a minimum of 20–25 percent of the investment. In addition, the agency requires varying amounts of collateral, up to 100 percent of the loan, as well as personal and corporate guarantees for all loans.

Application Procedure

The procedure for obtaining FmHA guarantees is long and tedious, requiring a stack of forms and the involvement of several agencies. But the FmHA provides a mechanism for entrepreneurs to determine whether the grueling application process is likely to bear fruit: the preapplication. Once a borrower finds a bank willing to make a loan with an FmHA guarantee, the two parties can draft a letter of intent that briefly describes the business—its history, finances, and future plans—and the purposes of the loan. The letter comprises a preapplication, and from it the FmHA will advise the parties whether the business is eligible for FmHA assistance and, if so, the potential weaknesses that exist in the request. Though the preapplication is submitted entirely at the borrower's option, it is a sensible option, since the FmHA response can save much future time and energy.

Entrepreneurs who receive encouraging responses from their preapplications can plunge into the full application. According to the FmHA, the application requirements are not too different from those for bank and SBA loans. Applicants must provide personal histories, balance sheet, and profit-loss data for the previous three years; cash-flow statements; and financial projections looking ahead three years. In addition, applicants must show that their businesses comply with federal pollution standards and various other federal regulations.

All applications must also be reviewed by the Department of Labor to determine the business and labor competition for the area in which each applicant is located and also to determine if the applicant is actually creating jobs or merely transferring jobs from one area to another.

The whole process, according to the FmHA, takes two to three months. Once again, the importance of being prepared with the right information cannot be overemphasized. *Venture* magazine, in a May 1979 article on FmHA loans, observed that "Six-month ordeals are not uncommon, but they are generally the result of incomplete applications or gaps in the business plan, rather than bureaucratic inefficiencies." An FmHA official seconds that; he maintains that 95 percent of delays in processing applications are caused by applicant errors or negligence.

DEPARTMENT OF ENERGY

There are two Department of Energy-sponsored programs of particular interest to start-up businesses. The first is run by DOE together with the National Bureau of Standards (NBS), which is an agency of the Commerce Department. Essentially, the NBS acts as a screening agency, sending the most promising invention proposals to the DOE for final decisions. Funding for energy-related inventions is supplied by the DOE.

Initial letters should include a request for NBS Form 1019 and should be sent to:

Office of Energy-Related Inventions
National Bureau of Standards
Washington, DC 20234
(301) 921-3694

For inventions that qualify, the program "is prepared to offer one-time assistance, usually amounting to one year of financial and technical backing," according to the DOE. "Assistance is negotiated directly with the inventor or small businessman," the agency adds.

Money obtained through the program does not have to be repaid, and any technical assistance received is free. Thus, entrepreneurs can wind up with the equivalent of a one-year scholarship to get things going, courtesy of the government. Grants thus far have averaged $70,000, and those who do not receive grants get a consolation prize: a written evaluation of their invention.

The rules and procedures for applying for such funds are fairly simple. The odds for obtaining grants and the time required for ultimate approval are another matter, however.

Anyone can apply for funding by filling out the simple two-page NBS Form 1019 and returning it with both a description of the invention and any material needed to support claims for the invention. NBS examiners evaluate the inventions by asking three key questions:

1. Is the invention technically competent and unique?
2. Will it save a significant amount of energy, or is it a new source of energy?
3. Does it have a reasonable chance of becoming a commercial success if given appropriate government assistance?

Certain types of proposals are not acceptable, including those that are nuclear-energy-related; those that are technically flawed, such as perpetual-motion machines; and those that are merely proposals to invent with no specific invention yet involved.

Both NBS and DOE say that they are very sensitive to inventors' concerns about security and that, consequently, they hold all submitted materials in strictest confidence. The program also allows inventors to keep the rights to any patents that result from research with government money.

Not surprisingly, the NBS receives many proposals—more than it can hope to fund. By the end of 1979, more than 11,500 proposals had been evaluated; of those, 119 had been referred to DOE for consideration of financial and technical assistance, and 57 had received grants or contracts. The NBS calculates that, of each 100 proposals it receives, 55 are immediately rejected for failing to qualify within the basic program requirements; of the remaining 45, only two can be expected to survive the agency's two-stage evaluation process and thus qualify for DOE evaluation. Once at DOE, the chances of approval become a bit better than 50 percent.

Those entrepreneurs who eventually receive money must possess not only exceptional inventions, but also remarkable patience. The NBS states flatly that it requires about six months to take inventions through its entire evaluation process. DOE says it then requires an additional four to five months for an invention to go through that agency's evaluation procedure. All in all, then, up to a year can elapse before an invention is approved for funding.

The second DOE program is solely under the jurisdiction of the Department of Energy, as follows:

Appropriate Energy Technology Program
Department of Energy
Washington, DC 20585
(202) 252-9104

Information for the Appropriate Energy Technology Program is available in Washington, as well as at ten regional Department of Energy offices located in Boston, New York, Philadelphia, Atlanta, Chicago, Kansas City (MO), Dallas, San Francisco, Seattle, and Lakewood (CA).

Entrepreneurs who have an idea or concept for utilizing energy sources, as opposed to an invention, should investigate the DOE's Appropriate Energy Technology Program. The program makes grants of up to $10,000 to develop ideas "in areas ranging from new concepts of energy sources to the new application of existing procedures or systems," DOE says. Awards of up to $50,000 are made to transform a concept into a useful technology or to test a technology's potential commercial applications.

Grants are held to a maximum of $50,000, in line with the concept behind the program that projects that this concept

> be small in scale; conserve non-renewable energy; use renewable resources; be simple to install, operate, and maintain; use local labor and local resources; and be environmentally sound.

Applicants must submit their own proposals, which describe the project, explain the research, describe the benefits, and outline a budget. For guidance in presenting the application material formally, potential applicants should contact DOE. Decisions on grants are made by selection panels in each DOE regional office.

As in the case of the inventions program jointly sponsored by the Department of Energy and the National Bureau of Standards, entrepreneurs must have extreme patience and be prepared for rejection. DOE itself says that decisions in the Appropriate Energy Technology Program take six to eight months. And the chances of actually winning a grant are less than one in twenty: in a recent year, 584 grants were awarded out of a total of 12,876 applications.

SOURCES FOR EXISTING BUSINESSES

Small-business owners tend to look with disdain at federal government financing programs. They are put off by the prospect of dealing with bureaucrats who have never worked in the business world. They are also put off by the prospect of handling government forms and seemingly interminable red tape. And, although they do not usually verbalize it, many small-business owners would rather not become involved in financial dealings with the government for fear that the Internal Revenue Service may eventually get curious about all the forms being filed; no one wants to arouse the IRS's curiosity.

But, as has been pointed out previously in this chapter, the federal government can turn out to be the only friend a small-business owner has. When money gets tight and banks are servicing mainly their large corporate clients, a federal loan, guarantee, or grant can be a lifesaver.

Of course, federal money is no cinch to obtain. Despite the government's poor image among business owners, there are still many more applicants than there is financing available. Thus, those applicants making the most complete and convincing cases will usually be the ones to get what they are seeking.

All of the agencies described earlier in this chapter, in the section dealing with financing for start-up businesses, also make funds available for existing businesses. Rather than repeat background information about these agencies and their requirements, readers will be referred to earlier material where appropriate. This section will confine itself to the specific programs and requirements that are different from, or in addition to, those for start-up businesses.

SMALL BUSINESS ADMINISTRATION

Office of Financing
U. S. Small Business Administration
1441 L St., NW
Washington, DC 20416
(202) 653-6570

Information and assistance is also available from more than 100 local offices scattered among the nation's large- and medium-sized cities. (For a list of local offices, see Appendix A.)

For existing businesses, two aspects of the Small Business Administration's (SBA) lending approach have traditionally proven frustrating. First, the agency's standards for determining which businesses qualify for SBA help and which do not are quite complicated and seemingly arbitrary. Second, the $500,000 loan guarantee limitation and the relatively short-term nature of SBA loans make SBA financing only a partial or limited solution for many businesses.

(For additional background information on the SBA, see pp. 80–84.)

The agency recently proposed simplifying its size standards, but when that change might occur is uncertain.

The criteria for determining whether a business is indeed "small," and thus eligible for SBA financing, vary according to the type of business. The basic criteria are as follows.

- Manufacturing businesses, depending on their industry, may have up to 250 employees, though in a few cases, they can have up to 1,500 employees.
- Wholesaling businesses, for the most part, must have annual sales of less than $9.5 million, but certain types can range up to $22 million.
- Service businesses must have annual sales of less than a maximum of (depending, again, on their industry) $2 million to $10 million.
- Retailing businesses generally must have under $2 million in annual sales, though exceptions allow various types of retailers up to a maximum of $7.5 million in annual sales.
- General (construction) contracting businesses must have average annual receipts not exceeding $9.5 million for the three most recently completed fiscal years; special trade (construction) contracting businesses must

have average annual receipts for the three most recent years not exceeding $1 million or $2 million, depending on the trade.
• Agricultural businesses cannot exceed $1 million in annual receipts.

These basic criteria are only the tip of the iceberg. For the various exceptions allowed specific businesses, owners should contact the nearest SBA office.

The proposed revised size standards would simplify the situation greatly; eligibility for SBA loans would be determined solely on the basis of number of employees. The number of employees allowed, however, would vary from industry to industry.

Loan Programs

Until recently, the SBA had essentially two broad loan categories: regular business loans and special interest group loans targeted to business owners in certain businesses or in various other categories such as minorities and women. As noted earlier in this chapter (p. 81), the special interest group loans were consolidated into the program of regular business loans, sometimes referred to as its "Section 7(a)" loans.

In addition, the SBA had several specialized types of business loans to assist small businesses hurt by such problems as seasonal fluctuations, government regulations, and energy shortages. These programs were consolidated into something named the Federal Action Loan Program, but the program at the time this book went to press seemed unlikely to receive any funding. One specialized loan type that apparently will continue in existence is known as Economic Injury Loans, which assist businesses whose prospects have been adversely affected by military base closings, federal construction projects, and similar occurrences. The SBA will also continue making emergency loans to help businesses hurt by natural disasters.

Types, Amounts, and Terms of Loans

The SBA's standard types, amounts, and terms of loans, which were described in this chapter's section on start-up businesses (pp. 81–82), are also applicable to existing businesses. Existing businesses should be aware that, historically, the SBA has catered to the nation's smallest businesses: small retail stores and service businesses. Relatively substantial manufacturing and high-technology businesses have encountered more difficulty obtaining SBA financing. The SBA's approach is reflected in statistics that show, traditionally, less than 25 percent of the agency's loans have been in the $100,000 to $500,000 category.

Existing businesses not owned by the handicapped should be prepared in the future to obtain SBA-guaranteed bank loans rather than direct loans. The SBA has moved in this direction in recent years and plans to move even further toward making the majority of its loans guaranteed loans, and cutting back on direct loans.

The Application Procedure

The application procedure described for start-up businesses (pp. 82–84) is similar in most respects for existing businesses. Existing businesses, however, have a few advantages over start-ups in obtaining SBA loans. Existing businesses can use business assets, such as land, buildings, and equipment, as collateral. In addition, they do not need to provide so much market data to convince the SBA of their business's viability; a relatively successful track record, as demonstrated in the most recent three years' financial results, is the most convincing evidence of promising future prospects.

Healthy existing businesses requesting relatively small loans can also expect fairly quick action on their applications. "The more established the business, the more profitable and financially secure it is, and the smaller the amount of money requested, the shorter the time from research to approval," advise Rick Stephan Hayes and John Cotton Howell in their book *How to Finance Your Small Business with Government Money: SBA Loans.*

FARMERS HOME ADMINISTRATION

Farmers Home Administration
Business and Industry Loan Program
Department of Agriculture
14th St. and Independence Ave., SW
Washington, DC 20250
(202) 447-7967

Assistance and information may be obtained from approximately 1,750 offices which serve every rural county. These branch offices are generally located in county seats.

Existing small businesses that seek financing from the Farmers Home Administration (FmHA) are often in competition with relatively large companies for money, since the agency places no limit on either the size of applicants' companies, or the amounts they can seek. When Chrysler Corporation got into a serious financial bind, it sought $250 million from FmHA, though the company eventually cut its request to one fifth of that amount. Nearly 20 percent of the loan guarantees granted by FmHA in a typical year are for more than $1 million, with a few exceeding $10 million. The average FmHA guarantee in a recent year was $820,000. (Additional background on FmHA is provided on pp. 84–87.)

Loan Terms

Despite the competition from large companies, FmHA is an important potential financing source for existing rural-area small businesses that need more than the SBA is allowed to lend or guarantee. Loans guaranteed by FmHA can be used for acquiring businesses, purchasing land and equipment, building and modernizing, pollution control, and various nonoperating costs. Proceeds cannot, however, be used to move businesses, repay other federal loans, pay creditors more than the value of the collateral, or pay off owners or other shareholders. Additional details on loan terms are provided on pp. 85–86.

Application Procedure

As with SBA, the FmHA application procedure is usually easier for existing businesses than for start-up businesses. Collateral is easier to come by, and the equity requirement is less—a minimum of 10 percent for a project, versus the 20 percent required for start-up businesses.

The application procedure is extended an extra two to three months for businesses seeking more than $1 million, however, since such applications must be evaluated and approved by the central FmHA office in Washington. Otherwise, the application procedure for existing businesses is the same as that for start-ups described on pp. 86–87.

ECONOMIC DEVELOPMENT ADMINISTRATION

Office of Private Investment
Economic Development Administration
U. S. Department of Commerce
Washington, DC 20230
(202) 377-5067

Information and assistance are available either through Commerce Department offices, which are located in most cities, or through regional EDA offices in Philadelphia, Atlanta, Chicago, Denver, Seattle, and Austin.

The Economic Development Administration (EDA) is another of those lending agencies that finds its existence somewhat precarious. The Reagan administration proposed eliminating the agency completely, but

94

at the time this book went to press, it appeared that the agency would survive, though only barely—it was granted only about one third of the funding it once had—and it could still find itself abolished in the near future.

One purpose of the EDA has been to make loans to businesses with financing needs that go beyond the SBA's $500,000 guarantee limits. Its loans can run for as long as twenty-five years.

The EDA has always been a tough source from which to extract dollars. Only a small fraction of the several thousand applications filed each year are ultimately approved for financing. The simple, initial application eventually requires reams of supporting material. On top of that, the EDA's red tape is perhaps the most copious of any government financing agency: one and a half years from application approval to disbursement of funds is not unusual. The recent budget cuts will likely only exacerbate the situation.

The above facts are not meant to steer small-business owners away from the EDA. Rather, they are intended to provide a note of caution: if there is any federal agency where it is important to know the rules and be prepared with complete business information, it is the EDA.

Businesses seeking EDA financing must, above all, demonstrate that proposed projects will provide new jobs. Such EDA loans are available only in areas deemed to be in need of economic development. The areas so designated are constantly changing, so potential applicants should check first with the EDA to determine whether or not their area is eligible.

EDA also makes loans to businesses of all sizes that have been adversely affected by competitive imported products. Companies that can show that their sales, production, or workforce have declined because of imports can receive loans that allow them to develop new business areas. In addition, companies can receive grants of up to $10,000 to help pay consultants for help in drawing up plans for development of these alternative business areas. Information on the program can be obtained from EDA Trade Adjustment Assistance Centers located in Los Angeles, Atlanta, Boston, New York, Trenton, Philadelphia, Chicago, Little Rock, Harrisburg (PA), and Binghamton (NY).

Types, Amounts, and Terms of Loans

Like the SBA, the EDA is a lender of last resort and seeks evidence that proposed projects for financing have been rejected by commercial sources. The agency makes direct loans and, alternatively, guarantees bank loans up to 90 percent.

While the EDA has no limits on what it can lend or guarantee, it uses a guideline of limiting itself to no more than $10,000 of financing for each job created or saved. Interest rates on direct loans are usually somewhat lower than prevailing bank rates. For guaranteed bank loans, the EDA requires that interest rates be very close to existing prime rates. Loans or guarantees in one recent year ranged from a low of $250,000 to a high of $5.2 million.

Working capital loans, lease guarantees, and interest subsidies must usually be repaid within five years. Other types of loans, though, may extend up to twenty-five years, though fixed-asset loans are limited in duration to the useful life of the assets being acquired. Also, direct fixed-asset loans may not exceed 65 percent of the total cost of land, buildings, machinery, and equipment acquired, which means that other financing sources may have to be attracted to the project as well.

The agency requires that a minimum of 15 percent of the cost of a project involving direct fixed-asset loans be in the form of equity capital or a subordinated loan. In addition, at least one third of the 15 percent must be supplied by the state or by a nongovernmental community or area organization. (The EDA can waive this last requirement about state or other organization support in certain hardship cases.)

EDA also requires collateral on both direct loans and guarantees in the form of liens on fixed assets, assignment of life insurance on key business personnel, and personal and corporate guarantees.

Application Procedure

As noted earlier, the EDA's initial four-page application form is somewhat beguiling. It requires only a brief project explanation and the most basic financial details.

EDA eventually requires more than the checking off of appropriate boxes and the filling in of a few numbers, though. According to an EDA brochure:

> Because of the complexity of most EDA projects, preparation of the application often entails considerable time and expense for the applicant. Similarly, processing can also entail additional time and expense.

Indeed, the difficulties only begin with the completion of the initial four-page application. When that form has been deemed appropriate, the agency begins requesting such information as market-share studies and various financial and engineering feasibility documentation; it also requires reviews by the Equal Employment Opportunity Commission and the Environmental Protection Agency to assure compliance with federal regulations.

DEPARTMENT OF HOUSING AND URBAN DEVELOPMENT

Urban Development Action Grants
Community Planning and Development
U. S. Department of Housing and Urban Development
451 Seventh St., SW
Washington, DC 20410
(202) 472-3947

Information can also be obtained from HUD area offices, which are usually based in each state's largest city.

Although the Department of Housing and Urban Development (HUD) has several programs of potential use to small businesses (its Community Development Block Grants and Rehabilitation Loan program, among others), the Urban Development Action Grants program comprises its main effort to encourage business development. This program is an extremely flexible one; it makes grants available to cities and towns, which can then use the money in any of a number of ways to aid businesses. The money is awarded to cities and towns that are able to convince HUD, first, that their economies and neighborhoods face serious hardships and, second, that the grants will generate significant investment and development. Localities that obtain such grants can acquire and then lease to businesses land or plant facilities, or they can make direct grants or loans to businesses.

The amounts of money involved are significant. In one recent year, grants to small cities ("small" being defined as cities with under 50,000 in population) ranged from $56,000 to $6.7 million, with the average grant being $852,000. The range in large cities was from $75,000 to $14.2 million, with an average grant of $2.7 million. Grants have been used to modernize and reopen closed plants; build new manufacturing facilities; and acquire land for hotels, parking garages, and retail facilities.

While the Action Grants program is quite flexible, business owners should be aware of a few overall guidelines before they attempt to procure such funds. First, business owners should be thinking along the lines of using the HUD money for a specific expansion project, such as building a new plant or hotel, rather than for working capital. Second, business owners should be prepared to work closely with local officials to prepare an application to HUD; previous personal and business contacts with city officials can be extremely helpful in laying the groundwork for a cooperative working relationship. Finally, business owners should be aware that HUD gives preference to project proposals that have obtained financing commitments from state or other federal agencies, such that the

HUD grant complements those funds; HUD also requires that any private funding, such as venture capital or bank loans, be firmly committed.

Business owners must negotiate terms for the HUD money directly with their city, which is, after all, the actual applicant. Some cities might want a long-term, low-interest loan arrangement, while others might be willing to make the money available as a grant in return for a percentage of a company's earnings for a certain number of years.

HUD says it makes decisions on applications for action grants in sixty to ninety days.

DEPARTMENT OF ENERGY

Office of Conservation and Solar Energy
U. S. Department of Energy
20 Massachusetts Ave., NW
Washington, DC 20585
(202) 376-4934

Information is also available through ten regional offices located in Boston, New York, Philadelphia, Atlanta, Chicago, Dallas, Kansas City (MO), San Francisco, Seattle, and Lakewood (CA).

Because of the United States' serious energy problems, Congress has allocated to the Department of Energy (DOE) hundreds of millions of dollars to encourage research aimed at saving energy and developing new energy sources. Funds, in the form of research grants, are available to businesses of all sizes, as well as to universities, to explore ways of increasing energy efficiency and developing economically feasible solar systems.

While money is ostensibly available to any size business, the DOE has been criticized by small-business lobbyists for relying too heavily on large corporations to do the research. The magazine *In Business,* in its July/August 1979 issue, argued:

> The issue is significant because it appears that small businesses are better suited to produce the innovative kinds of research that solar energy requires. Consequently, the government may be getting less back for its research buck by favoring big business.

Small-business owners who wish to pursue this funding avenue can get an early reading on their chances by going through a preapplication procedure. The DOE's Washington office (listed above) has standard application forms for this process. In requesting the forms, potential applicants should briefly describe the research project they envision.

If they are encouraged enough by the response to the preapplication, small-business owners can then submit a detailed, formal proposal describing the planned research. The DOE supplies a number of pamphlets that describe the elements of a complete formal proposal.

The DOE sets no limits on the size of its conservation and solar energy research grants. Applicants should "normally" expect to wait three to six months for an answer to a formal proposal, according to the DOE.

While the conservation and solar energy program offers the best overall potential for small business, DOE has a number of additional research and grant programs available to appropriate small businesses. Small-business owners can consult the *Catalog of Federal Domestic Assistance,* described at the end of this chapter under "Additional Information Sources"; they can also contact the following DOE office for guidance:

Unsolicited Proposal Section
Procurement and Contracts Management Directorate
U. S. Department of Energy
Washington, DC 20585
(202) 252-9200

The DOE has also started, on a limited basis, programs to guarantee bank loans made to develop coal mines and geothermal energy sources. The agency guarantees up to 80 percent of loans for coal mine development, to a maximum of $30 million; and up to 75 percent of loans for geothermal projects, to a maximum of $100 million per project and $200 million per borrower. The average coal loan guarantee has been $1.1 million, and the average geothermal guarantee has been $10.8 million. The agency takes three to four months to decide on coal loan guarantees and four to six months for geothermal loan guarantee decisions.

For further information on the coal loan guarantees, contact:

Director
Office of Coal Loan Programs
Department of Energy
1200 Pennsylvania Ave., NW (Room 3515)
Washington, DC 20461
(202) 633-8200

For further information on the geothermal loan guarantees, contact:

Program Manager
Geothermal Loan Guarantee Program
1200 Pennsylvania Ave., NW (Room 7112)
Washington, DC 20461
(202) 633-8760

National Science Foundation

Office of Small Business Innovation Research
Directorate for Engineering and Applied Science
National Science Foundation
1800 G St., NW
Washington, DC 20550
(202) 632-7388

Information regarding the formulation of funding proposals may be obtained from the Washington office at the above address.

The National Science Foundation (NSF) makes the bulk of its research grants available to universities, and its officials are most comfortable dealing with universities. As a consequence, most NSF officials are unfamiliar with and disinterested in the needs and capabilities of small businesses in the area of scientific research. Only in the last few years, at the specific urging of Congress, has the NSF made any effort to direct some of its research funds to scientifically and technically oriented small businesses.

In recent years, the agency has made grants of $5–10 million annually available to between 60 and 100 fortunate small businesses to do scientific research intended to lead ultimately to commercially feasible products and processes.

The NSF considers businesses "small" if they have fewer than 500 employees. Research areas appropriate for NSF grants are physics, chemistry, mathematics, biology, psychology, and engineering. The research should involve experiments that seek to prove theories, rather than develop proven concepts for commercial purposes or for market research. The agency will also not fund research that is already funded through other federal grants, such as projects sponsored by the Department of Energy.

NSF grants are awarded under a three-phase system. *Phase 1* consists of feasibility research to determine whether the approach or concept being explored makes scientific sense and is worthy of further consideration. *Phase 2* research is open only to those companies that have been awarded funds under the first phase; it constitutes the principal part of the research. *Phase 3* work involves the commercial development of the previously done research and must be privately funded.

Phase 1 grants are for a maximum of $25,000; the research under Phase 1 is to be completed within six months. Phase 2 grants can range anywhere from about $50,000 to $1 million, with the average grant being about $200,000. Phase 2 research projects are expected to last one to two years. In order to obtain Phase 2 grants, however, companies must have a commitment (assuming promising results) for venture-capital or other private funding that will enable them to proceed to Phase 3.

To apply for NSF funding, companies must formulate concise research proposals, usually of twenty pages or less, which describe the research objectives and plans and which include a detailed budget. Applications for Phase 2 grants must include a (conditional) commitment from a venture-capital firm or other private financing source to fund Phase 3. Details on composing NSF proposals are available from the agency at the address listed previously.

Applicants for NSF grants must take great care, both in selecting their research ideas and putting together their written proposals, because competition for the money is keen. Only 10–12 percent of applicants for Phase 1 grants are successful. The percentage of successful applicants rises substantially for Phase 2 applicants, however. Companies applying for either Phase 1 or Phase 2 funds should expect to wait at least six months before receiving an answer.

The NSF grant program has won some praise as an example of a straightforward, easy-to-apply-for government financing mechanism. An article about the program in the July 1980 issue of *Venture* magazine observed that ". . . the number of applications is mushrooming[,] as scientists and engineers discover that[,] for once, government grants can carry less red tape and fewer restrictions than private capital." The article also noted that most of the grants have gone to companies with ten or fewer employees.

FEDERAL LOAN CONSULTANTS AND PACKAGERS

Entrepreneurs who start down the seemingly endless path of applying for federal loans usually wonder at some point if there might be a way of farming out the tasks of filling out the forms and making the right bank and federal agency contacts, so as to improve the prospects of success.

Well, there is a way of farming out the tasks, but no assurance exists that it will improve the chances of success. Entrepreneurs can even wind up wasting valuable time and thousands of valuable dollars dealing with incompetents and con artists.

The people to whom these tasks are often farmed out are the dozens of consultants and loan packagers scattered around the country, who claim to be able to prepare loan applications and aid in getting businesses through the proper government channels. The consultants tend to specialize in helping obtain Small Business Administration, Farmers Home Administration, and Economic Development Administration loans.

But financing experts and government officials tend to frown on the consultant/packager approach for a number of reasons. Financing experts in particular argue that entrepreneurs should go through the process, with the aid of their accountants, of personally assembling the financial information necessary to fill out the loan applications. The process, the financing experts say, is an educational one that can help both those starting a business and those who already own businesses to understand better the strengths, weaknesses, and needs of their enterprise. Delegating the process to outsiders not only means passing up an important opportunity, but also placing an extremely important task in the hands of individuals who may only be concerned with the goal of obtaining a single loan.

Federal officials claim that loan applications that are conscientiously prepared by entrepreneurs have the same chances of success as those prepared by competent consultants. Indeed, if consultants are charging what a federal agency such as the SBA or FmHA considers to be exorbitant rates, applications may be rejected on that basis alone.

In addition, entrepreneurs who hire consultants/packagers run the risk of being taken for a ride. An article in the June 1980 issue of *INC.* magazine pointed out that "unscrupulous loan packagers have been descending on small businesses, offering relief from high interest rates and scarce money." The article noted that officers of a California loan packaging firm were arrested and charged with bilking twenty-five entrepreneurs out of between $1,500 and $4,738 each by promising government loans that were never received.

Even among legitimate consultants/packagers, entrepreneurs will find a wide disparity in charges. And, because the consultants and packagers are not regulated or required to register anywhere, there is no sure way of knowing whether their fees are appropriate. Some consultants/packagers require an advance fee, plus a fee after the applications are completed; some of them charge by the hour; and some charge a percentage of the loan sought. Generally speaking, fees of several thousand dollars are not uncommon.

For those entrepreneurs who are in a hurry to prepare their loan applications, who feel intimidated by the application procedure, or who, for any other reason, want the services of a consultant or packager, financing experts and government officials suggest taking great care in the selection process. The best place to start for recommendations is with one's accountant or banker.

Once armed with names, entrepreneurs can do some comparative shopping on rates and services. Government officials advise entrepreneurs to stay away from consultants/packagers who demand advance fees, as well as those who solicit by telephone or through newspaper advertisements that promote guarantees of success. Local bureaucrats can also advise whether proposed fees seem excessive. Entrepreneurs can ask consultants/packagers for the names of satisfied clients and then talk with those clients about their experiences.

The SBA declined to give us the names of packagers with whom it had worked and found to be honest and competent. Some of the organizations and consultants listed in Chapter 2, "Consultants and Management Assistance," and Chapter 7, "Assistance for Minority Businesses," do loan packaging.

ADDITIONAL INFORMATION SOURCES

Catalog of Federal Domestic Assistance. Issued by the Office of Management and Budget; available from the Superintendent of Documents, U. S. Government Printing Office, Washington, DC 20402; $20; published annually.

This approximately 1,000-page catalogue is an exceptional document for the entrepreneur who wants to explore every possible source of federal assistance. It lists and briefly describes each and every federal loan, grant, training, and assistance program. Included within each program description are vital statistics, such as the total amount of funds available, expected future funds, the number of grants or loans made, and where to get further information. The one drawback to the volume is that it requires some patience to use, because business-related program information is mixed in with education, defense, and social welfare program information.

Business Services and Information, The Guide to the Federal Government. Management Information Exchange; John Wiley & Sons, Inc.; 1979; $37.50.

This 300-page book is a directory of federal services and information of specific interest to businesses of all sizes.

Small Business Guide to Government. Issued by and available from U. S. Small Business Administration, Office of Advocacy, 1441 L St., NW, Washington, DC 20416; free.

This seventy-two-page booklet lists names, addresses, and telephone numbers of government agencies that are of particular interest to small-business owners. It provides a similar listing for small-business trade groups.

Business Loans: A Guide to Money Sources and How to Approach Them Successfully. Rick Stephan Hayes; CBI Publishing Co.; 1980; $22.50.

This book about small-business financing devotes some sixty pages to describing and advising about government loan programs. It also devotes more than two hundred pages to the mechanics of preparing loan proposals. Much of the material on government loans reads as though it came straight from government manuals and has become outdated with the Reagan administration cutbacks, but the book contains some useful information on agency attitudes and approaches.

How to Finance Your Small Business with Government Money: SBA Loans. Rick Stephan Hayes and John Cotton Howell; John Wiley & Sons; 1980; $14.95.

The first 24 pages of this 165-page book are devoted to explaining the various SBA lending programs. The remainder of the book is purportedly a guide to preparing SBA loan applications, but, in reality, it is a guide to preparing a loan proposal for any number of potential lenders. It instructs readers on putting together market surveys, *pro forma* balance sheets, cash-flow statements, and other basic financial information required by any lender.

National Institute for Continuing Professional Development
P.O. Box 3107
Dallas, TX 75221
(214) 528-2500

The National Institute for Continuing Professional Development (NICPD) sponsors various educational seminars, including one entitled "Government Loan and Loan Guarantee Programs." The seminar on government loan programs consists of a one-day workshop in major cities around the country. Workshop leaders are generally consultants with experience in arranging and understanding government loan programs for individuals and small businesses. The leaders explain the types of loans available and how to go about applying for them. Fees for the seminar range from $155 to $215.

On pp. 104–17 are some sample SBA loan application forms. SBA Form 4 is filed to obtain a direct SBA loan, while SBA Form 4-I is filed for an SBA-guaranteed bank loan. For both applications, key items required are the company balance sheet and profit-and-loss statement, along with earnings projections for one year. The personal financial statement form seeks detailed information on assets and liabilities.

OMB # 1001-R-0081

SBA Form 4
U.S. Small Business Administration

Loan Number

APPLICATION FOR LOAN

I. Applicant/Information About You

Name

Street Address

City, State, Zip Code

Telephone

II. Information About Your Business

Name of Business

Address of Business

City, State, Zip Code

County	Telephone
Type of Business	Date Established

Number of Employees | IRS Employer I.D. Number

Present: ____ After Approval: ____

Bank Where Your Business Has An Account

III. Information About Management: List the name of all owners (having 20% or greater interest), officers, directors, and/or partners. Provide the percent of ownership and the annual compensation.

Name and Title		% of Ownership
Address	Annual Compensation	
Name and Title		% of Ownership

VI. Assistance

List the names of attorneys, accountants, appraisers, agents, or other persons rendering assistance in preparation of this form.

Name and Occupation	Total Fees Paid
Address	Fees Due
Name and Occupation	Total Fees Paid
Address	Fees Due

INSTRUCTIONS FOR APPLICATION FORM

Sections I, II, III. Please provide the information requested. "You" refers to the proprietor, general partner or corporate officer signing this form.

Section IV. Use of the loan money; if your use of the loan fits one of the categories listed on the application form, please fill out this section. If you use "other", submit a list on a separate sheet of paper and label the list Exhibit A.

Section V. Summary of collateral: if your collateral consists of (A) Land and Building, (B) Inventory, and/or (C) Accounts Receivable, fill in the appropriate blanks. If you are using (D) Machinery and Equipment, (E) Furniture and Fixtures, and/or (F) Other, please provide an itemized list (labeled Exhibit B) that contains serial and identification numbers for all articles that had an original value greater than $500.

Address			Annual Compensation
Name and Title		% of Ownership	
Address			Annual Compensation
Name and Title		% of Ownership	
Address			Annual Compensation

IV. How You Plan to Use the Loan Money

Building			
☐ New ☐ Purchase ☐ Renovate	Amount for Building $	Amount for Land $	
Amount for New Equipment $	Amount for Notes Payable $		
Amount for Working Capital $	Amount for Equipment Repair $		
Amount for Accounts Payable $	Other (See Instructions) $		

Total Loan Requested ➜ $

Term of Loan ➜ Years: Months:

V. Summary of Collateral

	Present Market Value	Present Mortage Balance	Cost Less Depreciation
A. Land and Building			
B. Inventory			
C. Accounts Receivable			
D. Machinery and Equipment			
E. Furniture and Fixtures			
F. Other			
Total Collateral $			

SBA Form 4 (9-78) Previous Editions Are Obsolete

Section VI. Provide the information requested for all professional services used while preparing the application. You will be asked to complete another form **after loan closing** that will itemize compensation actually paid for services rendered in connection with this application.

CHECKLIST FOR APPLICATION PACKAGE

Yes	No	
☐	☐	All Exhibits must be signed and dated by person signing this form.
☐	☐	1. Have you submitted **SBA Form 912** (Personal History Statement) for each person e.g. owners, partners, major stock holders, etc.; the instructions are on **SBA Form 912?**
☐	☐	2. Have you filled out a personal balance sheet (**SBA Form 413** may be used for this purpose) for each stockholder (with 20% or greater ownership), partner, officer, and owner. Label this Exhibit C.
☐	☐	3. Have you included the statements listed below: **1,2,3** for the last three years; **1,2,3,4** dated within **90** days of filing the application; and statement **5**? This is Exhibit D.(Management Assistance has **Aids** that help in the preparation of financial Statements.) 1. Balance Sheet 2. Profit and Loss Statement 3. Reconciliation of Net Worth 4. Aging of Accounts Receivable and Payable 5. Earnings projections for at least one year (If Profit and Loss Statement is not available, explain why and substitute Federal Income Tax Forms.)
☐	☐	4. Have you completed a list which contains the original date and amount, present balance owed, interest rate, monthly payment, maturity and security for each loan or debt that your business currently has? Please indicate whether the loan is current or delinquent. An asterisk (*) should be placed by any of these debts that will be paid off with the **SBA** loan. This should be labeled Exhibit E. *(over)*↓

Yes No

☐ ☐ 5. Have you provided a brief history of your company and a paragraph describing the expected benefits it will receive from the loan? If not, you must do so. Label it Exhibit F.

☐ ☐ 6. Have you provided a brief description of the educational, technical and business background for all the people listed in Section III under management? If not, you must do so. Please mark it Exhibit G.

☐ ☐ 7. Do you have any co-signers and/or guarantors for this loan? If so, please submit their names, addresses and personal balance sheets as Exhibit H.

☐ ☐ 8. Are you buying machinery or equipment with your loan money? If so, you must include a list of the equipment and the cost. This is Exhibit J.

☐ ☐ 9. Have you or any officers of your company ever been involved in bankruptcy or insolvency proceedings? If so, please provide the details as Exhibit K.

☐ ☐ 10. Are you or your business involved in any pending lawsuits? If yes, provide the details as Exhibit L.

☐ ☐ 11. Do you or your spouse or any member of your household, or anyone who owns, manages, or directs your business or their spouses or members of their households work for the **Small Business Administration, Small Business Advisory Council, SCORE or ACE?** If so, please provide the name and address of the person and the office where employed. Label this Exhibit M.

☐ ☐ 12. Does your business have any subsidiaries or affiliates? If yes, please provide their names and the relationship with your company along with a current balance sheet and operating statement for each. This should be Exhibit N.

AGREEMENTS AND CERTIFICATIONS

Agreement of Nonemployment of SBA Personnel: I/We agree that if SBA approves this loan application I/We will not, for at least two years, hire as an employee or consultant anyone that was employed by the SBA during the one year period prior to the disbursement of the loan.

Certification: I/We certify: (a) I/We have not paid anyone connected with the Federal Government for help in getting this loan. I/We also agree to report to the **SBA Office of Security and Investigations, 1441 L Street N.W., Washington, D.C., 20416** any Federal Government employee who offers, in return for any type of compensation, to help get this loan approved.

(b) All information in this application and the Exhibits is true and complete to the best of my/our knowledge and is submitted to SBA so SBA can decide whether to grant a loan or participate with a lending institution in a loan to me/us. I/We agree to pay for or reimburse SBA for the cost of any surveys, title or mortage examinations, appraisals etc., performed by non-SBA personnel provided I/We have given my/our consent.

(c) I/We give the assurance that we will comply with sections 112 and 113 of volume 13 of the Code of Federal Regulations. These Code sections prohibit discrimination on the grounds of race, color, sex, religion, martial status, handicap, age, or national origin by recipients of Federal financial assistance and require appropriate reports and access to books and records. These requirements are applicable to anyone who buys or takes control of the business. I/We realize that if I/We do not comply with these non-discrimination requirements SBA can, call, terminate, or accelerate repayment or my/our loan.

Authority to Collect Personal Information: This information is provided pursuant to Public Law 93-579 (Privacy Act of 1974). **Effects of Nondisclosure:** Omission of an item means your application might not receive full consideration.

I/We authorize disclosure of all information sumitted in connection with this application to the financial institution agreeing to participate in the loan.

As consideration for any Management and Technical Assistance that may be provided, I/We waive all claims against **SBA** and its consultants.

I/We understand that **I/We** need not pay anybody to deal with **SBA**. **I/We** have read and understand Form **394** which explains **SBA** policy on representatives and their fees.

For Guaranty Loans please provide an original and one copy (Photocopy is Acceptable) of the Application Form, and all Exhibits to the participating lender. For Direct Loans submit one original copy of application and Exhibits to **SBA**.

It is against SBA regulations to charge the applicant a percentage of the loan proceeds as a fee for preparing this application. If you make a statement that you know to be false or if you over value a security in order to help obtain a loan under the provisions of the Small Business Act you can be fined up to $5,000 or be put in jail for up to two years, or both.

_____
Signature of Preparer if Other Than Applicant

_____
Print or Type Name of Preparer

_____
Address of Preparer
If Applicant is a proprietor or general partner, sign below:

_____   _____
By: Date
If Applicant is a corporation, sign below:

Corporate Seal   _____
                                         Date

By: _____
         Signature of President

Attested by: _____
         Signature of Corporate Secretary

© U.S GOVERNMENT PRINTING OFFICE: 1979--293-442/5294

---

13. Do you buy from, sell to, or use the services of any concern in which someone in your company has a significant financial interest? If yes, provide details on a separate sheet of paper labeled Exhibit P.

14. If your business is a franchise, have you included a copy of the franchise agreement? Please include it as Exhibit R.

15. If you or any principals or affiliates have ever requested government financing, list the name of the agency (including **SBA**), the amount requested or approved, date of request or approval, present balance, and status (i.e. current, delinquent). This should be Exhibit S.

CONSTRUCTION LOANS ONLY

16. Have you included in a separate exhibit (Exhibit T) the estimated cost of the project and a statement of the source of any additional funds? If not, please do so.

17. Have you filed all the necessary compliance documents (**SBA Form Series 601**)? If not, loan officer will advise which forms are necessary.

18. Have you provided copies of preliminary construction plans and specifications? If not, include them as Exhibit U. Final plans will be required prior to disbursement.

DIRECT LOANS ONLY

19. Have you included two bank declination letters with your application? These letters should include the name and telephone number of the persons contacted at the banks, the dates and terms of the loan, the reason for decline and whether or not the bank will participate with **SBA**. In towns with 200,000 people or less, one letter will be sufficient.

SBA Form 4 (9-78)   Previous Editions Are Obsolete

FOR SBA USE ONLY
Loan Number

SBA Form 4-I
U.S. Small Business Administration

Lender's Application for Guaranty or Participation

INSTRUCTIONS: Please provide the information requested in the left hand column. These items pertain to the borrower and the terms of the loan. The list in the right hand column is a checklist of the information that must be supplied with the application package. The lender has the OPTION of submitting a photocopy of a working paper or using the space on the reverse of this form to provide the information requested. For each item, place a check mark in the box to the left of the request if a working paper will be submitted; place no mark in the box next to an item if the reverse of this form is used.

LENDER INFORMATION
Name of Lender

Street Address

City, State, ZIP Code

Telephone

Name of Applicant

Name of Applicant's Business

LOAN INFORMATION
Loan Characteristics:
☐ Guaranty ☐ Immediate Participation

Amount: _____ Interest Rate:

$ _____ _____ % A.P.R.

Term of Loan:

☐ 1. The financial spread from the lender's credit analysis. Label working paper **Exhibit 1.**

☐ 2. Ratio analysis of applicant's business. Label working paper **Exhibit 2.**

☐ 3. A schedule of the borrower's fixed obligations during the next 4 years. Label working paper **Exhibit 3.**

☐ 4. A list of the collateral and lien positions and an analysis of the adequacy of the collateral. Label working paper **Exhibit 4.**

☐ 5. A paragraph describing the lender's credit experience with the applicant. Label working paper **Exhibit 5.**

☐ 6. Comments on the applicant's management skill. Label working paper **Exhibit 6.**

7. An analysis of the applicant's repayment ability. Label working paper **Exhibit 7.**

☐

8. A schedule of insurance, standby agreements and other conditions required by the loan agreement. Label working paper **Exhibit 8.**

☐

9. A list of the lender's employees, officers, directors, or substantial (greater than 10%) stockholders or any immediate family member of the above who has any financial interest in the applicant. If none, write **"None"** in the box to the left of this question; otherwise provide an explanation of the relationship. Label it **Exhibit 9.**

☐

Years   Months

If interest rate is variable

Base rate: Spread:

Bank Share: SBA Share:

_____ %   _____ %

Payment: (including interest and principal)

$ _____ Per month

(Payment must be in even dollar amounts)

If payment is not monthly:

$ _____ Per _____

Lender's Loan Officer Summary and Recommendation

_____

Signature   Title:
                 Date:

Comments of Lender's Official taking final action:

I approve this application to **SBA** subject to the terms and conditions outlined above. Without the participation of **SBA** to the extent applied for we would not be willing to make this loan, and in our opinion the financial assistance applied for is not otherwise available on reasonable terms.

_____

Signature   Title:
                 Date:

SBA Form 4-I (9-78)

Exhibit 1 FINANCIAL SPREAD

Balance Sheet as of: ___ Fiscal Year Ends: ___ Audited ☐ Unaudited ☐

	Debit	Credit	Pro forma
Assets			
Cash $			
Accounts Rec.			
Inventory			
Other			
Total Current Assets			
Fixed Assets			
Other Assets			
TOTAL ASSETS			
Liabilities and Net Worth			
Accounts Payable $			
Notes Payable			
Taxes			
Other			
SBA			
TOTAL CURRENT LIAB.			
Notes Payable $			
SBA			
Other			
TOTAL LIABILITIES			
NET WORTH			
TOTAL Liab. & Net Worth $			

Profit and Loss	Year:	Year:	Year:	Year:
Sales				
Depreciation				
Income Taxes				
W/D Office comp				
NET PROFIT AFTER TAX, DEPRECIATION & COMPENSATION				

Exhibit 2: RATIO ANALYSIS

Debt/Net Worth _____ ,Current Ratio_____ ,Working Capital_____

Comment on ratio analysis (including any apparent trends)

Exhibit 3: SCHEDULE OF FIXED OBLIGATIONS

Year 1 $__ __ __ __ Year 2 $__ __ __ Year 3 $__ __ __ __ Year 4 $__ __ __ __

Exhibit 4: COLLATERAL OFFERED AND LIEN POSITION: ANALYSIS OF ADEQUACY OF COLLATERAL

Exhibit 5: LENDER'S CREDIT EXPERIENCE WITH THE APPLICANT

Exhibit 6: COMMENTS ON THE MANAGEMENT SKILL OF THE APPLICANT

Exhibit 7: LENDER'S ANALYSIS OF REPAYMENT ABILITY

Exhibit 8: SCHEDULE OF INSURANCE REQUIREMENTS, STANDBY AGREEMENTS AND OTHER REQUIREMENTS

Exhibit 9: LIST OF LENDER'S EMPLOYEES, ETC. WITH A FINANCIAL INTEREST IN THE APPLICANT

SBA Form 4-I (9-78)   GPO 932 841

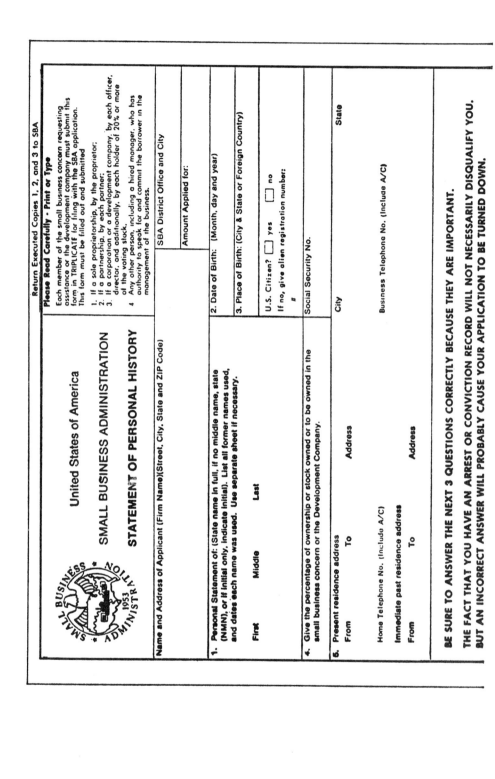

Return Executed Copies 1, 2, and 3 to SBA

Please Read Carefully - Print or Type

Each member of the small business concern requesting assistance or the development company must submit this form in TRIPLICATE for filing with the SBA application. This form must be filled out and submitted

1. If a sole proprietorship, by the proprietor;
2. If a partnership, by each partner;
3. If a corporation or a development company, by each officer, director, and additionally, by each holder of 20% or more of the voting stock.
4. Any other person, including a hired manager, who has authority to speak for and commit the borrower in the management of the business.

United States of America

SMALL BUSINESS ADMINISTRATION

STATEMENT OF PERSONAL HISTORY

SBA District Office and City
Amount Applied for:

Name and Address of Applicant (Firm Name)(Street, City, State and ZIP Code)

1. **Personal Statement of:** (State name in full, if no middle name, state (NMN), or if initial only, indicate initial). List all former names used, and dates each name was used. Use separate sheet if necessary.

First   Middle   Last

2. Date of Birth: (Month, day and year)

3. Place of Birth: (City & State or Foreign Country)

U.S. Citizen? ☐ yes   ☐ no
If no, give alien registration number:
#

Social Security No.

4. Give the percentage of ownership or stock owned or to be owned in the small business concern or the Development Company.

5. Present residence address

From   To   Address   City   State

Home Telephone No. (Include A/C)   Business Telephone No. (Include A/C)

Immediate past residence address

From   To   Address

BE SURE TO ANSWER THE NEXT 3 QUESTIONS CORRECTLY BECAUSE THEY ARE IMPORTANT.

THE FACT THAT YOU HAVE AN ARREST OR CONVICTION RECORD WILL NOT NECESSARILY DISQUALIFY YOU. BUT AN INCORRECT ANSWER WILL PROBABLY CAUSE YOUR APPLICATION TO BE TURNED DOWN.

6. Are you presently under indictment, on parole or probation?

☐ Yes ☐ No   If yes, furnish details in a separate exhibit. List name(s) under which held, if applicable.

7. Have you ever been charged with or arrested for any criminal offense other than a minor motor vehicle violation?

☐ Yes ☐ No   If yes, furnish details in a separate exhibit. List name(s) under which charged, if applicable.

8. Have you ever been convicted of any criminal offense other than a minor motor vehicle violation?

☐ Yes ☐ No   If yes, furnish details in a separate exhibit. List name(s) under which convicted, if applicable.

9. Name and address of participating bank

The information on this form will be used in connection with an investigation of your character. Any information you wish to submit, that you feel will expedite this investigation should be set forth.

Whoever makes any statement knowing it to be false, for the purpose of obtaining for himself or for any applicant, any loan, or loan extension by renewal, deferment or otherwise, or for the purpose of obtaining, or influencing SBA toward, anything of value under the Small Business Act, as amended, shall be punished under Section 16(a) of that Act, by a fine of not more than $5000, or by imprisonment for not more than 2 years, or both.

Signature	Title	Date

1. SBA FILE COPY

Form Approved
OMB No. 100-R-0081

PERSONAL FINANCIAL STATEMENT

Return to:

Small Business Administration

For SBA Use Only

SBA Loan No.

As of _____ , 19 ___ .

Complete this form if 1) a sole proprietorship by the proprietor; 2) a partnership by each partner; 3) a corporation by each officer and each stockholder with 20% or more ownership; 4) any other person or entity providing a guaranty on the loan.

Name and Address; Including ZIP Code   *(of person and spouse submitting Statement)*

This statement is submitted in connection with S.B.A. loan requested or granted to the individual or firm, whose name appears below:

Name and Address of Applicant or Borrower, Including ZIP Code

SOCIAL SECURITY NO. _____

Business *(of person submitting Statement)*

Please answer all questions using "No" or "None" where necessary

ASSETS		LIABILITIES	
Cash on Hand & In Banks . . . . $		Accounts Payable . . . . $	
Savings Account in Banks		Notes Payable to Banks	
U. S. Government Bonds		(Describe below - Section 2)	
Accounts & Notes Receivable		Notes Payable to Others	
Life Insurance-Cash Surrender Value Only . .		(Describe below - Section 2)	
Other Stocks and Bonds		Installment Account (Auto)	
(Describe - reverse side - Section 3)		Monthly Payments $	
Real Estate		Installment Accounts (Other)	
(Describe - reverse side - Section 4)		Monthly Payments $	
Automobile - Present Value		Loans on Life Insurance	
Other Personal Property		Mortgages on Real Estate	
(Describe - reverse side - Section 5)		(Describe - reverse side - Section 4)	
Other Assets		Unpaid Taxes	
(Describe - reverse side - Section 6)		(Describe - reverse side - Section 7)	
		Other Liabilities	
		(Describe - reverse side - Section 8)	
		Total Liabilities	
		Net Worth	
Total . . . . $		Total . . . . $	

Section 1. Source of Income
(Describe below all items listed in this Section)

Salary................$
Net Investment Income...........
Real Estate Income...........
Other Income (Describe)*...........

Description of items listed in Section 1

___

CONTINGENT LIABILITIES

As Endorser or Co-Maker...........$
Legal Claims and Judgments...........
Provision for Federal Income Tax...........
Other Special Debt...........

___

*Not necessary to disclose alimony or child support payments in "Other Income" unless it is desired to have such payments counted toward total income.

Life Insurance Held (Give face amount of policies - name of company and beneficiaries)

SUPPLEMENTARY SCHEDULES

Section 2. Notes Payable to Banks and Others

Name and Address of Holder of Note	Amount of Loan		Terms of Repayments	Maturity of Loan	How Endorsed, Guaranteed, or Secured
	Original Bal.	Present Bal.			
	$	$	$		

SBA FORM 413 (12-78) REF: SOP 50 50   Edition of 8-67 May Be Used Until Stock Is Exhausted

Section 3. Other Stocks and Bonds: Give listed and unlisted Stocks and Bonds (Use separate sheet if necessary)

No. of Shares	Names of Securities	Cost	Market Value Statement Date	
			Quotation	Amount

Section 4. Real Estate Owned. (List each parcel separately. Use supplemental sheets if necessary. Each sheet must be identified as a supplement to this statement and signed). (Also advises whether property is covered by title insurance, abstract of title, or both).

Title is in name of _____

Type of property _____

Address of property (City and State)

Original Cost to (me) (us) $ _____
Date Purchased _____
Present Market Value $ _____
Tax Assessment Value $ _____

Name and Address of Holder of Mortgage (City and State)

Date of Mortgage _____
Original Amount $ _____
Balance $ _____
Maturity _____
Terms of Payment _____

Status of Mortgage, i.e., current or delinquent. If delinquent describe delinquencies

Section 5. Other Personal Property. (Describe and if any is mortgaged, state name and address of mortgage holder and amount of mortgage. terms of payment and if delinquent, describe delinquency.)

Section 6. Other Assets. *(Describe)*

Section 7. Unpaid Taxes. *(Describe in detail, as to type, to whom payable, when due, amount, and what, if any, property a tax lien, if any, attaches)*

Section 8. Other Liabilities. *(Describe in detail)*

(I) or (We) certify the above and the statements contained in the schedules herein is a true and accurate statement of (my) or (our) financial condition as of the date stated herein. This statement is given for the purpose of: *(Check one of the following)*

☐ Inducing S.B.A. to grant a loan as requested in application, of the individual or firm whose name appears herein, in connection with which this statement is submitted.

☐ Furnishing a statement of (my) or (our) financial condition, pursuant to the terms of the guaranty executed by (me) or (us) at the time S.B.A. granted a loan to the individual or firm, whose name appears herein.

Signature _____

Signature _____ Date _____

CHAPTER 4

State and Local Government Assistance

INTRODUCTION: RAPIDLY EXPANDING SOURCES OF AID

There's good news and bad news for entrepreneurs who wonder what kind of financing and other assistance might be available from their state and local authorities.

The good news is that state and local officials are becoming increasingly aware of and sensitive to the needs of smaller businesses.

The bad news is that state and local concern with smaller businesses has not yet spread to all states; thus, *where* a business is located makes a big difference in the kinds of assistance available.

The simple fact that state and local authorities are becoming attuned to the importance of small businesses is an extremely significant development, however. In the years immediately following World War II, the predominant approach to business development among state and local politicians and bureaucrats was to convince big companies to locate in their areas. States frequently competed with each other to lure big corporations, offering tax breaks and low-interest loans as inducements.

That approach to business development isn't entirely passé. Representatives of large industrial states, along with representatives of less developed small states, engage in stiff competition to get a company such as Volkswagen or IBM or Digital Equipment to open plants in their state.

But since the late 1960s and early 1970s a growing number of states have soured on the big score. Instead, they have become convinced that the key to encouraging business development lies in encouraging their existing smaller businesses to grow and develop. More than half the states in the country now have some kind of special program directed to encouraging small-business development; these programs take the form of small-business offices, procurement programs, or loan programs.

The changes in attitudes and approach stem from a growing volume of evidence which suggests that small businesses, rather than large corporations, account for the bulk of new jobs being created. Because politicians at all levels tend to equate business development with new jobs, such evidence carries important weight.

According to an article in *Venture* magazine's April 1980 issue on states' interest in small businesses,

> . . . indications are growing that entrepreneurs and small businessmen may be courted with more fervor in the future. The principal reason for this budding new focus is mounting evidence from state, federal, and private surveys that small, young businesses create more jobs than do large, mature companies.

Because attitudes are in something of a transitional period, the types and quality of assistance available to small businesses vary widely from state to state. It is only in a few states, such as Connecticut, Massachusetts, and New Jersey, that extensive programs are in place that focus on developing small businesses. A number of other states, such as Delaware and Idaho, have no special programs to aid small businesses. And in other states, particularly in the South, aggressive business development programs still tend to focus on attracting large company plants, but initial efforts are under way to focus more attention on small-business needs.

Much the same change in attitude is occurring in many of the nation's largest cities. Instead of trying to attract outside corporations to locate in their cities, officials are becoming increasingly adept at arranging attractive financing packages to encourage their existing businesses to stay put and expand in their home cities.

OBTAINING AID

Though the type and quality of state and local assistance vary widely, a few generalizations can be offered about what is available. First of all, although such assistance is available mostly to existing businesses, a growing number of states offer start-up businesses a chance of benefiting.

State and local assistance can also be difficult to track down and apply for. Simply understanding *which* state and city agencies can do *what* is a major task, usually requiring a fair amount of investigation. State and city agencies frequently draw on a number of local and federal lending sources, which can mean much red tape and lengthy delays before getting decisions.

And unlike the situation with most federal financing agencies, political connections and personal rapport can be important in dealing with state and local agencies. That is partly a reflection of the nature of state and local government in general.

Despite the advantage of knowing the right people, there is no discounting the importance of a sound balance sheet in obtaining state and local assistance. Though such assistance is supposed to be geared toward companies unable to attract commercial financing, a stable conservative balance sheet generally receives the most favorable action. That means that dynamic, fast-growing companies may encounter resistance. Because they require continuous, large amounts of cash, their balance sheets often look shaky.

STATE ASSISTANCE

State assistance can come in any number of forms, ranging from tax breaks to assistance in site selection for new plants to direct loans. This chapter will confine itself to considering the most direct forms of financing available to businesses of all sizes, along with programs directed specifically to small businesses. The most common forms of assistance are the following.

1. Special small-business assistance programs; these can include procurement programs, loan and venture-capital programs, and special complaint-handling departments, all geared specifically to small businesses. Definitions of small businesses are usually spelled out by the states.
2. State-sponsored direct loans and guarantees of bank loans, usually to encourage existing businesses or entice outside businesses to build new plants. Such financing is usually available to companies of all sizes, but may be directed predominantly to small businesses. Loans can vary widely in size, from a few thousand dollars to hundreds of thousands of dollars.
3. Financing from quasi-public agencies and private nonprofit corporations which have combinations of public and private funds available for businesses of all sizes. The most common of such organizations are business development corporations, which are nonprofit corporations that have been established in about thirty states. They are usually funded by groups of commercial banks to make loans to businesses that can't obtain direct bank financing. They can also obtain special Small Business Administration funds available to states, SBA guarantees of their loans, and other types of federal and state assistance that result in financing packages from several sources.
4. Industrial revenue bonds. Such bonds are the most common form

of state-authorized financing assistance. Actually, state and municipal agencies borrow funds from private and public investors, usually banks, by issuing bonds; the money is then typically used to construct or expand plants or to build pollution-control facilities. Companies then usually lease the plants or facilities from the issuing agency for the life of the bonds, which range from fifteen to twenty-five years, and can generally acquire the facilities for nominal fees at the end of the leases.

Industrial revenue bonds, as both the most common form of state assistance and the most intricate, warrant further discussion. They have advantages for companies, investors, and states. Companies can get 100 percent financing, instead of the 80 percent or 90 percent they would get with a mortgage. Interest rates are usually 1¼ to 2½ percent lower than interest rates on comparable bank financing. The lower interest rates stem from the fact that interest received by investors on the bonds is exempt from state and federal taxes, so long as the total bond issue and the company's local capital expenditures for both the three years preceding and succeeding the issue do not together exceed $10 million. Such bonds allow states to encourage development of areas underutilized by business where unemployment is considered excessive.

Almost all states allow revenue bonds, either for business expansion or pollution-control equipment, although some states use the device more frequently than others. In recent years, such bonds have become an important small-business financing mechanism. Altogether, more than $7 billion of revenue and pollution-control bonds were issued in a recent year for projects under $10 million.

Businesses considering going the bond route for financing should take into account the likelihood that the areas where it is easiest to get state or municipal authorization for bonds are usually the least desirable from the viewpoints of transportation, appropriately trained labor supply, and other factors. Otherwise, enough businesses would be present that state officials would not be interested in further business development.

To obtain bond financing, companies must first obtain authorization from the appropriate political body for issuance of bonds. Success in obtaining such authorization depends in part on the government's interest in developing the area which the business proposes to expand, as well as the procedures set up to decide on issuing authorization; some locales require extensive study of proposals, and others require very little study.

Next, companies must demonstrate interest in the bonds on the part of public or private investors. Some jurisdictions help in this process, but it is usually wise to have help from an investment banking or law firm specializing in bonds.

Because investors tend to be most interested in sound-appearing balance sheets, fast-growing, capital-hungry companies can encounter obstacles in seeking financing through such bonds. But skilled investment bankers and lawyers can frequently find ways around such obstacles—for example, by obtaining guarantees from backup companies to assume leases of facilities built with bond proceeds.

The idea is to reassure state or local officials in charge of issuing the bonds that someone will be around to make the required payments should the company seeking the financing fail. Experienced investment bankers and lawyers frequently have the contacts necessary to make such arrangements.

Industrial revenue bonds are usually issued for a minimum of $400,000 to $500,000, simply because the legal and assorted other costs associated with obtaining such funds make them uneconomical in lower amounts. Federal law limits revenue bonds to a maximum of $10 million.

One potential disadvantage of industrial revenue bonds is that, when the amount of the bonds covers only a portion of the funds needed for projects, the SBA and other federal agencies will not get involved in financing additional amounts. Thus, financing packages consisting of funds from both tax-exempt bonds and federal loans are impossible to arrange. States would have no objection to such combination packages, but the federal government is against them. It doesn't like the idea of promoting tax-exempt bonds, because such bonds reduce federal tax revenues.

Small businesses seeking industrial revenue bond funds should be prepared with the same kind of information needed to obtain bank loans. Lawyers can assist in presenting the information in correct form for state officials and potential investors. Legal fees are usually based on a flat percentage of the bond issue amount and tend to range from $15,000 on up. The whole process of obtaining industrial revenue bond financing usually takes from two to six months.

STATE SOURCES

What follows in this section is a brief description of the small-business and other direct financial assistance programs in each of the fifty states as well as the District of Columbia and Puerto Rico. Together with each description is the title, address, and phone number of the main economic development official, along with the phone number of any small-business assistance office in the state.

The descriptions and office listings are not meant to be all-inclusive. Rather, they are meant to give readers an idea of the scope of assistance potentially available in each state, as well as provide a place to start in the gathering of detailed information. Within some state descriptions, additional state and other agencies and the cities in which they are located are referred to; readers can usually obtain further information on such agencies by contacting the main economic development office listed or by finding the phone number and calling the agency directly. In some cases economic development officials may prove to be ignorant of other programs in the state; in such cases entrepreneurs can usually get help from the governor's office or from their state legislator. It was not possible to include further details on programs and contacts here because of space limitations.

The information contained in the listings was drawn from a number of sources: a book issued by the U. S. Small Business Administration's office of the Chief Counsel for Advocacy, entitled the *Directory of State Small Business Programs; Sourceguide for Borrowing Capital* by Leonard E. Smollen, Mark Rollinson, and Stanley M. Rubel; *Site Selection Handbook* and *Industrial Development* magazine, both of which are published by Conway Publications, Inc., of Atlanta; and the National Association of State Development Agencies, a trade group of state economic development officials based in Washington. We were also assisted by Joseph P. Furber, President of the American Industrial Development Council, a Kansas City, Missouri, organization that promotes state and local development.

ALABAMA

Director
Alabama Development Office
c/o State Capitol
3734 Atlanta Highway
Montgomery, AL 36130
(205) 832-6011
(205) 832-6980
(205) 832-6400

Alabama has a special small-business procurement program whose goal is to award a minimum of 10 percent of any department's or agency's total purchases to small businesses. Small businesses are defined as independently owned and operated businesses with either fewer than fifty employees or less than $1 million in gross annual receipts.

Alabama also has one of the most active industrial revenue bond programs in the country, typically issuing several hundred million dollars in bonds annually. In addition, the State assists expanding or relocating companies with employee training programs.

ALASKA

Commissioner
Department of Commerce and Economic Development
Pouch D
Juneau, AK 99811
(907) 465-2500

Small-business office in Fairbanks branch of
   Department of Commerce and Economic Development:
(907) 452-8182

Alaska has a number of financing programs of special interest to small businesses. It has a Small Business Revolving Loan Fund which makes fifteen-year loans at 9.5 percent interest rates for a maximum of $500,000 to small businesses. To be considered small, businesses must have fewer than 200 employees and less than $10 million in gross receipts.

The State has other revolving loan funds to assist businesses associated with tourism, fishing, agriculture, and child care.

The State also has the Small Business Development Corporation of Alaska, which is designed to finance plant construction and expansion.

Alaska's most recent and innovative effort to assist fledgling companies is the Alaska Renewable Resources Corporation, a public corporation that uses proceeds from mineral leases, rentals, and royalties to finance start-ups and existing companies involved in forest products, fishing, agriculture, and renewable-energy resources. Financing is available in various forms, including loans, equity investments, and direct grants.

The small-business office is overseen by a Small Business Development specialist, who aids start-up entrepreneurs in selecting sites, preparing business plans, and lining up supply sources. The specialist also provides management assistance to small businesses that are experiencing operating difficulties.

Though industrial revenue bonds are permitted, Alaska has been relatively inactive in this area.

ARIZONA

Executive Director
Arizona Office of Economic Planning and Development
1700 W Washington
Phoenix, AZ 85007
(602) 255-4331
(602) 255-5374

Arizona has no special programs of direct assistance for small businesses. Its municipalities can issue revenue bonds, but activity in this area has been only modest; since the program was started in 1964, only fourteen bond financings, for a total of $38 million, have been undertaken.

ARKANSAS

Executive Director
Department of Economic Development
One Capitol Mall
Little Rock, AR 72201
(501) 371-2052

Small Business Assistance Division:
(800) 482-9659

The Small Business Assistance Division is primarily a referral service, offering small-business owners information on state services and programs available to them. The division also has plans to establish seminars and continuing-education classes on small business at various education centers in Arkansas.

The State has two business development corporations that lend funds to businesses unable to obtain commercial financing and that also arrange federal financing packages.

Arkansas also has an active revenue bond program that is particularly helpful to businesses that might otherwise be unable to raise money, because the program includes the option of a state guarantee to pay off the bonds, up to $500,000 apiece.

CALIFORNIA

Director
Department of Economic and Business Development
P.O. Box 1499
Sacramento, CA 95805
(916) 322-1394
(916) 322-5665

Office of Small Business Development in Department of
   Economic and Business Development:
(916) 445-6545

California has traditionally been able to attract sufficient numbers of new businesses of all sizes on the basis of its attractive economic and physical climate and has only recently started creating business assistance programs. It became one of the last states to start an industrial revenue bond program, beginning January 1, 1981.

California now has an Office of Small Business Development that can provide loan guarantees, management assistance, and public relations services. The State has a small-business procurement program, under which small businesses are to be given preference if their bids are within 5 percent of the lowest responsible bidder. Small businesses, for this purpose, are defined as those which are independently owned and operated, not dominant in their field, and based in California.

The State also has a variety of loan programs available to small businesses. Under a Small Business Loan Program administered by the banking superintendent, loans are made directly by banks to small businesses that might not qualify for ordinary business loans. Businesses that receive ordinary bank loans, as well as lenders and the State, are charged loan premiums, which go into the Small Business Loan Reserve Fund to cover defaults.

California has also established an Office of Local Economic Development in Sacramento. This office utilizes federal and state funds to make loans to small businesses that create jobs in specific high-unemployment areas. Loans are for between $100,000 and $350,000 at below-market interest rates.

In addition, California has licensed two business development companies, First California Business & Industrial Development Corp. and Statewide California Business & Industrial Development Corp., both located in Newport Beach. These companies specialize in long-term loans and equity investments for small businesses. Most recently, these companies have moved to increase their leverage by making extensive use of federal loan guarantees and then selling the guaranteed loans to private investors.

Three other loan outlets known as Regional Small Business Development Corporations have been established; they are in San Francisco, Fresno, and Los Angeles. Loans and loan guarantees are provided to small businesses that are unable to obtain ordinary commercial financing. Funds come from both federal loan programs and private California financial institutions.

COLORADO

Director
Division of Commerce and Development
500 State Centennial Building
Denver, CO 80203
(303) 839-3045

Small Business Assistance Center at University of Colorado in
   Boulder:
(303) 492-8211

Though once active in seeking to encourage business development,
Colorado has, in recent years, moved away from aiding businesses of any
size.

The Small Business Assistance Center, which is funded jointly by
federal and state government, provides various management assistance to
small businesses, including start-up help, marketing research, feasibility
studies, organization analysis, and financial counseling.

Colorado allows cities, towns, and counties to issue revenue bonds.
Since the program started in the mid-1960s, more than $260 million of
revenue bonds have been issued.

CONNECTICUT

Commissioner
Connecticut Department of Economic Development
210 Washington St.
Hartford, CT 06106
(203) 566-3787

Office of Small Business Affairs in Department of Economic
   Development:
(203) 566-4051

Business Ombudsman:
(203) 566-7035

Connecticut has established one of the more comprehensive programs
in the country for assisting small businesses. The Office of Small Business
Affairs lobbies to obtain state loans for small businesses, administers a
procurement program for small businesses, and serves as liaison on behalf
of small businesses with federal, state, regional, and local agencies.

> Established in the summer of 1977, the Office of Small Business Affairs
> has proven conclusively the validity of consolidating virtually *all* state gov-
> ernmental functions relating to small business in a single agency,

concluded Laurence Collins, a Boston *Globe* reporter, in a 1979 research
report on state and local assistance for small companies that he wrote for
the Small Business Administration's Office of Advocacy.

Connecticut's procurement program seeks to grant to small business
between 15 percent and 25 percent of all contracts let. Its small-business
loan program makes loans for up to one year for a maximum of $100,000
at interest rates usually somewhat below market rates. For both the

procurement and loan programs, small businesses are defined as those with annual sales of less than $1 million.

Connecticut, in recent years, has also established a quasi-public corporation, Connecticut Product Development Corporation (CPDC), to provide venture capital for the development of new products. The corporation has provided more than $1.3 million of risk capital from state and federal funds to approximately twenty companies to develop new products. In most situations the CPDC puts up 60 percent of product development costs, and the small business puts up 40 percent. The CPDC receives its return from royalty payments on the new products; it does not fund start-up businesses, however.

In addition, Connecticut has a business development corporation, Connecticut Development Credit Corporation, in Meriden, which makes loans to companies unable to obtain commercial credit. The State allows issuance of revenue bonds through municipalities and through the Connecticut Development Authority, a state agency. The authority can also issue a general obligation bond for groups of mortgage loans for property and equipment on behalf of companies otherwise unable to obtain the loans.

DELAWARE

Director
Delaware Department of Community Affairs and Economic
    Development
630 State College Road
P.O. Box 1401
Dover, DE 19901
(302) 736-4254

Delaware has no programs specifically directed to small businesses. However, the State has been relatively active in allowing issuance of industrial revenue bonds and aids businesses that might not otherwise be able to qualify for bonds by guaranteeing some bonds.

DISTRICT OF COLUMBIA

Director
Office of Business and Economic Development
DC Building (Room 201)
1350 E St., NW
Washington, DC 20004
(202) 727-3511

The District of Columbia's main source of assistance to small businesses is a business development corporation. Businesses must have been turned down by a commercial bank in order to qualify for loans.

FLORIDA

Chief
Division of Economic Development
Florida Department of Commerce
107 W Gaines St.
Tallahassee, FL 32301
(904) 488-9360

The Division of Economic Development has a small-business office that assists and advises small businesses on dealing with government agencies, regulations, and procurement at federal, state, and local levels. Florida also permits local governmental bodies to issue revenue bonds for business development; and the State has a business development corporation, Industrial Development Corporation of Florida, in Orlando, that makes loans to companies unable to obtain ordinary commercial financing.

GEORGIA

Commissioner
Georgia Department of Industry and Trade
1400 North OMNI International
Atlanta, GA 30303
(404) 656-3556

Georgia has established a goal of seeking to direct a "fair" proportion of its total purchases, contracts, and subcontracts to small business, which it defines as those with fewer than 100 employees or less than $1 million in gross annual receipts. The State also has an active industrial revenue bond program, with bonds issued by counties and municipalities; along with a business development corporation, the Business Development Corporation of Georgia, in Atlanta, which lends funds to businesses unable to get commercial financing.

In addition, state officials are backing an effort sponsored in part by Georgia Tech's Advanced Technology Center to provide financing to high-technology businesses; the funds will come from private investors.

HAWAII

Director
Hawaii Department of Planning and Economic Development
Kamamula Building
250 S King St.
Honolulu, HI 96804
(808) 548-3033
(808) 548-4616

Hawaii's main source of assistance to small businesses is through its Capital Loan Program, under which funds are lent for plant construction, conversion, and expansion, as well as for land acquisition for expansion, equipment and machinery purchases, and working capital. Businesses are defined as small if they meet SBA definitions of small businesses. Loans are available for a maximum of $50,000 and twenty years at a 7½ percent interest rate.

Several hundred businesses have received loans under the program since it was started in 1964. Funds for the program have been provided by the State, the SBA, and other sources.

Hawaii also has a loan program for purchasing, building, and repairing small fishing vessels under terms similar to the Capital Loan Program, except loan term is limited to ten years. Hawaii is one of only three states that doesn't permit issuance of industrial revenue bonds.

IDAHO

Administrator
Division of Tourism and Industrial Development
Capitol Building
Boise, ID 83720
(208) 384-2470

Idaho has virtually no special programs of direct assistance for businesses of any size. It also does not permit revenue bonds of any kind.

ILLINOIS

Director
Illinois Department of Commerce and Community Affairs
222 S College
Springfield, IL 62706
(217) 782-7500

Small Business Information Office (in the Governor's Office of
  Manpower and Human Development):
(312) 793-6885

The Small Business Information Office assists small businesses in
dealing with federal, state, and local agencies. Illinois also has a small-
business procurement program which seeks to direct a "fair" proportion
of state purchases and contracts to small businesses. For construction
contracts, 25 percent to 40 percent for small companies is considered appropriate. The State defines small businesses variably, according to the
number of employees and sales and depending on the industry.

Illinois also has an active revenue bond program, which has helped
finance more than 100 industrial projects with several hundred million
dollars. Another source of state assistance is the Illinois Industrial Development Authority, in Marion, which is a quasi-public agency that has, in
recent years, made loans ranging from $16,000 to $150,000 for up to
twenty-five years to small businesses, including start-up loans. Interest
rates are below market rates. The Authority also makes loans together
with federal agencies to businesses seeking to expand in high-
unemployment areas.

INDIANA

Executive Director
Indiana Department of Commerce
440 N Meridian St.
Indianapolis, IN 46220
(317) 232-8800

Small Business Ombudsman Office:
(317) 232-3376

Indiana has a small-business procurement program under which
awards can be set aside for small businesses if a reasonable expectation
exists that at least two capable small businesses will bid. Definitions of
small business vary according to industry.

The State also has an active industrial revenue bond program that
has generated more than $2 billion in assistance. In addition, Indiana has
a Mortgage Guarantee Loan Program, under which companies unable to
secure ordinary commercial mortgages can obtain state guarantees for up
to $1 million, or 90 percent of a project, whichever is less, to repay com-
mercial lenders.

The Small Business Ombudsman Office is in the formative stages. It
is designed to handle complaints about state forms and regulations and to
attempt to solve the related problems.

IOWA

Director
Iowa Development Commission
250 Jewett Building
Des Moines, IA 50309
(515) 281-3619

General Ombudsman Office:
(515) 281-3592

Though Iowa has no programs specifically designed to assist small businesses directly, it has an active industrial revenue bond program and a business development corporation, the Iowa Business Development Credit Corporation in Des Moines. The State's industrial revenue bond program has generated in excess of $400 million for more than 100 different projects since the program was started in 1963. The Iowa Business Development Credit Corporation makes loans up to $300,000 (though they average between $100,000 and $150,000) and mature within ten years. Interest rates are negotiable.

Iowa is in the process of establishing a small-business ombudsman office; in the meantime, entrepreneurs with complaints and questions about state agencies and officials should call the General Ombudsman Office, which handles complaints from all citizens.

KANSAS

Secretary
Kansas Department of Economic Development
503 Kansas Ave.
Topeka, KS 66603
(913) 296-3481

Kansas has a small-business procurement program that seeks to direct at least 10 percent of state purchases to businesses defined as small. Definitions vary according to the business area.

Kansas also has an active industrial revenue bond program which has generated more than $500 million for over 500 projects in recent years. And Kansas has an active business development corporation, the Kansas Development Credit Corporation, located in Topeka, which has made several hundred loans since it was started in the mid-1960s.

KENTUCKY

Commissioner
Kentucky Department of Commerce
Capitol Plaza Towers
Frankfort, KY 40601
(502) 564-4270

Small Business Development Section in Kentucky
  Department of Commerce:
(502) 564-4270

The Small Business Development Section provides management assistance in such areas as obtaining financing, developing exports, and becoming involved in government procurement programs. The section has published fliers listing programs and sources available to assist small businesses at the local, commonwealth, and federal levels. Kentucky has also recently started a procurement program for setting aside unspecified amounts of commonwealth purchases for small businesses.

Kentucky has an active industrial revenue bond program that has seen more than $1 billion raised over recent years. The Kentucky Industrial Development Finance Authority, a commonwealth agency, has, during the 1970s, been a source of low-interest working capital loans to small businesses unable to obtain ordinary commercial loans. And the Business Development Corporation of Kentucky, in Louisville, has made loans available to small businesses on a limited basis.

LOUISIANA

Director of Economic Development
Louisiana Department of Commerce
P.O. Box 44185
Baton Rouge, LA 70804
(504) 342-5361

Louisiana has a procurement program designed to direct up to 10 percent of state purchases of goods and services, excluding construction, to small businesses. Businesses are defined as small in accordance with their business area. The State also has an active industrial revenue bond program, which is its main source of financial assistance to businesses.

The State has plans for establishing an office of small-business assistance, which would handle complaints and provide management assistance.

MAINE

Director
State Development Office
193 State St.
Augusta, ME 04333
(207) 289-2656

Maine's principal effort to assist small businesses specifically is a loan insurance program under the Maine Small Business Loan Authority. It can ensure repayment of up to 80 percent of commercial mortgage loans involving a principal obligation of under $30,000. Maine also has a moderately active industrial revenue bond program, as well as a state agency known as the Maine Guarantee Authority, which is empowered to make direct loans or guarantee commercial loans for businesses of all sizes. The Maine Guarantee Authority recently made an express commitment to increase the amounts loaned to small businesses.

The State recently created the Maine Development Foundation to aid start-up and existing businesses by forming a state-backed venture-capital firm to be known as Maine Capital Corp. and providing site selection and trade development assistance.

MARYLAND

Secretary
Maryland Department of Economic and Community Development
Office of Business and Industrial Development
1748 Forest Drive
Annapolis, MD 21401
(301) 269-3265
(301) 269-3727
(301) 269-3514

Maryland has two programs specifically geared for small businesses: a procurement program that seeks to direct a "fair" proportion of state purchases to small businesses, and a loan program designed to assist small businesses. Under the procurement program, small businesses can be awarded orders only if their bids do not exceed by 5 percent bids received by other acceptable larger businesses. Businesses are defined as small based on their industry, number of employees, and annual sales. The loan program is designed to provide working capital to small businesses that need funds to complete work on local, state, or federal government contracts; thus, small businesses must have government contracts to obtain such loans.

Maryland also has several other financing programs that can be used by small businesses. It has a fairly active business development corporation, the Development Credit Corporation of Maryland, in Baltimore, which makes loans to businesses unable to obtain ordinary commercial loans. The State also has an active industrial revenue bond program, under which counties and municipalities issue the bonds. And the Maryland Industrial Development Finance Authority guarantees industrial mortgage loans for businesses that might not otherwise be able to receive the loans.

Maryland has an Office of Minority Business Enterprise at (301) 269-2682.

MASSACHUSETTS

Secretary
Massachusetts Department of Commerce and Development
100 Cambridge St.
Boston, MA 02202
(617) 727-3221

Division of Small Business Assistance:
(617) 727-4005

Though Massachusetts well deserves its derisive nickname of "Taxachusetts" and the reputation of being less than friendly to businesses of all sizes, the Commonwealth, in recent years, has moved aggressively to promote business development. The result is one of the more impressive overall lists of assistance options available to small businesses anywhere in the country. The assistance includes venture capital for start-up businesses, consulting, and procurement aid. Briefly, the programs are as follows.

- The Division of Small Business Assistance provides information on federal and commonwealth programs, as well as consulting aid.
- A procurement program directs that a minimum of 5 percent of commonwealth purchases go to small businesses. Businesses are defined as small according to their industry, sales, and number of employees.
- Massachusetts Community Development Finance Corporation, apparently the nation's only state-financed venture-capital firm. It was started in 1975 with $10 million of commonwealth funds and has since invested more than $3 million in a variety of start-up ventures and existing businesses. According to an article on the program in the July 1980 edition of *Venture* magazine, ". . . if

one measure of CDFC's performance is job creation . . . the Massachusetts organization deserves high marks."
- Massachusetts Technology Development Corporation, a commonwealth-created public corporation funded with $2 million of federal funds, provides, in collaboration with private sources, loans and investments to start high-technology businesses.
- Massachusetts Capital Resource Corporation is a private partnership funded to the tune of $100 million by seventeen Massachusetts insurance companies, in consideration of a reduction of their tax rates. It mostly makes loans to fast-growing small companies that might otherwise be unable to obtain financing.
- An active business development corporation in Boston, known as Massachusetts Business Development Corporation, makes loans ranging from $75,000 to $500,000 to companies that are unable to secure commercial financing.
- An active industrial revenue program is administered through the Massachusetts Industrial Finance Agency. It also provides insurance of commercial industrial mortgages.
- A commonwealth-run consulting/counseling network, known as the Business Information Center Network, was established in 1979. When it is finally operational, the Network, according to the November 16, 1979, issue of *New England Business* magazine, will have thirty-six intensively trained coordinators, some with previous business experience, placed in twenty-six offices statewide. There they will offer a "Business Planning Guide" and provide market analysis, site selection, financing referrals[,] and demographic breakdowns to help people decide, first, if they are going into the right business at the right time, and then, how to do it.

The Network has already assisted small businesses in obtaining more than $25 million of financing.

MICHIGAN

Director
Office of Economic Development
Michigan Department of Commerce
P.O. Box 30225
Lansing, MI 48909
(517) 737-3530

Small Business Development Division (in Department of Commerce):
(517) 373-0637
(800) 292-9544

Michigan's major effort to assist small businesses consists of its Small Business Development Division, which provides technical assistance, develops seminars, and aids in dealing with state requirements and regulations. The State has a small-business procurement program designed to ensure that small and minority businesses obtain a "fair proportion" of state purchases and contracts. The State distributes straightforward fliers to small businesses explaining how to participate in the program.

Michigan has a relatively active program for industrial revenue bonds; the bonds are issued by municipalities. The State is also in the process of establishing a business development corporation.

MINNESOTA

Commissioner
Department of Economic Development
Hanover Building
480 Cedar St.
St. Paul, MN 55101
(612) 296-2755

Small Business Assistance Center within Department of Economic
    Development:
(612) 296-5011

Minnesota has both procurement and consulting/information programs designed specifically for small businesses. The procurement program is supposed to direct about 20 percent of state purchases to small businesses; businesses are considered small if they have twenty or fewer employees or less than $1 million in annual revenues. Its consulting/information program is administered by the Small Business Assistance Center. It provides management assistance and information on federal, state, and local programs for small businesses.

Minnesota has several loan programs for small businesses. Its Small Business Finance Agency makes available "the benefits of tax-exempt bond financing to small businesses in one larger bond issue," according to the State; funds can be used for expansion or pollution-control facilities. The State's Indian Business Loan Program is available to Indians living both on and off reservations.

The State also has a program known as The Minnesota Area Redevelopment Administration, in Duluth, which provides financing for projects partially financed by the federal government. Minnesota has an active industrial revenue bond program; bonds are issued by municipalities. And its Equal Business Opportunity Division in the Department of Economic Development assists minority businesses seeking to sell goods and services to the State.

MISSISSIPPI

Director
Mississippi Department of Economic Development
P.O. Box 849
1202 State Office Building
Jackson, MS 39205
(601) 354-6711

Small Business Assistance Division in Agricultural and Industrial
  Board:
(601) 354-6487

Mississippi's primary assistance directed to small businesses is its loan guarantee program, under which it guarantees repayment of a maximum of 74 percent of loans up to $100,000. The program is geared to assist business start-ups and expansion of existing businesses. The Small Business Assistance Division manages the program.

In addition, a privately funded organization known as the Mississippi Economic Development Corporation helps businesses of all sizes put together loan packages from commercial, state, and federal sources and sometimes provides a small amount of its own financing. Mississippi also has one of the oldest and the more aggressive industrial revenue bond programs in the country; bonds can be issued by municipalities. Since the program was started in 1936, more than $1.2 billion has been raised for in excess of 1,200 projects.

Mississippi also sponsors workshops and courses on starting and operating small businesses in conjunction with the Small Business Administration.

MISSOURI

Director
Division of Community and Economic Development
1014 Madison St.
Jefferson City, MO 65102
(314) 751-4241

Existing Business Administration (Division of Community and
  Economic Development) acts as small-business referral and
  complaint agency:
(314) 751-4855

The Existing Business Administration program handles complaints about state business practices and provides information about state programs of potential assistance to small businesses. It also publishes a directory of state business programs.

Missouri has a moderately active business development corporation, the First Missouri Development Finance Corporation in Jefferson City; and a moderately active industrial revenue bond program under which municipalities issue bonds. The State also seeks to encourage banks to make loans to businesses by agreeing to deposit a percentage of the amounts lent with the lending banks.

MONTANA

Director
Office of Commerce and Small Business Development
State Capitol Building
Helena, MT 59601
(406) 449-3111
(406) 449-3923

Montana has a broad goal of increasing procurement opportunities for small businesses. The State also has a moderately active business development corporation, the Development Credit Corporation of Montana, in Helena, which makes loans to businesses turned down by commercial sources. Montana has a modestly active industrial revenue bond program, under which municipalities can issue bonds; a large proportion of bond proceeds have been directed to pollution-control projects.

Montana has a small-business loan program funded recently at only $200,000 annually; the State has hopes of expanding the program so that it can make debt-equity investments in businesses to aid them in qualifying for federally guaranteed bank loans. With U. S. Department of Commerce funding, Montana has, since 1977, helped sponsor the Center for Innovation in Butte to assist inventors in developing and marketing products. The center evaluates the commercial potential of inventors' ideas and gives small grants of a few thousand dollars to support inventions judged to have the greatest potential. The center can be reached at (406) 494-6256.

NEBRASKA

Director
Nebraska Department of Economic Development
P.O. Box 94666
301 Centennial Mall S
Lincoln, NE 68509
(402) 471-3111

Nebraska's business assistance efforts consist mainly of an active industrial revenue bond program and a moderately active business development corporation, the Business Development Corporation of Nebraska in Lincoln. More than 200 projects have been assisted with in excess of $250 million by industrial revenue bonds in recent years. The State has no programs directed specifically to small businesses.

NEVADA

Director
Nevada Department of Economic Development
Capitol Complex
Carson City, NV 89710
(702) 885-4322

Nevada makes no special efforts to assist small businesses specifically and only a slight effort to aid businesses in general through a relatively inactive industrial revenue bond program.

New HAMPSHIRE

Commissioner
Department of Resources and Economic Development
P.O. Box 856
Concord, NH 03301
(603) 271-2411

New Hampshire has been one of the most successful states in the country in attracting businesses of all sizes to relocate and build plants in the State. Though the State has no special programs to assist small businesses directly, it has an active industrial revenue bond program operated by the New Hampshire Industrial Development Authority in Concord. The Authority can also guarantee industrial mortgage loans. In addition, New Hampshire has a business development corporation, the New Hampshire Business Development Corporation, which tends to make loans in conjunction with individual banks.

NEW JERSEY

Director
Division of Economic Development
Department of Labor and Industry
P.O. Box 2766
Trenton, NJ 08625
(609) 292-7757

Small Business Development Unit within Division of Economic
   Development:
   (609) 984-3416
   (609) 292-9587

Along with Connecticut and Massachusetts, New Jersey has one of
the most innovative combinations of programs designed to promote small-
business development. The Small Business Development Unit assists in
arranging financing packages, helps obtain state and federal contracts, and
provides management assistance and information. An Office of Business
Advocacy, (609) 292-0700, handles complaints about and problems between businesses and government agencies at all levels.

The State also encourages development of companies with new products through its Office for Promoting Technical Innovation (OPTI),
which started operations in 1979. OPTI provides technical evaluations,
marketing surveys, aid in locating financing, and consulting help, along
with small loans and guarantees of bank loans.

New Jersey's active industrial revenue bond program, administered
by the New Jersey Economic Development Authority, has been more inclined than bond issuers in most other states to make funds available to
smaller businesses. It also guarantees bank loans and makes direct loans
to urban retail businesses.

In addition, the New Jersey Urban Loan Authority, a state agency,
makes loans to small businesses that relocate or expand into deteriorating
urban, suburban, and rural areas of the State.

NEW MEXICO

Existing Industry Liaison
Economic Development Division
Department of Commerce and Industry
Bataan Memorial Building
Santa Fe, NM 87503
(505) 827-5571

Except for a relatively generous employee training program available
to businesses of all sizes, New Mexico has few programs to encourage
business development. It has a little-used industrial revenue bond program and has authorized a business development corporation, Development Credit Corporation of New Mexico; movement to fund the corporation has been slow, however. Various New Mexico communities provide
loans through chambers of commerce and other local organizations for industrial development.

The Existing Industry Liaison provides information to businesses of
all sizes about how they can best use state and federal programs.

NEW YORK

Commissioner
Department of Commerce
99 Washington Ave.
Albany, NY 12245
(518) 474-4100

Division of Ombudsmen and Small Business Services Division in the
New York City Office of the Department of Commerce:
(212) 949-9303

The Division of Ombudsmen and Small Business Services Division arrange seminars, assist in procurement, and serve in an ombudsman role on behalf of small businesses in New York. However, the State has a number of programs through which small businesses can obtain financing. The New York Job Development Authority can make long-term loans for up to 40 percent of construction costs for building, expanding, or equipping plants.

New York has an active industrial revenue bond program with bonds issued by local industrial development agencies. In addition, New York has the largest business development corporation in the country. New York Business Development Corporation in Albany makes about $6 million in loans to more than thirty companies annually. The loans are usually either secured by fixed assets or 90 percent guarantees from the SBA.

NORTH CAROLINA

Executive Director
Business Assistance Division
North Carolina Department of Commerce
430 N Salisbury St. (Suite 294)
Raleigh, NC 27611
(919) 733-6003

Small Business Development Section with Business Assistance
Division:
(919) 733-7980

The Small Business Development Section was established in 1980 to provide assistance in the areas of procurement, education, and financing. Workshops and conferences have been scheduled on such subjects as selling to the State, basic bookkeeping, advertising, taxation, and women in business. The State's procurement policy is that a "fair proportion" go to small businesses. And the State is in the formative stages of developing a policy to encourage high-technology businesses.

North Carolina also has a relatively modest industrial revenue bond program, with bonds issued by county authorities. The State has a business development corporation, the Business Development Corporation of North Carolina, in Raleigh, which makes a handful of loans each year.

North Dakota

Director
Business and Industrial Development Department
513 E Bismarck Ave.
Bismarck, ND 58505
(701) 224-2810

For a state its size, North Dakota is fairly active in encouraging business development. It has no specific programs directed to small businesses, but it has a fairly active business development corporation, the North Dakota State Development Credit Corporation, in Bismarck, which makes loans, together with banks or on its own, to companies which cannot obtain commercial loans. The corporation has tended to show a preference for financing smaller companies.

North Dakota also has a moderately active industrial revenue bond program, with bonds issued by municipalities and counties.

Ohio

Director
Department of Economic and Community Development
30 E Broad St. (25th Floor)
Columbus, OH 43215
(614) 466-3379

Office of Small Business Assistance in the Department of Economic and Community Development:
(614) 466-4945

The Office of Small Business Assistance provides technical and financial information to small businesses, handles complaints, provides guidance on state regulations, and makes contacts with state agencies for procurement purposes.

Ohio has an active industrial revenue bond program that has seen well over $1 billion raised in recent years. Bonds can be issued by county or municipal organizations, as well as by the Ohio Development Financing Commission (ODFC), a state agency in Columbus. ODFC also guarantees up to 90 percent of loans of up to $1 million for companies unable to obtain commercial loans on their own credit.

The State's Department of Economic and Community Development has issued a publication entitled *Starting and Operating a Small Business in Ohio.*

OKLAHOMA

Director
Industrial Development Department
Office of the Governor
Oklahoma City, OK 73105
(405) 521-2401

Oklahoma has a fairly active business assistance program. Its Industrial Development Department assists small manufacturers in planning layouts and controlling inventories. The State has a business development corporation, the Oklahoma Business Development Corporation, in Oklahoma City, which makes a handful of loans each year, usually together with commercial sources.

The Oklahoma Industrial Finance Authority in Oklahoma City is a state agency that provides mortgage loans of up to $1 million to small manufacturers. In addition, the State has a relatively active industrial revenue bond program; bonds can be issued by the State, counties, and municipalities.

A newly started Innovative Technology Research and Development Program, funded by the U. S. Department of Commerce through Southeastern Oklahoma State University, provides technical assistance for product development, with an emphasis on small and minority-owned businesses.

OREGON

Director
Department of Economic Development
155 Cottage St., NE
Salem, OR 97310
(503) 373-1200

Small-business matters are handled by the special assistant to the Director for Business-Government Relations in the Department of Economic Development, at the above telephone number.

Oregon has a reputation as a state that favors environmental quality over business development. But, according to an article in the February 1980 issue of *INC.* magazine, that attitude is changing. "Oregon needs jobs for its growing population and . . . the state is looking to small business to provide a lot of them," the article noted. "It's looking especially hard to high-technology firms and for manufacturers that can exploit the state's timber resources."

The special assistant to the Director for Business-Government Relations provides assistance and information to small businesses on making the best possible use of local, state, and federal programs; the special assistant also plays an informal ombudsman role. The State provides free counseling to small businesses that seek to become involved in international trade.

Oregon also recently started an energy loan program under which low-interest loans are made to small enterprises, employing fewer than 100 people, for developing renewable-energy resources. The State has authority to issue industrial revenue bonds but has used the authority infrequently.

In addition, the State has a permit coordination center which assists any business to determine what permits and licenses are required to do business in Oregon. And the Department of Economic Development has put out two publications especially for small businesses: *Guide to Government Services for Small Business* and *Financing Small Business in Oregon.*

PENNSYLVANIA

Secretary
Pennsylvania Department of Commerce
419 South Office Building
Harrisburg, PA 17120
(717) 787-3003

Small Business Office in the Department of Commerce:
(717) 783-1592

Pennsylvania has a useful array of business development programs, most of which can be used by small businesses.

The Small Business Office serves mainly in an ombudsman role, by helping to solve problems businesses have with the Commonwealth's government. Small businesses can also benefit from the Pennsylvania Technical Assistance Program (PTAP), which provides technical information to any Pennsylvania business that requests it. A small-business owner who had used the program wrote, in the April 1980 issue of *INC.* magazine:

"I know that the program's technical specialists respond rapidly to company requests and are helpful and thorough." Information on PTAP is available through the Commonwealth's Department of Commerce.

A recently created Small Business Service Center in the Department of Commerce centralizes the process of obtaining permits and provides information on public and private financing and technical assistance programs for small businesses.

In addition, Pennsylvania has among the most active industrial revenue bond programs in the country, with more than $4 billion in bonds issued in recent years; bonds can be issued by local authorities.

And Pennsylvania has an agency, the Pennsylvania Industrial Development Authority, that makes loans to businesses that are building or acquiring plants in areas of high unemployment. It can finance up to half of a project, depending on the unemployment rate in the area of the project.

Finally, Pennsylvania has three business development corporations: the RIDS Investment Development Fund in Pittsburgh, the Southeastern Pennsylvania Development Fund in Philadelphia, and the Pennsylvania Development Credit Corporation in Harrisburg. They generally make loans to businesses that are unable to obtain commercial loans, with an emphasis on small companies.

RHODE ISLAND

Director
Rhode Island Department of Economic Development
One Weybossett Hill
Providence, RI 02908
(401) 277-2601

The Department of Economic Development attempts to act as a one-stop center to advise small businesses on financing programs in the State. It also assists small businesses in obtaining financing from other sources. The programs available in Rhode Island include a business development corporation, a program of guaranteeing industrial mortgages, and several vehicles for industrial revenue bonds.

The Business Development Corporation of Rhode Island makes a handful of loans to businesses of various sizes each year. Applicants do not necessarily need to have been turned down first by commercial lenders.

The mortgage guarantee program is administered by the Rhode Island Industrial Building Authority in Providence. It can guarantee up to 90 percent of mortgages for acquiring or building facilities and up to 80 percent of loans for purchasing machinery.

Industrial revenue bonds have been issued on a relatively infrequent basis; they can be issued by the State and individual communities, as well as by a state-run corporation, the Rhode Island Port Authority and Economic Development Corporation, in Providence.

SOUTH CAROLINA

Director
South Carolina State Development Board
P.O. Box 927
Columbia, SC 29202
(803) 758-3145

South Carolina's great success in luring businesses of all sizes to build plants in the State is symbolic of the business boom enjoyed throughout the Sunbelt. Yet the State does little to aid businesses directly. It has no special small-business programs. Its main effort on behalf of business development has been a fairly extensive industrial revenue bond program that has seen more than $500 million raised for various projects in recent years.

SOUTH DAKOTA

Director
South Dakota IDEA
221 South Central
Pierre, SD 57501
(605) 773-5032

South Dakota provides very little in the way of direct business assistance. Its only real effort is a relatively inactive industrial revenue bond program, under which municipalities in the State can issue bonds.

TENNESSEE

Commissioner
Economic and Community Development
1007 Andrew Jackson Building
Nashville, TN 37219
(615) 741-1888
(800) 342-8470 (from within Tennessee)
(800) 251-8594 (from outside Tennessee)

Tennessee's most direct efforts at business development consist of an extensive industrial revenue bond program and a mortgage guarantee program. The State has no formal small-business program, but it is planning to establish a small-business assistance office to provide information about public and private programs for small businesses and to handle complaints.

Tennessee's industrial revenue bond program has raised more than $900 million for over 600 projects. Bonds can be issued by cities, towns, counties, and organizations.

The Tennessee Industrial Development Authority, a state agency in Nashville, can guarantee up to half of first mortgages issued by commercial lenders, to a maximum of $250,000.

TEXAS

Executive Director
Texas Industrial Commission
Capitol Station; Box 12728
410 E Fifth St.
Austin, TX 78711
(512) 472-5059

For a state of Texas's size and influence, where everything is supposedly giant size, the efforts at business development seem minuscule. The State has a small-business procurement program, under which all state agencies seek to award 10 percent of their purchases to businesses with either fewer than 100 employees or less than $1 million in gross receipts. The State also has a relatively inactive industrial revenue bond program.

UTAH

Business Development Coordinator
Economic and Industrial Development Division
2 Arrow Press Square
165 South West Temple
Salt Lake City, UT 84101
(801) 533-5325

Office of Small Business Development in Economic and Industrial Development Division at above number.

Utah's Office of Small Business Development, in the Economic and Industrial Development Division, provides both long-term and short-term management assistance to start-up and existing small businesses. The Office also attempts to serve as a liaison between small-business owners and government bureaucrats, particularly in the area of procurement. In addition, it aids start-up businesses in applying for Small Business Administration loans. The Office has published a booklet, *Starting a Small Business in Utah*.

The State has relatively inactive industrial revenue bond and business development corporation programs; the business development corporation is the Utah Business Development Corporation.

VERMONT

Commissioner of Economic Development
Vermont Agency of Development and Community Affairs
109 State St.
Montpelier, VT 05602
(802) 828-3221
(802) 828-3236

Vermont has a number of financial assistance programs that have potential use for small businesses. The Vermont Industrial Development Authority, a state agency, operates a mortgage loan guarantee program under which businesses, otherwise unable to obtain a commercial mortgage, can obtain guarantees for repayment of up to 80 percent of their loans.

The Authority also can make direct mortgage loans for up to 40 percent of a project's cost. And it can, along with municipalities, issue industrial revenue bonds, though few bonds have been issued.

Vermont has a business development corporation, the Vermont Development Credit Corporation, in Montpelier, which has been relatively inactive.

And a unique program known as Vermont Job Start makes loans— some as small as $1,500 at 5 percent interest—available to quite small ventures which create employment.

VIRGINIA

Director
Virginia Division of Industrial Development
1010 State Office Building
Richmond, VA 23219
(804) 786-3791

Virginia's efforts to promote business development consist mainly of a fairly active industrial revenue bond program and a business development corporation. Revenue bonds can be issued through municipalities and counties. The Virginia Industrial Development Corporation in Richmond makes loans to businesses that are unable to obtain commercial financing, and it has a preference for smaller companies.

WASHINGTON

Director
Department of Commerce and Economic Development
101 General Administration Building
Olympia, WA 98504
(206) 753-7426

Small Business Division of Department of Commerce and Economic Development:
(206) 753-5614

The Small Business Division serves both an advocacy and assistance role for small businesses in the State. It seeks to promote the interests of small business among state agencies; it also encourages state agencies to increase their purchases from small businesses, which are defined as independently owned firms with fifty or fewer employees. The division assists small businesses in obtaining technical, consulting, and financial assistance as well.

Washington also has two relatively active business development corporations: the Business Development Corporation of Eastern Washington, in Spokane, and the Business and Industrial Development Corporation of Washington in Seattle. The State has no industrial revenue bond program.

Washington has been experimenting in recent years with a one-stop licensing center to save businesses time and red tape in obtaining necessary licenses.

WEST VIRGINIA

Director
Governor's Office of Economic and Community Development
State Capitol
Charleston, WV 25305
(304) 348-0190

Small Business Service Unit in Governor's Office of Economic and Community Development:
(304) 348-0010

The Small Business Service Unit aids entrepreneurs in getting businesses started, provides consulting and loan packaging assistance, and helps small businesses get state procurement awards. It also serves as small business' ombudsman.

In addition, a number of programs in the State are potentially available to finance small-business development. The State's Economic Development Authority in Charleston can provide low-interest loans for up to 50 percent of the cost of new plants and equipment; most of those loans have gone to small businesses. The State has a business development corporation, the West Virginia Business Development Corporation, in Charleston, which has been fairly active in providing loans to businesses unable to obtain them commercially. And West Virginia has a relatively active industrial revenue bond program, under which more than $600 million has been raised in recent years. The bonds can be issued by counties or municipalities.

WISCONSIN

Secretary
Department of Business Development
123 W Washington Ave.
Madison, WI 53702
(608) 266-3222

Small Business Ombudsman:
(608) 266-9465

The Small Business Ombudsman mainly acts as a small-business advocate and handles small-business complaints about state agencies. The Council of Small and Minority Business Opportunities seeks to encourage state agencies to direct more of their purchases to businesses with less than $1.5 million in annual sales.

Wisconsin also has a relatively active industrial revenue bond program, under which municipalities within the State are allowed to issue bonds; and the State recently established an Office of Economic Development, which may include a mechanism similar to the Massachusetts Community Development Finance Corp. for making state-funded venture capital available to fledgling businesses. In addition, Wisconsin has several hundred thousand dollars available to support alternative energy ventures.

Within Wisconsin, the Madison Development Corp., a private, nonprofit investment company established by the City of Madison, makes low-interest loans available to small businesses in the area, mostly with the purpose of rehabilitating commercial property.

WYOMING

Executive Director
Department of Economic Planning and Development
Barrett Building
Cheyenne, WY 82002
(307) 777-7284

Considering its meager population, Wyoming has a substantial program of business assistance. It has no formal small-business program, but it has an active business development corporation and an active industrial revenue bond program.

The Wyoming Industrial Development Corporation, in Casper, provides loans to both start-up and existing small businesses that are unable to obtain commercial loans. The State also permits counties and municipalities to issue industrial revenue bonds; more than $400 million in loans have been issued in recent years.

PUERTO RICO

Deputy Administrator
Puerto Rico Economic Development Administration
Continental Operations Branch
1290 Ave. of the Americas
New York, NY 10019
(212) 245-1200
     or
Administrator
Puerto Rico Economic Development Administration
G.P.O. Box 2350
San Juan, PR 00936

For entrepreneurs trying to start businesses or open new plants, Puerto Rico tries hard to be accommodating. Because it is part of the United States, its businesses are eligible for federal financing programs, and economic development officials will assist in arranging packages. The island's biggest lure, however, lies in its tax benefits. Depending on where companies locate, their profits are exempt from up to 90 percent of taxes for up to twenty-five years. And, for smaller businesses with profits of under $500,000, the first $100,000 is completely exempt from taxes for from ten to twenty-five years, thanks to recent legislation.

The exhibit on p. 154 summarizes State Assistance Programs available in each of the fifty states and Puerto Rico.

LOCAL SOURCES

Just as states have come to recognize the importance of economic development, so have cities. And, like a growing number of states, many cities are paying an increasing amount of attention to small businesses.

Because most cities are on even tighter budgets than are states and the federal government, they usually do not have much of their own money to lend. What they are learning to do quite skillfully, however, is to draw on private, state, and federal financing sources to put together financing packages for small businesses in their communities that are unable to raise the needed cash from commercial sources alone.

In an article in the November–December 1980 issue of the *Harvard Business Review*, Samuel Beard, President of the National Development Council (a nonprofit organization active in arranging urban business loans), observed that many cities now employ financial professionals who are skillful in assessing the financing needs of small businesses and in negotiating and putting together financing packages. Often the financial professionals working in city agencies have the expertise and connections with private, state, and local sources to be able to inform small-business owners quickly about their prospects for obtaining financing. But because financing usually comes from several sources, the paperwork and red tape involved in getting a final decision can take many months. The agencies should be approached by business owners only after the owners have put together a specific plan for the kind of project they wish to undertake.

All of the nation's fifty largest cities now have an agency involved in economic development. These agencies can be located most easily by contacting the mayor's office and asking for the agency involved in economic or community development.

In addition, would-be and existing entrepreneurs based in poorer urban areas should check with economic development officials about the existence of Community Development Corporations (CDCs) near them. CDCs are nonprofit community groups that attempt to encourage local economic development, partly by investing in new and existing businesses. While the bulk of CDC funding has come from the federal government, most CDCs obtain additional financial support from foundations, banks, and their communities.

CDC financial assistance is most commonly in the form of equity investments, through which CDCs gain partial or complete ownership of the businesses. CDCs can also obtain bank loans, federal agency loan guarantees, and other types of assistance to supplement their own funds. Individual investments can range from a few thousand dollars to a few hundred thousand dollars.

EXHIBIT

State Assistance Programs

State	Small-Business Office	Small-Business Procurement Program	Small-Business Loan Guarantee Venture-Capital Program	General Business Loan or Loan Guarantee Program	Business Development Corporation or Similar Private Loan Program	Industrial Revenue Bond Program
Alabama		X				X
Alaska	X		X	X	X	X
Arizona						X
Arkansas	X				X	X
California	X	X	X		X	X
Colorado	X					X
Connecticut	X	X	X	X	X	X
Delaware						X
District of Columbia					X	
Florida	X				X	X
Georgia		X			X	X
Hawaii			X			
Idaho						
Illinois	X	X	X	X		X
Indiana	X	X		X		X
Iowa	X				X	X
Kansas		X			X	X
Kentucky	X	X		X	X	X
Louisiana	X	X				X
Maine			X	X		X
Maryland		X	X	X	X	X
Massachusetts	X	X	X	X	X	X
Michigan	X	X			X	X
Minnesota	X	X	X	X		X
Mississippi	X	X			X	X
Missouri	X				X	X
Montana	X	X	X		X	X
Nebraska					X	X
Nevada						X
New Hampshire				X	X	X
New Jersey	X		X			X
New Mexico					X	X
New York	X			X	X	X
North Carolina	X	X			X	X
North Dakota						X
Ohio	X			X		X
Oklahoma				X	X	X
Oregon	X		X			X
Pennsylvania	X			X	X	X
Rhode Island				X	X	X
South Carolina						X
South Dakota						X
Tennessee	X			X		X
Texas		X				X
Utah	X				X	X
Vermont				X	X	X
Virginia				X	X	X
Washington	X				X	
West Virginia	X			X	X	X
Wisconsin	X		X			X
Wyoming					X	X
Puerto Rico						X

ADDITIONAL INFORMATION SOURCE

Sourceguide for Borrowing Capital, by Leonard E. Smollen, Mark Rollinson, and Stanley M. Rubel (Wellesley Hills, MA: Capital Publishing Corp., 1977)

This book contains two quite useful chapters on state financing sources. One chapter, by the late Stanley M. Rubel, is a description and listing of business development corporations and other organizations. A second chapter, by Mark Rollinson, examines in detail revenue bond programs in each state. Both chapters also contain useful advice about exploiting state financing sources. The book's only real weakness is that it is beginning to become somewhat outdated as new state programs are added and others are changed.

CHAPTER 5

Commercial Finance

INTRODUCTION: TENSION AMID A CHANGING LENDING CLIMATE

A festive mood enveloped the conference room as nearly thirty lending officers and other officials of Citicorp, the world's second largest bank, gathered after dinner not long ago. Walter Wriston, chairman of the board, strolled into the room and took a lone chair at the front. After warming the group with a few humorous one-liners, for which he is so noted, he made a surprise announcement. He had just come from an emergency meeting involving the default of a $75 million Citicorp loan, he said.

A very audible moan rushed through the room, followed by silence and low whispers among the bankers present. A $75 million write-off was substantial, even for a bank with $100 billion of assets. The implications were clear: loan officers responsible for the loan would find this a major blot on their track records.

This anecdote illustrates a basic fact of life about commercial finance: margins on bank and other commercial loans are so thin that all losses are painful. Bad loans are a sure one-way ticket to the loan officers' graveyard. Whether a loss is for $75 million at Citicorp or $10,000 at a small country bank, the problems, fears, and consequences are similar.

All of which helps explain the tensions and misunderstandings that frequently accompany relations between entrepreneurs and commercial lenders.

Small businesses are by nature filled with risk. Thousands fail each year. Many of those that survive seem to be operating on the edge of disaster. If the businesses are growing at all, their cash requirements seem unending.

Bankers, though, are always seeking to minimize their risks. Small businesses with their seemingly endless cash crunches and their owners who frequently have grandiose expansion plans amid such difficulties make commercial lenders uncomfortable. Not surprisingly, bankers tend to feel most comfortable with big companies, since such customers usually have been in existence for many years and tend to be growing steadily and predictably. Big companies also tend to have substantial cash cushions.

Add to these normal tensions a sluggish economy, roller-coaster interest rates, inflation, and tight federal credit policies, and it's easy to see how entrepreneurs and commercial lenders might have little to talk about.

Indeed, for start-up entrepreneurs, the lending situation is almost of a Catch-22 variety, as *The Wall Street Journal* noted in a January 22, 1980, article: "Banks won't make one of those 18% loans to a new business unless it seems likely to survive and prosper; but its chances of surviving and prospering are lower if it has to pay 18% on its money."

FAVORABLE FUTURE TRENDS

For all the hopelessness that seems to have permeated the small-business lending climate in recent years, there are some hopeful signs on the horizon. Primary among the optimistic signs are some dramatic shifts taking place in the financial services industry; these shifts should favor small businesses.

For instance, an outgrowth of legislation passed in the 1970s has been to open the once protected banking industry to competition from other financial institutions. According to an article in the *Harvard Business Review* of September–October 1980, major industrial companies, foreign banks, insurance companies, and pension funds—once major bank customers—are becoming the banks' biggest competitors.

The article's author, a partner in a venture-capital and financial advisory firm, predicted that "smaller corporations . . . will have a greater number of services available, like asset financing through leasing, inventory, and accounts receivable financing."

A June 1979 article in *INC.* magazine supports the view that options are increasing for smaller businesses.

> If a local bank can't meet needs, to whom can a company turn? That brings up another common myth—that insurance companies, pension funds, foundations, and branches of bank holding companies are available only to large corporations. That's not the case.

Another note of encouragement is the growing list of commercial banks nationwide that have a "small business prime" interest rate that is generally one to two percentage points below the prime rate available to large corporations. Dozens of banks offer such loans, usually to companies which fit the following criteria: annual sales of less than $5 mil-

158

lion, assets of $300,000 to $500,000 or less, and borrowings below $250,000 to $400,000. A list of banks with the small-business prime is available from:

Office of Financing
Small Business Administration
1441 Vermont Ave., NW
Washington, DC 20416
(202) 653-6570

START-UP
OPTIONS

Most start-up entrepreneurs misunderstand banks and other lending sources. While the entrepreneur views the venture as an investment with future payoffs in return for the risks that are overcome, a bank sees the situation differently. A bank is concerned with its security and needs to be convinced that the loan will be repaid even if the venture doesn't succeed. Thus, if the loan application has substantial collateral behind it, or if the entrepreneur can pledge substantial personal net worth to ensure repayment, a bank is quite likely to make the loan.

But most start-up entrepreneurs lack such personal financial strength and cannot look to banks, leasing companies, and other commercial lenders for support. Personal funds, friends, relatives, and associates are the dominant sources of funding for start-ups.

Start-up entrepreneurs with a prior track record of business success along with the know-how to prepare and present a well-thought-out business plan can often secure start-up loans and other financing. Many such entrepreneurs complain that they can get a start-up loan, but only because they are so financially secure that they do not need it. Even then, a personal signature and collateral to guarantee the new venture's loan may be required.

Growing competition among commercial financial institutions may eventually ease the difficulties start-up entrepreneurs have obtaining commercial funding, but for now commercial financing is a limited option. A 1980 survey of 1,597 business owners by the National Federation of Independent Business found that personal savings funded 48 percent of start-ups, while friends contributed to 13 percent. Banks and other institutional lenders were sources for 29 percent of the start-up entrepreneurs, while venture capitalists and government helped less than 1 percent each. (The types of businesses surveyed isn't known and could have influenced the results in one direction or another.)

Existing-
BUSINESS OPTIONS

The picture is quite different for existing businesses. Banks, leasing companies, commercial finance companies, factors, insurance companies, and small-business investment corporations (SBICs) usually view small, existing businesses as important customers. Commercial lenders are in the business of making loans, secured by such assets as machinery and equipment, buildings, inventory, and receivables, to ongoing firms. To minimize their risks, commercial lenders tend to be very collateral-minded, though certain unsecured loans are made as well.

The result is that many well-established and profitable small businesses obtain loans relatively easily. But many other newer or more marginally profitable businesses encounter obstacles. Most bankers look at fifteen to thirty opportunities for each business loan made; the rejects typically have little in the way of collateral, net worth, or track records, and also tend to lack business plans and financial projections.

What can business owners do to improve their chances of obtaining commercial loans? They can, of course, work at formulating business plans and financial projections. (For information on handling such chores, see the books and articles noted at the end of this chapter and Appendix C on developing and using a business plan.) In addition, business owners should attempt to understand their commercial lending options. If their local bank won't take the proposal seriously, what other sources of credit and loans are available? What are the types of short-, medium-, and long-term debt available for existing businesses, and who has them? What are the application procedures for various types and sources, and what criteria are used to evaluate the proposals or requests? What terms and conditions can be expected with the various types of financing and institutions? And what are some of the principal advantages and disadvantages of the various options?

This chapter addresses these and other pertinent financing questions for small businesses. For those readers who are less familiar with the terminology and concepts commonly used by bankers, lessors, factors, and others, a glossary has been included at the end of the book, beginning on p. 391. A sample commercial loan application, including statements of covenants and agreements between the lender and borrowing business, is included as well, on pp. 185–93.

The chapter does not separate start-up and existing firms, since this is an inappropriate distinction for the vast majority of commercial financing. Commercial lenders are predominantly interested in existing businesses, and generally are not a source of start-up capital, unless the entrepreneur has substantial collateral, net worth, and will personally guarantee any loans.

This chapter differs somewhat from other chapters in that it doesn't attempt to pinpoint specific sources by name. Since there are thousands of banks and other financial institutions, it was unfeasible to research and distinguish between them or to discuss individual institutions in a representative way as we do elsewhere.

What did make sense was to examine generically the various options available to the small businesses according to the duration of loans for short-, intermediate-, and long-term financing (see Table I). To assist readers in easily examining these sources, several tables are included in the chapter:

- Table I, *Commercial Financing Sources,* summarizes the principal sources and time periods of financing, and whether money is available for start-up and existing firms.
- Table II, *"Sources and Uses" Chart,* summarizes the principal uses of funds, lender industry preferences, and key factors to prepare for a first meeting and loan proposal.

TABLE I

Commercial Financing Sources

| Source | TYPES OF BUSINESSES AIDED | | PRINCIPAL USE OF FUNDING | | |
	Start-ups	Existing	Short-term <1 Yr.	Intermediate-term 1–5 Yrs.	Long-term >5 Yrs.
Commercial Banks	occasionally, if collateralized	yes	most frequent	some	rare
Commercial Finance Companies	rare	yes	most frequent	yes	rare
Factors	rare	yes	most frequent	some	no
Mutual Savings Banks; Savings and Loans	rare	yes (real estate)	no	no	yes (real estate)
Leasing Company	difficult	yes	no	most frequent	occasionally
Small Business Investment Corporations (SBICs)	occasionally	yes	no	yes	yes
Insurance Companies	rare	yes	no	no	yes

TABLE II

"Sources and Uses" Chart

Source	Use of Loan	Appropriate Industries	"Ideal" Preparation for First Meeting w/Lender
Commercial Bank (<1 yr.)	Seasonal financing of receivables, inventory, other working capital needs (loans repaid from sale of assets financed). Low risk to bank, so relatively easy to get; good way to establish credit rating to help get future longer-term financing.	No prohibitions. Nonprofits need specific purpose & payback method.	• 1–2 page business description, history & future plans • Resumes of key management • Details on loan use • CPA-prepared financial statements for past 3 years, audited • Cash-flow projections for term of loan • Company tax returns
(1–5 yrs.)	Working capital, machinery & equipment, retirement of higher-interest borrowings.	Typically, "high-risk" areas are avoided. These may include seasonal businesses like resorts, or entertainment and high-technology firms (where change is rapid and value of inventory can drop suddenly).	for past 3 years • Statement of company owners' personal assets & liabilities • List of major customers & suppliers (trade refs for credit check) • Receivables & payable aging lists • Schedule of company's assets • List of other financial institutions company involved with
Commercial Finance Company or Factor (<1–5 yrs.)	Working capital, interim turnaround financing, acquisitions & buyouts. Short-term uses when unsecured financing unavailable.	Generally considered unsuitable for consignment sales, products with slow turnover or low gross margins, high tech, large contracts with partial payment terms, or service industries with client receivables.	• Same information as for bank • Aged receivables list & cash-flow statement very important • Schedule of any other assets being financed or used as collateral
Leasing Company (<3–6 yrs.)	Use of fixed assets without major capital investment; leveraged buyout financing.	No prohibitions.	• Same information as for bank • Cash flow very important
SBIC (5–20 yrs.)	Semipermanent capital to refund short-term debt, add to plant & equipment, expand into new markets, increase working capital, acquire other firms.	Small business as defined by the SBA; varies by industry (typically, assets <$9.0 million, NW <$4.0 million). Industry preferences vary widely among SBICs.	• Same information as for bank • Financial projections for at least 3 years • Emphasis on detailed plans for future growth

Source	Use of Loan	Appropriate Industries	*"Ideal" Preparation for First Meeting w/Lender*
Insurance Company (10–15 yrs.)	Same as for SBIC	Manufacturing generally favored. Prohibitions vary with lenders: e.g., Prudential does no business with high-tech firms, banks, or insurance companies, while Equitable bars liquor, tobacco, & firearms industries. Borrower must be a corporation.	• Same information as for bank, except that tax returns aren't usually required • Historical earnings coverage of proposed debt service is crucial

• Tables III, IV, and V (pp. 163, 171, and 177) summarize the principal sources of short-, intermediate-, and long-term financing, respectively, and the primary preferences, procedures, and criteria used by each source to evaluate loan proposals.

While no single table could encompass the variations and nuances of thousands of sources, we attempt to capture the principal characteristics and details to aid entrepreneurs in making an initial screening of possible sources. Most of these sources can be found in or near the nation's fifty largest cities.

SOURCES OF SHORT-TERM FINANCING

Duration: Less than one year (often 60–90 days)

Principal Uses: Working capital for seasonal financing, receivables, inventory, work-in-process, and other temporary needs; trade payables.

Principal Sources: Commercial banks (note or loan, line of credit); factors (pledge receivables, inventory, or equipment as collateral); commercial finance company.

COMMERCIAL BANKS (see Tables I–III)

When small-business owners consider applying for commercial financing, they usually think first of trying a local bank. As even the most casual observer knows, each metropolitan area typically has dozens of commercial banks, and even the smallest town usually has several to choose from (there are 14,000 commercial banks nationally). Because all banks advertise friendly and efficient service, it's natural to assume that they're pretty much alike.

But nothing could be further from the truth. According to an article by James McNeill Stancill in the *Harvard Business Review* of March–April 1980, on how small-business owners should choose banks,

> Choosing a bank is one of the most important business decisions confronting the developing firm. Too often, though, the decision is made on the basis of the bank's convenient location.

Banks can differ widely in their criteria for evaluating loan applications and the terms they offer when they do extend loans, the article noted. It cautioned readers, for instance, to beware of promised low interest rates, since they have a way of creeping up. The article also advised business owners to question whether their banks will make unsecured loans; lend 80 percent or more on receivables, and 50–70 percent against inventory; and whether they require compensating balances, or will negotiate on this point.

TABLE III

Principal Short-term Financing Sources
(Note or line of credit, less than one year)

Procedures and Criteria	Commercial Bank	Commercial Finance Company	Factor
Preferred size and stage of borrower	Any size; several years' history; occasional start-up	Sales over several million; no start-ups, unless team proven	Same
Size of loan	$5,000 to $60 million	$100,000 to $30 million; average $3 million	Same
Interest rate	Prime + 3–4%; some two-tier rates	Prime + 4–8%	Prime + 2–6%
Collateral required	None; ¼ time require compensating balances	Receivables; plant, equipment, inventory; owner's assets	Receivables purchased
Time to obtain decision	Few days to 2 weeks	One week or more	Same
Type of credit references needed	Personal and trade	Same	Same
Financial statements required	Personal; last 3 years of business, audited if possible	Same	Same
Business tax returns	Sometimes	Sometimes	Usually
Customer list	Sometimes	Sometimes	Very important
A/R[1] & A/P[2] aging list	Sometimes	Sometimes	Very important
Sales backlog examined	Sometimes	Sometimes	Closely
Cash flow & financial projections	Definitely, cover term of loan	Same	Same
Restrictions and covenants	Standard note or loan agreement	Same; may have prepayment penalties, changes in borrowing limits	Same

[1] Accounts Receivable
[2] Accounts Payable

Entrepreneurs are also advised to promote their businesses with their bankers, even after a loan has been obtained. Observed a successful entrepreneur in an article in the October 1980 issue of *INC.* magazine:

> I guess I'd always assumed bankers were experts on any business. That isn't true. If you want them to deal with your needs intelligently, you've got to spend time going over every last nut and bolt.

Perhaps the cardinal rule in dealing with bankers is to avoid surprises. They signal a possible loss of control and risks that are beyond the tolerance of most lending officers.

APPLICATION PROCEDURES (see Tables II and III)

A lender is most concerned with a borrower's cash flow and profits and how a loan will affect those areas; the idea is to be able to project the likelihood that the loan will be repaid on time. Bank loan officers usually are most impressed by applicants who demonstrate a thorough knowledge of the business and a clear understanding of how much of a loan is needed, for what purposes, and how and when it will be repaid.

Entrepreneurs meeting for the first time with an unknown banker improve their chances immensely by having a business plan (for start-ups) or business information to support their loan requests (for existing firms). (See Appendix C for a business plan guide.) Such information usually includes brief sales and earnings history, background of principals, details on how the loan will be used, cash-flow and profit-loss projections, lists of key customers, trade and credit references, an aging of receivables and payables, and any financial statements prepared or audited by a certified public accountant.

While different banks have their own particular paperwork requirements, a thorough preparation of the sort just described will provide the details necessary to comply with most requirements. (See the end of this chapter for a representative loan application.)

EVALUATION CRITERIA (see Table III)

Bank lending is a person-to-person business, according to Lincoln Morison, a senior vice president at the First National Bank of Boston. "A loan officer's first impression of management is crucial," he says. "It's important for the borrower to demonstrate a knowledge of the business and to make a clear presentation at the first meeting." The lending officer will judge the track record and credibility of the borrower to be sure the loan will be repaid, and also with the hope of acquiring a growing new customer for the bank.

As is evident in Table III, quite broad criteria are used. While they prefer an existing business whose past record, sales backlog, customer list, accounting system, and even audited financial statements provide credibility, banks will on occasion lend to new businesses. The more evidence entrepreneurs can provide to enhance their business credibility, the easier it becomes to secure a loan. The entire process can take as little as one day, but usually takes one to two weeks.

TERMS AND CONDITIONS (see Table III)

Interest rates for small businesses usually run three to four percentage points above the prime, unless the bank has a special two-tier lending rate structure, which gives small businesses lower rates. Short-term working capital loans are generally unsecured, but often a compensating balance, amounting to 15–20 percent of the loan, is required to remain on deposit at the bank. These notes typically are renewable each ninety days and must be paid off completely once a year. The founders of a start-up business may be required to guarantee with their personal net worths the new firm's loan. And in very uncertain economic times, personal guarantees have been required of the principals of well-established businesses with several million dollars of profitable sales. Generally, no other operating restrictions are required.

ADVANTAGES OF COMMERCIAL BANKS

Commercial banks are more organized and professional than informal sources, such as friends or relatives, and are the least expensive of the commercial loan sources. Borrowing from a bank is better for a small business' credit rating than borrowing from other sources. The more aggressive banks want new business and also want to see the small-business customers prosper. The larger banks offer a multitude of services that can be of considerable help to a business as it grows; these services include computerized payroll and tax preparation, letters of credit, international services, trust and estate services, money market and securities sales and purchases, lease financing, and cash management tools. Most importantly, a skillful loan officer can be an invaluable financial adviser for the growing business.

DISADVANTAGES

Historically, banks have not been customer- and market-oriented; rather, they wait for customers to come through the door. While this attitude appears to be shifting, small companies usually will not find bankers out hustling business. Bankers' concerns about risk and the high failure rate of small businesses create a considerable obstacle; lending officers tend to be more skeptical and less enthusiastic about small businesses, especially if they are new or young. Thus, banks are the most difficult of commercial sources for small businesses to secure loans from.

Banks can also be quite bureaucratic, with a lending committee making most decisions. This not only takes time, but may prevent entrepreneurs from making their proposals in person to the decision-makers. Banks demand more technical detail and information than most other lending sources before deciding on loans. Because they are government regulated, banks are especially careful to avoid bad loans and thus monitor borrowers more closely and more frequently than other lending sources.

COMMERCIAL FINANCE COMPANIES
(see Tables I–III)

The principal difference between banks and commercial finance companies, according to the book *Sourceguide for Borrowing Capital* (by Leonard E. Smollen, Mark Rollinson, and Stanley M. Rubel) is that:

> the bank is primarily relying on the business to continue to be successful and to generate adequate cash flow with which to repay the loan . . . Finance companies are secured lenders . . . They are primarily concerned with the quality of the collateral that has been pledged to secure their loan.

The collateral usually consists of accounts receivable and inventory.

Because commercial finance companies not only require collateral on loans but also charge higher interest rates than banks, entrepreneurs are generally advised to try banks first for loans. If banks won't grant loans, entrepreneurs can choose from many commercial finance companies; possibly 1,500 currently operate in the U.S. and they are playing an increasingly important role in the financing of growing firms. They are usually more receptive than banks to making loans to businesses which have experienced losses or other financial setbacks. (Some banks, though, have commercial finance subsidiaries.)

APPLICATION PROCEDURES (see Tables II and III)

The loan application that is prepared for but rejected by a commercial bank contains much the same information that is required by a commercial finance company. However, since the commercial finance company is often dealing with riskier companies than banks will handle, the most important information concerns the nature, quality, and value at liquidation of the applicant's receivables or inventory. Such things as audited financial statements, detailed aging of receivables and payables, most recent three years' tax returns, and cash-flow projections should thus be a part of any financing request to commercial financing companies. A business plan which discusses the management team, the trends and patterns in the industry, competition, and a marketing plan can help calm commercial finance company fears about risk. (See Appendix C for a summary of a business plan.) Decisions on applications are typically made in one week or more.

EVALUATION CRITERIA (see Tables II and III)

Commercial finance companies are concerned about the quality of management, cash flow, and financial position, but they look primarily at the liquidation value of the collateral should the customer fail. Thus, commercial finance companies may actually approve loans to companies viewed by banks as quite shaky financially; the banks may be put off by such problems as an excessive debt-to-equity ratio and low profits. Finance companies generally consider loans for 75–85 percent of the invoice value of receivables to be used as collateral. Inventory typically is collateralized for 25–50 percent of its appraised value.

TERMS AND CONDITIONS (see Table III)

Typically, accounts receivable are either factored (purchased outright) or used as collateral for short-term loans. Those receivables less than ninety days old can justify loans of 75–85 percent of invoices. Compensating balances are not required, and interest rates of 3–6 percent above the prime rate are typical, but only on those funds actually used. Usually, there is a charge for bank-clearing days to cover the float while checks are deposited and verified.

ADVANTAGES OF COMMERCIAL FINANCE COMPANIES

Their primary advantages are that they make loans that banks avoid and generally provide more flexibility in the loan agreements than banks do. Interest is paid only so long as businesses are still viable; the asset collateral makes up any unpaid balance.

Such loans can be more attractive than selling stock to investors or having to adhere to the often onerous restrictions of bank or SBA loans.

DISADVANTAGES

The interest rates are generally higher by 2 percent or more than loans from commercial banks and even some factors. Owners of closely held businesses are generally required to personally guarantee the loans. In addition, any existing loans by officers to a company are subordinated to the finance company's loan, and no new loans to officers are permitted. Once a receivable is over ninety days old, the borrower is typically required to repurchase it. Thus, a weak credit and collections department could rapidly undermine an existing weak financial situation. Finally, visits by the commercial finance company's field audit staff take time and can be distracting to employees.

FACTORS (see Tables I and III)

Factoring is often confused with accounts receivable financing, but there is an important difference; factors actually *buy* receivables from companies and rely on their own credit and collection expertise. Accounts receivable financing involves receivables pledged as collateral.

With "old line" factoring, cash is advanced immediately after orders are shipped, which can be especially helpful to new and rapidly growing businesses. "Maturity" factoring advances cash on the average due date of invoices.

As is the case with commercial financing, factoring is a financial tool used mostly by companies unable to obtain bank loans. In the early part of this century, factoring was confined to the textile industry. But more recently factoring has become acceptable in such industries as plastics, toys, shoes, clothing, furniture, and carpet making. It is occasionally used for seasonal inventory and equipment loans.

Generally, a business must have a minimum of $500,000 to $750,000 in annual sales and a minimum net worth as low as $50,000 to $100,000 to attract a factor. (Factoring is also a principal activity of most commercial finance companies.)

APPLICATION PROCEDURES (see Tables I and III)

All the financial, operating, and management data required for commercial bank loan applications are required by factors. In addition, because factors must carefully analyze the nature, quality, and value of customers, considerable additional information must be provided. None of it is difficult to produce if a company's accounting system includes details on accounts, bad debts, and inventory. Factors want to assess such things as average size of invoices, each customer's peak purchases, terms of sales, historical returns, allowances and disputes, detailed aging of receivables, and due dates by customer. A loan decision usually takes one week or more.

Terms and conditions (see Table III)

Factors usually require a reserve of 5–10 percent of the gross amount of the receivables sold. In addition, they charge a commission of ½–1½ percent of the gross amount of invoices sold, along with fees for investigation and for covering the float in bank clearing. The funds advanced to small businesses by factors have a typical interest rate of 2–6 percent above the prime rate. Most factoring arrangements can be cancelled by either party on 60 days' notice, but initially are for a one- to two-year period.

Evaluation criteria (see Tables I and III)

Though factors prefer companies that have annual sales of more than $10 million, they will often work with smaller companies which show substantial growth potential. Start-ups are rare customers, but can occasionally persuade a factor if they have experienced and impressive management teams and business plans.

The key evaluation criteria for factors are the quality and value of a company's receivables, since factors buy receivables outright and must collect them to make a profit.

Unattractive to factors are products sold on consignment, products with low turnover and low margins, faddish items, and professional services. The larger an applicant's sales volume and average invoice size, the more impressed factors will be.

Advantages of factoring

The principal benefits of factors are the elimination of credit risk, bad debts, and the department responsible for credit and collections. Small businesses with factors can thus concentrate on selling, even to unknown or marginal customers whose creditworthiness they are unable to assess carefully themselves. Rapidly growing small firms can generate immediate cash through factoring and reduce the need for equity capital. Businesses with fluctuating sales and limited working capital can also benefit from the quick cash infusion factors provide.

Factors usually make their decisions more rapidly than commercial banks. Compared to accounts receivable financing by commercial finance companies, which typically provide 75–85 percent of invoices as loans, factors advance 90–95 percent of gross invoices, further accelerating cash flow.

DISADVANTAGES OF FACTORING

The full cost of factoring is difficult to calculate, but generally will be greater than the cost of commercial bank loans. Also, business owners can expect to make a major time investment to learn how factoring might apply to their business and to investigate and negotiate arrangements.

SOURCES OF INTERMEDIATE-TERM FINANCING
(refer to glossary beginning on p. 391 if terms are unfamiliar)

Duration: Secured and unsecured term loans, more than one year, but less than five to seven years.

Principal Uses: Growth and working capital, machinery and equipment, plant improvement, other fixed assets, turnaround financing, acquisitions, leveraged buyouts, retiring higher-interest loans.

Principal Sources: Commercial banks, commercial finance companies, factors, leasing companies.

COMMERCIAL BANKS (see Tables II and IV)

Banks are a major source of secured loans for intermediate-term financing. The basic guidelines that apply to short-term bank loans and dealing with lending officers are also applicable here (see pp. 163–66).

APPLICATION PROCEDURES (see Tables II and IV)

The process and procedures are fundamentally the same as noted earlier for short-term bank loans. A brief business plan (see Appendix C for guidelines) which provides company history, trends and prospects in the industry, current and planned assets, track record of management, financial projections, and justification of the need and use of funds is the core of the loan proposal. Typically, a decision is made in a few days to two weeks.

EVALUATION CRITERIA (see Tables II and IV)

Existing businesses of nearly any size can secure such loans, but start-ups usually can't. Particular emphasis is placed on the borrower's entrepreneurial and managerial record. Most financings exceed $25,000, and typically range from $100,000 to $250,000. The lender's major concern is the effective use of the loan to generate future cash flow to ensure timely repayment. Machinery, equipment, or business property used as

TABLE IV

Principal Intermediate-term Financing Sources
(1 to 6 years, term loan)

Procedures and Criteria	Commercial Bank	Commercial Finance Company	Factor	Leasing Company
Preferred size and stage of borrower	Any size; 3rd stage; occasional start-up	Sales over $10 million; proven teams for start-ups	Same	Any size; 2nd or 3rd stage; some start-ups
Size of loan	$25,000+	$100,000 to $30 million; average $3 million	Same	$3,000 to $5 million
Interest rate	Prime + 3–4%	Prime + 3–6%	Prime + 4–6%	Prime + 1–6%
Collateral required	Secured by inventory, equipment, A/Rs[2]	Plant, equipment, inventory, A/Rs[2]	A/Rs[2]	2–3 months' advance payment
Time to obtain decision	Few days to 2 weeks	1 week or more	Same	1 day to 2 weeks
Type of credit references needed	Personal and business	Same	Same	Sometimes trade credit
Financial statements required	Personal if guarantee loan; 3 years business, audited if possible	Same	Same	Same
Business tax returns	Sometimes	Usually	Usually	Sometimes
Customer list	Sometimes	Yes	Yes	No
A/P[1] & A/R[2]	Sometimes	Yes	Yes	Depends on size
Sales backlog examined	Sometimes	Yes	Yes	Depends on size
Cash flow and financial projections	Definitely, for term of loan	Very important, over 1–2 years minimum	Same	Yes, from 1 year to term of loan
Restrictions and covenants	Variable, such as: • Min. working capital • Min. net worth, current ratio, debt ratio • Dividend payment restrictions • Sales & acquisition of assets • Salaries • Pledging other assets	Generally none; watch for prepayment penalties	Same	None

[1] Accounts Payable
[2] Accounts Receivable

collateral is appraised at auction value. The loan is typically limited to 100–150 percent of that auction-appraised value. If other collateral is pledged, such as marketable securities, the loan is limited to 50–75 percent of securities' market value.

TERMS AND CONDITIONS (see Table IV)

Loans are usually made for periods up to five years, though sometimes for as long as seven years, with a repayment schedule of regular equal installments. Sometimes a significant portion of principal can be deferred until the end of the loan term, when a "balloon payment" is made. Interest rates on intermediate-term loans may be somewhat higher than short-term loans (prime plus 3–4 percent) unless a two-tier rate is available. Compensating balances of 15–20 percent of loans are usually required.

Banks typically impose a number of other covenants and restrictions to reduce their risk exposure. For instance, they may prohibit, or require their approval of, additional borrowing, mergers, payments of dividends, sales of assets, reduced working capital, and changes in management. Such restrictions vary from bank to bank and are negotiable.

ADVANTAGES AND DISADVANTAGES OF COMMERCIAL BANKS
(see earlier discussion on commercial banks, pp. 163–66)

COMMERCIAL FINANCE COMPANIES
(see Tables I, II, and IV)

Commercial finance companies are a major alternative source of intermediate-term financing for businesses rejected by banks. Any viable business with assets whose liquidation value can be determined is a possible candidate for a secured loan.

APPLICATION PROCEDURES (see Tables II and IV)

Besides the standard information banks require, commercial finance companies have some unique additional requirements. They usually like to have the latest comparative financial statements—preferably audited; an aging schedule of accounts payable; the last three years' tax returns; a business plan with cash-flow projections; information on management; and data on accounting and control systems. Information about particular assets that might serve as collateral should include the purchase dates and costs, serial numbers, depreciation schedules, and any recent appraiser's reports. One week or more is typically required for a lending decision to be made.

EVALUATION CRITERIA (see Tables II and IV)

The fundamental question commercial finance companies ask to evaluate a prospective secured term loan is straightforward: will pledged assets (plant, equipment, machinery, etc.), if sold at liquidation (bankrupt) prices, cover the value of the outstanding loan? Many smaller companies can get a favorable answer to this question—even though a bank was negative—because commercial finance companies will take greater risks, and lend to financially weaker businesses. According to the book *Business Loans*, by Rick Stephan Hayes, commercial finance companies will "take as security or collateral certain items banks are more selective about . . . In short, commercial finance companies are a lot more flexible than banks."

Commercial finance companies prefer as customers companies with sales of $10 million or more, but are interested in smaller, growth-oriented ventures. Financings average $3 million, and range from $100,000 to $30 million.

TERMS AND CONDITIONS (see Tables II and IV)

The loan agreement is similar to that for secured loans made by banks. The amount typically is 75 percent of the auction appraisal of pledged assets; the percentage can be more, depending on competition at the time of the loan. The interest rate usually is 3–6 percent above the prime rate, and occasionally can go as high as twice the prime for high-risk loans. Personal guarantees are required by closely held companies; the lender also enjoys discretionary rights to alter the percentage of the collateral used to secure the loan. This major power gives the lender protection, should repayment of the loan become threatened. Finally, periodic field audits are conducted to verify the borrower's condition and collateral.

ADVANTAGES

In addition to those pluses noted in the section on short-term financing (p. 167), commercial finance companies have other advantages for intermediate-term loans. Commercial finance companies are more flexible than banks. Their officials usually do not suffer as much from the conservatism and risk aversion of many career bank loan officers. Thus, a bank's rejection does not necessarily eliminate a business as possibly a quite reasonable prospect for a commercial finance loan.

DISADVANTAGES

Two factors that weigh against this source are the higher interest rates than banks and the powerful discretionary rights of the lender. In addition, the actual field audit of assets may take a substartial amount of time and be somewhat of a nuisance to a business's employees.

FACTORS (see Tables I, II, and IV)

In addition to purchasing accounts receivable as a form of short-term financing, factors also make intermediate-term loans against inventory and fixed assets for three- to five-year periods, with monthly or quarterly amortization.

APPLICATION PROCEDURE (see Tables II and IV)

Basically, applicants need the same information required for a commercial bank loan. Valuation of the assets used as collateral is particularly important. A period of a week or more is typically required for a loan decision.

EVALUATION CRITERIA (see Tables II and IV)

The factor examines the loan proposal in much the same way that a commercial bank does, except the factor tends to be less conservative. The proposal is carefully examined to determine whether a loan can be profitably used on plant improvements, machinery, equipment, or whatever. The cushion sought by the factor is typically one to one and one half times the appraised auction value, to ensure recovery of the loan if liquidation of the business should occur.

TERMS AND CONDITIONS (see Table IV)

Factor loans usually run 4–6 percent above the prime rate. An agreement similar to a bank loan is executed so that the factor has a lien against the collateral.

ADVANTAGES OF FACTORS
(see previous discussion on p. 169)

The principal advantage of factors is that they are an important alternative to commercial banks and finance companies. Factors often make loans that banks have rejected and also tend to be more flexible. Factoring can be especially advantageous in accelerating cash flow.

DISADVANTAGES OF FACTORS
(see previous discussion on p. 170)

The factor loan costs as much as 2–4 percent more than the bank rate, to compensate for the increased risks.

LEASING COMPANIES (see Tables I, II, and IV)

Leasing has in recent years become a major source of intermediate-term financing for small companies. Approximately 700 to 800 leasing companies are scattered around the country, along with thousands of commercial banks and many commercial finance companies which also do leasing. Virtually any kind of fixed asset can be financed through a leasing arrangement, including typewriters and office equipment, automobiles and trucks, computers, machinery, and equipment. For new ventures, leasing can be an important means of conserving cash and lowering capital requirements, whether debt or equity. Financings for as little as $2,000 to $3,000 to as much as $5 million are possible, usually for periods of three to six years.

APPLICATION PROCEDURES (see Tables II and IV)

Like a bank, a leasing company wants to be quite certain that the applying company and its management are sound. It will, therefore, request much of the same information required to secure a bank loan for purchasing assets. Because the leasing company retains ownership of, and title to, assets, it has what amounts to collateral. The leasing company is especially interested in cash-flow projections over the life of the lease. Various statements, history, tax returns, management backgrounds, and related facts are also required. Usually a decision on leasing requests is made in one day to two weeks.

EVALUATION CRITERIA (see Tables I, II, and IV)

Virtually any size business can potentially be a customer of a leasing company. For example, even a single-proprietor service business can arrange to lease such things as a typewriter, microcomputer, or furniture. The applicant's cash-flow projections are most critical in the evaluation, since monthly payments are required for most leases.

Terms and conditions
(see Table IV)

A wide and flexible variety of leasing arrangements exists to meet the needs of particular industries and businesses. Typically, about 10 percent of the value of the asset being leased is required up front in the form of two or three months' advance payment on the lease. The total cost of a lease is greater than an outright purchase or a commercial loan to finance the asset, and the asset is usually not owned at the expiration of the lease. For an additional cost, arrangements can often be made to acquire the asset. The effective rate of interest for leasing is typically 1–6 percent above the prime rate.

Start-ups and early-stage businesses can often find support from a leasing company, provided the founders are prepared to personally guarantee the lease or pledge additional collateral.

Advantages of
leasing companies

The biggest advantage is that they enable start-up or growing ventures to conserve cash and to reduce the total capital they require. Only 10 percent of the asset's value is needed up front, compared to 20–25 percent for a bank financing or down payment for purchase. At later stages of growth, small businesses can avoid additional debt or the need for outside equity by leasing fixed assets. Leasing can also be a means of acquiring additional financing for companies with existing bank or other loan restrictions, since leasing doesn't usually count as a loan under such loan covenants. Leasing also provides a tax advantage, since businesses can write off as an expense all current lease payments, instead of having to depreciate the asset over a longer period. Finally, leasing companies make reasonably rapid decisions, usually in one day to two weeks.

Disadvantages

New accounting rules are likely to require reporting of leases on the balance sheet as a liability. Leasing is also more costly than most other financing methods. The 1980–81 credit crunch is likely to topple some smaller leasing firms, suggesting that a fair amount of time and care should be given to locating a sound lessor.

COMMERCIAL FINANCE

TABLE V

Principal Long-term Financing Sources
(5+ to 20-year term loans)

Procedures and Criteria	SBICs	Life Insurance Companies
Preferred size and stage of borrower	Assets less than $9 million; net worth less than $4 million; after-tax income below $400,000; later stages; some start-ups	Later stages; sales $10 million; net worth $1 million +; 5 years' operating history
Size of loan	$500,000 to $75 million; average $3 million	Less than $100,000 to $1 million or more; $500,000 to $75 million; average $3 million
Interest rate	Negotiable; prime + 3%; equity kickers	Baa to Baa bond rating + 2–3%; equity kickers
Collateral required	Usually none	Usually none
Time to obtain decision	2 to 4 weeks or more	2 weeks minimum; average 3 months
Type of credit references needed	Trade credit	Trade credit
Financial statements required	Sometimes personal; business past 3–5 years, audited preferred	Basically same
Business tax returns	Sometimes	No—but many want last IRS-cleared date
Customer list	Yes	Yes, at least major customers
A/P¹ & A/R²	Usually	Yes
Sales backlog examined	Yes	Yes
Cash flow and financial projections	Yes—to cover at least 3 years	Very important, 1–5 years
Restrictions and covenants	• Minimum net worth, working capital, net assets • Promptly pay fees, taxes, assessments • Number and who on board • Keep investor current with reports, financial statements, etc. • Approval to sell, borrow, acquire, issue stock, etc.	Same plus: • Dividend payments • Stock repurchase • Discretionary payments to subordinated debtors • Limits on debt, notes, asset disposal • No additional liens on assets, etc.

¹ Accounts payable
² Accounts receivable

SOURCES OF LONG-TERM FINANCING
(see Tables I, II, and V)

Duration: Usually more than five to seven years and up to fifteen to twenty years.

Principal Uses: Semipermanent and permanent capital to retire short-term or intermediate-term debt; expand real estate, plant, facilities, and equipment; develop and expand into new markets, market new products; increase working capital; make acquisitions; finance leveraged buyouts.

Principal Sources: Small Business Investment Corporations (SBICs) and insurance companies.

Long-term lenders of the sort discussed in this section are not prime sources of financing for the vast majority of small businesses. These lenders make long-term loans mostly to well-established, profitable, and fast-growing small companies which already have annual sales of at least several million dollars. This section, therefore, is relevant primarily to such established and growing small companies.

SMALL BUSINESS INVESTMENT
CORPORATIONS (SBICs)
(see Tables I, II, and V)

The 1958 Small Business Investment Act led to the creation of SBICs; the SBICs were financed largely with special Small Business Administration (SBA) loans. In the go-go days of the 1960s, over 700 SBICs existed. During the 1970s, the number diminished to around 300, as many SBICs were unable to make enough profit on their investments to repay their SBA loans.

Today SBICs can be found in thirty-eight states and in Puerto Rico, with five states accounting for nearly half: New York (53), California (36), Texas (27), Connecticut (17), and Massachusetts (16). Nationwide, the SBICs are backed by about $600 million in SBA loans, and $500 million in private capital.

SBICs have been an important small-business financing source; since their inception some 50,000 small businesses have secured about $3.5 billion of financing in a wide range of businesses and industries. Financings average about $100,000, consisting of both debt and equity.

A listing of SBICs, their capitalization, and investment preferences is available from a trade association of SBICs:

National Association of Small Business
    Investment Companies
618 Washington Building
Washington, DC 20005
(202) 638–3411

APPLICATION PROCEDURES (see Tables II and V)

SBICs, like other long-term lenders and venture-capital investors, are especially concerned about the quality of management and the prospects for profitable growth. In addition to the detailed financial statements, history, and other facts banks require, SBICs like to see a complete business plan (see Appendix C for guidelines). A business plan, in advance of a face-to-face meeting, is the principal guide used to initially assess a venture. Without one, the chances of successful financing are drastically reduced. Decisions are usually made in about two to four weeks.

EVALUATION CRITERIA (see Tables I, II, and V)

Most SBICs make loans and equity investments in a diverse assortment of ventures. Some specialize in particular areas such as real estate, rentals and leasing, high technology, and health care. Typically, few startups are funded; the emphasis is on businesses with several years of operating experience. SBA limitations on size restrict loans to businesses with assets of $9 million or less, net worth of $4 million or less, and average net income after taxes of $400,000 or less yearly. Within these broad guidelines, the quality of management and the future growth and earnings potential are most critical to obtaining backing.

TERMS AND CONDITIONS (see Table V)

Loans must be made for more than five, but not longer than twenty, years. The interest rate on loans cannot exceed by 7 percent the cost of money paid by the SBIC for its capital. An SBIC may want stock as part of the deal, but may not acquire more than 49 percent of any business, nor may it lend more than 20 percent of its capital to any single business.

Various restrictions and covenants are common to long-term loan agreements with SBICs. These restrictions and covenants may include such things as: minimum net worth, working capital, and net assets; prompt repayment of all taxes, fees, and assessments; board memberships; periodically informing the SBIC with financial statements and reports; and approval of such things as selling or acquiring assets, change in management compensation, and change in the nature of the business.

ADVANTAGES OF SBICs

They are knowledgeable, experienced, and heavily involved with small businesses—more so than other long-term lenders. They are used to dealing with risky businesses and are flexible and creative in working out arrangements to offset risks so as to make loans. The SBIC can become a valuable outside adviser to the board of directors of a closely held company, providing significant advice, contacts, and credibility. For fast-growth businesses, a carefully chosen SBIC can become an important link to other venture-capital firms and investors when additional financing is needed.

DISADVANTAGES

A previously debt-free, closely held company is likely to perceive the covenants and restrictions of an SBIC loan agreement as too burdensome and restrictive. Clearly, the founders can no longer enjoy their substantial discretionary decision-making. Some SBICs are criticized for relying too much on loans rather than equity investments so as to earn enough current income to support their overhead. They might urge a higher portion of debt for a small business than a conventional venture-capital firm might encourage (see Chapter 6, "Venture Capital"). Finally, for growing businesses which expect to be too large in a few years to qualify for SBIC backing, conventional venture-capital firms may provide better long-term financial partners.

LIFE INSURANCE COMPANIES
(see Tables I, II, and V)

In the June 1980 issue of *Nation's Business,* a vice president of Massachusetts Mutual Life Insurance Company noted that small growing businesses often encounter problems finding long-term financing. "What may not be so well-known," he stated, "is that many small firms are turning to private, long-term loans from institutional lenders such as insurance companies." While most small businesses—even those with a net worth of $500,000 or more and sales exceeding several million dollars annually—will find this source very difficult to tap, life insurance companies should not be overlooked. Though start-up financings are rare, leveraged buyouts and unsecured ten- to fifteen-year loans are made. Moreover, some life insurance companies have a record of aggressive lending to small businesses; two such national life insurance companies are the following:

The Equitable Life Assurance Society
Regional Corporate Finance Department
1290 Ave. of the Americas (Suite 3400)
New York, NY 10019
(212) 554-1455
(Seven regional offices: Atlanta, Boston, Chicago, Houston, Los Angeles, New York, San Francisco)

The Prudential Insurance Company of America
Prudential Plaza
Newark, NJ 07101
(201) 877-6000
(Thirteen field offices: Atlanta, Boston, Chicago, Cincinnati, Dallas, Detroit, Houston, Los Angeles, Milwaukee, Minneapolis, Newark, San Francisco, Toronto)

APPLICATION PROCEDURES (see Tables II and V)

Life insurance companies are most interested in cash-flow projections which look ahead several years. The projections should be based on receipt of the loan being requested, to convey the soundness of the long-term financing plan. Life insurance companies seek evidence of good relationships with past and current creditors. They also examine various information about management and performance normally sought by banks, SBICs, and other lenders. The average decision on a loan proposal requires three months, though decisions are sometimes made sooner. The best ways to approach life insurance companies are through personal contacts and referrals by CPAs or bankers.

EVALUATION CRITERIA (see Tables II and V)

"Probably no other factor . . . ranks as high as management quality" in evaluating applicants for insurance company loans, observed the article in the June 1980 issue of *Nation's Business*. "Performance, of course, is the ultimate test of management quality, and return on invested capital (of 8%) is a good indicator."

Typically, the prospective insurance company borrower looks like the cream of the small business crop. For example, annual sales are usually $10 million or more, net worth exceeds $1 million, and earnings appear to be one to two times interest and principal on the long-term debt. Basically, the business is considered financially sound by most conventional ratio analyses of industry standards.

Certain types of business are shunned by insurance companies, according to the book *Financing the Growing Business* by Thomas J. Martin. These include finance, leasing, construction, personal service, and personal holding companies; companies relying on government or defense contracts, or overly dependent on one customer or source of supply; franchise holders; and brokerage-type operations.

TERMS AND CONDITIONS (see Table V)

Loans typically extend ten to fifteen years, and in recent years have had effective interest rates in the 11–13 percent range. Borrowers must pay a commitment fee of ½–1 percent of the loan amount and legal fees of $5,000 to $20,000. Expensive prepayment penalties are often included in agreements. A moratorium on early principal payments along with balloon payments at maturity are also possible. Equity kickers can occasionally be negotiated, enabling the insurance company to realize a capital gain, should the company perform well.

Various covenants similar to those required for SBIC loans may be required in the agreement. These covenants impose limitations and restrictions in such areas as working capital and current ratio, dividend payments, stock repurchases, short-term notes, and asset disposal, among other areas.

ADVANTAGES OF LIFE INSURANCE COMPANIES

The main advantage is that loans are unsecured, which potentially frees assets for additional borrowing if necessary. Unlike banks, insurance companies do not require compensating balances. Their long-term loans can be inexpensive, even at 12 percent, when inflation is taken into account, and can replace more costly short- and medium-term financing. Such long-term loans can also represent an alternative to selling stock, thus preventing dilution of the founders' shares.

DISADVANTAGES

Only a relatively small segment of all small businesses are potential candidates for such loans. If small businesses are so sound, numerous other financing options may also exist, such as SBICs, venture capital, and private or public placements. The cost of such loans is generally greater than selling a bond or debenture through a public offering.

ADDITIONAL INFORMATION SOURCES

BOOKS

Business Loans: A Guide to Money Sources and How to Approach Them Successfully, 2nd ed., by Rick Stephan Hayes. (Boston: CBI Publishing Company, Inc., 1980)
Discussion of commercial, private, and government funding sources plus detailed instructions on preparation for requesting a loan and a sample application package.

The Small Business Guide to Borrowing Money, by Richard L. Rubin and Philip Goldberg. (New York: McGraw-Hill Book Company, 1980)

Conceptually similar to the Hayes book, though a little shorter with fewer sample forms. Includes selected listings of venture-capital firms and SBICs; good discussion of how to work with different sources.

Sourceguide for Borrowing Capital, by Leonard E. Smollen, Mark Rollinson, and Stanley M. Rubel. (Wellesley Hills, MA: Capital Publishing Corporation, 1977; rev. ed. due in 1981)
Excellent discussion of all institutional funding sources and advice on using them, via articles written by experts in each area; directories of commercial finance and leasing companies, SBICs, and other sources. New edition should provide needed updating.

Financing the Growing Small Business, by Thomas J. Martin. (New York: Holt, Rinehart and Winston, 1980)
An excellent book on financing the small firm. It contains many practical examples, guidelines, and suggestions. Also includes a glossary, valuation guides, and present value tables.

ARTICLES

"Business Plans that Pass the 'Snicker Test,'" *Venture,* October 1979.

"CPA Assistance in Business Financing," *CPA Journal,* April 1978.

"Capital Acquisition: In Financing, Think High-Yield Debt—Not Equity," *INC.,* April 1979.

"Getting the Most from Your Banking Relationship," by James McNeill Stancill, *Harvard Business Review,* March–April 1980.

"Growing a Company," *INC.,* October, November, December 1979 (3-part series).

"How to Go Public but Stay Private," by Deborah Bartlett, *INC.,* January 1980.

"Look to Receivables and Other Assets to Obtain Working Capital," by Robert I. Goldman, *Harvard Business Review,* November–December 1979.

"Raising Money a Better Way: Use Subordinated Debt," *The Business Owner,* May 1980.

"Small Business—An Owner's View of Banking," by William Hart, *Journal of Commercial Bank Lending,* November 1978.

"When Talk Turns to Financing Don't Believe All You Hear," by Russell Hindin, *INC.,* June 1979.

"Working with Your Lenders," by A. David Silver, *Venture,* October 1979.

PUBLISHERS OF
DIRECTORIES OF
COMMERCIAL FINANCING
SOURCES

National Commercial Finance Conference (provides referrals to suitable asset-based lenders in all areas of the country)
One Penn Plaza
New York, NY 10001
(212) 594-3490

The Corporate Finance Sourcebook (asset-based lenders and large commercial banks)
40 Central Park S
New York, NY 10019
(212) 759-1972

National Association of Small Business Investment Companies (NASBIC)
618 Washington Building
Washington, DC 20005
(202) 638-3411

American Association of Equipment Lessors
1700 N Moore St. (Suite 1930)
Arlington, VA 22209
(703) 527-8655

United States League of Savings Associations (S&L associations)
111 E Wacker Drive
Chicago, IL 60601
(312) 644-3100

National Association of Mutual Savings Banks
200 Park Ave.
New York, NY 10166
(212) 973-5432

Below is a typical initial bank loan application form for small businesses. Additional business financial information such as profit-and-loss figures and balance sheets may be required either to accompany such an application or after the application has passed an initial screening.

APPLICATION
Small Business Term Loan

TO: THE FIRST NATIONAL BANK OF BOSTON
BOSTON, MASSACHUSETTS 02110

Date..

The undersigned hereby submit(s) application for a loan in the net amount of

.... Dollars $ [   ]

For the purpose of...

....

....

to be repaid in..............monthly payments on the ☐ 5th ☐ 10th ☐ 15th ☐ 20th ☐ 25th ☐ 30th day of the month.

BUSINESS RECORD

☐ Corporation
☐ Partnership
☐ Proprietorship

Name of Business...
(Please Print)

Kind of Business... Phone No. ....

Address...
(Street)   (City or Town)   (Zone)   (State)

Year Business Established..........................Annual Rent $........................Lease Expires...................

Business Checking Account...
(Name of Bank)

PRINCIPALS

Name.. Date of Birth....................................

Residence...

Residence Telephone No. .... No. of years at present residence .... Number of Dependents ....

Previous Residence..

Checking a/c (bank)..Title of account.....................................Balance $...........

Savings or Cooperative a/c (bank)..a/c no..Balance $...........

Real Estate Owned..Date Purchased....................Mtge. held by...................

Cost $................Valuation $...............Original Mortgage $................Present Balance $.............Monthly Payments $...............Rental Income $...............

Life Insurance: Face Amt. Carried $.................................Cash Value $...............Subject to Loan of $................

Other Assets: Securities Mkt. Value $...............................Auto (Make & Year)...............................

Open loans	To Whom Owed	Original Amount	Unpaid Balance	Monthly Payment	Collateral
	.... $..............	.... $.............	.... $.............		....
	.... $..............	.... $.............	.... $.............		....

Name.. Date of Birth....................................

Residence...

Residence Telephone No. .... No. of years at present residence .... Number of Dependents ....

Previous Residence..

Checking a/c (bank)..Title of account.....................................Balance $...........

Savings or Cooperative a/c (bank)..a/c no..Balance $...........

Real Estate Owned..Date Purchased....................Mtge. held by...................

Cost $................Valuation $...............Original Mortgage $................Present Balance $.............Monthly Payments $...............Rental Income $...............

Life Insurance: Face Amt. Carried $.................................Cash Value $...............Subject to Loan of $................

Other Assets: Securities Mkt. Value $...............................Auto (Make & Year)...............................

Open loans	To Whom Owed	Original Amount	Unpaid Balance	Monthly Payment	Collateral
	.... $..............	.... $.............	.... $.............		....
	.... $..............	.... $.............	.... $.............		....

Borrower, in consideration of Bank making the loan to Borrower, hereby warrants, represents and agrees as follows:

1. If Borrower is a corporation, Borrower is duly organized and existing under the laws of..
and is duly qualified as a foreign corporation in the States of..

2. Borrower will cause the following present indebtedness of Borrower is be subordinated to the loan by a Subordination Agreement satisfactory to Bank.

Name of Creditor of Borrower   *Amount*

....

....

....

....

3. The execution, delivery and performance hereof and any security instruments or guarantees called for or delivered hereunder are (if Borrower is a corporation) within its corporate powers, have been duly authorized, are not in contravention of the terms of Borrower's Articles of Incorporation or By-laws or any amendment thereof and (whether or not Borrower is a corporation) are not in contravention of law or of any indenture, agreement or undertaking to which Borrower is a party or by which Borrower is bound.

4. All financial statements, profit and loss statements, statements as to ownership and other statements heretofore or hereafter given to Bank in connection with this agreement are or will be true and correct subject to any limitation stated therein and Borrower is the owner of all property in which Borrower has given or is giving a security interest to Bank, free from all encumbrances and Borrower will so own all property in which Borrower hereafter gives a security interest to Bank.

5. Borrower will maintain executive personnel and management satisfactory to Bank.

6. Borrower will maintain adequate fire (including so-called extended coverage), public liability and other insurance as Bank may require, in such form and written by such companies as may be satisfactory to Bank and will upon request of Bank deliver to it the policies concerned. All policies covering property given as security for the loan shall have a loss payable clause in favor of Bank.

GENERAL INFORMATION

Has the business, or any of the principals ever been involved in any judgments, attachments or other legal proceedings other than divorce, custody, alimony or separate support proceedings?

☐ Yes ☐ No. If "yes," attach memorandum giving details.

Name of Accountant :...Tel. No..

Address :..

Name of Insurance Agent :...Tel. No..

Address :..
The foregoing statements and any supplementary information are warranted by the undersigned to be true and are furnished to induce you to make the loan applied for, which, if made, will be used only for the purpose above stated.

The Bank is authorized to obtain from any source any information which it may require to enable or assist it to pass upon this application. If this application is approved, I also authorize the Bank to give credit information to others.

The undersigned knows that you rely and will continue to rely thereon until written notice of any change therein is received by you. The undersigned will give you immediate written notice of any material change in the undersigned's financial condition, including any law-suit, begun or threatened, the effect of which may be to materially alter the said condition.

The undersigned will furnish you with such financial statements and data at such times and with such certifications as you may require, without expense to you. You, and your agents and accountants, may at any time inspect the undersigned's books and accounts.

This application shall remain the property of the Bank, whether approved, not approved, withdrawn, or if the loan is paid.

Signed this   day of   , 19

It is unlawful to deny or stop credit or services or to damage anyone's credit standing because of his or her sex or marital status.

....(SEAL)
                                                                                     Name of Applicant

By ....
                                                                                     Title, if any

By ....
                                                                                     Title, if any

A typical bank loan agreement, which specifies conditions borrower must meet to avoid defaulting on the loan.

BUSINESS LOAN AGREEMENT

TO: THE FIRST NATIONAL BANK OF BOSTON

The undersigned_____

_____(hereinafter called "Borrower") hereby applies to THE FIRST NATIONAL BANK OF BOSTON (hereinafter called "Bank") for a loan (hereinafter called the "loan") to be evidenced by a promissory note which includes the following provisions or such other provisions as to which Borrower and Bank may agree in writing:

Amount of Note: $_____ Date of Note: _____

_____, 19_____

Payable: _____

Borrower, in consideration of Bank making the loan to Borrower, hereby warrants, represents and agrees as follows:

1. The business operations of Borrower are as follows: _____

(Insert type of business, i.e., machine shop, bakery, etc.)

and said business is a_____

(Indicate whether sole ownership, partnership, corporation or trust)

2. Borrower will continue said business, will not engage in any other business without permission of Bank, and will use the proceeds of the loan only in connection with said business and for the following purposes:

3. Borrower's balance sheet as at_____

_____ 19_____and the related statement of income and retained earnings for Borrower's fiscal year ending on such date, both of which have been delivered to Bank, are complete and correct and have been prepared in accordance with generally accepted accounting principles consistently applied throughout the period involved. There are no liabilities of Borrower contingent or otherwise not disclosed in said balance sheet and since the date of such balance sheet there has been no change in the assets, liabilities, financial condition or business of Borrower shown thereon other than changes in the ordinary course of business, the effect of which has not been in the aggregate materially adverse.

4. So long as any amount remains unpaid under the loan:

4.1 Borrower's current business assets will exceed Borrower's current business liabilities, both determined in accordance with generally accepted accounting principles consistent with those applied in preparation of the financial statements referred to in Paragraph 3, by at least_____

_____ Dollars ($_____). If left blank, this provision is not applicable.

4.2 Borrower's current ratio (the relationship of current assets to current liabilities) will be maintained at not less than   . Classification of current assets and current liabilities shall be computed in accordance with generally accepted accounting principles consistently applied.

4.3 Borrower's debt to tangible net worth ratio (the relationship of current and total indebtedness to tangible net worth) shall not exceed
_____. For purposes of this Agreement, "tangible net worth" shall mean the aggregate book value of the assets of the Borrower (after deduction therefrom of all applicable reserves and allowances) minus (a) total liabilities, (b) any write-up in the value of assets occurring after the date hereof, and (c) all intangibles including but not limited to goodwill, leasehold improvements, patents, trademarks and the like.

4.4 Borrower's tangible net worth will not be less than $

4.5 Borrower will maintain compensating demand deposit account balances of at least_____of the outstanding loan balance. If such balances are not maintained, Borrower will be charged a deficiency fee equal in amount to the product of (X) the difference between the required compensating balance and the balance maintained, and (Y) the rate stated in the note of even date herewith for the number of days actually elapsed based on a 360 day year.

4.6 Borrower will furnish to Bank within ninety days after the close of each fiscal year of Borrower, a balance sheet of Borrower as of the close of such year and an income statement and statement of retained earnings for such year for Borrower (or if Borrower is an individual, for Borrower's business) certified by independent public accountants satisfactory to Bank; will furnish to Bank unaudited balance sheet and operating figures for each_____within thirty days after the end of each of said periods, and such other data as Bank may request; and will at all times permit representatives of Bank to inspect and make extracts from Borrower's books and records.

4.7 Borrower will maintain its books and records relating to its financial affairs at all times in accordance with, and all financial statements provided for herein shall be prepared in accordance with, generally accepted accounting principles consistent with those applied in preparation of the financial statements referred to in Paragraph 3.

4.8 Borrower will not pay any dividends on any class of capital stock or make any other distribution or payment on account of or in redemption of capital stock, or permit any withdrawals from or distributions of the assets of Borrower, or if Borrower is an individual, the business assets of Borrower, except as salary or compensation for services rendered after the date hereof; provided, however, that total payment for services rendered (in cash or otherwise and including dividends, withdrawals, distributions, salary and compensation) in any month to the following may equal but shall not exceed the following amounts:

Name	Monthly Amount

4.9 Borrower will maintain financially sound and reputable insurers, insurance with respect to Borrower's properties and business against such casualties and contingencies and in such types and such amounts as shall be in accordance with sound business practices.

4.10 Without the prior written consent of Bank, Borrower will not:

4.10.1 Incur, assume or permit to exist indebtedness for borrowed money except from the bank.

4.10.2 Sell, factor or borrow on the security of Borrower's accounts receivable with or without recourse, guaranty, endorse (other than for collection or deposit in the regular course of business) or become or remain liable in respect of any indebtedness, obligation or liability of any other person, firm or corporation or permit any such secondary responsibility to exist;

4.10.3 Create or permit to exist any mortgage, pledge or other lien or encumbrance on any of Borrower's property except (i) those arising from attachments or similar proceedings, pending litigation, judgments or taxes or assessments whose validity or amount is currently being contested in good faith by appropriate proceedings and for which adequate reserves have been established and maintained in accordance with generally accepted accounting principles, or taxes and assessments which are not due and delinquent; (ii) liens of carriers, warehousemen, mechanics and materialmen and other like (iii) pledges or deposits made in connection with workmen's compensation, unemployment or other insurance, old age pensions or other social security benefits, and good faith deposits in connection with tenders, contracts or leases to which Borrower is a party, or deposits to secure, or in lieu of, surety, penalty or appeal bonds, performance bonds and other similar obligations; (iv) encumbrances consisting of easements, rights of way, zoning restrictions, restrictions on the use of real property and similar encumbrances and minor irregularities in title; (v) landlord's liens under leases; and (vi) in favor of Bank.

4.10.4 Purchase or acquire any securities of or make any loans or advances to or investments in any person, firm or corporation except obligations of the United States government or any agency of the United States government or certificates of deposit issued by any one of the fifty largest banks in the United States;

4.10.5 Merge or consolidate or sell or dispose of all or a portion of Borrower's assets other than in the ordinary course of business, or in any way or manner alter Borrower's capital structure, including the sale, transfer or redemption of any shares of the Borrower.

4.10.6 Hire or discharge any officer or retain the services of any independent contractor or professional, except in the ordinary course of business and only where the management of the Borrower is not materially affected or changed.

4.10.7 In any twelve month period spend or become obligated to spend any sum in excess of_____ Dollars ($_____) for the acquisition, construction or installation of properties to be carried in Borrower's books as fixed assets. If left blank, this provision is not applicable.

4.10.8 Incur or assume rental obligations for any current or future period of twelve consecutive months under leases of real or personal property aggregating more than $_____or aggregating more than $_____ _____at any one time outstanding.

5. The loan and any and all other obligations of Borrower to Bank, direct or indirect, absolute or contingent, due or to become due, now existing or hereafter arising (the "Obligations") shall at Bank's option become immediately due and payable without notice or demand at any time after (a) default in the payment or performance of any Obligation; (b) default in the observance by Borrower of any

of the terms of this Agreement; (c) death, dissolution, termination of existence, insolvency, business failure, appointment of a receiver of any part of the property of, assignment for the benefit of creditors by, or the commencement of any proceedings under any bankruptcy or insolvency laws by or against Borrower or any party secondarily liable under any of the Obligations.

6. Any deposits or other sums at any time credited by or due from Bank to Borrower and any securities or other property of Borrower in Bank's possession may at all times be held and treated as security for payment of the Obligations. In the event any one or more of the events of default set forth in Paragraph 5 shall have occurred or be continuing, then regardless of the adequacy of any collateral, any deposits or other sums credited by or due from Bank to Borrower may be set off against any and all of the Obligations.

7. Borrower will at all times execute and deliver such further instruments and take such further action as may reasonably be requested by Bank in order to carry out the intent and purposes of this Agreement.

8. No failure or delay on Bank's part in exercising any right hereunder shall operate as a waiver thereof or any other right. No waiver hereunder shall be effective unless in writing and a waiver on any one occasion shall not be a waiver of any right or remedy on any future occasion.

9. In case of a default in the performance of the Obligations, Borrower will pay to Bank such further amount as shall be sufficient to cover the cost and expense of collection including (without limitation) reasonable attorneys' fees and expenses.

10. This Agreement shall be deemed to be a sealed contract under the law of Massachusetts and shall be construed in accordance with such law.

11. Borrower agrees to additional provisions as follows:

_____
_____
_____
_____
_____
_____
_____
_____
_____

IN WITNESS WHEREOF, Borrower has executed and delivered this Loan Agreement this_____
day of_____, 19_____.

_____

_____

SECURITY AGREEMENT

_____
NAME

_____
STREET AND NUMBER   CITY   STATE

(hereinafter called "Debtor"), hereby grants to THE FIRST NATIONAL BANK OF BOSTON (hereinafter called "Bank"), to secure the payment of $_____ as provided in the Debtor's note(s) of even date herewith and also to secure the payment and performance of all other obligations of Debtor to Bank, whether direct or indirect, absolute or contingent, due or to become due, now existing or hereafter arising (all of the foregoing, including said notes, being hereinafter called the "Obligations"), a security interest in the following personal property of Debtor and any and all additions, substitutions, accessions and proceeds thereto or thereof (all of the same being hereinafter called the "Collateral"):

Debtor hereby warrants and covenants that—
1. The Collateral will be kept at_____ until such time as written consent to a change of location is obtained from Bank.

2. Except for the security interest granted hereby, Debtor is the owner of the Collateral free from all encumbrances and will defend the same against the claims and demands of all persons. Debtor will not pledge, mortgage or create, or suffer to exist, a security interest in the Collateral in favor of any person other than Bank, and will not sell or transfer the Collateral or any interest therein without the prior written consent of Bank.

3. The Collateral shall remain personal property irrespective of the manner of its attachment to any real estate. If the Collateral is attached to real estate prior to the perfection of the security interest granted hereby, Debtor will on demand of Bank furnish to Bank a disclaimer or disclaimers, signed by all persons having an interest in the real estate, of any interest in the Collateral which is prior to Bank's interest. Debtor will notify Bank in writing of any intended sale, mortgage or conveyancy of any real estate to which the Collateral is at any time attached, and will give written notice of the terms and conditions of this agreement to any prospective purchaser, mortgagee, grantee or other transferee of the real estate or any interest therein.

4. Debtor will immediately notify Bank in writing of any change in address from that shown in this agreement, shall at all reasonable times and from time to time allow Bank, by or through any of its officers, agents, attorneys or accountants, to examine, inspect or make extracts from Debtor's books and records, and shall do, make, execute and deliver all such additional and further acts, things, deeds, assurances and instruments as Bank may require more completely to vest in and assure to Bank its rights hereunder or in any of the Collateral.

5. Debtor will keep the Collateral at all times insured by such insurance as Bank may from time to time require, and in any event and without specific request by Bank, will insure the Collateral against fire, including so-called extended coverage, theft, and, in the case of any motor vehicle, collision, all insurance to be with such insurance companies as Bank shall approve, with loss thereon to be payable to Bank and Debtor as their respective interests may appear. All policies of insurance shall provide for not less than ten days' notice of cancellation or change in form to Bank and, if requested by Bank, shall be delivered to and held by it until all of the Obligations have been fully performed.

6. Debtor will keep the Collateral in good order and repair, and will not use the same in violation of law or any policy of insurance thereon. Bank may inspect the Collateral at any reasonable time, wherever located. Debtor will pay promptly when due all taxes and assessments upon the Collateral or for its use or operation or upon this agreement.

7. In its discretion, Bank may discharge taxes and other encumbrances at any time levied or placed on the Collateral, make repairs, thereof and place and pay for insurance thereon and pay any necessary filing fees. Debtor agrees to reimburse Bank on demand for any and all expenditures so made, and until paid the amount thereof shall be a debt secured by the Collateral. Bank shall have no obligation to Debtor to make any such expenditures nor shall the making thereof relieve Debtor of any default. Bank may act as attorney for Debtor in making, adjusting and settling claims under any insurance covering the Collateral.

8. Debtor may have possession and use of the Collateral until default. Upon the happening of any of the following events or conditions, namely: (a) default in the payment or performance of any of the Obligations, of any liability or obligation to Bank of any indorser, guarantor or surety of or for any of the Obligations, or of any covenant or liability contained or referred to herein or in any note, instrument, document or agreement evidencing any Obligation; (b) any representation or warranty of Debtor in this agreement or made to Bank by Debtor to induce it to enter into this agreement or to make a loan to Debtor proving false or erroneous in any material respect; (c) loss, theft, material damage, destruction, sale, or encumbrance of or to the Collateral, or the making of any levy thereon or seizure or attachment thereof by legal process; (d) death, dissolution, termination of existence, insolvency, business failure, appointment of a receiver of any part of the property of, assignment for the benefit of creditors by, or the commencement of any proceeding under any bankruptcy or insolvency laws by or against Debtor, or any indorser, guarantor or surety of or for any Obligation; (e) such a change in the management or ownership of Debtor as in the opinion of Bank increases its risk; thereupon, and as long as such default continues, Bank may without notice or demand declare all of the Obligations to be immediately due and payable, and Bank shall then have in any jurisdiction where enforcement hereof is sought, in addition to all other rights and remedies, the rights and remedies of a secured party under the Uniform Commercial Code of Massachusetts, including without limitation thereto the right to take immediate possession of the Collateral, and for the purpose Bank may, so far as Debtor can give authority therefor, enter upon any premises on which the Collateral, or any part thereof, may be situated and remove the same therefrom. Debtor will upon demand make the Collateral available to Bank at a place and time designated by Bank which is reasonably convenient to both parties. Bank will give Debtor at least five days' prior written notice of the time and place of any public sale of the Collateral or of the time after which any private sale thereof is to be made. From the proceeds of the sale, Bank shall be entitled to retain (i) all sums secured hereby, (ii) its reasonable expenses of retaking, holding, preparing for sale and selling, and (iii) reasonable legal expenses incurred by it in connection herewith and with such sale. No waiver by Bank of any default shall be effective unless in writing nor operate as a waiver of any other default or of the same default on another occasion.

9. Debtor waives demand, notice, protest, notice of acceptance of this agreement, notice of loans made, credit extended, collateral received or delivered or other action taken in reliance hereon and all other demands and notices of any description. With respect both to the Obligations and the Collateral, Debtor assents to any extension or postponement of the time of payment or any other indulgence, to any substitution, exchange or release of collateral, to the addition or release of any party or person primarily or secondarily liable, to the acceptance of partial payment thereon and the settlement, compromising or adjusting of any thereof, all in such manner and at such time or times as Bank may deem advisable. Bank shall have no duty as to the collection or protection of the Collateral or any income thereon, nor as to the preservation of rights against prior parties, nor as to the preservation

of any rights pertaining thereto beyond the safe custody thereof. Bank may exercise its rights with respect to the Collateral without resorting or regard to other collateral or sources of reimbursement for liability. Bank shall not be deemed to have waived any of its rights upon or under the Obligations or the Collateral unless such waiver be in writing and signed by Bank. No delay or omission on the part of Bank in exercising any right shall operate as a waiver of such right or any other right. A waiver on any one occasion shall not be construed as a bar to or waiver of any right on any future occasion. All rights and remedies of Bank on the Obligations or the Collateral, whether evidenced hereby or by any other instrument or papers, shall be cumulative and may be exercised separately or concurrently.

10. This agreement and all rights and obligations hereunder, including matters of construction, validity and performance, shall be governed by the law of Massachusetts. This agreement is intended to take effect as a sealed instrument.

IN WITNESS WHEREOF, Debtor has executed_____original counterparts of this agreement on this_____ day of_____, 19___.

SIGNED AND SEALED
IN THE PRESENCE OF   _____

By_____

_____

WITNESS

CHAPTER 6
Venture Capital

INTRODUCTION: IN VOGUE AGAIN

Of all the forms of financing available to entrepreneurs, venture capital is probably the most glamorous. After all, the companies that attract venture capital are thought by the professional investors who run venture-capital firms to have the best chances of becoming the next generation of Xeroxes, IBMs, and Polaroids.

From a short-term operating viewpoint, venture capital also has appeal to entrepreneurs. It is typically an investment—risk money—which is totally unsecured and doesn't have to be repaid in regular installments like bank loans or other debt arrangements. Thus, companies which obtain venture capital usually don't have the immediate financial pressures they would have if the same money were borrowed; in some cases, venture-capital firms have taken to making their financings in combinations of loans and investments.

For all the glamor and financial luxury venture capital affords, though, it usually poses a serious dilemma for entrepreneurs who seek it out. That is because in exchange for venture capital, entrepreneurs must give the venture capitalists a sizable chunk of their companies—often up to 70 percent or 80 percent ownership. Giving up most of the ownership of a company with excellent growth potential to strangers waving a wad of money is a painful experience for most business owners.

It is an experience that is becoming increasingly commonplace in the 1980s, however. After having been in short supply during most of the 1970s, venture capital has suddenly become more available than at any time since the go-go days of the 1960s, when it seemed as if anyone with an idea for a new business could obtain venture capital.

An estimated $1 billion became available for venture-capital investments in start-up and existing businesses during 1981, versus less than $50 million four years earlier, according to *Venture Capital Journal.*

As a consequence, the number of venture-capital investments seem certain to continue an upward trend that already became apparent during the late 1970s. A survey of fifty-five private venture-capital firms—only about one fourth of the private firms in existence—sponsored by the National Venture Capital Association, a trade group, showed them making 600 venture-capital investments worth $244 million in 1979, versus only 252 investments worth $83.9 million in 1977.

What's more, a wider variety of small companies seems likely to qualify for venture capital than has in years. Venture capital, during the 1970s, at least, became identified nearly entirely with well-established high-technology companies. Now, though, ". . . venture capitalists are taking a fling in a variety of enterprises, ranging from start-ups in electric wiring and cable television to leveraged buyouts in direct mail firms and Hawaiian jewelry," reported the October 1980 issue of *Venture.* That doesn't mean the venture capitalists are doing a complete about-face; most of the twenty we interviewed say they still tend to be most receptive to high-technology companies, though they admit their horizons are definitely expanding.

Why the sudden availability of funds for venture capital? For one thing, a reduction in the capital gains tax in 1978 made the potential profits from venture-capital investments more attractive to the wealthy families, private investors, insurance companies, and others who make funds available to venture-capital firms. In addition, a liberalizing of federal pension regulations in the late 1970s made it easier for pension funds to commit money to venture-capital investments. And finally, the increase in stock market prices and resulting interest by the public in new stock issues enabled venture-capital firms to sell their investments to the public at sizable profits; the firms could then use the profits for investments in other start-up and existing businesses.

WHO SHOULD SEEK VENTURE CAPITAL?

For all the changes going on in the area of venture capital that widen its availability, it still remains a very difficult form of financing to obtain. Venture capitalists are interested mainly in businesses and entrepreneurs who meet certain tough criteria.

For one thing, venture capitalists, unlike commercial lenders, are interested in businesses with growth potential. The faster the growth, the better. Venture capitalists make their money when they sell their investment—whether to the public via a stock offering, to large corporations, or back to the entrepreneurs who started the business. Most of those venture capitalists we interviewed indicated that their goals are for their investments to increase in value about 100 percent annually, so that after three years they've tripled their original investment, after five years they've quintupled it, and so on.

Venture capitalists also place a high premium on management quality. They are primarily interested in the previous experience of start-up entrepreneurs and owners of young businesses. Those entrepreneurs who have succeeded in other ventures or management positions are likeliest to pique the interest of venture capitalists. In the same vein, venture capitalists tend to be attracted to small businesses headed by teams of entrepreneurs with complementary business skills, rather than single-person operations.

In addition, venture capitalists want more than convincing talk from investment-seeking entrepreneurs—they want comprehensive business plans as well. Since venture-capital firms tend not to have formal application forms like commercial lenders, the business plan becomes the primary means of evaluating applicants. Those business plans which accentuate the qualifications of the chief managers and demonstrate a thorough understanding of markets stand the best chance of securing funds for entrepreneurs. (For details on putting together a business plan, see Appendix C.)

Because of the stringent guidelines venture capitalists use, most entrepreneurs who seek out venture capital come away empty-handed. Generally speaking, between 1 percent and 3 percent of all proposals and business plans received by venture capitalists are approved for funding, usually within three or four months. About 90 percent of requests are rejected in less than a day, say venture capitalists. The reasons for rejection are usually either inexperienced management, an inadequately skilled team, or a poor or nonexistent business plan, note the venture capitalists.

VENTURE-CAPITAL OPTIONS

For those entrepreneurs who feel confident enough about their business' growth potential and their own managerial abilities, there are many venture-capital options to pursue. All totaled, more than 600 venture-capital firms are in operation. Most make available financial and technical assistance to companies they back and operate nationally. They frequently team up in syndicates of three to eight firms when investments of more than several hundred thousand dollars are required. Venture-capital firms break down into three basic categories as follows:

1. *Private firms,* which include between 200 and 250 professional partnerships and corporations backed by funds primarily from insurance

companies; pension funds; and wealthy families like the Rockefellers, Paysons, and Whitneys. Most of these firms consist of only a few partners, who are usually experienced investment analysts. They make the final investment decisions themselves, usually taking six weeks to three months on businesses they don't weed out in initial screenings.

Most of their investments are in the range of $300,000 to $800,000 apiece, though they will often go as low as $50,000 and as high as $3 million. The bulk of their investments tend to go into high-technology businesses, though they are open to consideration of most all areas except real estate and construction.

2. *Corporate venture groups,* which are set up by the nation's largest corporations as a way for them to develop fast-growing subsidiaries or new technologies for the future. About sixty major corporations—including Exxon, General Electric, Dow Chemical, and Monsanto—have set up venture-capital arms in recent years, but as of late 1980 only twenty to thirty of these were still active investors.

The number of active corporate venture groups has declined because they have generally fared poorly on a financial basis. According to a Harvard Business School study, private venture-capital firms have performed substantially better in choosing investments than have corporate groups. The reasons aren't totally clear, but seem to stem from the inexperience of corporate venture analysts, big-company bureaucracies which delay and diffuse decision-making responsibility, and an inability of corporations to understand the needs and aspirations of entrepreneurs. For instance, some corporate groups insist on 90 percent or even 100 percent ownership of the businesses they invest in and expect the businesses to become corporate subsidiaries, regardless of what the entrepreneur-founders would like.

Some corporations are somewhat more enlightened, though, and have begun giving their venture groups more independence both in deciding which businesses to invest in and in extending investment terms to entrepreneurs. Stumbling on the right corporate group can provide entrepreneurs another advantage—access to large amounts of cash. Corporate groups have been known to invest between $10 million and $15 million in ventures they consider particularly promising.

3. *Small Business Investment Companies* (SBICs), which are private firms licensed and financed to a large extent by the Small Business Administration. SBICs must have a minimum of $500,000 of their own money (raised usually from corporate and individual investors) and are entitled to borrow up to four times that amount from the SBA. Slightly more than 300 SBICs are scattered around the country, some of them operated by the same corporations and investment groups which have private centure-capital firms.

Because SBICs have to pay back the money they borrow from the
SBA, with interest, they need to ensure that small businesses they invest
in are generating an immediate and continuing cash flow. The best way to
do that is to lend money rather than invest it, or to package financings as
combinations of debt and equity.

Because of the need for cash flow, only about one third of the nation's SBICs are actively involved in making equity-type investments. The
other two thirds or so limit themselves primarily to extending loans and
thus are really not venture-capital firms, but commercial lenders. The
lending policies of these SBICs are described in more detail on pp.
178–80 of Chapter 5, "Commercial Finance."

Those SBICs that make actual investments tend to be somewhat
more conservative in the kinds of companies they will fund than other
venture-capital firms. Such SBICs are interested in growth, but they are
also interested in stability; thus, they tend to avoid start-up situations. The
amounts available for investment are similar to amounts extended by private venture-capital firms—$300,000 to $800,000 on average, with as little as $50,000 and as much as $3 million invested.

In addition, about 100 Minority Enterprise Small Business Investment Companies (MESBICs) provide loans and investments to businesses owned by racial minorities; these firms are described in more detail on pp. 231–37 and pp. 241–47 of Chapter 7, "Assistance for
Minority Businesses."

The rest of this chapter is devoted to describing twenty of the nation's most active venture-capital firms, which we contacted individually.
The firms are divided into two broad sections based on whether they
make substantial investments in start-up businesses or concentrate on
existing businesses. In addition, several tables summarize the investment
policies of these twenty firms. We have also provided a listing of thirty additional active venture-capital firms; space and time limitations did not
allow a detailed breakdown of their investment policies. We did survey
those thirty firms, however, and the results are reported in table form
in the September 1981 issue of *INC.* magazine. (For a reprint, contact
INC. at the address listed on p. 375.)

We have undoubtedly left out of our listings many active and high-
quality venture-capital firms. Therefore, we have also included a listing of
the most reliable and useful directories and books on venture capital,
some of which comprehensively list all venture-capital firms. Readers
should also refer to a glossary of financial terms beginning on p. 391
and the outline of a venture-capital investment agreement in Appendix D.

We were aided considerably in developing our listing of venture-capital firms by Stanley Pratt, whose Capital Publishing Co. produces a
monthly journal, *Venture Capital Journal,* as well as a directory to venture-capital sources, listed at the end of this chapter.

SOURCES FOR START-UP BUSINESSES

As noted in the introduction, one of the more noteworthy venture-capital trends has been the increased availability of such funds to start-up entrepreneurs. A recent survey by the National Venture Capital Association of 287 venture-capital deals found that nearly one fourth involved start-ups; that was more than triple the 1974 rate. Our survey of twenty active venture-capital firms showed about half the firms making 35 percent or more of their investments in start-ups; indeed, three firms said 50–80 percent of their investments are in start-ups.

More than any other business owners, however, start-up entrepreneurs offered venture capital face the dilemma of giving up sizable chunks of their companies. Venture capitalists will usually demand in return for providing capital somewhere between 50 percent and 90 percent ownership of the new company, with 70 percent fairly typical.

TABLE I

Overview of Venture Capital Sources

	Private Venture Capital Firms	Small Business Investment Companies (SBICs)	Corporate/Industrial Venture Capitalists
Estimated ₦–1980	200–250	305+	Perhaps 60 in business; 20–30 active (Exxon, GE, Monsanto, 3M, Inco, etc.)
Principal objectives & motives	Capital gains 25–40% compounded after tax per year 5–10x original investment in 5–10 years	Capital gains Same range as private	Windows on technology; tap new talent; acquire new markets; spawn new suppliers; diversification; public relations; use surplus cash; philanthropy; capital gains
Typical size, range of investments	$300,000 to $4 million Survey av.: $700,000		$10–15 million not unusual
Stage of ventures sought	All stages 20–30% start-ups more common		Later stages; rarely start-ups; seeking markets of $100–200+ million
Outside approval of deals done by firm	Unusual, perhaps 10–12% of firms		Very common, 75% of decisions; review boards and directors

TABLE II

Overview of Company Characteristics

Venture Capital Source	Stages Funded*	Industry Preferred	Reg'd Size Potential
ARD	All	High-tech	None
1st Capital Corporation of Boston	All	None; do a lot of high-tech	None
Greylock Mgt. Corporation	All	High rate of innovation	No: "smaller" company range
The Palmer Organization	Up to pub. offering	High-tech	None
T. A. Associates	All	High-tech	None
Business Development Services Inc.	All	High-tech	Varies with industry
Oak Investment Partners	All; preferred early	High-tech	Varies with industry
Pioneer Investors Corporation	All	None; leaving RE	None
Sprout Group	Start-up; 2nd	High-tech	$1m minimum
DSV Associates	Start-up; 2nd	High-tech	None
Lubrizol Enterprises	All	High-tech chemical	$200m in 10–12 years
Continental Illinois	All	None; no RE	Varies with industry
1st Capital Corporation of Chicago	All	None	None

* *Note:* "All" excludes seed unless otherwise noted.

Geographic Preference	Start-ups Done Past 5 Yrs.	1979 New Deals/ Amount	1979 Portfolio Size	Number Proposals Rec'd Month	% Funded
U.S.	40%	3/$3m	17	20	1%
U.S.; N.E. if lead investor	40%	11/$2.7m	50	12 good	10%
U.S.; N.E. if young company	10%	NA	NA	12 good	5%
U.S.	30%	5/$2m	19	20 good	2%
U.S.; N.E. if young	10%	NA	NA	125	1%
U.S.; N.E. if leader	50% in 2	5/$4m	22	25	2%
N.E.	10%	8/$5m	8	40	<5%
U.S.	10%	8/$4m	25	10	2%
U.S.	10%	13/$17.4m	35	100	1%
U.S.	>80%	5/$1.6m	39	25	1%
U.S.	25%	3/$19m	4	100	<1%
U.S.	35%	8/$16m	NA	40	3%
U.S.	35%	15/$20m	64	150	<1%

TABLE II
Overview of Company Characteristics

Venture Capital Source	Stages Funded*	Industry Preferred	Reg'd Size Potential
NW Growth Fund	All	High-tech; no RE	None
Texas Capital Corporation	1st & 2nd	No RE, construction	$20m minimum
BankAmerica Capital Corporation	All	Manufacturing oriented, preferred electronics & computers	None
Brentwood Associates	All	High-tech, medical, energy	None
Mayfield Fund	All	None	None
Sutter Hill	All	Tech-oriented manufacturing companies	None
WestVen	All	Technology, manufacturing, services, distribution	$100–200m for start-ups

TABLE III
Typical Requirements

Venture Capital Source	Business Plan	In-place Team	Size of Initial Investment ($000s)		
			Min.	Max.	Avg.
ARD	Yes	Yes	400	1,000	700
1st Capital Corporation of Boston	Yes	Yes, will fill in	100	1,000	300
Greylock Mgt. Corporation	Yes	No; will fill in	250	1,200	600
The Palmer Organization	Yes	No	250	1,000	400
T. A. Associates	Yes	Yes; will fill in	500	3,000	1,500
Business Development Services Inc.	Yes	Yes; never fill in	250	2,000	NA

Geographic Preference	Start-ups Done Past 5 Yrs.	1979 New Deals/ Amount	1979 Portfolio Size	Number Proposals Rec'd Month	% Funded
"Backyard" for start-ups	15%	11/$NA	55	45	1%
U.S.	5%	4/$1.8m	22	10 good	5%
U.S.	2%	6/$16m	40	10	1%
U.S.	40%	16/$11m	16	30 good	3%
West Coast	35%	8/$8m	8	60	<2%
U.S.	50%	10/$6.5m	40	45	<2%
None	25%	13/$9m	21	50	2%

TABLE III
Typical Requirements

Range of Ownership Sought	Controlling 51%	ROI Desired
Varies	No	25% in 5 years
0–50%	No	25–35% in 5–10 years
Varies	No	No formula
<60%	No	No formula
Varies	No	25–35% in 5 years
<50%	No	40% in 3–5 years

TABLE III
Typical Requirements

Venture Capital Source	Business Plan	In-place Team	Size of Initial Investment ($000s)		
			Min.	Max.	Avg.
Oak Investment Partners	Yes; founder's own	Yes	250	1,500	750
Pioneer Investors Corporation	Yes	Yes	17	10,000	400
Sprout Group	Yes	Yes	1,000	None	NA
DSV Associates	No	No	100	500	300
Lubrizol Enterprises	Yes	No, though preferred	150	15,000	NA
Continental Illinois	Yes, informal	Yes; will fill in	200	1,000	NA
1st Capital Corporation of Chicago	Yes	Yes	1,000	None	NA
NW Growth Fund	Yes; will help	No; will fill in	250	1,500	600
Texas Capital Corporation	Yes, eventually	Yes; will fill in	250	600	400
BankAmerica Capital Corporation	Yes	Yes; will fill in	500	3,000	1,500
Brentwood Associates	Yes	Yes; will fill in	500	2,000	1,000
Mayfield Fund	Yes	Yes	50	1,000	750
Sutter Hill	Yes	Yes; will fill in	50	2,000	800
WestVen	Yes; will help complete	Yes; will fill in	400	1,800	500

TABLE IV
Structuring the Deal

Venture Capital Source	Approach Preferred	Time Between 1st Contact & Funds Commitment		
		Min.	Max.	Avg.
ARD	Directly or referred	3 wks.	13 mos.	6 wks.
1st Capital Corporation of Boston	Submit business plan	1 mo.	4 mos.	2.5 mos.

Range of Ownership Sought	Controlling 51%	ROI Desired
<60%	No	40% in 5 years
4–100%	Rarely	5–10x in 5–7 years
30–90%	Often	Flexible; 5–10 years
Varies	No	Flexible
Minimum 20%	No	25%; LT inv.
Varies	No	NA
Varies	No	Varies
Ltd. as SBIC	No	3–5x in 3–7 years
Varies	No	Varies; 7 years
Varies	No	No formula
Varies	Usually not	30–50% in 5–10 years
Varies	No	10x in 5 years
Up to 50%	No	10x in 5–7 years
10–30%, more for start-ups	Rarely	30% in 5–7 years

TABLE IV
Structuring the Deal

Preferred Instruments Debt Equity Warr. Capital Debt	Preferred Vehicle for Capital Gain	Buyback by Founders
Combination even convertible to CS	Don't care	Yes
X	Whatever makes sense	Yes

TABLE IV
Structuring the Deal

Venture Capital Source	Approach Preferred	Time Between 1st Contact & Funds Commitment		
		Min.	Max.	Avg.
Greylock Mgt. Corporation	Phone or letter	2 wks.	2 yrs.	—
The Palmer Organization	Don't care	1 mo.	3 mos.	6 wks.
T. A. Associates	Submit business plan	22 hrs.	NA	2 mos.
Business Development Services Inc.	Phone or letter	24 hrs.	NA	1 mo.
Oak Investment Partners	Submit business plan; no intermediaries	1 mo.	1 yr.	2 mos.
Pioneer Investors Corporation	Don't care	4 days	1 yr.	6 mos.
Sprout Group	Phone followed by written proposal	1 mo.	6 mos.	6 wks.
DSV Associates	Don't care	3 mos.	>1 yr.	5 mos.
Lubrizol Enterprises	Search out investors	5 mos.	2 yrs.	—
Continental Illinois	Don't care	1 mo.	4 mos.	2 mos.
1st Capital Corporation of Chicago	Prefer referral	1 mo.	3 mos.	2 mos.
NW Growth Fund	Don't care	2 mos.	8 mos.	3 mos.
Texas Capital Corporation	Don't care	45 days	120 days	75 days
BankAmerica Capital Corporation	Don't care	2 mos.	6 mos.	4 mos.
Brentwood Associates	Phone followed business plan	1 wk.	3 mos.	1½ mos.
Mayfield Fund	Submit business plan	2 wks.	2 mos.	2 mos.
Sutter Hill	Don't care	1 mo.	4 mos.	45 days
WestVen	Phone or brief written proposal	1 wk.	3 mos.	45 days

Preferred Instruments				Preferred Vehicle for Capital Gain	Buyback by Founders
Debt	*Equity*	*Warr.*	*Capital Debt*		
	X	X	X	Don't care; LT inv.	Never happ'd but OK
	CS	X	X	What's best for firm	Never happ'd but OK
X	CS if early	X	X	Depends on market	Yes, in SBIC only
X	CS+ PS	X	X	Depends on market	Yes
	PS annually			Usually merger	Yes
X		X		No preference	Yes but when considered to be unsuccessful business
No ST	X	X	X	Cash or marketable securities	Yes
	X			Merger or pub. offering	Discouraged
Combination generally convertible to CS				Whatever makes sense	Yes
	X		X	Whatever makes sense	Yes
	X			Whatever makes sense	Yes
	X	X	X	Going public	Not encouraged
X	PS	X	X	No preference	Will consider
X	X	X	X	No preference	Yes
	X	X	X	Merger or pub. offering	Usually not
X	X	X	X	Pub. offering	No
	CS			No preference	Never happ'd
	X		X	Depends on situation	Yes

Start-up entrepreneurs may have some negotiating leeway, though, as increasing amounts of venture capital become available and competition among venture capitalists for attractive opportunities heats up. If several venture capitalists express interest in a new business, the owners may be able to whittle down the amount of ownership they have to give up. The owners may also be able to arrange either some kind of combination debt-equity package that minimizes the amount of ownership turned over or else a buyback option that gives the owners first crack at repurchasing their ownership at some point in the future.

For start-up entrepreneurs, a prior managerial or entrepreneurial track record is paramount in gaining the interest of venture capitalists; entrepreneurs without a track record should look to other financing sources to get started, then several years after establishing their companies successfully, perhaps try for venture capital.

In addition to considering the nine venture-capital firms we identified as being very receptive to start-up businesses, entrepreneurs should also refer to the descriptions of the eleven firms which invest primarily in existing businesses, since those firms also invest at least somewhat in start-ups; a few even indicated they are attempting to increase the number of start-up investments they make.

American Research and Development
One Beacon Street
Boston, MA 02108
(617) 523-6411
A division of Textron, Inc.

American Research and Development (ARD) was started in 1946 as the country's first private venture-capital company. It prefers a balanced portfolio of start-ups, young businesses, and mature companies; it feels that too much staff time is spent working with start-ups if they predominate. Still and all, about 40 percent of ARD's investments during the past five years have been in start-ups.

ARD invests as little as $400,000 and as much as $1 million initially, with an average investment of about $700,000 in individual businesses. Its current industry preferences are high technology, including medical technology and computer-related businesses.

ARD typically takes about six weeks to make investment decisions. It relies heavily on its feelings about the entrepreneurs. Observes an official: "It comes down to gut feeling. We look for potential in people who have no operating experience; a lot are not managers when they come to us. We look for people who can recognize their own weaknesses."

Lack of prior operating experience in entrepreneurs doesn't sanction the absence of business expertise, though. "If a guy was a stock clerk wanting to put out a new video game, we're not going to pay attention to him," says the official. "We're looking for a combination of things: product concept as well as previous experience."

ARD bases its calculations for rate of return on a five-year time frame, but does not usually liquidate that soon. Rather, like many corporate venture-capital divisions, it looks for companies that might become suitable acquisitions for Textron.

Brentwood Associates
11661 San Vicente Boulevard (Suite 707)
Los Angeles, CA 90049
(213) 826-6581
Private ownership, with SBIC subsidiary

Between 40 percent and 50 percent of Brentwood Associates' recent investments have been start-ups. Initial investments have been as low as $100,000, although $500,000 is the minimum amount the firm likes to invest, and $2 million is not an unusual initial investment in a well-established business.

Brentwood has been focusing on energy-related companies in California, although it doesn't exclude any industries or geographic locations from consideration. Brentwood funds an average of one of the thirty or so serious proposals it considers each month, which are screened from around 100 inquiries. Its decisions come in anywhere from a week to three months. An initial phone call to ascertain Brentwood's interest is preferred; a business plan is required before the first interview takes place.

Brentwood typically seeks a 30–50 percent annual return on its investment, compounded, in five to ten years, but is not rigid about this requirement. It prefers to realize its capital gains through mergers or public offerings, but occasionally allows buybacks by the founders based on market value (a prearranged formula agreement is not possible).

Business Development Services, Inc.
3135 Easton Turnpike
Fairfield, CT 06431
(203) 373-2067
Wholly owned subsidiary of General Electric Company

Business Development Services, Inc. (BDSI) prefers to fund companies it figures have $100 million annual sales potential, but it will fund lesser potential companies which show promise for developing new technologies. BDSI's initial investments typically range from $250,000 to $2 million; the firm has a preference for larger deals. BDSI usually funds high-technology businesses and will get involved in joint ventures with other venture-capital firms anywhere in the U.S. About 50 percent of the past two years' investments have been start-ups.

BDSI says it is unusually flexible, having made investment decisions in as little as twenty-four hours, though a month is more typical. It does have some guidelines, however. While it does not care how it is approached initially, its president says an entrepreneur "has to have a good excuse" if he or she doesn't have a completed business plan. Also, the business and technical members of the management team must be in place, preferably along with the marketing and manufacturing members as well. (BDSI says it will help find the finance person, if necessary, feeling that that is the least important slot.)

BDSI says it never seeks more than 50 percent ownership, but looks for ten times its investment in five years with start-ups and three to five times its investment in three to five years with more mature businesses. It looks for a positive cash flow in all its projects after a maximum of two years.

Continental Illinois Venture Corporation
231 S LaSalle St.
Chicago, IL 60693
(312) 828-8023
SBIC, wholly owned subsidiary of Continental Illinois Corporation

Continental Illinois Venture Corporation (CIVC) says it seeks "growth-oriented companies whose principals have prior management experience in their industry." Defining a start-up as a business having a developed product and an in-place management team (rather than "an engineer who has an idea"), CIVC says 40 percent of its investments have been in start-ups over the past five years.

Initial investments have ranged from $200,000 to $10 million, depending on the stage of the business. Its financings generally include the issuance of convertible subordinated debt and convertible equity, although the firm will sometimes accept all common stock as well.

CIVC says it can make a financing commitment in two weeks. CIVC likes some kind of financing commitment from entrepreneurs it backs, depending on their situations. A CIVC official also becomes an active board member of all portfolio companies.

CIVC's current industry preferences include manufacturers, wholesalers, retailers, service companies, and jobbers; high-technology ideas with operative prototypes are considered. CIVC bought into Apple Computer in 1978 and recently became heavily invested in a chain of retail stores that sell videotape and large-screen TVs.

DSV Associates
221 Nassau St.
Princeton, NJ 08540
(609) 924-6420
Limited partnership

Of a recent succession of thirty-nine investments DSV Associates made, thirty-four were in start-ups. It prefers to make initial investments ranging from $100,000 to $500,000 and will take the lead in syndications for larger investments. DSV is especially receptive to start-ups exploiting technology involved in digital electronics, molecular biology, and efficient energy use. The firm will often help in formulating the final business plan and filling out the management team, besides investing funds, when it has been presented with only a concept and some capital. In these cases especially, track record is important. "I want to bet on the guy who has shown the ability to win," says an official. "It's safer to start a company with him."

DSV doesn't seek absolute voting control, feeling that the worst thing that can happen to a young company is for the venture capitalist to own too much of it. The firm always seeks in its agreements the power to change managements. DSV generally realizes its profits through mergers or public offerings, and frowns on buyback agreements for entrepreneurs.

First Capital Corporation of Boston
100 Federal St. (17th Floor)
Boston, MA 02110
(617) 434-2442
SBIC, wholly owned subsidiary of First National Bank of Boston

First Capital Corporation, New England's oldest SBIC, has historically emphasized investments in small- to medium-sized high-technology companies in electronics, broadcasting, and manufacturing. But an official says the company considers investments in all industries because "if you do one thing for long, you develop a bias." A recent funding was a start-up book publisher, carried out with a combination of debt and equity.

Of twenty-six new investments during the past five years, eleven have been in start-ups. First Capital Boston typically finances one of the twelve or so "serious" proposals it reviews each month, deciding in an average of two and a half months. Initial investments typically range from $100,000 to $1 million.

First Capital Boston requires a written business plan and prefers to see it before being otherwise contacted by entrepreneurs. It also requires a "significant" financial investment from entrepreneurs it backs ($10,000 out of a net worth of $50,000 is significant; $10,000 from a net worth of $1 million is not). If an entrepreneur has little or no net worth, his or her time commitment is important.

First Capital Corporation of Chicago
One First National Plaza (Suite 2628)
Chicago, IL 60670
(312) 732-5400
SBIC, wholly owned subsidiary of First Chicago Corporation

First Capital Corporation considers companies in all industries and areas of the country. Current investments include a movie company, cable TV companies, timber holdings, and oil exploration and development companies.

First Capital Chicago's brochure says it will invest as little as $250,000 in a new company, but a company official said First Capital usually won't put up less than $1 million, because smaller investments aren't worth the time involved. In 1979, First Capital Chicago furnished $20 million to fifteen companies, including seven start-ups. The firm prefers syndicated deals to taking on the whole amount of funding itself. First Chicago specifies the means by which it will sell its holdings in the original funding agreement worked out with entrepreneurs.

Though First Capital Chicago doesn't insist on board representation of companies it funds, a representative attends board meetings and generally acts as an adviser or consultant to portfolio companies. Although entrepreneurs can contact the company directly, First Capital Chicago's "listening ability goes up when they have been referred to us," says the official.

Mayfield Fund
2200 Sand Hill Road
Menlo Park, CA 94025
(415) 854-5560
Limited partnership

The Mayfield Fund invests mostly in high-technology companies involved in the following areas: computer memory, earth station equipment for satellite communications, genetic engineering, energy, and warehouse computerization and automation. A Mayfield official says the firm is primarily interested in teams of superior managers of high-technology enterprises; the products or processes are secondary. Mayfield also frequently participates in joint ventures with other venture-capital firms.

Mayfield prefers common stock investments for start-up financings, but will consider both debt and equity financings for established businesses. Its investments range from $50,000 to $1 million. The firm takes anywhere from ten days to two months to make investment decisions. It typically funds one of the sixty or so proposals it reviews every month and limits its financings to West Coast businesses.

Mayfield seeks a return of ten times its investment in five years, preferably by the company's going public; buyback by the founders is not allowed. The firm prefers to be approached through the submission of a written business plan.

Sutter Hill Ventures
Two Palo Alto Square (Suite 700)
Palo Alto, CA 94304
(415) 493-5600
Limited partnership

Sutter Hill Ventures was the only venture-capital firm we contacted that said it actually prefers start-ups. Over half its investments in the past five years have been in start-ups, although it also likes to buy public companies in financial trouble. The firm looks for technology-oriented manufacturing companies and avoids companies in construction, food, hotels, motels, restaurants, motion pictures, and real estate.

Sutter Hill doesn't care how it is approached initially, although it does require a written business plan. It will assist in filling out an incomplete management team. Even though most of its investments happen to be located in the West, it says it has no geographic limitations on businesses it will consider.

Sutter Hill works closely with its companies, especially the start-ups, providing board membership and help in such areas as raising additional equity, strategy development, and long-range planning. The degree of equity it seeks varies with the risk undertaken, but the firm doesn't presently own more than 50 percent of any company. It seeks a return of ten times its investment in five to seven years, and says it has never had a founder who wanted to buy back Sutter Hill's share of the company.

SOURCES FOR EXISTING BUSINESSES

Venture capitalists usually feel most comfortable dealing with well-established, profitable, and growth-oriented small businesses, for the simple reason that they have demonstrated their ability to compete in the marketplace. The risks for the venture capitalists are thus reduced; in some cases, an infusion of cash is really all that is required for a small company to accelerate its growth.

The availability of increasing amounts of venture capital has sharpened the competition among venture capitalists for such solid and dynamic small companies. The competition is good news for business owners, since it gives them much more freedom of maneuver in negotiating terms with venture capitalists. A company with one to three years of successful operations behind it, an impressive management team, and a comprehensive plan for future growth may be able to obtain venture capital for somewhere in the range of 20 percent to 50 percent of ownership. A similarly successful company with more than three years of successful growth behind it might get a substantial amount of capital by giving up as little as 10 percent to 15 percent of ownership.

Business owners who find painful the idea of giving up substantial ownership—even 15 percent or 20 percent—are often in a good position to negotiate some kind of debt to reduce the amount of equity sold. Venture capitalists are increasingly interested in the immediate returns they get from financings that include a loan.

Owners of established businesses are especially advised to seek out venture-capital firms that suit the businesses' particular needs. A fast-growing maker of computers or medical instruments with annual sales of $10 million to $15 million and hopes of eventually going public should not seek out a small SBIC. On the other hand, a profitable but slower growing manufacturer of machinery with no interest in selling stock to the public and with smaller financing requirements might do best with a small SBIC.

The venture-capital firms which follow concentrate on investments in existing businesses. Owners of existing businesses should also refer to the listing of venture-capital firms in the section immediately preceding for start-up businesses, since those venture-capital firms also invest in established businesses.

BankAmerica Capital Corporation
555 California St.
San Francisco, CA 94104
(415) 622-2582
Has SBIC and limited partnership, both funded by BankAmerica Corporation

Founded more than twenty years ago, BankAmerica Capital Corporation seeks investments in high-technology, manufacturing-oriented concerns. It avoids companies in services, real estate, and motion pictures, but has no geographic constraints. It funds all stages of development; only about 2 percent of its investments during the past five years have been in start-ups.

The firm takes from two to four months to review proposals it considers seriously. In 1979, BankAmerica Capital invested $16 million in six businesses. Initial financings have ranged from $500,000 to $3 million each, averaging about $1.5 million. BankAmerica Capital is open to various debt-equity combinations.

BankAmerica Capital says it doesn't care how it is approached, but it does require a completed business plan and at least a core management team which it will help fill out. It looks for the classic factors in evaluating investments: experienced management teams, expanding markets, and distinctive product lines. The range of ownership BankAmerica Capital seeks varies widely, but rarely exceeds 50 percent. BankAmerica Capital works closely with its companies; it recently invested in an established electronics manufacturer for 30 percent of common stock plus board membership.

Greylock Management Corporation
One Federal St.
Boston, MA 02110
(617) 423-5525
Private venture-capital firm

An official of Greylock Management Corporation said the firm looks for "good people with good ideas" at any stage of development. The well-known company has been funding an increasing number of start-ups over the past ten years; about 10 percent of its investments have been in start-ups in recent years.

Greylock prefers companies in industries undergoing high rates of innovation, such as medical equipment and communications businesses. No geographic or company-sized requirements are specified.

The company initially invests an average of $500,000 to $700,000, although it has provided as little as $250,000 and as much as $1.2 million. Greylock funds perhaps one of the ten to twelve proposals that receive its careful attention each month, taking anywhere from a few weeks to two years to make a commitment.

Greylock likes to examine written business plans, references, and evidence of the lead entrepreneur's track record. It does not require an in-place management team, though, and will work with companies to find the necessary people. The firm can be approached through a phone call or letter and often will contact companies it understands to be promising.

Lubrizol Enterprises
29400 Lakeland Boulevard
Wickliffe, OH 44092
(216) 943-4200
Wholly owned subsidiary of Lubrizol Corporation

Lubrizol Enterprises is a young corporate subsidiary that calls itself a business development group rather than a venture-capital company. It had funded only four businesses by the end of 1980—three of them existing businesses. Lubrizol Enterprises sought out all four businesses. Although it is currently getting 100 or so proposals a month because of recent publicity, Lubrizol says it is extremely selective and often looks for teams to implement ideas it originates. Lubrizol likes to help formulate business plans and prefers a team to a single entrepreneur with a good idea but no practical experience. The company prefers that entrepreneurs invest at least $50,000, but that's not a strict rule. It looks for its early-stage investments to break even in three to four years.

In 1979, Lubrizol invested $19 million in three companies, including $15.2 million for 23.5 percent of Genentech, Inc.

Northwest Growth Fund, Inc.
960 Northwestern Bank Building
Minneapolis, MN 55402
(612) 372-8770
SBIC, wholly owned subsidiary of Northwest Bancorporation

Also owns:

Cascade Capital Corporation
1300 SW Fifth Ave. (Suite 3018)
Portland, OR 97201
(503) 223-6622

Central Investment Corporation of Denver
1108 15th St. (Suite 811)
Denver, CO 80202
(303) 825-3351

Since it was founded in 1961, Northwest Growth Fund (NWGF) has invested over $50 million in more than 150 companies. It is one of the relatively small number of SBICs that always seeks an equity position, using convertible subordinated debentures, convertible preferred stock, subordinated debt with warrants, and common stock. A typical investment ranges from $250,000 to $600,000, although NWGF can invest up to $1,100,000 in a single company and will act as a lead investor with other venture-capital companies to raise a larger amount.

NWGF funds all stages of development, from start-ups (around 10 percent to 15 percent in the last five years) through well-established companies. Although around 60 percent of its investments are in high-technology firms, NWGF will look at anything except real estate, and its portfolio has included an amusement park, an iron foundry, a large-scale scientific computer manufacturer, and recently the Sesame Street Touring Company and a Mexican restaurant chain. NWGF prefers to realize its capital gains through public offerings. It funds perhaps one of the forty to fifty proposals it receives each month. NWGF prefers to fund only local start-ups on its own, but will participate with other firms in joint ventures in any other geographic location.

In addition to a written business plan including resumes and personal histories of principals (and, from ongoing firms, an audited financial statement), Northwest looks for flexibility and openness on the part of the applying entrepreneurs toward the investors. The firm doesn't care how it is approached initially. NWGF looks for a return of three to five times investment in three to seven years.

Oak Investment Partners, Inc.
2 Railroad Place
Westport, CT 06880
(203) 226-8346
Limited partnership

Oak Investment Partners prefers young companies in high-technology industries with national or international market potential. About 90 percent of its recent investments have been in existing companies, mostly in the office automation and data communications industries. Oak prefers to take common or preferred stock for up to 60 percent ownership, with initial investments ranging from $250,000 to $1.5 million.

The firm generally acts on proposals within two months, accepting perhaps one or two of the forty it considers each month. It prefers to receive a business plan written by the founder before conducting any interviews.

Typical recent fundings have included a computer-aided design equipment start-up in which Oak invested $1.5 million in return for 60 percent ownership.

The Palmer Organization
183 Essex St.
Boston, MA 02111
(617) 423-4355
Limited partnership

The Palmer Organization prefers young high-technology firms. About 60 percent of its investments are in New England and about three quarters in high-technology firms.

Palmer funds perhaps one of the twenty "worthy" proposals it sees each month, usually acting in about six weeks. The company buys up to 60 percent of companies it invests in. Palmer frowns on buyback agreements with entrepreneurs but has no specific prohibition against such agreements.

Pioneer Investors Corporation
One Battery Park Plaza
New York, NY 10004
(212) 248-2759
Privately held SBIC and partnership

Pioneer Investors Corporation says it is interested in all stages of financing, although about 90 percent of its investments in the past five years have been in existing businesses. It claims no preferred industries; it recently provided $250,000 to a very-early-stage manufacturer of laser surgical systems. It has provided as little as $17,000 and as much as $10 million in a single investment; typical initial investments range from $300,000 to $500,000. It uses debt-equity combinations for financing and looks for a return of five to ten times its investment in five to ten years. Pioneer typically funds two or three of the 120 proposals it evaluates each year. It takes anywhere from four days to a year to respond, although six months is an average length of time.

Pioneer has between 1 percent and 100 percent ownership in its various investments, depending on the situation, but rarely seeks a controlling interest. The company will consider buybacks by founders, but feels the investment was not a success if this occurs, reasoning that the founders would not be able to afford to buy Pioneer out if the company grew as anticipated.

Sprout Group
140 Broadway
New York, NY 10006
(212) 943-0300
Limited partnerships

Sprout Group prefers well-established companies—more than 90 percent of its investments over the past five years have been in existing businesses. But the percentage going to start-ups is likely to increase, according to an article in the January 28, 1980, issue of *Fortune* magazine, because Sprout discovered that the $13 million it invested in start-ups up to 1979 returned 37 percent annually, more than twice the average yield of the $49 million put into later-stage deals.

The firm generally makes a minimum investment of $1 million, usually for a controlling interest. Each new investment is assigned to a Sprout staff member, who works closely with the company's management, setting stringent performance goals and maintaining an active role in company management. Unlike many other venture-capital firms, Sprout avoids joint ventures with other firms and generally maintains a low profile in the venture-capital industry.

Sprout says it prefers to be approached via a phone call followed by a written proposal. It prefers high-technology businesses and recently financed a recombinant DNA firm and several industrial component manufacturers. Sprout typically funds one of the 100 proposals it receives each month, taking an average of six weeks to reach a decision.

T. A. Associates
111 Devonshire St.
Boston, MA 02109
(617) 725-2300
Management of several partnerships and an SBIC

T. A. Associates concentrates on well-established companies, though it plans to increase its start-up investments to more than 10 percent. It invests from $500,000 to $3 million ($1.5 million is typical) in a range of industries anywhere in the country. Recent investment areas include data communications, computer software, cable TV, data-based management companies, instrumentation, and process control.

T. A. Associates requires a knowledgeable management team that knows the market for its product and has a detailed marketing plan as part of the business plan. It funds from one to three of the 100 to 150 proposals it sees each month, many of which it solicits.

T. A. Associates accepts annual returns of between 20 percent and 25 percent compounded on an SBIC investment, but it seeks a minimum of 30 percent in a private equity investment. It prefers to realize its gain by going public or otherwise selling its interests within five years. Buyback by founders is possible in an SBIC deal only. T. A. prefers that interested companies submit a written business plan before seeking a meeting with the staff.

Texas Capital Corporation
2424 Houston Natural Gas Building
Houston, TX 77002
(713) 658-9961
SBIC, wholly owned subsidiary of Telcom Corporation

Although it prefers existing businesses with annual revenues of more than $2 million, the Texas Capital Corporation will fund an occasional start-up; around 5 percent of the past five years' initial investments have been start-ups. The firm has a diversified portfolio, excluding only real estate and construction businesses from consideration. Texas Capital Corporation has no geographic constraints and will invest between $250,000 and $600,000 in firms that have a minimum sales potential of $20 million. The company says it takes seriously about ten proposals a month and funds an average of one every other month, typically taking two and a half months to act on a proposal. In 1979, the firm invested $1.8 million in four businesses.

This SBIC historically has preferred debt-equity packages as its investment vehicle, although it sees a trend toward more use of stock. Texas Capital recently participated with other venture capitalists in a $3 million expansion of an oil-well service company, for which the venture-capital investors received one third of the company.

Texas Capital wants detailed financial statements and financial analyses, demonstrated or near-term profitability, and a clear competitive edge such as a proprietary product for its investments.

WestVen
555 California St. (Room 3325)
San Francisco, CA 94104
(415) 622-6864
Limited partnership

Although WestVen prefers technology-oriented enterprises, its port-folio of approximately twenty companies also includes food, insurance, and auto parts businesses. WestVen seeks equity investments, sometimes combined with loans, of around $500,000 initially and a total of $1 million eventually, although it has invested as much as $1.8 million in a single business. The partnership funds about a dozen of the 600 proposals it receives each year, taking anywhere from a week, where principals are well-known, to three months to make decisions. In 1979, the firm initially invested $9 million in thirteen businesses.

WestVen says it is flexible in achieving its desired 30 percent annual compounded return in five to seven years, claiming that it does not push companies to be acquired or go public; buyback by founders is generally possible, especially when WestVen has participated in a leveraged buyout.

Between 1976 and 1980, existing-business investments comprised 75 percent of activity and start-ups represented about 25 percent. In start-ups, WestVen looks for businesses that are not capital intensive and which offer potential revenues of $100 to $200 million a year. There are no geographic limitations. WestVen is an active investor and generally seeks board membership in its investments.

ADDITIONAL ACTIVE VENTURE-CAPITAL FIRMS

Allsop & Associates
3100 Oakland Road, NE
Cedar Rapids, IA 52402
(319) 363-7248

Allstate Insurance Company
Allstate Plaza
Northbrook, IL 60062
(312) 291-5736

Bessemer Securities Corporation
245 Park Ave.
New York, NY 10012
(212) 949-7813

Burr, Egan
(their West Coast office)
475 Sansome St.
San Francisco, CA 94123
(415) 396-4417

Burr, Egan, Deleage & Company
175 Federal St.
Boston, MA 02110
(617) 482-8020

Capital Southwest Corporation
12900 Preston Road (Suite 700)
Dallas, TX 75230
(214) 233-8242

The Charles River Partnership II
133 Federal St.
Boston, MA 02110
(617) 482-9370

Fidelity Venture Associates
82 Devonshire St.
Boston, MA 02109
(617) 726-0450

First Dallas Capital Corporation
P.O. Box 83385
Dallas, TX 75283
(214) 744-8050

Golder, Thoma & Co.
120 S LaSalle St.
Chicago, IL 60693
(312) 853-3322

Hambrecht & Quist
235 Montgomery St.
San Francisco, CA 94104
(415) 433-1720

Harrison Capital, Inc.
2000 Westchester Ave.
Harrison, NY 10650
(914) 253-7845

Heizer Corporation
20 N Wacker Drive
Chicago, IL 60606
(312) 641-2200

Hixon Venture Company
341 Milam Building
San Antonio, TX 78205
(512) 225-3053

Innoven Capital
Park 80 Plaza West 1
Saddlebrook, NJ 07662
(201) 845-4900

Institutional Venture Associates
3000 Sand Hill Road
Menlo Park, CA 94025
(415) 854-0132

Interwest Partners
235 Montgomery St.
San Francisco, CA 94104
(415) 391-1545

Kleiner, Perkins, Caufield & Byers
Two Embarcadero Center (Suite
2900)
San Francisco, CA 94111
(415) 421-3110

Carl Marks & Company, Inc.
77 Water St.
New York, NY 10004
(212) 437-7080

Massachusetts Capital Corporation
100 Federal St.
Boston, MA 02110
(617) 426-2488

Narragansett Capital Corporation
40 Westminster St.
Providence, RI 02903
(401) 751-1000

New England Enterprise Capital
Corporation
28 State St.
Boston, MA 02106
(617) 742-0285

Pathfinders Ventures, Inc.
One Corporate Center III (Suite
585)
7300 Metro Boulevard
Minneapolis, MN 55435
(612) 835-1121

Alan Patricof Associates, Inc.
One E 53rd St.
New York, NY 10022
(212) 753-6300

Republic Venture Group, Inc.
P.O. Box 5961
Dallas, TX 75222
(214) 653-5942

Research and Science Investors,
Inc.
405 Lexington Ave.
New York, NY 10017
(212) 986-7977

Schooner Capital Corporation
141 Milk St.
Boston, MA 02109
(617) 357-9031

Venrock Associates
30 Rockefeller Plaza (Room
5600)
New York, NY 10020
(212) 247-3700

Wells Fargo Investment Co.
475 Sansome St. (15th Floor)
San Francisco, CA 94111
(415) 396-3292

Welsh, Carson, Anderson & Co.
45 Wall St.
New York, NY 10005
(212) 422-3232

J. H. Whitney & Co.
630 Fifth Ave.
New York, NY 10020
(212) 757-0500

ADDITIONAL INFORMATION SOURCES

READINGS

Capital Publishing Corporation
Two Laurel Avenue, P.O. Box 348
Wellesley Hills, MA 02181
(617) 235-5405

Capital Publishing Corporation has long been recognized as the most authoritative source of information on the venture-capital industry, with its monthly *Venture Capital Journal,* reference books on business development, and seminars for entrepreneurs and investors. Capital Publishing has also recently developed an information services, research, and consulting division called Venture Economics, which uses a proprietary data base built up over the past twenty years. Venture Economics clients are generally investors looking at industry trends, but entrepreneurs should find the *Journal* and the book *Guide to Venture Capital Sources* extremely valuable.

Guide to Venture Capital Sources, 5th ed., by Stanley M. Rubel, 1981. $62.50.
Contains articles written by experts on such subjects as business plan preparation techniques, guidelines for working with venture capitalists, raising and using venture capital, going public. It also contains information on more than 600 venture-capital companies and more than sixty small-business underwriters.

Venture Capital Journal. $365/year.
Monthly bulletin of news and trends in business development; details on current financings.

Venture magazine publishes an annual directory of venture capitalists in a late-fall issue. For details on *Venture,* see pp. 375–76 in Appendix B.

ORGANIZATIONS

National Venture Capital Association
2030 M St., NW (Suite 403)
Washington, DC 20036
(202) 659-5756

The National Venture Capital Association is a trade association that lobbies on and monitors legislation and government regulations affecting the venture-capital industry. It has no information on how its members invest their funds, though, and its free membership directory lists only the names, addresses, and phone numbers of the approximately ninety members.

Western Association of Venture Capitalists
3000 Sand Hill Road (Bldg. 2, Suite 260)
Menlo Park, CA 94025
(415) 854-1322

This trade association's membership directory lists around seventy venture-capital firms located in the western half of the United States and gives information on levels of initial and total investment, states of funding, and industry preferences for each member.

National Association of Small Business Investment Companies
(NASBIC)
618 Washington Building
Washington, DC 20005
(202) 638-3411

NASBIC's free annual directory lists about 300 members and associates by geography, investment policy, and industry preferences, along with providing a brief overview of SBICs and MESBICs. The Association also encourages entrepreneurs to call or write it for additional information.

CHAPTER 7
Assistance for Minority Businesses

INTRODUCTION: LOOKING BEYOND STEREOTYPES

If there is an area of small business in which stereotypes are particularly prevalent, it is in the area of minority business. Two stereotypes seem to predominate.

One is the "George Jefferson" stereotype. George Jefferson is the hard-driving, fast-talking, immensely successful black entrepreneur of the television series "The Jeffersons." Through sheer determination and hard work, George Jefferson has built a thriving chain of dry-cleaning stores and has long since economically bypassed his onetime neighbor and racial nemesis Archie Bunker. The message is simple: by employing such determination and hard work, black entrepreneurs can be as successful as white entrepreneurs.

The other stereotype might best be referred to as the "government handout" stereotype. Minority entrepreneurs who are not so hard driving as George Jefferson, the stereotype has it, simply take advantage of federal handouts in the form of loans, procurement programs, and management assistance. Starting a business then becomes a snap, although a few recipients simply pocket the money and let their businesses fold, leading to widely reported scandals—again, according to the stereotype.

Not surprisingly, the reality is much different than the stereotypes would suggest. Despite the existence of many minority entrepreneurs who are quite as determined and industrious as the fictitious George Jefferson, and despite the availability of various forms of special federal assistance, racial minorities have simply not achieved the cumulative kind of business success their percentage representation in the population should produce.

STATE OF MINORITY BUSINESSES

According to an article by Richard America, a Small Business Administration official, which appeared in the May/June 1980 issue of the *Harvard Business Review*, "minority business receipts for 1978 were about $35 billion in a $2 trillion economy, or not quite 2% of total receipts." Mr. America projected that, even with increased government and corporate purchases from minority businesses, "minority receipts in 1982 may reach $75 billion in what will then be a $2.5 trillion economy, or perhaps 3% of total receipts." Considering that racial minorities comprise more than a quarter of the nation's population, such statistics suggest that minorities are significantly underrepresented in the business sector.

Another set of statistics that reinforces this unfavorable documentation regarding the importance of minority businesses to the country's economy comes from the annual listing of the 100 largest black companies as compiled by *Black Enterprise* magazine. According to the 1980 list, the largest black-owned company, a record production company, had annual sales of about $65 million, while the one-hundredth largest company on the list was an auto dealership with annual sales of $5.2 million. The largest company would not even come close to penetrating the annual *Fortune* magazine listing of the top 500 American companies, while the one-hundredth largest black-owned company is downright puny in the corporate scheme of things.

Moreover, according to Mr. America of the SBA and others who have studied minority businesses, the types of businesses that minorities tend to start are not always those with the best long-term prospects. Minorities seem to be attracted mostly to slow-growing, low-profit retail and service businesses, rather than the more promising manufacturing and high-technology businesses.

GOVERNMENT ASSISTANCE PROBLEMS

As much as minority entrepreneurs might wish for easily available federal assistance, the fact of the matter is that such help is available on only a limited basis and is frequently of dubious value when obtained. True, the federal government has a grab bag full of programs directed specifically to minority entrepreneurs. But the programs are often difficult to understand, in part because they tend to duplicate each other. According to a report on "Minority Business Development" presented to the 1980 White House Conference on Small Business by conference organizers, "There are numerous, perhaps too many, overlapping government programs to assist minorities to join the mainstream of American business."

In addition, the purposes and quality of the programs have been questioned. For instance, federal procurement programs have, in some cases, been accused of fostering excessive minority business dependence on government purchases, so that the businesses are sometimes unable to compete in the real world. And government-sponsored consultants are sometimes so poorly trained or inexperienced that their advice is either worthless or, according to some critics, just plain wrong.

As if all these difficulties were not enough, federal minority business financing programs have been plagued with the phenomenon of white-controlled minority "fronts": businesses with minority presidents and other officers that are actually owned by whites. Such businesses pass themselves off as minority businesses to obtain government loans and contracts, but the profits flow to the white owners; the effect is to deprive legitimate minority businesses of financing and sales.

As with most stereotypes, there are a few elements of truth in the minority business stereotypes. For enterprising minority entrepreneurs willing to endure the confusion and red tape that surrounds federal minority business assistance programs, useful financing, procurement, and consulting help can be obtained. And some signs have begun to appear which indicate that the process of obtaining federal assistance may become more orderly, because the government recently started a process of organizing its programs more logically. The government is concentrating its efforts on eliminating the overlapping and duplication of programs within the Small Business Administration (SBA) and the Commerce Department's Minority Business Development Agency (MBDA).

Richard America, in his *Harvard Business Review* article on minority business, described the changes this way:

> Under the new policy that is evolving, the SBA will continue financing, training, and counseling both would-be entrepreneurs and owners of small enterprises and will merge various government purchasing programs. But the MBDA will direct more of its management and technical assistance and possibly long-term financing toward larger minority businesses with more attention to manufacturing. In some cases these businesses may have sales of $5 million and more and, at least in a few instances, the potential to become publicly held. These substantial manufacturing operations will likely be acquired from public corporations or from private holders by groups of experienced minority entrepreneurs.

Besides the federal government's direct-aid programs for minority business, a number of quasi-public and private organizations and businesses exist that can assist minority businesses. These include government-assisted venture-capital firms, minority banks, minority trade associations, and minority consulting firms.

WHO QUALIFIES AS A MINORITY?

Before considering in more detail the specific sources of assistance available to minority businesses, a definition of just who qualifies as a minority entrepreneur might be in order. Generally speaking, those considered by the federal government to be minorities are blacks, Hispanics, American Indians, Aleuts, and Asian-Pacific Americans. But Congress left open the possibility of other groups qualifying as minorities when it amended an SBA program by providing that socially and economically disadvantaged groups and individuals include, "But [are] not limited to, black Americans, Hispanic Americans, Native Americans, and other minorities." Congress left the authority to designate other minorities as eligible for special programs with the SBA.

A number of white groups, such as Hasidic Jews, have attempted to qualify under the government's broad description of minorities as being a "socially and economically disadvantaged" group. The SBA ruled recently, however, that Hasidic Jews as a group do not qualify for minority assistance, though individual Hasidic Jewish businessmen might qualify if they proved they suffered financially from discrimination, according to an article in the July 1980 issue of *Black Enterprise* magazine. The effect of this decision is to leave relatively intact the government's traditional definition of minorities but to leave open the possibility of exceptions. The issue is a sticky one, and the government, not surprisingly, has shied away from making any all-encompassing or unalterable rules.

FEDERAL ASSISTANCE PREDOMINATES

The issue is an important one, however, because, for all the jumble and confusion of sources of assistance for minority business, the federal government remains the most substantial single source. It provides loans, largely through SBA programs. It provides consulting assistance through the SBA and the MBDA. And, through the SBA and a variety of other federal agencies, the government seeks to direct purchasing orders and contracts specifically to minority firms.

The federal government's hand also looms large in various programs and projects that involve private investors and businesses. For instance, the SBA provides investment assistance to bolster funds provided by private investors to create venture-capital firms known as Minority Enterprise Small Business Investment Companies (MESBICs). Also, a recent federal law requires white businesses which receive government contracts to direct some of the federal funds to minority companies.

OTHER ORGANIZATIONS GROWING

While various organizations and businesses oriented toward aiding minorities lack the financial resources of the federal government, such concerns are growing in importance. For example, members of the National Minority Supplier Development Center, an organization of corporations seeking to direct corporate purchases to minority business suppliers, bought more than $3 billion of goods and services from minority businesses in 1979, as compared with $86 million in 1972. Minority trade associations, too, are doing more in the way of offering consulting and other services to their members than they did in the past. In addition, at least a half-dozen states have programs designed to provide information, management assistance, and procurement awards to minority businesses. The programs vary widely in scope and competence. The states that have been identified as having such programs are Michigan, Minnesota, New York, Tennessee, Virginia, and Wisconsin. For more information, minority entrepreneurs should contact sources in those states listed in Chapter 4, "State and Local Government Assistance."

The remainder of this chapter is devoted to listing and describing specific federal government programs and other organizations and businesses that can be of particular help to minority businesses. Some programs can, of course, be utilized by all types of entrepreneurs, including minority businessmen. Those programs, which are described more fully elsewhere, are listed with a reference to the more detailed description.

The listings which follow may be broken down into two broad categories: those most appropriate for start-ups and those most appropriate for existing businesses. Some sources are available to both types of entrepreneurs; in such cases, descriptions are given appropriate to the type of entrepreneur under discussion, and cross-references are indicated as needed. As is the case for entrepreneurs in general, many more sources are applicable to existing minority businesses than to start up minority businesses.

FINANCING FOR START-UP BUSINESSES

Obtaining financing is probably the most difficult task facing any entrepreneur seeking to start or acquire a business, and it is usually even more difficult for minority entrepreneurs than for white entrepreneurs. Minority entrepreneurs often lack the business experience and training of their white counterparts and must deal with the additional problem of possible discrimination by white bankers and other private financing sources.

At the same time, though, the federal government has become increasingly sensitive to the financing problems of minority entrepreneurs and has established a few programs directed in significant part to minorities. The government has also sought to encourage agencies that make or guarantee loans to all entrepreneurs to direct more of their efforts to minorities.

Thus, federal agencies and the federally backed venture-capital program for minorities are the best potential sources for minority entrepreneurs seeking start-up financing. As is the case with entrepreneurs in general, the Small Business Administration offers the best overall hope of success to start-up minority entrepreneurs. Another agency that operates programs of potential aid to minorities starting or acquiring businesses is the Bureau of Indian Affairs. In addition, minority entrepreneurs should not overlook the various federal financing programs available to entrepreneurs of all races that are described in Chapter 3, "Federal Government Financing Sources." (See pp. 78–89.)

Minority start-up entrepreneurs should also explore the financing opportunities described throughout Chapter 5, "Commercial Finance," and on pp. 199–213 of Chapter 6, "Venture Capital."

SMALL BUSINESS ADMINISTRATION

Office of Financing
U. S. Small Business Administration
1441 L St., NW
Washington, DC 20416
(202) 653-6570

Information and assistance regarding SBA loans are also available from more than 100 local offices scattered among the nation's large- and medium-sized cities. (For a list of local offices, see Appendix A.) Minority entrepreneurs should seek out minority small-business development specialists, who offer guidance on seeking SBA assistance.

Regular Business Loans [Section 7(a) Program]

For many years, the SBA program of likeliest help to minority applicants was the Equal Opportunity Loan Program, which provided more liberal terms than conventional SBA loans. But that program, along with other special SBA programs, has been incorporated into the program of regular business loans, referred to by the SBA as its Section 7(a) program.

Even before this change, though, the 7(a) program of direct and guaranteed loans had established itself as an important source of minority business financing. In recent years, approximately 14 percent of the 25,000–30,000 loans generated and about 10 percent of the more than $3 billion available under this program have gone to minority entrepreneurs, according to federal statistics. Thus, between 3,500 and 4,000 loans, totaling more than $300 million annually, have gone to minorities. For further details on the 7(a) program's availability to start-up entrepreneurs, please see pp. 80–84 of Chapter 3, "Federal Government Financing Sources."

Construction Surety Bond Guarantee Program

Finally, an SBA program of immense potential to minority construction companies is the agency's program for guaranteeing surety bonds. The SBA can guarantee commercially issued surety bonds up to 90 percent on contracts valued up to $1 million. Surety bonds are really insurance policies to protect property owners if contractors fail to complete projects or to protect general contractors if subcontractors fail to complete their work. Small contractors, particularly minority-owned contractors, have encountered much difficulty in obtaining such bonding. Without it, though, construction companies cannot meet the requirements of most contracts. The effect of the SBA's program is uncertain; minority construction firms apparently encounter difficulties even with the SBA guarantees, since bonding companies tend to prefer dealing with large construction companies, which are rarely minority-owned.

BUREAU OF INDIAN AFFAIRS

Director
Office of Tribal Resources Development
Bureau of Indian Affairs
18th and C Sts., NW
Washington, DC 20245
(202) 343-5875

Information is also available from local BIA offices.

The Bureau of Indian Affairs (BIA) makes available loans of from $100 to more than $1 million for Indians on federal reservations to start or acquire businesses, or to expand existing businesses. Loans average about $100,000 and can be made either to Indian organizations for the purpose of starting businesses or lending money to individual Indians; or, alternatively, loans can be made directly to individual Indians. Individual Indians applying directly to the Bureau of Indian Affairs for such loans must document that they are members of federally recognized tribes and also must demonstrate that they are unable to obtain commercial financing.

The Bureau of Indian Affairs can also provide up to 90 percent guarantees of commercial financing, much the same way as does SBA. Applications must be filed at the local level. According to the Bureau, applicants can expect to be notified in sixty days whether or not their application has been approved, provided they furnished adequate financial information.

MINORITY ENTERPRISE SMALL BUSINESS INVESTMENT COMPANIES

Investment Division
Small Business Administration
1441 L St., NW
Washington, DC 20416
(202) 653-6848

or

American Association of Minority Enterprise Small Business
    Investment Companies
1413 K St., NW
Washington, DC 20005
(202) 347-8600

Up-to-date lists of Minority Enterprise Small Business Investment Companies (MESBICs) and limited information on investment policies can be obtained from both the above sources.

For minority entrepreneurs who seek to start or acquire businesses in such areas as manufacturing, high technology, the media, entertainment, retailing, and franchising, MESBICs are potential sources of either loans or investments funds. A MESBIC is a type of Small Business Investment Company (SBIC) that concentrates on investment in ventures owned by minority entrepreneurs. MESBICs thus are subject to SBA guidelines and eligible for SBA funding. (SBICs are described in more detail on pp. 178–80 of Chapter 5, "Commercial Finance," and pp. 197–98 of Chapter 6, "Venture Capital.")

Because MESBICs operate similarly to venture-capital firms, they place a heavy emphasis on entrepreneurs' past business experience. Those minority entrepreneurs who have demonstrated, either through their performances in large companies or through running their own businesses, that they have the expertise necessary to start or acquire a business, are likeliest to win MESBIC backing.

Though MESBICs have been in existence since 1970, they have only in recent years become reliable sources of capital for minority entrepreneurs. In the past few years, MESBICs have made between 450 and 475 investments annually, totaling approximately $30–35 million. According to the American Association of MESBICs, about 40 percent of the funds go to start-up businesses in a variety of areas, including manufacturing, retail establishments, and service businesses.

Many MESBICs established in the early 1970s folded, in part because they did not have enough funds and in part because their investment philosophy was too oriented toward being socially responsible, hence allowing for investments in ventures that had high-minded goals but were extremely risky. The federal government, which lends money to MESBICs through the SBA, has in recent years attempted to solve the problem of undercapitalization by requiring that organizers of MESBICs—which can include wealthy individual investors, corporations, banks, and other organizations—put up a minimum of $500,000, instead of the $150,000 originally required. The MESBICs can receive up to four times the amount of money they put up in the form of SBA loans. The MESBICs themselves have also tended to solve the problem of too many do-gooder investments by becoming hardheaded evaluators of investment proposals. This evolution has occurred as MESBIC staffs have become more experienced in evaluating possible investments.

In recent years, corporations in particular have seen increased promise in minority business investments and have established large MESBICs with several million dollars of private funds. "Super MESBICs" is how Richard America of the SBA referred to these corporate enterprises in his May/June 1980 *Harvard Business Review* article on minority businesses.

Super MESBICs seek to invest in fast-growing, highly profitable ventures in such areas as high technology and entertainment. In late 1979, four MESBICs helped put together a package of approximately $5.3 million in cash, loans, and services for a new record company started by a minority entrepreneur who had a successful track record in that business area. More recently, seven MESBICs raised $6 million toward the $28 million purchase of a Philadelphia television station by minority entrepreneurs.

The main criticism leveled at MESBICs is similar to that directed at SBICs in general—that they tend to rely too heavily on debt, rather than equity investments. Loans are a way of ensuring an immediate and steady income that helps MESBICs defray their operating expenses and repay their own SBA loans; for minority companies financed by MESBICs, though, too heavy a debt load can be disastrous during periods when business slows down. This criticism is not meant to imply that MESBICs make no equity investments, because they do. The Super MESBICs in particular are usually sufficiently capitalized by their corporate overseers so that they do not have to worry about generating immediate income on their investments. Minority entrepreneurs considering approaching MESBICs for financing should approach them much as they would any venture-capital firm. For more details on how venture-capital firms operate and act on investment proposals, please see Chapter 6, "Venture Capital."

At last count, there were well over 100 MESBICs scattered around the country, each having anywhere from $150,000 to several million dollars of capital; the amounts actually invested and the amounts available for new investment cannot be determined for each MESBIC; nor can the inclination of each individual MESBIC to invest in start-ups. Generally speaking, the larger the MESBIC, the likelier it will be to make investments outside its immediate geographic area. The largest MESBICs are national in scope and thus will consider minority entrepreneurs regardless of their location. MESBICs will also frequently combine resources to fund companies. And most either provide consulting or will arrange for competent consultants to aid entrepreneurs in running their companies.

We attempted to identify those MESBICs most likely to be receptive to backing entrepreneurs who want either to start businesses or acquire existing businesses. Particularly helpful in providing leads in that regard was Richard America of the SBA. Also of help were several articles dealing with MESBICs in *Venture* magazine. The American Association of MESBICs, a trade group that represents MESBICs, provided a few suggestions, although we found that the organization was quite reluctant to be specific about which MESBICs are doing what; whether the reluctance stemmed from ignorance, laziness, or privacy concerns is unknown, however. The SBA's investment division, which oversees the licensing and funding of MESBICs, was similarly recalcitrant about identifying the MESBICs most likely to be helpful to start-up entrepreneurs.

In most cases, we telephoned the MESBICs directly, though in a few cases data supplied by the SBA's listing of MESBICs was used. This listing includes the total capitalization and broad investment policies of each MESBIC. In most cases of MESBICs with incomplete investment information, resistance from the MESBIC about supplying the information or inability to contact appropriate officials was encountered. Those MESBICs that were determined to be amenable to the possibility of funding start-up entrepreneurs are listed below. Start-up entrepreneurs should also refer to the listing of MESBICs inclined most toward backing existing businesses on pp. 241–45, however, since those MESBICs occasionally back start-ups as well.

Alliance Enterprise Corp.
1616 Walnut St.
Philadelphia, PA 19103
(215) 972-4230

With slightly more than $4 million of its own and SBA funds, Alliance Enterprise is apparently the third largest MESBIC. It was started by Sun Co., the oil conglomerate; and, whereas it was once diversified in the kinds of investments it would back, it has recently been specializing in broadcasting ventures, such as a recent acquisition by minority entrepreneurs of a television station. An Alliance Enterprise official indicates, though, that the MESBIC will consider leveraged buyouts of companies with a minimum of $1.5 million of revenues or the potential for being made profitable within two years with a minimum of $5 million in sales in five years. (Leveraged buyouts usually involve officers of a corporate subsidiary obtaining loans from various sources, including venture-capital firms, to buy the subsidiary.) Alliance Enterprise says its typical investment is about $200,000 and its maximum is $800,000.

Allied Investment Developers Inc.
9999 NE Second Ave.
Miami Shores, FL 33138
(305) 757-6796

This individually owned MESBIC specializes in funding entrepreneurs starting fast-food franchises. Its own and SBA funding total $825,000.

Burger King MESBIC Inc.
P.O. Box 520783
Biscayne Annex
Miami, FL 33152
(305) 274-7011

As the name suggests, this MESBIC, established by Burger King, finances minority entrepreneurs who want to open Burger King franchises. Funding from Burger King and the SBA total $750,000.

Equico Capital Corp.
1270 Ave. of the Americas
New York, NY 10020
(212) 489-7033

Established by the Equitable Life Assurance Society of the United States, Equico is the nation's largest MESBIC, with nearly $12 million of capitalization. Though Equico is not wild about getting involved in start-up situations, it helped fund the start-up record company referred to previously and says it is open to other start-up situations in the areas of energy, high technology, and health care.

Equico's primary interest is in backing acquisitions by experienced minority entrepreneurs of existing businesses. The businesses should ideally have sales of $1 million to $15 million and be in the areas of communications, manufacturing, energy, high technology, or health care. Equico says it seeks to avoid investments in the areas of retailing and services, except for computer services.

Equico typically invests a combination of debt and equity totaling about $400,000, although it gets involved in larger investments with other MESBICs through syndicates. It has invested in acquisitions of radio stations and manufacturing companies.

MCA New Ventures Inc.
100 Universal City Plaza
Universal City, CA 91608
(213) 985-4321

After Equico, MCA New Ventures is among the largest MESBICs, with about $6 million of its own and SBA funds. As a subsidiary of the entertainment conglomerate MCA Inc., the MESBIC is, not surprisingly, most interested in ventures in the entertainment industry. It has been involved in funding new record companies and theatrical ventures, such as plays. Its funding usually takes the form of a combination of debt and equity. It will, in combination with other MESBICs, get involved in deals exceeding $1 million.

Minority Broadcasting Investment Corporation
1220 19th St., NW
Washington, DC 20036
(202) 293-2977

This MESBIC was started by Storer Broadcasting of Miami with $1 million of the television station chain's funds. It has been chiefly involved, since its inception in 1979, in helping minority entrepreneurs acquire radio and television stations. It will usually invest $150,000 to $200,000 of its own funds in a combination of debt and equity but will pool its money together with that of other MESBICs on acquisitions ranging from $1 million to $4 million.

Minority Broadcast Investment Fund
1771 N St., NW
Washington, DC 20036
(202) 293-3574

This fund resulted from an ambitious project of the National Association of Broadcasters to create a MESBIC devoted to aiding minorities to acquire television and radio stations. The MESBIC was still being organized as this book went to press, but the organizers hoped to have at least $10 million available for debt, equity, and combination investments. Not surprisingly, it expects that entrepreneurs it backs will have solid experience in operating television or radio stations.

Motor Enterprises Inc.
6-248 General Motors Building
Detroit, MI 48202
(313) 556-4273

Motor Enterprises was started by General Motors (GM) and confines its investments to businesses located near GM plants. Each GM plant has a Motor Enterprises office, at which entrepreneurs can inquire about backing.

Motor Enterprises is quite receptive to funding start-ups, particularly in the area of manufacturing; but it has also backed retail and service businesses. During one recent six-month period, six of eleven investments made by the MESBIC were in start-ups.

This MESBIC's average investment is about $60,000; its maximum is usually about $150,000, though it says it would go as high as $250,000. Motor Enterprises says it will back an entrepreneur who is completely without capital, but only if he or she has solid experience in the industry of his or her new business. The MESBIC also says it places a heavy premium on providing management expertise to entrepreneurs to help ensure success.

MANAGEMENT ASSISTANCE FOR START-UP BUSINESSES

Start-up minority entrepreneurs have a number of options for obtaining training, consulting, and technical assistance. Assistance can be obtained at no cost primarily through two federal agencies: the Small Business Administration and the Minority Business Development Administration of the Commerce Department.

But, like anything that is given away free, the value of government-sponsored management assistance is questionable. According to the report "Minority Business Development," issued at the 1980 White House Conference on Small Business by conference organizers,

> Management and technical assistance provided by both the SBA and MBDA have been marginally successful. These programs have been characterized as being "too little, too late." . . . In short, whether the level and quality of management assistance provided by MBDA and SBA has been

adequate to make a significant difference in the chances of success . . . is questionable.

Another option for start-up minority entrepreneurs is to hire their own consultants, based on the recommendations of knowledgeable business people and interviews of potential consultants. But, because entrepreneurs just starting out are usually extremely short of cash, paying consultants hundreds of dollars daily may be out of the question.

Minority entrepreneurs considering seeking outsider advice would probably do well to decide exactly what services they need. Are you looking to understand business terminology approaches better, find a banker, put together a business plan, or make a substantial acquisition? Each such service requires a different type of assistance and level of expertise. Entrepreneurs seeking to broaden their business knowledge might do best with a course or seminar, such as is periodically offered by the SBA. Experienced business managers wanting to acquire substantial businesses via complex financing arrangements would probably be better off approaching the MBDA, along with possibly private consultants and MESBICs.

Generally speaking, the SBA and MBDA are good places for start-up entrepreneurs to begin their search for outside assistance. Neither agency requires that entrepreneurs be receiving government loans to qualify for management help. Usually these agencies will attempt to guide entrepreneurs toward the specific type of assistance programs they consider most appropriate; if the entrepreneur tries the agency's suggestions, though, and finds them inappropriate, he or she should feel free to request alternatives.

What follows is an overview of the management and technical assistance for minorities that is available from the SBA and the MBDA. Start-up minority entrepreneurs who feel that neither of these agencies can provide the kind of consulting help they need might want to consider seeking out private consultants, such as the consultants described in Chapter 2, "Consultants and Management Assistance." Also potentially helpful are some of the minority information groups and trade organizations on pp. 254–56 of this chapter.

SMALL BUSINESS ADMINISTRATION

Assistant Administrator for Management Assistance
Small Business Administration
1441 L St., NW
Washington, DC 20416
(202) 653-6894

Information and assistance are also available from more than 100 local SBA offices scattered among the nation's large- and medium-sized cities. (For a list of local offices, see Appendix A.) Minority entrepreneurs should seek out minority small-business development specialists, who offer guidance on seeking SBA assistance.

Call Contracts Program

The SBA's main management assistance program, designed specifically for minorities, is known as its Call Contracts Program. Under this program, the SBA contracts with professional management consultant firms to provide services to minority entrepreneurs; the SBA then refers the entrepreneurs to the consultants. The services can include assistance in such things as assembling a business plan, doing market research, evaluating new business opportunities, and providing legal advice.

The SBA usually tries to reserve the Call Contracts Program either for start-up entrepreneurs who are well along in establishing their businesses or for entrepreneurs running existing businesses who have SBA loans which are in danger of not being paid back because the businesses are doing poorly. The SBA will usually try to steer start-up minority entrepreneurs in the formative stages of planning a business to its other programs, which are open to entrepreneurs of all races.

There is no indication that the Call Contracts Program is any better for start-up minority entrepreneurs than is any other program available to all entrepreneurs. In general, minority entrepreneurs are probably better off, at least initially, taking the advice of the agency's minority small-business development specialists as to which program is best for them. If they feel that programs to which they are referred are inappropriate, then they should request information regarding other programs they feel might be more suitable.

Other Programs

Among the other programs that can prove useful to start-up entrepreneurs are SBA's Small Business Development Centers, its Small Business Institutues, its Service Corps of Retired Executives (SCORE), its Active Corps of Executives (ACE), and its various short-term seminars on starting businesses. These programs are all described in greater detail in Chapter 2, "Consultants and Management Assistance."

One point minority entrepreneurs looking to the SBA for management assistance should keep in mind is that the SBA is best at aiding small retail and service ventures to get started and keep going. The agency is usually not equipped to provide the more complex types of assistance frequently required by large-scale and fast-growing manufacturing and high-technology businesses, so entrepreneurs about to start or acquire such businesses should look instead to the Minority Business Development Agency.

MINORITY BUSINESS DEVELOPMENT AGENCY

Minority Business Development Agency
Department of Commerce
Washington, DC 20230
(202) 377-3165

Information also available at fifteen regional and district offices located in San Francisco, Washington, Atlanta, Chicago, New York, Dallas, Phoenix, Los Angeles, Miami, New Orleans, Boston, Albuquerque, Philadelphia, Memphis, and San Antonio.

The Minority Business Development Agency (MBDA) is the new name given the old Office of Minority Business Enterprise (OMBE), and with the new name has come a new direction. Whereas OMBE attempted to dispense management assistance to minority entrepreneurs of all types, MBDA is hoping to concentrate management and technical help on entrepreneurs seeking to establish or acquire substantial and fast-growing manufacturing, high-technology, communications, health services, and other such businesses. As was noted in the introduction to this chapter, federal officials expect to steer minority entrepreneurs starting more traditional retailing and service businesses to the SBA.

The MBDA provides the bulk of its management assistance through about 100 Business Development Organizations, which are primarily management consulting firms and nonprofit community economic development organizations. While the Business Development Organizations have, in the past, been sometimes less than capable and sometimes even less than honest in using government grants, the MBDA has of late made a major effort to upgrade the quality of Business Development Organizations.

The MBDA wants to use the Business Development Organizations to help implement its goal of encouraging substantial and fast-growing minority-owned enterprises. Business Development Organizations can do that by helping to scout out potential acquisition candidates for large-scale ventures on behalf of experienced minority entrepreneurs and aiding in putting together complex multimillion-dollar financing packages that can include loans and investments from a variety of sources.

In addition, the Business Development Organizations are helping to implement the MBDA's Technology Commercialization Program, which is designed to aid minority entrepreneurs transform new technologies into commercial products. The Business Development Organizations aid entrepreneurs in obtaining financial and technical assistance from other federal agencies and from commercial financing sources.

Thus, minority entrepreneurs with solid management experience in large corporations or successful smaller businesses, who are interested in starting their own fast-growing ventures or in acquiring substantial businesses, should look to the MBDA for management guidance and, possibly, for assistance in arranging financing or finding acquisition candidates. How successful the agency will be in its new goal remains to be seen.

FINANCING FOR EXISTING BUSINESSES

Minority entrepreneurs seeking loans or equity investments to expand existing businesses will encounter less resistance and a wider range of potential sources than start-up minority entrepreneurs. All the sources described as potentially useful for start-up entrepreneurs are even more likely to back existing businesses; in fact, some sources available to existing businesses will not even consider start-ups.

This is not meant to imply, however, that obtaining financing is a piece of cake for minority entrepreneurs with existing businesses. They will still encounter stiff competition for sources that cater to minorities, and they will run up against both competition and potential discrimination when seeking help from sources that serve all types of business owners.

Minority owners of existing businesses can seek financing not only from Small Business Administration programs to assist minorities and Minority Enterprise Small Business Investment Companies (MESBICs), but also from a few private minority venture-capital firms and about 100 minority banks. Minority entrepreneurs should also consider the financing opportunities described in Chapter 3, "Federal Government Financing Sources"; Chapter 5, "Commercial Finance"; and Chapter 6, "Venture Capital."

SMALL BUSINESS ADMINISTRATION

U. S. Small Business Administration
1441 L St., NW
Washington, DC 20416
(202) 653-6570

Information and assistance are also available at more than 100 local SBA offices, which are scattered among the nation's large- and medium-sized cities. (For a listing of these offices, see Appendix A.) Minority entrepreneurs should seek out minority small-business development specialists, who offer guidance on seeking SBA assistance.

Minority-owned businesses needing up to $500,000 should look into the SBA's program of regular business loans, known as its 7(a) program. Most regular business loans are made by banks at their regular rates, with 90 percent SBA guarantees on repayment in the event the business defaults.

For further details on the availability to minorities of regular 7(a) business loans, please see pp. 229–30 of this chapter. Additional details on SBA programs available to entrepreneurs in general can be found on pp. 80–84 and 90–92 of Chapter 3, "Federal Government Financing Sources."

BUREAU OF INDIAN AFFAIRS

Director
Office of Tribal Resources Development
Bureau of Indian Affairs
18th and C Sts., NW
Washington, DC 20245
(202) 343-5875

Information also available from local BIA offices

Financing information on start-up minority businesses, which is described on pp. 230–31 of this chapter, is also applicable to existing businesses.

MINORITY ENTERPRISE SMALL BUSINESS INVESTMENT COMPANIES

Investment Division
Small Business Administration
1441 L St., NW
Washington, DC 20416
(202) 653-6848

or

American Association of Minority Enterprise Small Business
  Investment Companies
1413 K St., NW
Washington, DC 20005
(202) 347-8600

Both sources can provide up-to-date lists of Minority Enterprise Small Business Investment Companies (MESBICs) and limited information on MESBIC investment policies.

The bulk of MESBICs' funds go into existing minority businesses in the form of loans or investments or some combination of the two. Much like other sorts of venture-capital firms, MESBICs are most interested in financially healthy, fast-growing companies in need of funds to fuel their growth.

Some MESBICs prefer to make mostly loans, while others prefer investments whereby the MESBIC acquires partial ownership of the minority company. Those MESBICs that lean toward loans are likely to be most interested in a company's overall financial strength, which influences its ability to repay loans. MESBICs inclined to make equity investments, on the other hand, are most interested in fast growth, since that usually increases the value of their investment.

Generally speaking, retail, service, and franchised businesses will be likeliest to impress MESBICs inclined to make loans; and manufacturing, high-technology, and media/entertainment businesses will usually be the fast-growth businesses preferred by MESBICs that make equity investments. However, that rule of thumb should not be construed to imply that a fast-growing retail business will be unable to obtain a MESBIC equity investment or that a stable, slow-growing manufacturing company will be unable to obtain a MESBIC loan.

According to the "Minority Business Development" report issued in preparation for the 1980 White House Conference on Small Business,

> The typical business financed by a MESBIC during 1979 was a profitable corporation less than three years old employing 27 people with gross revenues just under $900,000. . . . Growth and diversity are the words that best characterize recent MESBIC investments, as specialized financing has enabled minorities to enter business arenas [that were] previously unattainable.

For more background on MESBICs, readers should refer to pp. 231–36 in this chapter: the MESBICs listed on those pages are all open to financing existing minority businesses in addition to start-ups, and those listings will not be repeated in this section of the chapter. This section of the chapter will list additional MESBICs available nearly exclusively to existing businesses. Our sources of information on MESBICs for this section of the chapter were the same as for the earlier section. Minority owners of existing businesses should also refer to Chapter 6, "Venture Capital," for background on the way in which venture capitalists evaluate businesses, since operators of MESBICs use much the same criteria.

Associated Southwest Investors Inc.
2425 Alamo, SE
Albuquerque, NM 87106
(505) 842-5955

Associated Southwest Investors, with a total of $2.4 million in capitalization, has most recently been focusing on investments in communications and manufacturing businesses, but the MESBIC says it is open to other business areas. It usually invests between $75,000 and $200,000, generally in the form of debt which is convertible into equity. Among its recent investments have been a television station, a manufacturer of kitchen appliances, an oil drilling company, and an office building. Associated Southwest confines nearly all of its investments to existing businesses in its immediate area. Its ventures outside New Mexico occur when it gets involved in syndicated investments. It provides some management assistance.

Chicago Community Ventures Inc.
19 S LaSalle St.
Chicago, IL 60603
(312) 726-6084

Chicago Community Ventures was started by seventeen corporations in 1972. It currently has a total of $2 million in capitalization. The MESBIC prefers backing existing manufacturing businesses, the primary objective being to create employment. It usually invests between $50,000 and $300,000 in the form of debt and concentrates on Chicago-area businesses, except when working with other MESBICs or banks.

Community Equity Corporation of Nebraska
5620 Ames Ave.
Omaha, NE 68104
(402) 455-1500

With a total capital base of only $600,000, Community Equity keeps its investments relatively small—usually from $10,000 to $35,000 up to a maximum of $80,000. Its investments thus far have been in the form of debt. It has invested in a real estate company, a trucking company, an electronics company, and an editorial services company. Community Equity has thus far confined its investments to Nebraska.

Fulcrum Venture Capital Corp.
2021 K St., NW
Washington, DC 20006
(202) 833-9590

Fulcrum invests in existing minority businesses that have sales of more than $1 million. It also gets involved in leveraged buyouts involving minority employees of corporate subsidiaries who seek to buy the subsidiaries. It has total capitalization exceeding $7 million, making it one of the largest MESBICs around.

Massachusetts Venture Capital Corp.
141 Milk St.
Boston, MA 02109
(617) 426-0208

Massachusetts Venture Capital will invest in almost any kind of business, except retail stores. It has total capitalization of $1.4 million; among its recent investments have been an electronics distributor, a producer of electrical equipment, an importing business, a printing company, a radio station, and a food-processing plant. Its typical investment is between $50,000 and $200,000, usually in the form of debt and equity combined. Most of its investments are in the Boston area.

MESBIC Financial Corp. of Dallas
7701 N Stemmons Freeway
Dallas, TX 75247
(214) 637-0445

This MESBIC, the largest in Texas and among the larger MESBICs nationally, with about $3 million of capitalization, tends to prefer making loans to existing manufacturing companies. Among its recent investments: an electronics distributor, a maker of automobile electrical systems, a giftware manufacturing representative, and a specialty construction company.

Metro-Detroit Investment Co.
18481 Ten Mile Road
Southfield, MI 48075
(313) 557-3818

A subsidiary of Melody Farms Dairy, Metro-Detroit specializes in making investments in retail food stores in Michigan. Metro-Detroit has nearly $3.5 million of capitalization; its investments are mostly in the form of loans of $10,000 to $150,000 that go into expanding existing stores.

Metro-Detroit says it is open to start-up proposals. It adds that it does not get involved in working with other MESBICs to fund minority businesses, but that it sometimes works together with a bank.

Metro-Detroit declined, however, to provide specific information as to how many stores it has invested in of late and how many were start-ups versus existing businesses; the MESBIC also declined to provide information on typical investments in terms of amounts and situations.

Minority Equity Capital Co.
275 Madison Ave.
New York, NY 10016
(212) 686-9710

Minority Equity Capital prefers relatively large, fast-growing companies in communications and manufacturing. Its investments usually range between $200,000 and $300,000 and tend to be equity-oriented.

Among its recent investments have been a record company, a television station, and a radio station. With about $3.9 million in total capitalization, it is one of the largest MESBICs in the country.

Opportunity Capital Corporation of California
100 California St.
San Francisco, CA 94111
(415) 421-5935

With $3.8 million in private capital and SBA loans, Opportunity Capital ranks as one of the nation's largest MESBICs. It tends to prefer making loans or equity investments in medium to large minority companies in the areas of radio and television, transportation, and manufacturing. About two thirds of its investments are in California, and one third are out of state. Opportunity Capital also likes to have a representative on the board of directors of each company it finances.

MINORITY BANKS

Minority business owners frustrated by their inability to obtain loans from white-owned banks might find help at minority-owned banks. At the very least, they will usually find bankers sympathetic to the problems faced by minority businesses.

Minority-owned banks are usually based in minority urban areas. Their primary purpose is to funnel loans to minority businesses in their metropolitan areas. Their main limitation in assisting minority businesses, however, is availability of cash. Of the country's 14,000 commercial banks, only about 100 are owned by minorities and they have assets averaging only about $15 million each, which is less than half the $35 million average of other banks, according to Richard America's article on minority business in the May/June 1980 *Harvard Business Review*.

Nonetheless, minority banks have managed to make efficient use of their assets by being aggressive in making loans which are 90 percent guaranteed by the SBA; such loans limit the banks' risks. Minority banks also tend to steer clear of backing start-up businesses. Of about ten minority-owned banks with which we talked, all said they tend to concentrate their loans on existing businesses.

Though minority banks usually try to make loans to minority businesses, their criteria for assessing businesses is much the same as other banks. For background on how banks evaluate potential customers, readers should refer to Chapter 5, "Commercial Finance."

What follows is a listing of a dozen of the largest minority banks, scattered geographically around the country, along with the minority group which has principal ownership and an estimate of the banks' assets.

For a complete listing of minority banks by state, readers should obtain the directory *Try Us,* published semiannually by the National Minority Business Campaign, a nonprofit organization that promotes minority business; a more complete description of the directory is contained at the end of this chapter. In addition, *Black Enterprise* magazine, in its June issue each year, ranks the nation's black-owned banks according to their assets.

Western United States

Bank of Finance
2651 S Western Ave.
Los Angeles, CA 90018
(213) 735-1031
  Black-owned; assets of $22.1 million

Cathay Bank of Los Angeles
777 N Broadway
Los Angeles, CA 90012
(213) 626-7691
  Chinese-owned; assets of $110 million

First Enterprise Bank
1632 Franklin Ave.
Oakland, CA 94612
(415) 839-6300
  Black-owned; assets of $38.4 million

Midwest

First Independence National Bank of Detroit
234 State St.
Detroit, MI 48226
(313) 964-2350
  Black-owned; assets of $52.2 million

Independence Bank of Chicago
7936 S Cottage Grove
Chicago, IL
(312) 487-4700
  Black-owned; assets of $98.3 million

Seaway National Bank of Chicago
645 E 87th St.
Chicago, IL 60619
(312) 487-4800
  Black-owned; assets of $80.9 million

Eastern United States

City National Bank of New Jersey
900 Broad St.
Newark, NJ 07102
(201) 624-0865
    Black-owned; assets of $27.5 million

Freedom National Bank of New York
275 W 125th St.
New York, NY 10027
(212) 678-1500
    Black-owned; assets of $58 million

Golden Pacific National Bank
241 Canal St.
New York, NY 10013
(212) 925-8880
    Chinese-owned; assets of $20 million

The South

Bank of Miami
100 E Flagler
Miami, FL 33131
(305) 579-3045
    Hispanic-owned; assets of $174 million

Citizens Trust Bank
175 Houston St.
Atlanta, GA 30303
(404) 659-5959
    Black-owned; assets of $48 million

Mechanic & Farmers Bank
116 W Parrish St.
Durham, NC 27702
(919) 683-1521
    Black-owned; assets of $44 million

FEDERAL GOVERNMENT PROCUREMENT ASSISTANCE FOR EXISTING BUSINESSES

Depending on whom one listens to, federal efforts to direct more government purchases to minority businesses are either a godsend or a charade.

Those impressed by government efforts point to the fact that federal agencies do more than $3 billion of business annually with minority businesses, as compared with only about $1 billion in fiscal 1977; and that hundreds of minority businesses have benefited from government purchases and contracts. They applaud the government's successful effort, as evidenced in a recent Supreme Court case, in defending the practice of setting aside specific percentages of business for minorities.

Critics of the government's attempts to buy more from minority businesses, however, argue that bureaucrats have dragged their heels and failed to comply with existing laws requiring government purchases from minority companies. Critics also charge that some minority businesses receiving government contracts without bidding have become dependent on the contracts and have been unable to become competitive with other businesses. And well-publicized instances of fraud in minority procurement assistance efforts raise questions about whether legitimate minority businesses are benefiting as much as the government says, critics contend.

The reality of government efforts to aid minority business development through procurement probably lies somewhere between the two viewpoints: the efforts do represent an admirable desire to assist minority businesses, but too often the efforts are bungled because of bureaucratic obstacles. What all this means for minority businesses is that the government should be viewed as a useful potential customer, provided minority businesses are prepared to encounter the frustrations inherent in dealing with federal agencies.

Federal efforts to direct more business to minorities fall into three broad categories of federal minority procurement assistance, as described below. Minority business owners who read about the special minority procurement programs and decide to explore them further are advised to read Chapter 10, "Government Procurement," which details the federal government's overall procurement procedures.

SBA PROCUREMENT ASSISTANCE PROGRAM

The Small Business Administration's procurement assistance program for minority businesses, better known as the SBA's Section 8(a) program, has been used since the late 1960s to direct government purchases to minority businesses. Under the program, the SBA contracts directly with federal agencies for procurement contracts and then subcontracts them to minority businesses which it determines can fulfill the contract specifications. Because subcontracts are awarded by the SBA on a noncompetitive basis, prices are usually higher than they would be through normal bidding.

There is no question that many minority businesses are benefiting on a short-term basis from the program: in one recent year $748.2 million in

8(a) contracts was awarded to nearly 1,200 minority businesses. There is one question that is being raised both within and outside the government, however, and that is whether the program is doing any long-term good. According to a June 12, 1980, *Wall Street Journal* article on the program,

> The SBA program is supposed to help minority businesses to eventually succeed in the private market, without preferential government help. But in the program's . . . history, only 174 businesses, or 4% of the entrants, have graduated to self-sufficiency. Some have been in the program for a decade.

The SBA has also admitted that, in past years, many of those subcontracts awarded may not have been completed satisfactorily, even though payments were made. Whether the apparent fraud was the result of dishonest SBA bureaucrats or disreputable minority business owners has not been clarified. Such criticisms and disclosures caused the SBA in 1981 to suspend, at least temporarily, the admission of additional businesses into the program.

The SBA, in accordance with recent legislation, now has the authority to provide recipients of 8(a) contracts with management assistance through its various consulting and management assistance programs. The agency has also stated that it will seek to grant 8(a) subcontracts to those minority businesses it feels have the best chances of achieving long-term growth and independence. And the SBA will limit the amount of time companies can remain in the program to possibly three or five years.

Thus, minority businesses seeking 8(a) subcontracts should be prepared to demonstrate, through both their past performance and likely future prospects, that they have the capacity, not only to deliver what the subcontracts provide, but also to develop on a competitive basis after the subcontracts are completed. Minority entrepreneurs should get in touch with SBA minority small-business development specialists, who can help guide them through the application procedure for being designated potential recipients of 8(a) subcontracts. Information can also be obtained from the SBA's central office at the following address:

Office of Business Development
Small Business Administration
1441 L St., NW
Washington, DC 20416
(202) 653-6813

MINORITY BUSINESS SET-ASIDES

This type of procurement assistance comes in a number of forms. Essentially, however, it amounts to federal, state, and local government agencies allotting a certain percentage of their purchases and contracts to minority businesses. Sometimes the allotments are actually set aside and minority businesses subsequently sought out to receive the business; but more often the set-asides are really goals of particular percentages that agencies strive to award to minority businesses. Set-asides are typically 10 percent or 15 percent of agencies' procurements.

Under recent federal legislation, each federal agency is required to establish an Office of Small and Disadvantaged Business Utilization to oversee efforts to use minority businesses as suppliers. According to the June 1980 issue of *Black Enterprise* magazine, some of the agencies, such as the Department of Transportation and the Department of the Interior, were aggressive in setting up and staffing their Offices of Small and Disadvantaged Business Utilization. That aggressiveness will have enabled the Department of Transportation to funnel about $1.4 billion—of the $15 billion the agency made available in fiscal 1981 for the building of mass transit, highways, airports, and other facilities—to minority construction firms and other minority concerns, according to the August 7, 1980, New York *Times*. Yet, *Black Enterprise* charged that other federal agencies, most notably the Environmental Protection Agency and the Veterans Administration, have dragged their heels in setting up Offices of Small and Disadvantaged Business Utilization.

Minority business owners can pursue set-asides through a number of channels. For example, SBA procurement specialists in SBA branch offices around the country can advise minority businesses about procurement opportunities in various agencies and can also attempt to seek out contracts for specific businesses. Information on the SBA's procurement assistance efforts can be obtained from its central office as well:

Small Business Administration
1441 L St., NW
Washington, DC 20416
(202) 653-6635

For entrepreneurs who wish to contact the Office of Small and Disadvantaged Business Utilization directly, information on getting in touch with specific agency offices can be obtained through the Office of Management and Budget's procurement office in Washington:

Office of Federal Procurement Policy
New Executive Office Building
726 Jefferson Place, NW
Washington, DC 20503
(202) 395-3455
(202) 395-5802

Some individual cities and states, and agencies within various cities and states, have their own set-aside guidelines. Some allusions to state minority procurement programs are contained in Chapter 4, "State and Local Government Assistance." In addition, information on state and local set-aside efforts can frequently be obtained by contacting state development officials, who are listed in Chapter 4. The minority information and trade groups listed and described on pp. 254–56 of this chapter can also provide information.

PUBLIC LAW 95-507

Under Public Law (PL) 95-507, which was passed in 1978, bidders on federal contracts of more than $500,000 ($1 million for construction contracts) are required to include, as part of their bids, plans for subcontracting some of the work to minority and other small businesses. The law does not specify any percentages of business that should go to minority firms. Rather, judgments as to whether minority subcontracting plans are appropriate are left to federal procurement officials, who base their assessments on the availability of qualified minority subcontractors in bidders' geographic areas.

According to the June 1980 issue of *Black Enterprise* magazine, the law got off to a slow start.

> . . . With this strong medicine in place, minority businesses should receive a multimillion-dollar shot in the arm each year through federal contracting opportunities.
>
> But the law is also a major departure from the traditional way the government's 150,000 procurement officers do business. Compliance requires extra work on the part of each federal agency and on the part of the firm bidding on a contract. It forces a shake-up in some of the "old boy networks" that so often dominate procurement activities in certain fields, such as defense. And it is, as so many bureaucrats involved in procurement like to say, "a complex law."

During the first six months in which the law was in effect, *Black Enterprise* stated that

> federal agencies had issued nearly $10 billion in contracts and contract solicitations that were in violation of the minority subcontracting mandates of PL 95-507.

The magazine added:

> Had it not been for the outcries of minority trade organizations and congressional watchdogs, PL 95-507's most meaningful provisions . . . would probably be forgotten. Instead, agencies are making reluctant but significant efforts to modify or cancel noncompliant contracts and to make sure that new contracts and solicitations meet the PL 95-507 standard.

Because white-owned companies that desire to comply with PL 95-507 are inclined to seek out lists and directories of minority businesses, minority entrepreneurs should attempt to be listed in as many places as possible. Many such lists are kept by the minority information and trade groups described later in this chapter and by the National Minority Supplier Development Council described in the next section.

Additional details on PL 95-507 are contained in Chapter 10, "Government Procurement."

PROCUREMENT ASSISTANCE FROM CORPORATIONS

Many of the country's large corporations are making intensive efforts to direct more of their purchases to minority firms. Their largesse is motivated by several factors: concerns about social responsibility, a fear of the federal government imposing quotas and otherwise interfering in corporate contracting, and a feeling that minority suppliers can frequently offer competitive prices and reliable delivery. Of course, some substantial corporations have done little or nothing to involve minority companies as suppliers, and others have programs that exist in name only.

The key to successful corporate minority purchasing efforts appears to be commitment from corporations' top management. In corporations where top managers are truly committed to involving minority firms as suppliers, pressure is exerted on lower-level managers to follow through on reaching purchasing goals from minority businesses. Such pressure is needed because purchasing officials are frequently reluctant to switch from long-standing white suppliers to new or less experienced minority businesses.

Minority firms that would like to find corporate customers should begin by establishing contact with one of the forty-seven local councils operated by the National Minority Supplier Development Council (NMSDC). The NMSDC, which, until a few years ago, was known as the National Minority Purchasing Council, consists of several hundred corporations seeking to obtain more minority suppliers. Member corporations pay annual dues of $500 to $5,000 (depending on their assets) to support the NMSDC's efforts to increase contact between corporations and minority businesses. The NMSDC devotes considerable effort to identifying minority-owned companies that might serve as suppliers to corporations. The effort has paid off for many minority companies: NMSDC members made more than $3 billion of purchases from minority companies in 1979, as compared with $1.8 billion in 1978 and $86 million during its first year in 1972.

The NMSDC publishes directories of potential minority suppliers for its corporate members. It also sponsors trade fairs, at which minority firm owners and corporate purchasing officials can meet, and free workshop-seminars at which minority entrepreneurs learn how best to go about obtaining corporate purchasing orders and purchasing officials learn how to find appropriate minority suppliers.

The NMSDC currently has more than 18,000 minority companies listed as potential minority suppliers. To become listed, minority firms must be certified by one of the forty-seven NMSDC regional councils. Certification entails filling out an application and being visited by a council representative. Every minority business wanting to be listed is included. Businesses listed range from creative artists and craftsmen to construction contractors.

The NMSDC will supply addresses, phone numbers, and contacts for its forty-seven local councils to minority entrepreneurs who contact its main office in New York at:

National Minority Supplier Development Council
1500 Broadway
New York, NY 10036
(212) 944-2430

MANAGEMENT ASSISTANCE FOR EXISTING BUSINESSES

Owners of existing minority businesses can avail themselves of the same government sources of training, consulting, and technical assistance as can start-up entrepreneurs. These sources include the Small Business Administration, which is geared toward aiding small retail and service businesses, and the Minority Business Development Agency of the Commerce Department, which specializes in assisting fast-growing businesses in such areas as manufacturing and high technology. Details on the minority business programs offered by those two agencies are on pp. 236–40 in this chapter.

While government management assistance programs can be beneficial to minority businesses and should serve as a starting point for minority business owners, those seeking specific advice on complex situations or projects might do well to explore the possibility of utilizing private consulting firms. Areas or projects which might benefit from consultants' advice include marketing research, cash-flow analysis, and inventory control systems. For further information on choosing private consulting firms and for descriptions of individual firms, please see Chapter 2, "Consultants and Management Assistance."

Minority consulting firms may be the answer for some minority businesses in search of management assistance. Such firms can frequently provide assistance in obtaining government minority set-aside contracts and subcontracts, corporate purchasing orders, and various types of financing. Moreover, minority consulting firms, like minority banks, tend to be more attuned to the special business problems minority companies encounter. In cases in which corporations or government agencies hire minority consultants to locate minority suppliers or provide other consulting services, the services are usually free to the minority firms. In other situations, fees similar to those charged by all consulting firms apply.

Specific minority consulting firms are listed in the directory *Try Us,* which is published by the National Minority Business Campaign, a nonprofit Minneapolis organization (described in more detail on p. 257).

Minority businesses interested in obtaining various types of consulting assistance should also explore the organizations listed under the section about minority information and trade groups, which immediately follows.

MINORITY INFORMATION AND TRADE GROUPS

Various nonprofit organizations have been established—most within the last twenty years—to promote minority business growth. These organizations perform a wide variety of services, including compiling lists of minority businesses for corporations, providing seminars and consulting services, and lobbying for more government assistance to minority businesses.

The main organizations we identified are as follows.

Interracial Council for Business Opportunity
800 Second Ave.
New York, NY 10017
(212) 599-0677

The Interracial Council for Business Opportunity (ICBO) was founded in 1963 by the National Urban League and the American Jewish Congress to help develop minority businesses through consulting and technical assistance. The ICBO focuses its efforts on minority businesses with the potential to achieve $1 million or more in annual sales. It provides assistance in obtaining government and private financing, making acquisitions, and expanding existing businesses. The organization is funded by corporations, foundations, and the Minority Business Development Agency. Its consultants are mostly corporation managers who provide the assistance on a volunteer basis. The ICBO has branch offices in Newark and New Orleans, but it claims to operate on a national scale.

Minority Business Information Institute Inc.
295 Madison Ave.
New York, NY 10017
(212) 889-8220

The Institute is a reference and research library for use by minority entrepreneurs. It provides information on publications, organizations, government programs, and other areas of relevance to minority business. The service, which is funded on a joint basis by the Commerce Department and Earl G. Graves, publisher of *Black Enterprise* magazine, is available without charge and may be used by phone or mail, as well as in person.

Minority Contractors Assistance Project Inc.
1750 K St., NW
Washington, DC 20006
(202) 833-1840

This nonprofit organization provides bonding and various sorts of financial, technical, and management assistance to minority construction contractors around the country. The organization prefers to work with contractors that gross more than $250,000 annually. Because it is funded by government grants and private sources, its services are free to minority businesses. It has regional offices in Atlanta, Oakland, Los Angeles, Wilmington (DE), and Columbus (MS).

National Association of Black Manufacturers
1910 K St., NW
Washington, DC 20006
(202) 785-5133

This organization lobbies the federal government and corporations on behalf of black-owned manufacturing companies. It also assists the government and corporations in locating appropriate black manufacturing companies to perform procurement contracts. It publishes two newsletter-magazines on legislative and other developments affecting black manufacturers. Membership dues range from $300 to $3,000, depending on the assets of the company.

National Business League
4324 Georgia Ave., NW
Washington, DC 20011
(202) 829-5900

Started in 1900 by Booker T. Washington, the black educator-writer, the National Business League is the oldest organization devoted to promoting minority business. The National Business League has 15,000 members and devotes the bulk of its efforts to lobbying the federal government and corporations on behalf of minority business, seeking equal treatment and expanded assistance. The League also sponsors research on minority business and publishes a newsletter on minority business developments. Membership dues range from $10 to $50 for individuals, depending on voting privileges; for businesses, dues start at $250 and head up to more than $5,000, depending on company size and membership privileges.

National Economic Development Association
1636 R St., NW
Washington, DC 20009
(202) 232-1666

The National Economic Development Association (NEDA) concentrates primarily on promoting the interests of Hispanic entrepreneurs. It provides assistance to minority businesses in preparing applications for bank and government loans, obtaining government and corporate procurement contracts, expanding operations, and locating business opportunities and resources. Because it is supported with federal government funds, its services are available without charge to minority business owners. Services are provided by a bilingual staff of more than 150 professionals with business training; there are twenty-six offices in the United States and Puerto Rico.

MINORITY PUBLICATIONS

BLACK ENTERPRISE

Earl G. Graves Publishing Co.
295 Madison Ave.
New York, NY 10017
(212) 889-8820

Black Enterprise offers the most comprehensive and entertaining coverage of minority business of any publication. It provides updates of developments in government assistance to minority business, along with profiles of successful black entrepreneurs. It also includes articles, similar to those in *Ebony* magazine, on black lifestyles and neighborhoods. Published monthly, the annual subscription rate is $10.

NATIONAL MINORITY BUSINESS CAMPAIGN

National Minority Business Campaign
1201 12th Ave. N
Minneapolis, MN 55411

This nonprofit organization publishes three directories and booklets on an annual or semiannual basis. These are:

Try Us; National Minority Business Directory
(known, simply, as *Try Us*);

Guide to Obtaining Minority Business Directories
(known, simply, as *Guide*); and

Purchasing People in Major Corporations
(known, simply, as *Purchasing People*)

Try Us lists 4,300 minority businesses that have at least regional sales, with a brief description of each company's products or services. Minority firms are listed without charge. The directory costs $14.

Guide lists by state 200 organizations that have compiled minority firm listings in their areas. It costs $3.

Purchasing People lists purchasing officials and minority vendor program coordinators of the 750 largest companies in the country. It costs $4.

CHAPTER 8

Assistance for Women

INTRODUCTION: DEVELOPING A NEW NETWORK

Women might well be viewed as the nation's newest entrepreneurs.

White men, of course, have always predominated as entrepreneurs in the United States. Then in the late 1960s and early 1970s, various efforts were started to encourage racial minorities to start their own businesses. These efforts included special federally and privately sponsored financing, management, and procurement programs. (For background and details see Chapter 7, "Assistance for Minority Businesses.")

Since the late 1970s, the entrepreneurship focus has shifted to women. The federal government, with encouragement from newly formed women's organizations, has placed a high priority on attracting women into the small-business arena.

There seems little doubt that such efforts are way overdue. Women have been notoriously underrepresented as small-business owners. Statistics compiled by the Census Bureau during the 1970s showed that though women comprise slightly more than half the total population, they own only a bit more than 4 percent of all businesses. Moreover, women-owned businesses account for less than 1 percent of all business receipts, and nearly 90 percent of the businesses don't even have any employees beyond the female owner.

THE DISCRIMINATION BARRIER

Why do women account for such a small proportion of the world of entrepreneurship? A combination of obstacles seems to be hindering women, according to investigators who have examined the role of women as business owners.

A report issued by organizers of the 1980 White House Conference on Small Business concluded, on the basis of testimony from would-be and existing women entrepreneurs,

> that women face many obstacles, such as lack of adequate capital, lack of marketing opportunities, and lack of management and technical skills due in part to discriminatory practices. The traditional business community is not yet ready to accept women on an equal footing nor do women belong to the "old boy" network. Thus, women . . . feel they are not taken seriously as business owners.

Another report, compiled in 1978 by a presidentially appointed Task Force on Women Business Owners, was more blunt in its assessment.

> After months of research and evaluation, the Task Force has concluded that if starting a new business is considered difficult, it is considerably more difficult for a woman. A systematic history of overt discrimination starts her on a course in life that steers her from a traditional "man's province," prevents her from training for careers that lead to entrepreneurship, diminishes her ambitions and aspirations for this career, and then places obstacles in her path as she tries to pursue it. For minority women these obstacles are even greater because of racism and cultural differences.

The obstacles become quickly apparent to most women who attempt to start businesses. Friends and relatives they seek out as investors tend to not take them seriously. Bankers may be indifferent or even derisive in turning down loan requests. And if the businesses actually get started, potential suppliers and customers are frequently equally cautious about getting involved with women entrepreneurs.

Discrimination against women even extends into the kinds of businesses open to them. When financing and credit are available, it is most often for women in retail and service businesses—boutiques, gift shops, employment agencies, and real estate firms. Other business areas that might offer more substantial long-term opportunities, such as manufacturing and high-technology businesses, seem to be considered off-limits to women.

Once they do get businesses established, women frequently encounter other sorts of problems. According to an article in *The Wall Street Journal* of July 7, 1980:

> Fear of accounting and math often discourages women from diagnosing the condition of their companies and from planning their direction. An aversion to asserting themselves sometimes keeps women from confronting workers who should be disciplined or fired. And worrying about slighting their other responsibilities as wives and mothers sometimes becomes a harmful preoccupation.

SHIFTING ATTITUDES

But changes are definitely afoot. The emergence of both working women as a growing social force and women's rights organizations as a significant political force has helped focus attention on the role of women in the business world.

The effect of the social and political changes on women as entrepreneurs could be profound. Evidence suggests that women are challenging the various barriers to business ownership. The Task Force on Women Business Owners, for instance, found through its own research that "the growth rate for self-employed women as a group was three times that of self-employed men from 1972 to 1977."

Women are also organizing themselves to help each other in much the same way that men have informally helped each other start businesses for years and years. The concept is referred to by women as "networking," which is modeled after the "old boy" approach of men whereby informal contacts result in financing, customers, professional services, and other essentials for any new business.

A number of women's business organizations have sprung up in recent years to provide training, moral support, and potential contacts to women entrepreneurs. The largest of the organizations—the National Association of Women Business Owners—has chapters in at least fifteen cities around the country, and is described in greater detail later in this chapter. At least eight women's banks have also been established in cities around the country to provide loans and business advice to women in an atmosphere of support and understanding.

The various women's business organizations have also been active in lobbying for support of women entrepreneurs among private financial institutions and government policy-makers at all levels. At a regional conference in Chicago in 1979 in preparation for the 1980 White House Conference on Small Business, women's business groups were among the most active participants; they set up a hotel hospitality suite in which they served homemade pastries and tried to corral as many private financial and government officials as possible to press their case for making small-business ownership easier for women.

IMPLICATIONS FOR WOMEN ENTREPRENEURS

The effect of all the complaints and consciousness-raising by women isn't entirely clear. The impact on private financial institutions such as banks and venture-capital firms is difficult to assess because they are so diverse. But it is no doubt fair to say that the men who usually run these institutions are at the least more aware than they were of women's aspirations and growing influence; that in itself should make many such men give more than cursory attention to female loan and investment candidates.

The entrepreneurship message has definitely been heard in Washington. Many federal agencies now say they are quite receptive to the idea of including women in training, financing, and procurement programs for entrepreneurs and they urge women to become involved. Some of the agencies have even set up special loan and training programs for women.

Possibly the most important effect of all the attention given the problems women encounter as entrepreneurs has been to awaken millions of women to the notion that they can even think about owning their own businesses. That can be a powerful notion, so long as would-be women entrepreneurs keep their developing opportunities in perspective.

That means women should be prepared to make use of all the new resources at their disposal for obtaining information, contacts, management training, and financing. These resources include mostly women's business organizations, women's banks, government programs designed to assist women, and publications directed to potential women entrepreneurs.

But women entrepreneurs must also be mindful of the fact that these new resources aren't guarantees of business success. They are only resources, or tools, that can help women to compete more equally with other business owners. In some instances these new resources are rudimentary tools; management training courses may be poorly taught, or government financing may take long months to be decided on.

Women, then, should be prepared to use not only the special organizations and programs designed for them, but other resources as well. In other words, women should be prepared to share or compete with men in obtaining management assistance, commercial financing, state and local government aid, and other resources available to would-be and existing entrepreneurs in general. Many of the other chapters of this book can be useful in steering women to what's available in these various categories.

The remainder of this chapter is devoted to identifying and describing resources specifically oriented to women entrepreneurs. Because the various programs and organizations tend to be very recent in origin, they aren't as specialized and thus as easily segmented as other types of sources, such as those for racial minorities. And because so few women own businesses, most of the resources are devoted to aiding women who seek to start new businesses. Thus, this chapter is divided basically into federal government and nongovernment sources and, in the case of the government sources, according to the type of assistance offered— management assistance, financing, and procurement help. This chapter is not subdivided into sections for start-up and existing entrepreneurs, as are some other chapters where such a subdivision is easily made.

FEDERAL GOVERNMENT INITIATIVES

The most noticeable reaction to women's complaints about barriers to entrepreneurship has come from the federal government. After the Task Force on Women Business Owners filed its report with President Carter in 1978, he issued an executive order directing federal agencies to attempt to involve women in businesses of their own. The agencies were to make special efforts to include women in programs designed to assist entrepreneurs in obtaining management training, financial aid, and procurement opportunities.

After the order was issued in May 1979, various federal agencies issued a flurry of announcements proclaiming their desire to help women start and expand their businesses. A few agencies, such as the Small Business Administration, the Federal Trade Commission, and the Farmers Home Administration of the Department of Agriculture, even announced such things as pilot loan and training programs for women and goals of increasing the amount of funds loaned to women.

The announcements certainly served one purpose: they created the impression that the federal government was committing substantial resources to assisting women become entrepreneurs.

But close examination of the announcements suggests more form than substance exists for many of the initiatives. As an article in the May 1980 issue of *Venture* magazine observed:

> Still stinging from sour experiences with minority aid programs of the past, the government has been reluctant to fall into a quota set-up in specifying funds for women. So when it comes to women, agencies speak of "targets" and "goals" rather than specific set-asides.

Targets and goals allow government agencies to make grandiose announcements in which they commit themselves to attempting to loan millions of dollars to women. Whether or not they meet their targets usually goes unnoticed. Set-asides, on the other hand, commit agencies to actually loaning the amounts specified to entrepreneurs and have been frequently used to assist minority businesses.

Some of the programs for women have also been initiated on a pilot basis, which means that they stay in effect for only a limited time, usually a year. After that period, they may or may not be renewed.

Other programs were announced as being under consideration and then either weren't funded or weren't even proposed for funding. Among the agencies that developed pilot programs that never got off the ground were the following: the Federal Trade Commission had a pilot program, which was scrapped, to inform women of their credit rights; the Tennessee Valley Authority proposed a management training program for women business owners, but the program failed to obtain funding; and the Overseas Private Investment Corporation announced a preferential program for women planning investments in less developed countries that, an information officer subsequently told us, simply didn't exist.

Even the few programs that were set up could fall victim in future years to the Reagan administration's cutbacks in federal spending. The Republican administration has also indicated that it has less interest in promoting entrepreneurship for women than the Carter administration had.

For the most up-to-date information on federal programs specifically directed to women entrepreneurs, the following committee consisting of representatives from sixteen federal agencies should be contacted:

Interagency Committee on Women's Business Enterprise
c/o Office of Women's Business Enterprise
U. S. Small Business Administration
1441 L St., NW
Washington, DC 20416
(202) 653-6087

For federal government purposes, women entrepreneurs must own at least 51 percent of their businesses and operate them on a day-to-day basis to qualify for assistance programs. In addition, women have been considered ineligible for programs designed for racial minorities; of course, minority women are eligible for such programs. (The programs are described in detail in Chapter 7, "Assistance for Minority Businesses.")

Our impression after contacting federal government agencies is that they have made only a modest beginning at best in their efforts to assist women entrepreneurs. We have divided this section on government initiatives into three subsections examining management assistance, financing programs, and procurement assistance. Readers of this section are also advised to refer to Chapter 2, "Consultants and Management Assistance"; Chapter 3, "Federal Government Financing Sources"; and Chapter 10, "Government Procurement."

MANAGEMENT ASSISTANCE

Small Business Administration
Assistant Administrator for Management Assistance
Small Business Administration
1441 L St., NW
Washington, DC 20416
(202) 653-6881

Information is also available through more than 100 local offices in cities around the country (a listing of these offices is in Appendix A).

The Small Business Administration (SBA) sponsors various workshops and seminars on starting and operating small businesses. It also has several programs for providing consulting assistance to operating business owners. (For details on SBA management assistance programs, see Chapter 2, "Consulting and Management Assistance.")

In recent years, the SBA has also offered seminars and workshops specifically for women. At one point, it offered one- and two-day seminars to provide background on the basics of successful entrepreneurship along with information on additional resources. It has also offered training for women in several major cities on operating franchises.

The major advantage of all the SBA's management assistance programs is that they're free. Not surprisingly, they vary considerably in their quality.

The programs specifically designed for women are offered sporadically, so women should check with their local SBA office or the Washington office on what's planned for the immediate future. If these offices aren't helpful, women can contact the SBA's Office of Women's Business Enterprise at the above address, (202) 653-6074 or (202) 653-8000.

General Services Administration
Office of External Affairs
General Services Administration
18th and F Sts., NW
Washington, DC 20405
(202) 566-1297

Information is available from regional offices in Boston, New York, Washington, Philadelphia, Atlanta, Chicago, Kansas City, Fort Worth, Houston, Denver, San Francisco, Los Angeles, and Seattle.

The General Services Administration's (GSA) primary duty is purchasing supplies for government agencies, but in recent years it has offered special seminars around the country for women interested in starting and expanding businesses. The seminars last from one to three days and have been addressed to both would-be and existing entrepreneurs. Though the seminars have been free in past years, except for travel and associated expenses, the GSA has considered adding a nominal charge for future programs. The seminars have attracted between 8,000 and 10,000 participants annually in past years.

FINANCING

U. S. Small Business Administration
Office of Women's Business Enterprise
U. S. Small Business Administration
1441 L St., NW
Washington, DC 20416
(202) 653-6074; (202) 653-8000

Information is also available through more than 100 local offices in cities around the country (a listing of these offices is in Appendix A, beginning on p. 368).

The Office of Women's Business Enterprise was established in 1980 to oversee the Small Business Administration's efforts to provide financing and other assistance for women entrepreneurs. The SBA set a goal during the fiscal year that ended September 30, 1980, of providing $50 million of loans to women entrepreneurs through its existing regular business loan, or Section 7(a), program. Such loans are available to both start-up and existing entrepreneurs. As the fiscal year ended, the SBA exceeded its goal, but then decided to dispense with setting new higher goals. (For details on applying for SBA loans, see pp. 80–84 and pp. 90–92 in Chapter 3, "Federal Government Financing Sources.")

Women who encounter difficulties in applying for SBA loans or assistance from other federal agencies should contact the SBA's Office of Women's Business Enterprise, which attempts to resolve such problems and act as an advocate for women entrepreneurs.

PROCUREMENT

The federal government during the Carter administration placed a high priority on attempting to steer more of its purchases to businesses owned by women. For the fiscal year ended September 30, 1980, about $200 million of federal procurement was from women-owned businesses and the goal was to triple that amount in two years. The Reagan administration has indicated that it places a lower priority on such goals.

To encourage fulfillment of the goals, the government has adopted regulations that stipulate that for all federal contracts over $10,000, contractors must agree to use their best efforts to subcontract to women-owned businesses. And winners of contracts over $500,000 must agree to establish an affirmative-action plan agreeable to government procurement officials to subcontract with businesses owned by women.

Women interested in selling products and services to the federal government should refer to Chapter 10, "Government Procurement," for further information. A source of assistance geared to the special needs of women attempting to sell to the government is the Association of Women Government Contractors (described on pp. 268–69 of this chapter).

WOMEN'S ORGANIZATIONS

Women's growing interest in entrepreneurship has led to the formation of dozens of organizations to serve the interests of women entrepreneurs. The concept behind most of the organizations is to establish a "network" of resources and contacts women entrepreneurs can turn to for financing, customers, suppliers, and various other business needs.

Broadly speaking, women's organizations fall into two groups:

1. Women's banks, which are oriented to provide financing and management guidance to women business owners;

2. Women's business groups, which primarily carry on lobbying and management assistance activities. Most of the groups are open to women entrepreneurs of all sorts, including those seeking to start businesses and those who already own businesses.

Besides their specific programs of assistance, the organizations serve another valuable purpose for women entrepreneurs—they put women who have similar interests and aspirations in contact with each other. That helps relieve the isolation all entrepreneurs tend to feel and allows women to share their particular problems and experiences with others in similar situations. Such sharing can be an important learning experience as well.

WOMEN'S BANKS

Since 1975, at least eight banks around the country have been established by women. The banks mostly started from the premise that they would serve as places where women would make deposits and obtain loans for various purposes, including starting and expanding businesses. Special banks for women were needed, it was reasoned, so that women would avoid discrimination and be able to do their banking business among others who understood their particular problems.

Many of the banks encountered financial difficulties, though. The banks often didn't get the volume of deposits they expected and some ran into problems because they made loans to businesses which failed.

Women's banks have since changed their focus somewhat as a consequence. They now say that their primary purpose is to operate successfully from a business viewpoint, and to do that they are willing to serve men as well as women and to be tougher in evaluating loan requests of all sorts. In other words, the banks have become more profit-oriented than they were originally.

Yet the banks remain staffed and operated mostly by women and thus retain their orientation to women's special difficulties starting and operating businesses. An article in the August 4, 1980, New York *Times* noted, "Despite their new tough-mindedness, however, the women's banks do still differ from other banks in the degree of personal attention they seem to pay to women who apply for loans."

Some of the women's banks even offer seminars and counseling to loan applicants, whether or not they are approved for loans. Some also attempt to provide information on other resources of potential help to women. Women seeking business loans are thus advised to start their search at a women's bank. The banks are as follows:

Western Women's Bank
235 Front St.
San Francisco, CA 94111
(415) 421-9890

Women's National Bank
1627 K St., NW
Washington, DC 20006
(202) 466-4090

First Women's Bank of California
12301 Wilshire Boulevard
West Los Angeles, CA 90017
(213) 820-4941

First Women's Bank of Maryland
1800 Rockville Pike
Rockville, MD 20852
(301) 770-1300

Women's Bank
724 17th St.
Denver, CO 80202
(303) 534-2265

First Women's Bank
111 E 57th St.
New York, NY 10022
(212) 644-0670

Connecticut Women's Bank
100 Mason St.
Greenwich, CT 06830
(203) 622-1066

Women's Bank
1007 E Main St.
Richmond, VA 23219
(804) 643-1106

WOMEN'S BUSINESS GROUPS

American Women's Economic Development Corp.
1270 Ave. of the Americas
New York, NY 10020
(212) 397-0880

The American Women's Economic Development Corp. (AWED) provides free business counseling and training to women who plan to start new businesses and those who already own businesses. The organization, which was started in 1976, has been able to provide its services at no cost because it has had funding from various federal and private sources.

AWED has about fifty-five full-time and part-time employees, including business school professors and professional business managers. The organizations provide two types of assistance:

1. A nationwide telephone counseling service. Women entrepreneurs must fill out an application to register for the service, which allows them to direct specific questions about their business operations to trained counselors. More than 6,000 women have received such counseling.

2. A one-year training program for women planning to start or already operating businesses. The program includes short courses in accounting, law, personnel, time management, advertising, and sales. Women must apply for admission and are judged on the basis of their ambition, knowledge of their field, and success potential of their businesses. Between 175 and 200 women go through the program each year. It is open to women anywhere in the country, but in reality applicants must be near New York to be able to participate.

The organization claims that only a handful of the several hundred women who have completed the training program have gone bankrupt. AWED attempts to promote the network concept by keeping tabs on graduates of the training program and putting them in touch with each other as requests for suppliers, investors, and so forth are made by participants.

AWED expects to expand by opening branch offices in other cities around the country.

Association for Women Government Contractors
1218 16th St., NW
Washington, DC 20036
(202) 347-5195

The Association for Women Government Contractors was started in 1980 to provide women with information on selling goods and services to the government and also to lobby for expanded procurement opportunities for women. The association plans at least half a dozen seminars annually on various aspects of selling to the government, including government contract regulations and bid protests.

The association has also been pressuring various government agencies to be more receptive to the needs of women entrepreneurs. For instance, it has been seeking some kind of set-aside program under which women-owned businesses would be guaranteed a certain amount of government business, to be administered through the Small Business Administration.

The association encourages members to work together to obtain government contracts, such as through joint ventures and subcontracting. It publishes a monthly newsletter which includes listings of members to aid them in getting together. By the end of 1980, the association had about seventy-five members, most of whom were based in the Washington, DC, area.

Dues are $55 annually for individuals and $200 annually for companies (which provides voting rights for up to ten employees).

Association of Women Entrepreneurs
1212 Lincoln Benefit Life Building
Lincoln, NE 68508
(402) 474-2058

The Association of Women Entrepreneurs is an independent organization started in 1979 that includes more than fifty would-be and existing women entrepreneurs from the Lincoln area.

The association sponsors panels, such as bankers advising on applying for loans, and seminars on starting businesses. It also refers members to sources of business counseling in the area. The association has plans for publishing a newsletter and a directory of women-owned businesses in Nebraska for use by companies that win government contracts which are seeking women subcontractors as well as by other businesses.

The association is also active in lobbying on behalf of women's business interests at the state level.

Dues are $50 annually.

Center for Women's Opportunities
American Association of Community and Junior Colleges
One Dupont Circle, NW
Washington, DC
(202) 293-7050

The Center for Women's Opportunities of the American Association of Community and Junior Colleges has developed a forty-five-hour course for women considering starting businesses; the course has been adopted by hundreds of community and junior colleges around the country. The Center has trained staff members of community and junior colleges to teach the course and hopes that several thousand women each year will take it.

The course is intended to provide women with basic business instruction and information about local resources to aid in starting businesses. Participants are also encouraged to develop their own business plans. The Center was assisted in setting up the course with funds and guidance from the U. S. Small Business Administration.

The course is being offered by community and junior colleges in all regions of the country. For information on the most conveniently located schools teaching the course, contact the Center for Women's Opportunities.

National Association of Bank Women
500 N Michigan Ave.
Chicago, IL 60611
(312) 661-1700

The National Association of Bank Women is an organization that represents the interests of more than 25,000 women bank officers and managers. It has become active in promoting the interests of women business owners by using some of its 280 branches to locate and assist women entrepreneurs to obtain financing.

The association received two grants to aid in its work. One grant from the Farmers Home Administration (FmHA) is intended for the association to help women who have been in business three to seven years obtain FmHA loans. The association is also using the FmHA grant to assist bankers who help arrange FmHA loans to identify and work with appropriate women-owned businesses.

A second grant from the Small Business Administration and a private foundation is designed to enable the association to assist women apply and negotiate for private bank loans. The program is also intended for the association to train bankers in working with women business owners. The focus of the effort is on women-owned businesses that have been in existence three to seven years.

Because both programs started on a pilot basis in 1980 with the intention of expanding gradually through 1981 and beyond, women entrepreneurs should contact the National Association of Bank Women to learn about the most conveniently located local association branches and banks involved.

National Association of Black Women Entrepreneurs
10 Witherell St.
Detroit, MI 48226
(313) 963-8766

The National Association of Black Women Entrepreneurs is an 800-member organization that consists predominantly of black women, but is open to women of all races. It holds monthly meetings in Detroit, though it has members around the country; it expects to be forming chapters in other locations.

Members are surveyed at the monthly meetings about the topics future workshops and seminars should cover. Those run in the past have been on the basics of marketing, financing, and government procurement.

Membership is open to would-be and existing business owners. Dues are $40 annually.

National Association of Women Business Owners
2000 P St., NW
Washington, DC 20036
(202) 338-8966

The National Association of Women Business Owners (NAWBO) is probably the largest and most influential of the women's business groups. It has 1,200 members nationally and through its fourteen local chapters scattered around the country.

NAWBO is geared mostly to the needs of women who own operating businesses. On a national level, it devotes itself largely to lobbying on behalf of women's business interests and promoting the network concept. It keeps track of members' products and services and attempts to match appropriate members to each other for business purposes. It also publishes directories for women-owned businesses in the Washington-Baltimore, Chicago, and Boston metropolitan areas for use by other women and by corporations seeking to purchase from women. (The directories are $10 each, or $25 for the three.)

Local NAWBO chapters provide managerial assistance and training. Dues collected by local chapters cover national dues as well; entrepreneurs who have no chapters in their areas can join the national organization for $100 annually plus an initial onetime registration fee of $15.

Local chapters are in New Orleans; Washington, DC; Baltimore; Roanoke, VA; Chicago; Houston; Los Angeles; Miami; St. Paul; Research Triangle Park, NC; Pittsburgh; Peoria, IL; Kansas City, MO; and Detroit. The chapters vary in their activities; to give readers an idea of what they do, we contacted a sampling of chapters as follows:

Baltimore Association of Women Business Owners (NAWBO
    chapter)
c/o LaRue Schneider
2633 N Charles St.
Baltimore, MD 21218
(301) 467-2611

The Baltimore Association of Women Business Owners was established in 1979 and has twenty-five members. The group publishes a monthly newsletter about its activities, has a hotline service for members in need of business counseling, and sponsors monthly meetings with guest speakers. Topics cover both business and nonbusiness subjects; recent speakers have advised women about maximizing their business expense and protecting themselves from violent crime. The association has also started an informal referral system for members seeking to do business with other members.

Dues are $100 annually.

Chicago Chapter of Women Business Owners (NAWBO chapter)
520 N Michigan Ave.
Chicago, IL 60611
(312) 467-0295; (312) 951-1020

The Chicago Chapter of Women Business Owners is one of the oldest NAWBO chapters, having been started in 1974. It has 275 members, most of whom own businesses in a variety of business areas.

The chapter publishes a newsletter every other month about its activities and keeps tabs on members' products and services so it can refer members to each other for business purposes. Before their monthly meetings, cocktail parties are held to allow members to exchange information.

The monthly dinner meetings feature experts to discuss such subjects as accounts receivable, cash-flow management, personnel practices, and government procurement. In addition, the chapter does business counseling by referring inquiring members to more expert members to answer questions. The chapter also offers seminars open to the general public on starting and operating small businesses.

And finally, the Chicago chapter engages in state and national lobbying on behalf of business issues of importance to women. Dues are $115 annually.

Greater Peoria Chapter of NAWBO
c/o Water Power, Inc.
8811 N Pioneer Road
Peoria, IL 61615
(309) 692-5511

The Greater Peoria Chapter of NAWBO was established in 1979 and has forty members. It holds monthly informational seminars on such subjects as accounting, business law, taxes, estate planning, accounts receivable, and business insurance. The chapter also offers counseling through its board members, who tend to be fairly experienced business owners.

In addition, the chapter places a high priority on counseling women who aren't members but are about to start businesses. It offers information on licensing, unemployment compensation, and taxes, and provides references to appropriate federal and state agencies which can provide assistance as well as to business courses.

Dues are $100 annually.

Los Angeles Association of Women Business Owners (NAWBO
chapter)
2410 Beverly Boulevard
Los Angeles, CA 90057
(213) 387-7432

The Los Angeles Association of Women Business Owners was started
in 1978 and has 100 members from the Los Angeles area. A key activity
is the monthly support group meeting, at which groups of twenty members assemble to consider various financial subjects, such as dealing with
crisis situations. The association also sponsors seminars open to women
who aren't members, on starting and operating small businesses. A
monthly newsletter lists upcoming events as well as major companies
that want to do business with women entrepreneurs.

The Los Angeles association also refers members to appropriate
government assistance programs. And it has a referral service for
members seeking to do business with other members.

Annual dues are $100.

Miami Association of Women Business Owners (NAWBO chapter)
c/o Dolly Alper
DuPont Plaza Center (Suite 400)
Miami, FL 33131
(305) 377-9240

The Miami Association of Women Business Owners was started in
1977 and has fifty members. Its primary activity consists of monthly
meetings at which a member usually showcases her business. It also maintains a referral service to aid members in doing business with each other;
it has published its own directory of women-owned businesses for the
Miami area, sold at $3 a copy.

The association doesn't have an official counseling program, but business problems raised by both members and nonmembers are handled informally by experienced members in similar businesses as those seeking
assistance.

Dues are $75 annually.

Michigan Association of Women Business Owners (NAWBO
chapter)
20600 Eureka Road
Taylor, MI 48180
(313) 281-1995

The Michigan Association of Women Business Owners was only
started in 1980, but has been actively recruiting members from around
the State. It had forty members after only a few months.

Its monthly meetings feature speakers on various business-related subjects like marketing and time management. The association has also started a referral service to match up both members and nonmembers for business purposes.

Dues are $100 annually.

Mid-America Association of Women Business Owners (NAWBO
    chapter)
c/o DeSenne Group, Inc.
3706 Broadway
Kansas City, MO 64111
(816) 756-2455; (816) 756-0600

The Mid-America Association of Women Business Owners was started in early 1980 and has thirty-five members. Its main emphasis is on the network idea; it maintains a referral service for local women entrepreneurs seeking to do business with other women, and each month a different member describes her business at the monthly meeting so that other members can be aware of potential business contacts.

The monthly meetings also feature speakers on business subjects such as improving cash flow and choosing an accountant. The association lobbies on behalf of women's business interests in both Kansas and Missouri.

Dues are $100 annually.

Minnesota Association of Women Business Owners (NAWBO
    chapter)
46 E Fourth St.
St. Paul, MN 55101
(612) 291-7983

The Minnesota Association of Women Business Owners was started in 1977 and has 200 members. Its services for members are largely in the area of business training. The association sponsors weekly Saturday seminars of various business subjects like pricing, personnel, and government procurement. It also sponsors an intensive three-weekend training program on business leadership, which costs members $200.

In addition, the association provides referrals for women seeking other women entrepreneurs to do business with. And it lobbies at the state level on behalf of women's business interests.

Dues are $100 annually plus an initial onetime $20 registration fee.

ADDITIONAL INFORMATION SOURCES

The federal government has published several booklets and directories specifically for women entrepreneurs which, unless otherwise indicated, are available from:

Superintendent of Documents
U. S. Government Printing Office
Washington, DC 20402

A Directory of Federal Government Business Assistance Programs for Women, free.
This guide to federal programs especially for women was put together by several federal agencies.

The Guide to the U. S. Department of Commerce for Women Business Owners, $2.75.
Describes Department of Commerce efforts to aid women entrepreneurs just starting out and already operating businesses.

Women and the Small Business Administration and *Women's Handbook: How the SBA Can Help You Go into Business.* Both publications, which describe SBA programs of potential use for women entrepreneurs, are available free from local SBA offices or the central SBA office:

U. S. Small Business Administration
Office of Women's Business Enterprise
U. S. Small Business Administration
1441 L St., NW
Washington, DC 20416

The Woman's Guide to Starting a Business: Revised Edition, by Claudia Jessup and Genie Hipps. (New York: Holt, Rinehart & Winston, 1979) $6.95
This book offers advice on starting and operating small businesses, with chapters on evaluating business ideas, financing, advertising, accounting, and marketing. It also includes interviews with thirty entrepreneurs, along with a bibliography and information source list.

Women and the Business Game: Strategies for Successful Ownership, by Charlotte Taylor. (New York: Cornerstone Library, 1980) $11.95
A thoughtful and clearly written guide to starting and operating a small business. The title is misleading, though, since the book's advice is mainly the sort addressed to entrepreneurs in general by various other guides to starting small businesses. At the end it lists other books and information sources of particular interest to women entrepreneurs.

The New Entrepreneurs: Women Working from Home by Terri P. Tepper and Nona Dawe Tepper. (New York: Universe Books, 1980) $10.95
This book essentially consists of forty profiles of women who started businesses at home, with their own accounts of how they learned to operate their businesses and the obstacles they encountered. Among the women profiled are a shoemaker, antique dealer, pastry chef, and craft specialists.

The Entrepreneurial Woman: How She Thinks and Copes: How She Starts and Succeeds in Her Own Business, by Sandra Winston. (New York: Newsweek Books, 1979) $8.95

This book, too, consists mostly of case histories of women who have started small enterprises. *INC.* magazine in its September 1979 issue was critical of the book for including "an endless series of self-help checklists" and being "condescending" to readers.

Women's Networks: The Complete Guide to Getting a Better Job, Advancing Your Career and Feeling Great as a Woman Through Networking, by Carol Kleiman. (New York: Lippincott & Crowell, 1980) $9.95

This book offers an overview of the network concept together with advice on setting up and using networks of different types. It also lists women's organizations around the country that promote the network concept.

CHAPTER 9
Franchising

INTRODUCTION: CONSTANTLY DEVELOPING OPPORTUNITIES

In an age of tight money and frequent recessions, which seem to make the possibility and actuality of ownership increasingly perilous, franchising remains an area of hope and excitement for would-be and existing entrepreneurs.

In recent years, between 100 and 300 companies annually have moved into franchising, and the number of franchisers now stands at approximately 2,000. Their economic impact is impressive: they account for more than 500,000 franchised outlets doing well over $300 billion in sales annually; in fact, the franchise companies account for nearly one third of all retail sales.

For all the current significance of franchising, the practice actually had its start early in this century, when the first automobile dealerships and affiliated gas stations were established. In the 1960s and 1970s, franchising became almost synonymous with fast-food and motel chains like McDonald's and Holiday Inn. More recently, real estate brokerage, weight-loss programs, quick-print photography, and automobile rust-proofing have become hot franchise areas. There seems to be almost no end to the kinds of businesses taking the franchising path; they now include in their numbers builders of underground homes, parent-child hair-styling shops, portable disco vans, and traveling cookie concessions.

Some franchise ideas have begun to pass by the wayside, though; auto dealerships and gas stations, for example, have lost their attractiveness because of the uncertain energy situation.

ADVANTAGES FOR FRANCHISEES

Franchising, according to a November 1979 *Money* magazine article, "amounts to paying someone else for the right to distribute his products and use his trademark for a set period of time, usually ten years." For would-be entrepreneurs, that proposition holds several attractions over starting a business independently. The main lure, according to the *Money* article, is that "A good franchise business can provide many of the same opportunities [as starting a business from scratch] with far fewer risks." Indeed, surveys taken by the International Franchise Association (IFA), a trade group of franchisers, suggest that less than 1 percent of franchised outlets fail. Other more conservative estimates put the failure rate during the first five years of franchise outlet operation at less than 10 percent. Though no one knows exactly how many independent small businesses fail, some estimates have that failure rate at 80 percent within the first five years. Certainly no observer of small business would suggest an independent business failure rate anywhere near as small as 10 percent.

Another attraction of franchises is that, in many cases, they allow entrepreneurs to buy the equivalent of a turnkey operation. Thus, the businesses are set up in key aspects by the franchisers: besides providing a proven and sometimes well-known product or service, franchisers frequently provide a location, hiring and accounting advice, and advertising. Franchisers will also keep tabs on franchises, helping to spot and resolve operating problems. And start-up costs can be as little as a few hundred dollars, although they are usually at least several thousand dollars.

ADVANTAGES FOR FRANCHISERS

For owners of small businesses with growth potential but without the cash to expand, franchising can be a way of growing quickly and relatively inexpensively. Instead of paying for the cost of new outlets—the type of growth that might be impossible during recessionary times—business owners can look to franchisees to cover certain start-up expenses, like the cost of buildings, supplies, and equipment. Franchisers who can cover at least some of the start-up costs find it easier to attract franchisees, though.

While franchisers do not reap anywhere near the profits they would if they owned the outlets, they stand to benefit from long-term royalty payments from franchisees, without having to worry about providing management of the outlets. Because the franchisees are themselves entrepreneurs, they can usually be expected to work more industriously than would hired managers.

FRANCHISING DRAWBACKS

For all its attractions, however, franchising has its perils for franchisees and franchisers alike. On the franchisee side, acquiring well-known franchises has become quite expensive. A fast-food franchise, such as a McDonald's, Burger King, or Wendy's, can easily require an investment of $300,000 to $500,000, assuming franchises are available—which they often are not (at least to the start-up entrepreneur). Many franchises are being sold to investor groups and corporations which specialize in operating franchises. In some cases, once franchisers become well established and financially prosperous, they open their own outlets to maximize profits. In one recent year, according to an article in the September 1979 issue of *Venture* magazine, McDonald's received about 25,000 inquiries from potential franchisees but granted only sixty stores to new entrepreneurs. The remaining 350 or so stores that were opened that year went either to existing McDonald's franchisees or remained in the direct control of the company itself.

Also, running a franchise is not quite the same thing as owning a business; all a franchisee really has is a contract to run the franchise for a certain amount of time (usually ten years), and the contract may or may not be renewed. As *Money* magazine's article in the November 1979 issue put it: "In a successful independent business, your equity grows. But with a franchise, you could be left with nothing but the building and equipment when your contract runs out in 10 years."

On the other side of the coin, small-business owners looking to franchise their businesses face some similar problems. The costs involved in setting up a franchising program can be so astronomical as to drain very quickly an otherwise successful business. The expenses include legal, accounting, and consulting fees; increased advertising costs; and personnel costs to hire franchising staff members to recruit and train franchisees. "With this kind of overhead, consultants warn that franchisers must be prepared to lose money for at least a two-year period," noted an article on franchising in the July 1980 issue of *Venture* magazine. The article also noted that "with today's uncertain economic conditions, franchisers may have to wait for profits even longer."

Besides coping with heavy financial costs, new franchisers must deal with the managerial strains of simultaneously setting up a franchising system and running their existing business. Establishing a franchise can quickly become a full-time task, so business owners must usually delegate responsibility for running already existing outlets to hired hands, a task which is easier said than done.

LEGAL CONCERNS

Because franchising is based on contractual arrangements between franchisee and franchiser, there are legal issues overhanging both parties. Disputes are frequent and sometimes wind up in court.

Recent court cases have involved suits in which franchisees have charged franchisers with unjustly refusing to renew contracts, with forcing franchisees to buy franchiser products at inflated prices, and with requiring franchisees to sell products at unfairly low prices. Other issues that commonly arise, but do not necessarily make it to court, are contentions by franchisees that they are not getting their money's worth from franchisers on required advertising fees and that franchisers are not enforcing contractual quality standards against poorly managed franchisees, a situation that can adversely affect the public image of all franchises.

According to an article in the October 1978 issue of *Journal of Small Business Management,* franchisees most likely to encounter legal problems with their franchisers are those involved in their first business undertaking who have failed to have their contract reviewed by an attorney, accepted contracts without modifying them to the peculiarities of their location or circumstances, and taken at face value franchiser sales and other estimates. "Franchisees who conduct their own market research, consult independent legal counsel, and have prior business experience tend to encounter few serious legal problems," the article concluded.

The legal issues raised by franchisees have in some cases been backed by judges or found to be true after unscrupulous or poorly run franchisers have gone bankrupt. However, the very frequency of complaints by franchisees convinced the federal government to require, through the Federal Trade Commission, that franchisers provide extensive disclosure to potential franchisees about their businesses, effective October 1979. Among the facts that must now be disclosed in writing by franchisers are their financial condition, their bankruptcy and litigation experience, information on initial training programs, contract termination procedures, and franchisee failure rates. At least fifteen states have enacted their own disclosure requirements as well which, in many ways, duplicate the FTC's requirements and, in a few ways, may even go further in prescribing the types of information franchisers must reveal.

The various regulations have, however, made life both expensive and complicated for new franchisers. Putting together a legal statement of fifty pages or more can easily cost many thousands of dollars; and simply understanding which federal or state regulations apply in which states can be complicated as well.

On the positive side, the regulations have made the process of evaluating franchisers somewhat easier for franchisees, who now can quickly have many questions answered that franchisers might formerly have refused to answer. Potential franchisees should remember, though, that no requirements exist that regulate which businesses can become franchisers; the federal and state regulations only govern the information franchisers must disclose.

The remainder of this chapter will attempt to shed further light on the opportunities available to entrepreneurs in franchising and also to provide information on regulations and information sources of importance to both franchisees and franchisers.

FOR PROSPECTIVE AND OPERATING FRANCHISEES

Would-be franchisees should consider three broad factors in deciding whether or not to acquire a franchise and which franchises offer the best opportunities.

First, entrepreneurs must decide what kind of business they want to operate and whether a franchise is the best way to get started. For an ethnic gourmet restaurant, for instance, an independently owned business might be most advisable; while, for a fast-food restaurant, a franchise might compete best.

Once having decided on a broad area of business, would-be franchisees must evaluate the potential franchises available—a difficult task, since, in most business areas, many types of franchises exist. For instance, in the automotive field alone, there are franchises available for muffler replacement, auto painting, transmission repair, and tune-ups. (Several of the franchising books and newsletters described on pp. 298–301 can offer guidance in this area.) Included in such an assessment should be consideration of the franchise's past growth record and potential for future growth, its approach to promotion and managerial assistance, and its plans for new products and other areas of development that will enable it to remain competitive.

The factors that help narrow the choice perhaps more than any other are franchise cost and terms. Franchises vary widely in the investment required to get started and the royalties required once the franchise is operating. Franchises also vary greatly in the kinds of demands they make of franchisees in such areas as the purchasing of equipment and supplies.

Prospective franchisees should remember that they are usually eligible for Small Business Administration loans and, possibly, other types of government loans to acquire franchises. For further details, refer to Chapter 3, "Federal Government Financing Sources." For minority entrepreneurs considering acquiring a franchise, several Minority Enterprise Small Business Investment Companies, as described on p. 234, provide financing for franchises. Banks and other commercial finance institutions also make loans to franchisees. For information on such loans, see Chapter 5, "Commercial Finance."

282

To give readers a flavor of the diversity, both of the franchises available and their requirements of franchisees, twelve franchises were investigated. Although some of the information contained in the following descriptions is available from several of the books listed at the end of this chapter, not all of it is available from other published sources. Each franchise listed here was contacted expressly for the purpose of filling in gaps in information published elsewhere, in such areas as royalty payments, supply purchasing, and advertising. Prospective franchisees are advised to obtain franchiser disclosure statements, which contain much more detailed information than is provided here, on any franchises they may be considering seriously.

For comprehensive listings and brief descriptions of the nation's 2,000 franchisers, readers should refer to the books and publications noted on pp. 298–301.

Baskin-Robbins Ice Cream Co.
31 Baskin-Robbins Place
Glendale, CA 91201
(213) 956-0031

2,400 retail ice cream store franchises in the United States, Canada, Japan, and Europe; established in 1945.

Start-up costs average about $20,000 per store. This cost includes a $7,500 general administration fee for five years. The franchisee leases the store and equipment from Baskin-Robbins and buys ice cream from Baskin-Robbins as well. Supplies and uniforms are purchased from distributors approved by Baskin-Robbins.

Baskin-Robbins is essentially an ice cream manufacturer that makes its long-term profits selling ice cream to its franchisees. The company collects no royalties, but franchisees are obligated to buy Baskin-Robbins ice cream. They must also buy toppings and uniforms from franchiser-approved distributors. Baskin-Robbins says this policy enables them to maintain quality control and allows for the reduced prices that accompany large purchase orders (economies of scale).

Baskin-Robbins provides for its franchisees free national advertising, but franchisees must pay 50 percent of the cost of regional advertising; franchisees do, however, have some say in regional advertising. Company representatives use franchise input to review and update the overall Baskin-Robbins marketing program on a quarterly basis.

Franchisee complaints about Baskin-Robbins have been similar to those voiced about a number of franchisers: franchisees contend restrictions that force them to buy supplies from approved distributors can cause financial difficulties if these distributors suddenly raise prices or cut service. Franchisees also complain that certain aspects of the company's promotional strategy, such as the giving of free ice cream cones on birthdays, help Baskin-Robbins as a company rather than the franchisee as an entrepreneur, because the franchisees, not the company, must absorb the cost of the freebies.

Burger King Corp.
P.O. Box 520783
Miami, FL 33152
(305) 596-7734

2,800 fast-food restaurant franchises in the United States and abroad; established in 1954.

Burger King requires franchisees to come up with start-up costs, which are around $110,000, from their own savings. Included in these costs is a $40,000 franchise fee which covers twenty years. Burger King estimates that first-year capital requirements may run another $160,000, which can emanate from bank loans or other financing.

Burger King collects a royalty equaling 3 percent of monthly sales. The company also collects 4 percent of monthly sales as a contribution toward advertising costs.

The franchiser's selection and training process is rigorous and thorough: prospective franchisees must demonstrate to Burger King that they have a net worth of at least $150,000 and liquid assets of at least $110,000 (the aforementioned start-up cost figure). Franchisees must successfully complete a fifty-hour training course before approval, and another six weeks of training once approval has been granted and before start-up. Ongoing assistance is provided by the company in the form of films, seminars, and additional training programs.

Century 21 Real Estate Corp.
18872 MacArthur Boulevard
Irvine, CA 92715
(714) 752-7521

7,600 real estate brokerage outlets in all fifty states; established in 1972.

Start-up costs depend on whether franchisees are beginning new businesses or converting existing brokerage firms into Century 21 outlets. All franchisees must pay a franchise fee of between $9,500 and $10,500, depending on the state. The franchise fee covers a five-year contract, which is renewable for five-year terms at a cost of $100. Special Century 21 signs, gold coats, office supplies, and additional equipage run between $1,500 and $4,000. Franchisees starting new operations have the additional expense of possibly buying office space and furnishing an office. In most states, the franchiser can provide ten-year loans through a commercial finance company to cover some start-up expenses. Century 21 assists in site selection and office layout.

Franchisees must pay a royalty of 6 percent of their gross commissions, as well as advertising expenses of 2 percent of their commissions.

Century 21 provides one week of intensive sales training to new franchisees and subsequent seminars and workshops on real estate sales and financing. The company also provides referrals of potential customers through its nationwide network.

Although Century 21 is now the largest real estate franchiser in the country, it is encountering increasing competition for franchisees from franchisers offering lower franchise fees and flat-fee royalties instead of a percentage.

Dunhill Personnel System Inc.
One Old Country Road
Carle Place, NY 11514
(516) 741-5081

300 personnel placement service outlets in the United States, Puerto Rico, Canada, and South America; established in 1952.

Dunhill outlets specialize in placing sales, administrative, technical, and skilled clerical personnel. The company has recently begun offering franchises for temporary personnel placement as well.

Dunhill estimates start-up costs at about $40,000. That cost includes a $20,000 franchise fee, $8,000 for office furnishings and various fees (including legal fees), and $12,000 to cover the first three to four months of operating expenses. When necessary, Dunhill will finance half of the franchise fee, deferring repayment of the $10,000 for ten months so that the money can come from franchisee earnings.

Dunhill claims 7 percent of cash receipts as royalties and 1 percent of same for advertising fees.

Dunhill provides a two-week training course for franchisees at its home office. The franchiser also provides training for franchisees' employment counselors and managers, follow-up visits by in-house field staff, and two or three regional workshops each year on topics selected by franchisees.

Dunhill is one of the relatively few franchisers which have established a franchisee advisory council to aid in communications with franchisees. The council is really an association of franchisees to keep Dunhill informed as to franchisee complaints and suggestions for improving operations.

H & R Block Inc.
4410 Main St.
Kansas City, MO 64111
(816) 753-6900

8,700 offices, of which 4,600 are franchised, for preparing individual income tax returns, across the United States; established in 1946.

The only new H & R Block franchises that remain are in small communities. These new franchises open at the rate of 100–150 annually. However, opportunities for acquiring H & R Block franchises exist by virtue of transfers from retiring franchisees, which are occurring at a rate of about 250 per year.

Franchise fees average about $1,500 for a five-year period. In the case of transfers, however, larger fees must be paid. The company says it will not "unreasonably withhold approval" of transfers, claiming it is not interested in increasing its percentage of company-owned outlets.

Annual royalties are steep: 50 percent of the first $5,000 of sales and 30 percent of the remainder. The company provides national advertising and specialized supplies, however, at no additional cost. Franchisees must arrange for their own offices and furnishings. Many begin operations in their own homes.

H & R Block prefers that franchisees have some bookkeeping or tax knowledge, but the franchiser provides seventy-five hours of training each fall for its new franchisees, as well as pretax-season training for all employees. The company keeps franchisees updated on tax law changes and court decisions, as well as providing ongoing managerial assistance.

Kwik-Kopy Corp.
5525 Hollister
Houston, TX 77040
(713) 939-1010

550 instant printing franchises in 39 states; established in 1967.

Start-up costs of a Kwik-Kopy franchise run between about $43,500 and $45,500. The cost includes a franchise fee of $29,500, which secures the franchise right for twenty-five years and is renewable at the option of the franchisee. Also included in the start-up cost estimate is $4,000 for equipment leasing and $10,000 to $12,000 of working capital to pay initial salaries and other expenses. Kwik-Kopy will, when necessary, finance up to $12,000 of the franchise fee. For an additional $3,000, franchisees can buy the company's recently developed in-store computer system that quickly estimates prices for complex jobs which would otherwise be too time-consuming to tabulate.

Five percent of annual gross sales are taken by the franchiser as royalties and 2 percent goes toward advertising.

Kwik-Kopy offers discounts of 10 percent off list prices to franchisees who purchase supplies from them and, alternatively, helps franchisees who want to use other suppliers to negotiate favorable contracts. The company selects sites, but franchisees must negotiate their own store leases.

Kwik-Kopy provides franchisees with three weeks of training at its headquarters. The company also provides ongoing managerial assistance and advice, beginning with one week of in-store supervision by its field staff. It will sometimes aid in local advertising, but franchisees have in many cases formed cooperative local advertising groups.

Midas Muffler Shops
Midas-International Corporation
222 S Riverside Plaza
Chicago, IL 60606
(312) 648-5600

1,100 outlets across the United States, Canada, and Puerto Rico; started in 1956.

Start-up costs for a Midas Muffler Shop outlet average $120,000. Included in that cost is a $10,000 franchise fee for twenty years. Midas requires that 50 percent of the initial $120,000 be in cash and does not provide any financing assistance. Franchisees must also pay to lease their land and building from Midas.

Franchisees must pay a flat annual fee of 10 percent of sales. This amount includes royalties and national advertising costs.

Midas screens prospective franchisees carefully. Franchisees must submit background information about themselves for review by both a special committee and field managers. Those applicants deemed suitable are invited to attend a two-day orientation seminar in Chicago to help them decide if they really want to make the financial commitment of becoming Midas franchisees. Those who decide in the affirmative then receive four weeks of training at a central Midas location. Midas continues to provide management assistance after the training session, in hiring and training employees, formulating local advertising programs, and advising franchisees on financial management procedures. Midas also provides free technical courses for dealers and managers.

Midas has an active franchisee association, which aids in relaying suggestions and complaints from franchisees to the company.

New England Log Homes Inc.
2301 State St.
P.O. Box 5056
Hamden, CT 06518
(203) 562-9981

Over 100 retail outlets around the country which sell kits for precut pine log homes or office buildings; established in 1970.

The company only approves franchise sites located along state or interstate highways. There are no royalties; instead, the franchiser pays the franchisee commissions on the log homes and offices sold. The higher the sales volume, the larger the franchisee's percentage of the take. Commissions also vary with the models sold. The company would not provide a range of commissions for our purposes.

Start-up costs cannot be estimated with total precision, because franchisees are not only expected to buy a log home kit and finishing supplies to serve as an office—the cost for which ranges between $32,000 and $50,000—but also to buy the land on which the office sits, which varies in cost by location and parcel size. The franchisee must also pay a "zoning fee" of $5,000 for an exclusive territory. On the positive side, franchisees are permanent owners of their office and land.

New England Log Homes provides national advertising without charge and reimburses franchisees for one fourth the cost of local ads that meet with its approval. Training varies, depending on the franchisee's background. Regular national and regional sales meetings are held; and sales, engineering, and operations staff officials are always available to provide assistance on questions or problems.

Ramada Inns Inc.
3838 E Van Buren St.
Phoenix, AZ 85008
(602) 273-4000

700 franchised hotels and motels in the United States and worldwide; established in 1959.

The Ramada Inn name can either be bought by builders of new hotels or motels, or it can be applied to existing units that meet Ramada's specifications. The company will grant franchises only to professional hotel or motel owners or managers or, alternatively, to investors who have professional management staffs. Royalties are 5.2 percent of gross room revenues.

Start-up costs vary widely, depending on whether the unit is new— size and location influence such costs—or existent. In addition to providing the hotel or motel, a franchisee must pay a franchise fee of $100 per room, or $20,000, whichever amount is greater.

Ramada feels that franchisees should be worth a minimum of $3 million. It does not offer financing but will assist in the preparation of loan applications.

The company provides plans to ensure reasonable conformity of units to its model physical plant. It also trains managers in what it calls the "Ramada concept" of doing business. Annual ten-day refresher training sessions are held in each region, and company staff officials visit several times yearly to provide assistance. A bonus to franchisees is hookup to the company's worldwide reservation system.

Sports Shacks Inc.
1310 E Highway 96
White Bear Lake, MN 55110
(612) 426-0072

750 retail sporting goods store franchises across the United States; established in 1974.

Start-up costs are a minimum of $35,000, which includes a $6,500 franchise fee covering four years (automatically renewable up to twenty years), initial inventory, equipment, and other predictable expenses. The company does not provide financing but will help to fill out loan applications.

Royalty payments are 3 percent of sales. Advertising costs are graduated depending on sales volume, but average about 1 percent of sales.

The company provides five days of training at its home office, two days of on-site training and supervision, and managerial assistance as needed from the home office. Franchisees also receive an operations manual, a monthly newsletter from the company, and management and merchandising bulletins.

Stretch & Sew Inc.
220 S Seneca Road
P.O. Box 185
Eugene, OR 97401
(503) 686-9961
(800) 547-2515

215 retail outlets in the United States and Canada selling special knit fabrics, patterns, and books, as well as offering instruction in sewing techniques; established in 1969.

Initial investment ranges from $56,000 to $100,000, depending on store size and location. Start-up includes costs for fixtures, initial inventory, training for teachers and management, and various legal and accounting expenses. It also includes a $15,000 franchise fee good for ten years of operation.

Stretch & Sew helps in site selection, but franchisees must negotiate their own leases. In the same vein, the company does not provide financing but will assist franchisees in preparing and presenting loan applications; however, Stretch & Sew does require that franchisees put up at least one third of the needed investment from their own savings. National advertising is provided at no additional charge, unless stores want their names used; local advertising is at the discretion of individual franchisees.

Royalties are 5 percent of annual gross sales for the first three years of operation, after which stores in metropolitan areas must pay the greater of $10,000 or 5 percent of sales annually, and stores in nonmetropolitan areas must pay the greater of $5,000 or 5 percent of sales.

The company provides two weeks of initial management training, plus three days of training in special sewing techniques for the first three sewing teachers, all without extra charge. The company also provides a two- or three-week internship at an established franchise. Stretch & Sew officials provide ongoing management assistance, and the company sponsors workshops and biyearly conventions. A franchisee association works at keeping franchisee concerns known to the company.

Taylor Rental Corp.
570 Cottage St.
Springfield, MA 01104
(413) 781-7730

More than 600 Taylor outlets in the United States, which rent commercial, industrial, and home equipment; established in 1945.

Start-up costs can vary widely, because franchisees must provide their own building and land for five years; consequently, purchase or lease costs figure into overall start-up costs. In addition, franchisees must put up an additional $38,500–$43,500 to cover a $6,000 franchise fee, a $22,500 down payment to Taylor for equipment and supplies (worth about $90,000), and $10,000 to $15,000 of working capital.

The company will help to arrange five-year bank loans to cover part of the start-up costs and will provide financing for future inventory growth. Taylor also helps franchisees in meeting its site specifications, which are fairly exacting, in that franchisees must provide a minimum of 3,200 feet of store space, plus parking for eight to ten cars and a fenced-in area for outdoor equipment.

Taylor collects 5 percent of sales income to cover royalties, life and health insurance, and use of the company's computer service; part of any unspent royalty is returned to dealers at year-end as an advertising allowance.

The company provides an initial ten-day training session and a subsequent one-week advanced training session at the franchise; franchisee staff members are also eligible for free training at a central location at any time.

CHECKING OUT FRANCHISERS

Once prospective franchisees have narrowed their choice of franchisers, they should carefully evaluate the franchises by learning not only about costs and terms, but also about the overall business practices of the franchisers and complaints of their current franchisees. This evaluation process has several parts.

First, and perhaps most importantly, franchising experts advise prospective franchisees to talk with operating franchisees of the franchises under consideration. It is preferable to conduct this survey with franchisees outside the immediate vicinity; they are not so likely to feel threatened by area competition and their advice, therefore, is not so apt to be negatively biased for reasons of personal gain. Franchisers should be asked for names of such franchisees. If they balk at supplying this or any other information, the entrepreneur should be wary. Once contacted, operating franchisees should be asked about what they see as the advantages and disadvantages of operating their particular franchise. They should also be queried as to how they get along with the franchiser. If they do not feel threatened, most franchisees will not mind sounding off a bit on the ins and outs of their business.

A second part of the evaluation process is investigating the legal and accounting aspects of the prospective franchises. Acquisition of a franchise involves fairly complex legal documents and the screening of reasonably sophisticated financial materials, some of which will contain information about the company's financial status and others of which may have to be signed by the entrepreneur; these may therefore affect him for some time afterward. Hence, an entrepreneur who is serious about acquiring a franchise should engage a lawyer who specializes in franchising. Prospective franchisees should also obtain disclosure documents and study them carefully, with the aid of an attorney or, if preferred, a financial analyst.

A number of organizations and government agencies can be of assistance in the whole process of checking out franchisers, and those appropriate to the situation should be contacted as part of the evaluation process. The same organizations and agencies can be of use to operating franchisees as well. A listing and description of these sources follows.

American Bar Association
1155 E 60th St.
Chicago, IL 60637
(312) 947-4000

The American Bar Association publishes a directory of those of its members who are active in the area of franchise law. Another way to find a good franchise lawyer is to check with franchisees in the fields being explored.

National Franchise Association Coalition
P.O. Box 366
Fox Lake, IL 60020
(312) 587-9501

A trade association of sixteen franchisee groups.

In a relatively small number of franchises, the franchisees have organized associations to aid in communicating with franchisers and each other. The associations are particularly helpful in allowing franchisees to make complaints and problems known to franchisers and in giving the weight of numbers and unity to particularly irksome or widespread franchisee difficulties.

The National Franchise Association Coalition (NFAC) represents approximately 25,000 franchisees drawn from 16 franchisee associations of the following franchises or kinds of franchises: McDonald's, Burger Chef, Popeye's, Montgomery Ward's independent catalogue sales agents, Dunkin' Donuts, Hertz, Kentucky Fried Chicken, Mister Donut, Dairy Queen, A & W International, 7-11 Stores, Midas, Arthur Treacher's, Shakey's, Ziebart, and independent news distributors.

Not every franchisee association belongs to the NFAC. It is still a fledgling group, having been established in 1975. Its executive director works only on a part-time basis.

Nonetheless, the NFAC can be a valuable resource for prospective franchisees seeking sources for learning how franchisers treat franchisees. And the Coalition can continue to be useful once the entrepreneur becomes a franchisee.

The NFAC publishes a newsletter about franchising industry trends and problems from franchisees' viewpoints, and it has a committee of consulting lawyers for referring members with legal problems. The NFAC also aids franchisees in organizing their own franchisee associations and lobbies for legislation to aid franchisees. Membership dues typically range from $25 to $100 per store annually, depending partly on ability to pay.

Program Adviser
Franchise and Business Opportunities Program
Federal Trade Commission
Washington, DC 20580
(202) 523-3625
(202) 523-3814

Responsible for enforcing franchiser disclosure regulations through its Washington office and through regional offices in New York, Atlanta, Denver, and San Francisco.

The key tool through which the FTC achieves this task is FTC Rule 436, which took effect on October 21, 1979, and which is considered a landmark accomplishment in franchising. Having taken about seven years to formulate, FTC Rule 436 is the first legal instrument which addresses franchiser informational disclosures to prospective franchisees. It stipulates that the franchiser must hand over a disclosure document to a prospective franchisee at the earliest of these three events:

1. ten business days before a contract is signed,
2. ten business days before money is due to be paid a franchiser, or
3. at the first in-person meeting between the two parties.

292

The document must provide specified information in each of twenty categories. Included in this information is the franchiser's business experience, the franchiser's litigation and bankruptcy history, initial and continuing payments required of franchisees, restrictions on goods and services purchased and sold by franchisees, financing assistance available from the franchiser, territorial protection, renewal and termination provisions, training provided, site selection procedures, franchiser financial statements, franchiser statistics on present franchises, and the names and addresses of other franchisees.

Franchisees should keep in mind that information contained in the disclosure statements has not been verified by the FTC or state agencies; however, if any of the information is found to be wrong or other violations of the FTC regulation occur, franchisers are subject to fines of up to $10,000 per violation, FTC injunctions to stop violations, and lawsuits by franchisees.

The FTC began its enforcement of the disclosure regulation in 1980 with a Washington staff of four, assisted by an additional eight people in the Denver, New York, San Francisco, and Atlanta regional offices. Franchisees who feel the disclosure rule has been violated or who have other complaints about franchisers should contact an FTC office. The FTC says it is also open to issuing advisory opinions to both franchisees and franchisers as to whether franchiser statements comply with the disclosure rule. In addition, the FTC's staff is open to informal questions and inquiries from prospective franchisees and franchisers seeking information.

How effective FTC enforcement efforts will be is uncertain, but some observers are pessimistic. An article on franchising in the February 1980 issue of *Venture* magazine, entitled "How the FTC Fails to Regulate," noted that "FTC officials concede privately that[,] because of its tiny staff, the agency cannot mount much of an enforcement effort." The article added:

> An additional stumbling block to enforcement may be the FTC's decision, early in the game, not to require franchisers to register and file their disclosure statements [with that agency]. This means the commission has no way of knowing—short of receiving complaints—whether franchisers have even bothered to prepare disclosure statements, let alone [to] do so properly and hand them out to prospective franchisees.

Franchising Industry Specialist
Service Industries Division
Office of Consumer Goods and Service Industries
Bureau of Industrial Economics
U. S. Department of Commerce
Washington, DC 20230
(202) 566-3400

The Commerce Department's Office of Consumer Goods and Service Industries collects and analyzes data on various industries, including franchising. It performs and publishes annual surveys on major franchises and on the role of franchising in the economy. (The publications are described on pp. 298–301 of this chapter, in the section dealing with franchising books and publications.) While the Office can provide useful statistical information, it will provide little in the way of judgments or inside information on individual franchisers.

STATE REGULATION

At least fifteen states have their own franchise disclosure requirements, some of which may be more stringent than the FTC rule and may also take precedence over the FTC rule. The existence of such regulations means that both prospective and operating franchisees in those states should check with the appropriate agency to find out what the regulations require and when and how they are enforced. The state agencies which supervise enforcement of franchise disclosure are as follows.

CALIFORNIA

Commissioner of Corporations
600 S Commonwealth Ave.
Los Angeles, CA 90005
(213) 736-2741

or

1025 P St.
Sacramento, CA 95814
(916) 445-7205

or

1350 Front St.
San Diego, CA 92101

or

600 California St.
San Francisco, CA 94108
(415) 557-3787

FLORIDA

Consumer Counsel
Department of Legal Affairs
The Capitol
Tallahassee, FL 32304
(904) 488-2719

HAWAII

Director of Regulatory Agencies
Business Registration Division
1010 Richards St.
Honolulu, HI 96813
(808) 548-4017

ILLINOIS

Chief
Consumer Protection & Franchise
  Division
Attorney General's Office
500 S Second St.
Springfield, IL 62706
(217) 782-4465

INDIANA

Securities Commissioner
State Office Building
Indianapolis, IN 46201
(317) 633-6681

MARYLAND

Securities Commissioner
One S Calvert St. (Room 1507)
Baltimore, MD 21202
(301) 383-3714

MICHIGAN

Director of Commerce
Corporation and Securities Bureau
5511 Enterprise Drive
Lansing, MI 48913
(517) 374-9444

MINNESOTA

Commissioner of Securities
Department of Commerce
500 Metro Square Building
Seventh and Roberts Sts.
St. Paul, MN 55101
(612) 296-5689

NORTH DAKOTA

Commissioner of Securities
State Capitol Building
Bismarck, ND 58505
(701) 224-2910

OREGON

Corporations Commissioner
Department of Commerce;
  Franchise Section
158 12th St., NE
Salem, OR 97310
(503) 378-4387

RHODE ISLAND

Director of Business Regulation
169 Weybossett St.
Providence, RI 02903
(401) 277-2405

SOUTH DAKOTA

Director of the Division of
  Securities
Department of Commerce and
  Consumer Affairs
Pierre, SD 57501
(605) 224-3241

VIRGINIA

Director
Division of Securities and Retail
  Franchising
1300 Travelers Building
11 S 12th St.
Richmond, VA 23219
(804) 770-7751

WASHINGTON

Securities Division
P.O. Box 648
Olympia, WA 98504
(206) 753-6928

WISCONSIN

Commissioner of Securities
448 W Washington Ave.
Madison, WI 53701
(608) 266-3414

FOR PROSPECTIVE AND OPERATING FRANCHISERS

BECOMING A FRANCHISER

The managers of successful small businesses with several retail outlets, who aspire to building large chains, have two basic choices. They can
gradually open a few new outlets each year, financing them from existing
profits or loans. Or they can franchise their operations and thereby possi-

bly open dozens of outlets annually. "Franchising is an effective way for companies to expand without a huge capital expansion," stated an article on the franchising of businesses which appeared in the November 1979 issue of *Venture* magazine. The article continued: "The growth can be carefully plotted and regulated. Moreover, the franchise system of distribution—which includes mass purchasing—can be exceedingly practical during economically hard times."

If franchising is the route chosen, the main problem for prospective franchisers to overcome, according to franchising experts, is to realize that the operation of their existing companies and franchising are two quite different businesses. Franchisers must sell their business concept to other entrepreneurs; teach others on a mass scale how to run their businesses; set up systems of franchising fees and royalties that make financial sense; and comply with complex government regulations. And the franchiser must do all this while still attending to the profitable operation of his or her own directly controlled businesses.

Thus, franchisers must essentially learn another business. They can learn by doing background reading (see pp. 300–1 of this chapter for suggestions) and by tapping the resources of the major franchising trade association, the International Franchise Association (IFA). Another source is franchise consultants, who can provide important advice on marketing and operating franchising businesses. Lastly, prospective franchisers can go to work for a franchise in a business similar to theirs to get a feel for what makes the franchising aspect of the operation tick.

Following are descriptions of the services offered by the IFA and a selection of franchising consultants. These sources can also provide information on finding appropriate attorneys and conforming with government regulations. For additional information on legal and regulatory sources, see the listings appropriate to franchisees on pp. 290–94 of this chapter. Readers may also wish to review the introduction to Chapter 2, "Consultants and Management Assistance," when considering the selection of franchising consultants.

International Franchise Association
1025 Connecticut Ave., NW
Washington, DC 20036
(202) 659-0790

The IFA is both a lobbying group and an educational organization that represents the interests of franchisers. A nonprofit organization founded in 1960, the IFA now represents more than 400 franchisers in the United States and abroad.

The Association has been active in attempting to affect both Federal Trade Commission and state regulations on franchising. It has published detailed information on franchising regulations in its "IFA Compliance Kit," which is described on p. 300.

The IFA keeps members updated on legislative developments that affect franchising through numerous publications. It sponsors workshops and symposiums around the country on managing franchise systems, franchising overseas, and dealing with legal issues. It also maintains a franchising library that is open to members. And it can provide guidance in choosing franchising consultants.

Membership is open to those franchisers who have been in business at least two years and have a minimum of ten operating franchises. The IFA says it screens applicants with regard to their qualifications and overall reputability. Membership fees range from $1,000 to $6,400 annually, depending on franchiser size and sales volume.

CONSULTANTS

Webb Lowe and Associates
2605 Laurel Canyon
W. Los Angeles, CA 90046
(213) 557-1844

This firm helps companies of all sizes to decide whether they want to grow internally or through franchising. If a firm should decide to franchise, Webb Lowe will assist in developing internal franchising capabilities, franchising staff, marketing programs, and pricing strategies.

Webb Lowe has a full-time staff of two and a national network of part-time consultants. The firm handles anywhere from four to twelve clients at any one time. Fees depend on a project's scope and interest to the firm; such fees have ranged from $1,200 to $5,000 per day, with variations depending on whether work is structured in accordance with monthly retainers or so as to be performed on a daily basis. The consulting firm is also open to equity participation in a client's business as a means of payment.

National Research Publications Inc.
720 S Colorado Boulevard
Denver, CO 80222
(303) 758-0131

This firm has been in business for twenty-seven years. It works for franchisers in the United States as well as in London and the Far East, helping them to develop franchising systems and programs from inception to completion. It will also research franchising opportunities for companies in specific areas. Consulting rates begin at $80 per hour, although most jobs are package deals ranging in cost from $25,000 to $65,000.

National Research Publications also publishes a semimonthly franchising newsletter, *Continental Franchise Review*. (See description on p. 301.)

The Franchise Group Inc.
3644 E McDowell Road
Phoenix, AZ 85008
(602) 267-9409

This firm, says an official, actually "becomes the franchise division of a company that wishes to go into franchising." Its procedure is to design and operate a franchising system until the franchiser is informed and organized enough to run it and incorporate it into his company. A typical consulting relationship lasts about five years.

The Franchise Group says it devotes the first year to testing the franchising concept through the operation of several franchise outlets; if the system shows no promise at the end of that year, the firm usually terminates its work and advises that the franchising effort be aborted. If the franchise system is operating successfully, however, the Franchise Group expands it and further involves the franchiser's personnel.

The Franchise Group has a regular staff of four, plus various part-time specialists who become involved with clients at different times in the franchising process. The firm declined to provide fee ranges, stating that fees are structured to fit a company's cash-flow projections over a typical five-year period, with annual adjustments made based on actual cash flow and other aspects of the company's financial picture.

Franchise Concepts Inc.
20200 Governors Drive
Olympia Fields, IL 60461
(312) 481-2900

This firm, with a staff of forty full-time and numerous part-time consultants, specializes in helping companies to set up franchising programs by formulating franchise policies, devising fee and royalty schedules, helping to draft franchise agreements and disclosure statements, developing marketing programs, and implementing sales programs. Franchise Concepts tries to achieve all these things over an initial three- to four-month period and then remain available to franchisers, as they take over the franchising tasks, for another eight or nine months. The comprehensive franchise development program costs between $30,000 and $80,000, depending on the scope of the task.

Franchise Concepts also performs other franchise-related consulting services, including feasibility studies and specific problem solving for established franchisers. Fees for these services vary accordingly.

American Franchise Institute
4545 42nd St., NW
Washington, DC 20016
(202) 363-5570

The American Franchise Institute specializes in helping small companies develop their own initial franchising programs. The firm aids the franchiser in drafting franchise agreements and disclosure statements, and it advises companies on selling franchises and negotiating with franchisee attorneys. It aims at familiarizing the company's staff with the entire franchise process.

Rather than maintaining a full-time staff, the American Franchise Institute puts together consultant teams on a project basis. Franchisers who are receptive to taking advice and doing a lot of their own work in developing regional franchise programs can get off with as little as $10,000 in consulting fees.

Seltz Franchising Developments Inc.
240 Madison Ave.
New York, NY 10016
(212) 889-6230

Seltz Franchising Developments specializes in implementing companies' franchising efforts over a period of two to three years. Seltz first assesses whether franchising is appropriate to the particular company, and, if it is, develops a marketing plan, arranges for written agreements and disclosure statements, and oversees the selling of franchises and the start-up efforts of franchisees. The firm then serves in an advisory capacity.

Seltz has a staff of eight, plus additional part-time experts. It handles up to six clients at any one time. It also has an affiliated legal department, which works with companies of all sizes. Seltz's fees for the two- to three-year implementation program range from $40,000 to $90,000. The firm's principal, David Seltz, has been a franchising consultant for more than twenty years and has written twenty-four books on franchising and related subjects.

ADDITIONAL INFORMATION SOURCES

FOR PROSPECTIVE AND OPERATING FRANCHISEES

Franchise Opportunities Handbook, United States Department of Commerce, available from Superintendent of Documents, U. S. Government Printing Office, Washington, DC 20402. $6.50.

This annual survey of about 900 franchisers provides probably the most extensive information on the franchises it covers of any publication. Information on each franchise includes number of outlets, length of time in business, capital needed for starting a franchise, financing assistance available from the franchiser, and training and managerial assistance available from the franchiser.

Your Fortune in Franchises, by Richard P. Finn (Chicago, IL: Contemporary Books Inc., 1979). $9.95.

Finn's book is a worthwhile introductory text for prospective franchisees. It explains such things as how to investigate opportunities, financial elements to consider, franchiser rights, site selection, training, promotion, financial management, and special opportunities for minority and female franchisees. Among the several hundred franchisers listed in the book are detailed appraisals of the six best franchising opportunities; there are also examples of franchises in each business category.

The Franchise Annual Handbook and Directory, Edward L. Dixon, ed. (Lewiston, NY: Info Press Inc.). $12.95.

This sourcebook lists about 2,000 American and Canadian franchises in each annual edition, as well as general information and advice for potential franchisees. Though it has more listings, it provides less information than does *Franchise Opportunities Handbook.*

IFA Membership Directory and *Investigate Before Investing: Guidance for Prospective Franchisees* (Washington, DC: International Franchise Association). $5 for both.

The *Directory* lists all IFA members, along with the number of franchises belonging to each, length of time in business, and investment required for enfranchisement. *Investigate Before Investing* is a booklet that explains how to evaluate franchising opportunities.

Franchise Index/Profile, the United States Small Business Administration, available from Superintendent of Documents, U. S. Government Printing Office, Washington, DC 20402. $2.

This book provides guidance on the pros and cons of franchising and on evaluating individual franchisers.

Franchising and Business Opportunities: Rules and Guides, Franchise and Business Opportunities Program, Federal Trade Commission, Washington, DC 20580. Free.

This booklet explains the FTC's disclosure rules in layman's terms.

1980 Directory of Franchising Organizations (New York: Pilot Books, 1980). $3.50.

This book contains a listing of only about 100 franchisers, with a one- or two-line description and oversimplified investment figures for each. It also has a superficial three-page discussion of franchising and a nine-point evaluation checklist. Overall, it contains the least amount of useful information of all the sources listed here.

The Dow Jones-Irwin Guide to Franchises, by Peter G. Norback and Craig T. Norback (Homewood, IL: Dow Jones-Irwin, 1978). $14.95.

This book is a disappointment, especially for the price. It lists 500 franchisers in the same format as the *Franchise Opportunities Handbook* and provides information about the International Franchise Association, the Small Business Administration, and the Commerce Department, none of which is especially helpful. In short, it provides half the information of the Commerce Department's *Franchise Opportunities Handbook,* but for twice the price.

FOR PROSPECTIVE AND OPERATING FRANCHISERS

Franchising in the Economy, the United States Department of Commerce, available from Superintendent of Documents, U. S. Government Printing Office, Washington, DC 20402. $4.75.

Published annually, this book is mainly a statistical compilation of the influence of franchises in the American economy. It also provides information on foreign franchise markets and general advice for the franchiser on approaching different countries as potential franchise markets.

FTC Franchising Rule: The IFA Compliance Kit, by Carl E. Zwisler III and Andrew A. Caffey (Washington, DC: International Franchise Association, 1979). $40 to members, $80 to nonmembers.

This book, which comes in a three-ring binder, contains a history and analysis of the Federal Trade Commission franchising disclosure rule so as to enable franchisers to comply with it. The book also provides an outline of state disclosure requirements.

How to Organize a Franchise Advisory Council (Washington, DC: International Franchise Association, 1979). $5 to members, $10 to nonmembers.

This book provides detailed advice and directions to franchisers on helping set up trade associations of franchisees to aid in communication and cooperation among franchisees and between franchisers and franchisees.

The Franchise Option, by DeBanks M. Henward III and William Ginalski (Phoenix, AZ: Franchise Group Publishers, 1980). $34.50.

This book provides advice on franchising businesses, with a view toward planning and implementing franchising systems.

Franchising: Proven Techniques for Rapid Company Expansion and Market Dominance, by David Seltz (New York: McGraw-Hill Publishing Co., 1980). $19.95.

This book discusses how to go about franchising a business. It also describes other types of business expansion techniques.

Franchising World, the International Franchise Association. $60 per year.

This monthly publication provides information on developing franchising trends, along with detailed information on IFA member public relations and advertising programs. It also includes updates on legal issues and industry profiles.

Continental Franchise Review, National Research Publications, Inc., 720 S Colorado Boulevard, Denver, CO 80222. $105 per year.

This newsletter is published twice monthly and provides an analysis of the existing franchising situation and climate.

FOR BOTH PROSPECTIVE AND OPERATING FRANCHISEES AND FRANCHISERS

Franchising Today, Franchise Technologies, 1201 San Luis Obispo Ave., Hayward, CA 94544. $18 per year.

This magazine comes out semimonthly and features profiles of successful franchisers and franchisees. The magazine reports on legal developments, international franchising, and new technologies. It also offers advice to both prospective franchisees and franchisers on getting started in their respective endeavors.

CHAPTER 10

Government Procurement

INTRODUCTION: A TOUGH, BUT ENTICING, MARKET

Selling to government agencies is much like obtaining loans and conducting other kinds of business with the government—it sounds like easy money when reading the brochures, but it's often exactly the opposite in practice.

Take the federal government, which will be the main focus of this chapter, but which is similar in its approach to state and local agencies. From the outside, it looks like a gold mine of opportunities for small businesses. Federal agencies purchase more than $100 billion of goods and services each year. In theory, businesses of all sizes are eligible to bid for orders, which are usually granted to companies offering the lowest prices and judged capable of performing adequately. Recently enacted laws and programs even attempt to aid small businesses in competing with large companies to obtain federal orders.

In reality, though, small businesses do relatively poorly in obtaining federal procurement awards. Of the $100 billion of federal purchases in a recent year, only about 25 percent went to small businesses; yet small businesses account for about half the nation's jobs and gross national product.

For certain key areas of federal procurement, the figures are even more discouraging for small businesses. In the area of research and development, for instance, which has been a particular strength of technologically oriented small businesses, less than 4 percent of the federal government's $26 billion R&D expenditure in 1978 went to small businesses.

The problems

Why aren't small businesses doing better in exploiting opportunities from what is the world's largest single purchaser of goods and services? A number of obstacles, mostly of the federal government's creation, make selling to the government a frustrating and sometimes even dangerous undertaking.

The first and perhaps most important obstacle facing small businesses is understanding just how to go about obtaining government orders. A summary of issues associated with federal procurement, which was distributed at a regional meeting in preparation for the 1980 White House Conference on Small Business by conference organizers, noted: "The framework of statutes and regulations governing federal purchasing may be needlessly complex, discouraging many small businesses from doing business with the federal government."

And those small businesses that decide to brave the regulatory maze sometimes wish they hadn't. They frequently encounter difficulties finding out which agencies buy what, submitting voluminous forms, and understanding the even more voluminous replies and contract language. They also discover that tentative bureaucrats seem to feel more comfortable with big-company suppliers than with small companies. And once small businesses become known to bureaucrats, the bureaucrats seem to have a way of moving on to new assignments, leaving small businesses to prove themselves to new, equally tentative, bureaucrats.

Small businesses that win federal procurement awards sometimes find that the specifications are different from what was originally understood. Or they discover that the government's time requirements for delivery are unreasonably short or that the time it takes to get paid is unreasonably long. All such problems have the potential for seriously undermining or even destroying small businesses.

Small businesses which attempt to cash in on federal orders by becoming subcontractors to large companies which have won contracts encounter some of the same obstacles. They must deal with government-mandated paperwork, a bias by big companies against small companies, and slow-arriving payments.

While the federal government must shoulder much of the blame for the difficulties small businesses face in obtaining government orders, small businesses in some cases do little to help themselves. Their most significant problem is a failure to communicate to government procurement officials exactly what their companies are capable of providing the government. Accustomed to trying to learn customers' wishes and then fill them, small-business owners too frequently are vague about what they can sell the government, say procurement officials. Such vagueness makes difficult the task of seeking out small businesses to bid on specific contracts, and it also doesn't help the confidence level of insecure bureaucrats.

POTENTIAL BENEFITS

The previous discussion might seem to suggest that small businesses should simply avoid selling to the federal government. That shouldn't necessarily be inferred, though. Understanding the government's procedures and making initial sales are difficult, and certainly few businesses should attempt to rely solely on federal procurement. Start-up businesses, in particular, should wait until their businesses are well established before attempting government sales.

But while penetrating the government market is tough, it's not impossible. Some small businesses are quite successful selling to the federal government, as the $25 billion of annual small-business sales to the government indicates.

The government also offers some distinct business advantages over other markets. For one thing, there's no doubt that the government will pay its bills, even if it is late. Being a government contractor can also provide a relatively new small business with credibility that can help in selling to private customers. In addition, the government buys nearly everything, from food to spark plugs to exotic scientific and technical equipment, and doesn't usually subject suppliers to the same kind of abrupt cancellations that can occur during recessions in private industry.

And in the view of some small-business owners, the government is actually a more objective purchaser than private companies. As the officer of a small Massachusetts instrumentation and control systems company that won government work stated in a May 1980 *INC.* magazine article: "We're convinced . . . that it's actually cheaper to do business with the government. Just compare it with the cost of doing business commercially." He went on to cite the costs of transportation, entertainment, and hotels to meet with prospective private customers in a far-off city. He added: "With the government, all we have to show is a capacity to meet the quality and paperwork requirements of a contract and be low bidder." He observed that the famous government paperwork can be worthwhile because it forces bidders to carefully calculate all production costs. "And with the government, everything is Dutch treat," he concluded.

ASSESSING THE GOVERNMENT MARKET

The natural tendency of entrepreneurs looking for the first time at the federal government as a potential customer is to view it almost as one huge company. It would be nice if the government operated that way, because then it would likely have a single centralized purchasing department that would monitor its needs and find suppliers.

Unfortunately, though, the government doesn't operate like a single company. Instead, it operates almost like a combination of several large companies with overlapping responsibilities and thousands of independent small companies.

One of the large companies might be considered to be the General Services Administration (GSA), which buys and distributes several billion dollars' worth of general use items like office furniture and light bulbs for all civilian agencies and military departments. Another large-company-type procurement agency is the Defense Logistics Agency (DLA) which buys billions of dollars' worth of general supply items like food, clothing, and textiles for the military services.

Because the GSA and DLA don't buy everything the civilian and military agencies need, the individual agencies have authority to make their own purchases, much like independent companies. Some of the purchases are made on a centralized basis and some on a decentralized basis. Thus, the Commerce Department buys various supplies and equipment on a centralized basis for its Washington and local offices. But area and district offices of the Mining Enforcement and Safety Administration of the Department of the Interior buy protective clothing for mine inspectors and mine safety equipment.

Procurement awards can be made via competitive bids or, in some cases, on a sole-source basis. Civilian agencies operate under one set of procurement regulations and military agencies operate under another set of regulations. Purchasing opportunities are publicized haphazardly, usually by inviting bids from companies known to be qualified and by listing bids in government publications. To be invited to bid, companies must fill out forms and be evaluated by appropriate agencies; since about 15,000 government locations have procurement offices, that can mean filling out quite a few forms and going through many evaluations. One business owner who won an $11,000 government contract discovered after it was over that the paperwork involved weighed five pounds.

If the whole situation sounds mind-boggling, that's because it is—at least at first glance. But in many respects, selling to the federal government is much like selling to private companies and individual consumers; initially the market looks hopelessly complex, but after study and investigation, it assumes the proportions of a tough market with its own special characteristics.

In certain respects, the federal government is similar to the world of private business. Despite the emphasis government brochures place on forms and regulations, selling companies must also establish relationships based on trust with government procurement officials. And just as company owners usually can't handle all their company's commercial sales, neither can they scout out all the potential government opportunities on a part-time basis—it takes a special sales force or a Washington representative akin to a manufacturer's representative.

OBTAINING ASSISTANCE

In at least one important respect, the government provides an advantage missing from commercial markets—it actually provides programs designed to assist small companies to become suppliers. Most of the assistance comes from the Small Business Administration (SBA) and General Services Administration (GSA), but thanks to legislation passed in 1978, all federal agencies are gearing up to encourage more small-business procurement.

The various procurement assistance programs are designed to put small businesses in touch with federal agencies that might need their products and to aid small businesses in obtaining a fair proportion of federal procurement awards. Most of the assistance programs are relatively new and indications are they have achieved some success; the percentage of federal procurement going to small businesses has increased to about 25 percent in recent years from 17.2 percent in 1969. Certainly any small company serious about selling to the government should explore how the assistance programs can help it through the procurement maze.

In addition to federal procurement assistance programs, small businesses can obtain information and guidance on selling to the government from other sources. Some private consultants specialize in helping small businesses obtain procurement awards. In addition, some colleges and other institutions offer courses on selling to the government. And a number of books attempt to explain the federal procurement process to novices.

Before seeking out either government or private consulting help, entrepreneurs should attempt to understand the overall procurement process. Thus, this chapter next describes the procurement procedure. The explanation is intended as an overview; because of space limitations, the explanation doesn't go into detail about specific regulations and procedures.

Following the overall explanation, this chapter lists and describes the various sources of government procurement assistance available. Then it lists and describes other sources of assistance, including consultants, courses, and books. Because government procurement is a realistic alternative only for established businesses, we have not devoted a section of this chapter to start-up businesses.

State and local government agencies handle their procurement in ways modeled after the federal government. Thus, this chapter can provide useful background in dealing with state and local procurement officials. Similarly, many states have in recent years enacted programs designed to direct more procurement to small businesses; for details on which states have special procurement programs, readers should refer to Chapter 4, "State and Local Government Assistance." Agencies listed in that chapter can usually provide assistance on further exploring procurement opportunities.

UNDERSTANDING THE PROCESS

As the introduction noted, selling to the government is in important respects similar to selling to consumers and private companies. Sellers must understand the rules of the game, identify likely customers, and effectively sell their product or service. All of these steps require much study and effort the first few times around. They become easier with experience.

THE RULES

The federal government makes the bulk of its purchases through competitive bidding. But it can award contracts, either for relatively small purchases or for products which only one company can provide, without competitive bidding.

Two basic forms of bidding are usually used. For commodity-type items such as nuts and bolts or foods, bidding is handled on the basis of price only; of course, all items must conform to certain standards the government sets. For products and services that can't be differentiated from competition on the basis of price alone, such as complex scientific equipment or research and development projects, bidding is based on more subjective factors such as performance, quality, and price.

While the heavy emphasis on competition can pit small businesses against better-financed and technically equipped large companies, recent legislation attempts to provide small businesses with some advantages. The legislation, known as Public Law 95-507, requires that purchases of under $10,000 be set aside for small businesses to compete for alone; for purchases of under $2,500, bidding isn't even required. And for contracts awarded in excess of $500,000 ($1 million for construction contracts), small-business subcontractors must be sought out.

Under the law, each government agency has established an Office of Small and Disadvantaged Business Utilization to monitor procurement that can be set aside for small businesses. Some offices are more effective and committed than others; unfortunately, commitment is important, since the law leaves to the offices various judgments associated with enforcing it. For instance, the offices must decide if adequate competition exists among small businesses for contracts under $100,000; if they decide it doesn't exist, they can open competition for such contracts to businesses of all sizes. (For discussion of how PL 95-507 affects minority businesses, refer to pp. 251–52 of Chapter 7, "Assistance for Minority Businesses.")

The federal government awards either of two basic contract types to suppliers: fixed-price and cost-reimbursement contracts. As the names suggest, a fixed-price contract is awarded for a prearranged and agreed-on price that cannot be changed later, while a cost-reimbursement contract allows for payment of costs as they accrue, plus a profit.

Perhaps the key factor to keep in mind about these and other procurement rules is that they are subject to seemingly endless exceptions and variations. The exceptions and variations are compounded by the fact that different government agencies rely on any of several sets of regulations. Thus, procurement officials have a certain amount of latitude in awarding many contracts. Small-business owners must be certain to understand what rules are being used when they bid on contracts to avoid wasting time or, even worse, avoid getting locked into contracts with unforeseen requirements that can easily result in serious financial losses.

One place to start in learning about federal procurement rules is with a copy of the *Federal Procurement Regulations,* which applies to most civilian agencies, or the *Defense Acquisition Regulations,* which applies to the Department of Defense. In addition, several courses and books can provide a basic knowledge of government procurement procedures. The regulations, courses, and books are described in greater detail later in this chapter.

IDENTIFYING CUSTOMERS

Broadly speaking, the federal government can be viewed as consisting of four markets: the General Services Administration (GSA), the Defense Logistics Agency (DLA), the thousands of other agency offices scattered around the country, and the winners of government contracts needing to subcontract some of their work. What small-business owners must do is learn what products and services each of these markets requires and decide whether their businesses can and should pursue sales to those markets.

The best way to learn what each government market requires is to determine what it has bought in the past and what it expects to order in the future. Unfortunately, no one source lists either all the things the government has bought or plans to buy. But collectively, a number of publications and federal agencies themselves can provide that information.

To learn what the government has bought in the past, business owners can consult the *U. S. Government Purchasing and Sales Directory* and the *GSA Supply Catalog*. In addition, a new government service, provided through the Federal Procurement Data Center in Roslyn, VA, can provide computerized data on all government purchases over $10,000.

To learn what the government is planning to buy in the future is a bit more tricky. The *Commerce Business Daily,* a daily publication issued by the Commerce Department, ostensibly lists all contracts the government is seeking bids on, but in reality it lists only about 10 percent of upcoming contracts. Finding out about the other 90 percent of planned purchases involves consulting with or writing to the GSA, DLA, or individual government agency offices to obtain applications necessary for getting onto bidder lists. Once businesses are on bidder lists, the businesses are notified about upcoming purchases so they can decide whether or not to submit bids.

For assistance in deciding which agencies to contact or in learning about upcoming purchases (aside from the GSA and DLA, which are centralized purchasing agencies and will assist small businesses in learning about opportunities in those agencies), small businesses should contact individual agencies' Office of Small Business Utilization, which can provide advice on selling to the agencies. The Small Business Administration (SBA) also assists small businesses in locating procurement opportunities, but its officials aren't aware of all the opportunities.

Information on subcontracting opportunities is available from the *Commerce Business Daily* and SBA subcontracting specialists. Neither of these sources has complete information, but SBA subcontracting specialists have access to directories and other resources that can identify the bulk of subcontracting opportunities for small businesses.

All the sources referred to in this discussion on identifying customers are described in greater detail later in this chapter.

Selling products and services

The textbook approach for successfully selling to the federal government is to find out about pending purchases—either through the *Commerce Business Daily* or by having gotten onto appropriate bidders' lists —and then to submit the proper applications and supporting information that comprise formal proposals. According to government officials, consultants, and magazine articles on selling to the government, that approach is all right for businesses selling commodity-type items at fixed prices. In such cases, the procedure for making awards—determining that bidding companies are capable of meeting the government's specifications, and then picking the company bidding the lowest price—is fairly cut and dried.

But for the billions of dollars' worth of contracts that are awarded based on a composite of factors that include quality, price, and supplier capabilities, the situation isn't as straightforward. Government procurement officials making decisions about such awards are in much the same position as corporate procurement officials. They want to get the best possible quality at the best possible price, but they want to feel comfortable that what they ordered will be delivered on time.

That means that businesses seeking such awards must convince the appropriate bureaucrats that they can perform. Such salesmanship can be done by telephone and letter, but it's usually most effectively done in person. And small businesses are usually operating at something of a disadvantage, since procurement officials tend to feel most comfortable with big companies in evaluating whether contracts will be completed on schedule.

The salesmanship doesn't end once a contract is won. It extends into negotiating advantageous final terms and getting paid within a reasonable amount of time. It also extends beyond one contract into learning about future contracts that might be appropriate for a particular company. Companies which are in touch with the right procurement officials frequently learn about plans for future purchases before they are publicized via *Commerce Business Daily* and bid solicitations; such information can give a company a valuable headstart over the competition in submitting a bid and winning a contract.

Such salesmanship requires the proper manpower, which is expensive. The president of a Boston energy consulting firm wrote in the September 1979 issue of *INC.* magazine, based on his unsuccessful efforts to win government work: "If you're going to do government contract work as an adjunct to your existing business with private industry, you are going to have to get into it all the way. . . . You'll need staff support and additional backup, not to mention the time to set up a full-time government contract division."

One alternative to setting up a full-time internal staff to go chasing after government contracts is to hire a Washington representative who specializes in finding government contracts—usually for a commission of between 1 percent and 20 percent of a contract's value.

Consultants specializing in government procurement can aid companies in setting up internal government procurement operations, in locating Washington representatives, and in pursuing the most promising markets. Descriptions of several procurement consultants follow later in this chapter.

GOVERNMENT AGENCY ASSISTANCE

With the preceding overview of the government procurement process as background, small-business owners can begin to exploit the government's own efforts to assist small businesses to become suppliers. As noted previously, several government agencies make special efforts to inform small-business owners about the procurement process and to direct small businesses to appropriate contract opportunities.

The most helpful sources for newcomers to the procurement game appear to be the GSA and the SBA. But others can be useful as well.

General Services Administration
18th and F Sts., NW
Washington, DC 20405
(202) 566-1240

Regional offices in Boston, New York, Washington, Philadelphia, Atlanta, Chicago, Kansas City, Fort Worth, Houston, Denver, San Francisco, Los Angeles, and Seattle.

The General Services Administration (GSA) arranges for the purchase of billions of dollars' worth of items that civilian agencies need in common, such as computers, automobiles, and office supplies. But for small businesses, the GSA actually provides two broad procurement services: first, it provides specifics on what it is buying and whether individual small businesses might qualify as suppliers; and second, it disseminates information and advice on selling to other federal agencies.

The GSA provides its services through Business Service Centers in each of its thirteen regional offices. The centers, according to a GSA booklet, "exist primarily to serve entrepreneurs in their search for government contracts." For businesses located outside the thirteen metropolitan areas with Business Service Centers, the GSA has what it calls a "Circuit Rider Program," under which GSA counselors visit outlying cities periodically.

The GSA's Business Service Centers are about the closest thing the federal government has to a centralized procurement operation. The centers can help guide business owners through the GSA's procurement maze, which includes six major subdivisions making a variety of purchase, lease, and construction procurement decisions.

And the centers' counselors "provide individuals and firms with detailed information about all types of government contracting opportunities," according to a GSA booklet. In addition to information, the centers issue applications for getting on bidders' mailing lists, furnish invitations for bids and specifications, and provide government publications that list bidding opportunities.

Small Business Administration
Associate Administrator for Procurement Assistance
Small Business Administration
1441 L St., NW
Washington, DC 20416
(202) 653-6635

Procurement assistance is available primarily through procurement representatives in each of ten regional offices—Boston, New York, Philadelphia, Atlanta, Chicago, Kansas City, Dallas, Denver, Seattle, and San Francisco.

The Small Business Administration (SBA) has in recent years become increasingly involved in the procurement process. The SBA's growing involvement stems primarily from Public Law 95-507, under which government agencies and prime contractors are required to set aside contracts and subcontracts for businesses deemed small under SBA regulations. Because the law allows both government agencies and prime contractors considerable latitude, the SBA has assumed the role of lobbyist to aid small businesses in obtaining the maximum amount of procurement possible.

The SBA provides essentially three types of procurement assistance (in addition to its 8[a] procurement program for minority businesses, described on pp. 248–49 of Chapter 7, "Assistance for Minority Businesses"):

1. The SBA has about sixty procurement center representatives who spend much of their time in major federal purchasing offices around the country reviewing purchases that have not been set aside for small-business bidders under PL 95-507. If procurement center representatives feel that small businesses should receive contracts or subcontracts that have instead gone to big companies, the representatives will try to persuade the purchasing agencies to reconsider their decisions.

Small-business owners can obtain from the SBA a list of procurement center representatives along with the purchasing agencies to which they are assigned. If the representatives are assigned to agencies small businesses would like to sell to, they can contact the representatives and seek assistance. The representatives can then let purchasing officers know of appropriate small businesses for specific orders.

2. One of the most valuable aids the SBA offers small businesses encountering difficulties obtaining government orders is its Certificate of Competency. When a small business is low bidder for a government contract but is rejected by purchasing officials after being judged financially

or otherwise incapable of performing the work, a Certificate of Competency can undo the rejection.

In such a case involving rejection of a low-bidder small business, involved purchasing officials must notify the SBA. The SBA then asks the business if it wishes to appeal the rejection. If an appeal is undertaken, the SBA has fifteen days to make its own determination as to whether the business is competent to fulfill the contract. If the SBA grants a Certificate of Competency, the original purchasing agency must award the contract to the business.

Although the certificate is valid only for a specific contract, it is an excellent way for a business to establish credibility with other government agencies in the future. The certificates also serve a broader purpose: they help save the government money by directing to small businesses contracts which might have gone to higher-bidding large businesses.

3. Since 1978, the SBA has solicited profiles of individual small businesses interested in selling to the federal government and stored them in its computerized Procurement Automated Source System (PASS). Federal purchasing officials and prime contractors interested in setting aside contracts for small businesses so as to comply with PL 95-507 can then draw on PASS.

The needs of purchasing officials and prime contractors are matched up with the qualifications of small businesses in the system. Companies whose qualifications appear to match specifications required may be notified and asked to bid on contracts.

The SBA has aggressively sought out small businesses that conform with its size standards to fill out a short application necessary to be included in PASS. The application seeks basic business information, including a brief explanation of company capabilities, annual sales in various categories such as exporting and domestic, and number of employees. The application and instructions for filling it out can be obtained from the SBA's main office or one of the regional offices.

As of late 1980, more than 30,000 businesses were in the system, versus only about 7,000 the prior year. More than 300 federal purchasing offices and about sixty prime contractors have made use of PASS during its brief existence to locate appropriate small-business suppliers.

Defense Logistics Agency
Small and Disadvantaged Business Utilization Specialist
Defense Logistics Agency
Cameron Station
Alexandria, VA 22314
(202) 274-7605

The Defense Logistics Agency (DLA) obtains food, clothing, textiles, medical, construction, and other supplies for the military services.

The DLA also manages the Defense Contract Administration Service, which aids in finding small-business subcontractors for large holders of defense prime contracts; such prime contracts, for sophisticated weapons and other systems, can amount to several hundred million dollars each, which means that substantial amounts of subcontracting opportunities are usually involved.

The DLA can assist small businesses both in exploring contracting opportunities it and other military services may have and can aid in tracking down appropriate subcontracting opportunities for small businesses. Procurement officials within DLA and other Defense Department agencies tend to be better trained than officials within civilian agencies, according to private procurement consultants.

Federal Procurement Data Center
1815 N Lyn St.
Roslyn, VA 22209
(202) 696-5069

The Federal Procurement Data Center serves as the equivalent of a marketing research source on federal procurement. Though it was only established in 1979, it is reasonably current on the procurement activities of all federal agencies.

Small businesses contemplating seeking out federal contracts can find out through the center which agencies have bought what products and services. The information includes total dollar amounts spent among various geographic locations of individual agencies. Thus, companies can get an idea of which agencies in their area might be likeliest to buy particular products and services and can then attempt to get on the bidding lists of the most promising agencies.

The information is generally based on contract awards of over $10,000. Companies can order standard reports or seek special inquiries for information tailored to their own needs. Specific breakdowns for a city or state run about $50, while a specially tailored nationwide file of information can cost $300 to $400. Individual standard reports are free.

Office of Federal Procurement Policy
New Executive Office Building
726 Jackson Place, NW
Washington, DC 20503
(202) 395-3455; (202) 395-5802

The Office of Federal Procurement Policy has responsibility for implementing uniform procurement regulations for all civilian and military agencies and for overseeing enforcement of PL 95-507. Its efforts on behalf of PL 95-507 have so far included resolving disputes in interpretation between the SBA and agency purchasing officials, and attempting to clarify ambiguities in the law.

Because the Office of Federal Procurement Policy is concerned primarily with matters of broad policy, it won't get involved in specific procurement problems encountered by small businesses. But staff members are available to answer questions on the government procurement process in general as well as implementation of PL 95-507.

Small businesses can also possibly influence future policy by letting the Office of Federal Procurement Policy know about their procurement problems and complaints, particularly with respect to implementation by federal agencies of PL 95-507. If enough similar complaints are registered, the Office can seek to rectify compliance and other problems.

CONSULTANTS

Because government regulations are so complex and the government market so diverse, entrepreneurs have good reason to want to turn to outside experts. As in most business areas, consultants exist who specialize in federal procurement.

Federal procurement consultants tend to be individuals who have worked either for the federal government or for large corporations handling procurement. Thus, they understand the regulations and know how the system works; they also frequently have a network of government procurement contacts in one or another area, such as the GSA or Defense Department.

Small-business owners who turn to consultants can use them in one of two ways. One approach is to use them as instructors and advisers—to learn what the regulations involve and which government agencies might offer the best procurement opportunities. A second approach is to use them simply as contacts and go-betweens to try and arrange government contracts on their own.

Small-business owners with government procurement experience recommend the first approach. By using consultants to learn the ropes and gauge opportunities, small-business owners stand the best chance of being able to explore procurement opportunities on their own after the consultant has left, the reasoning goes. Small businesses that obtain contracts solely on the basis of a consultant's contacts leave themselves dependent on the consultant, it is argued.

When arranging to use a consultant, small-business owners should be sure to determine that the consultant isn't representing any competitors; a written agreement with a consultant should specify that the consultant provide notification if he or she takes on a competitor. Small-business owners should seek out a written agreement with a consultant to cover other areas, such as financial arrangements, termination procedures, and specific tasks. Other aspects of dealing with consultants are described in Chapter 2, "Consultants and Management Assistance."

What follows are descriptions of several consultants specializing in federal procurement, whose names we obtained in conversations with small-business trade group officials and small-business owners. We talked with each consultant to obtain the background information provided. The consultants are as follows:

Fletcher Management Assistance Corp.
1990 M St., NW
Washington, DC 20036
(202) 331-1855

   or

5775 Sheridan Drive
Williamsville, NY 14221 (Buffalo)
(716) 633-8212

Fletcher Management Assistance Corp. specializes in working with small high-technology businesses to aid in procurement. The firm's principal, Harold K. Fletcher, was an SBA associate administrator and founder of a Buffalo high-technology company before becoming a full-time consultant in 1978.

The firm's basic consulting fee is $75 an hour, plus expenses, though overall project fees are subject to negotiation.

John T. Scruggs
145 Island Hills Road
Riverdale, GA 30296
(404) 997-0534

Mr. Scruggs began consulting full-time in 1978 after having worked twenty years as a procurement official in the SBA. He offers procurement assistance as well as general management assistance to small businesses. His basic consulting fee is $70 an hour, plus expenses; long-term fees depend on the scope of the project.

VanArsdale Associates
City Center Square
1100 Main St.
Kansas City, MO 64105
(816) 474-4588

VanArsdale Associates helps companies develop systems and techniques for selling to the federal government. The firm's usual procedure is to work with a company's management for several days, teaching managers how to go about discovering appropriate government markets and how best to present their company to procurement officials.

The firm's principal, Gene VanArsdale, is a former SBA procurement official. His firm's basic consulting fee is $80 an hour, plus expenses.

John H. Green & Associates
1008 140th Ave., NE
Bellevue, WA 98005
(206) 643-5556

John H. Green & Associates works with companies of all sizes on federal, state, and local procurement. The firm assists in helping with specific problems and situations or in developing overall approaches to exploiting procurement opportunities. It also aids companies selling to the government in establishing appropriate cost accounting systems, which can be a difficult task.

The firm's principal, John H. Green, was an armed forces procurement official for many years before becoming a full-time consultant in 1975. Fees range from $55 to $80 an hour, depending on the experience of the consultants involved.

COURSES, SEMINARS, AND CONFERENCES

A number of programs exist to provide background and guidance on selling to federal, state, and local agencies. The programs vary widely in cost and there's no indication of a direct relationship between quality and cost.

The least costly programs are free seminars on selling to the government held several times each year in Small Business Administration regional and district offices around the country. Other programs are sponsored by a variety of nongovernmental organizations. They are as follows:

Independent Study
University of California Extension
2223 Fulton St.
Berkeley, CA 94720
(415) 642-4124

The University of California Extension branch offers a correspondence course on government procurement entitled "Government Contracting in Business and Industry." The course is available to anyone, including non-California residents. Participants can sign up at any time and take up to a year to finish the twenty assignments, with a possible additional six-month extension if necessary. The course costs $110; Mastercard and Visa are accepted.

Sterling Institute
Waterfront Center
1010 Wisconsin Ave., NW
Washington, DC 20007
(202) 337-4000

Sterling Institute is a private firm that provides seminars and consulting services on various business subjects, including government procurement. It offers one- and two-day training programs on the government procurement process at the federal, state, and local level. Two-day programs are organized in cities around the country where twenty-five or more participants can be assembled; cost for the two-day programs is $200.

Federal Publications, Inc.
1120 20th St., NW
Washington, DC 20036
(202) 337-7000

Federal Publications, Inc., is a private firm which offers seminars of between two and five days on various aspects of government procurement, such as research and development contracting and subcontracting. The courses are offered in Washington and in cities and resort areas around the country. The seminars range in cost from about $500 to $700.

Conference and Products Exposition Director
National Institute of Government Purchasing
1001 Connecticut Ave., NW
Washington, DC 20036
(202) 331-1357

The National Institute of Government Purchasing is a national trade association of about 750 federal, state, and local government purchasing officials, which hosts a four-day conference each fall; businesses of all sizes can set up product displays for the officials. Reserving a display booth for the conference costs about $700, plus travel and lodging expenses. (Conferences are held in different cities each year.)

ADDITIONAL INFORMATION SOURCES

The $100 Billion Market: How to Do Business with the U. S. Government, by Herman Holtz (New York: AMACOM, 1980). $16.95

Offers a good overview of the federal procurement process. The writer's informal, breezy style makes for easy reading. His approach is hardheaded—he acknowledges the various obstacles to obtaining government contracts but argues that businesses that are best prepared can make out profitably in the procurement game. Besides advising the reader on how best to understand and exploit the system, he provides an extensive appendix of relevant publications and government procurement offices.

Government Contracts: Proposalmanship and Winning Strategies, by Herman Holtz (New York: Plenum Press, 1979). $19.50

This book is more specialized than the previous one, concentrating on negotiated contracts, as opposed to fixed-price contracts. Gives a good feeling for the breadth of opportunity available and amount of effort required to obtain negotiated contracts. Written in the same breezy style as the previous book.

How to Get Started in Government Business, by Eli Chappe (Suffern, NY: Danbury Press, 1979). $25.95

This is a manual that provides detailed instructions on selling products to the federal government. Though services are not covered, much of the material applies to services as well. The book is intended for novices in the area of federal procurement, but it actually assumes the reader has something of an overview of the procurement process. It sets out twenty-seven steps for small-business owners to follow in selling to the government along with describing markets and listing agencies and other contacts. Without some background on the process, however, the reader quickly becomes lost in going through the details of the twenty-seven steps. The 120-page manual is also packed with abbreviations that are confusing, even though they're explained in a two-page listing. Readers who have some familiarity with the procurement process, however, can benefit from the details and advice offered.

GOVERNMENT PUBLICATIONS

The federal government provides various publications which can aid small businesses that are serious about exploring the procurement situation. All except those noted can be obtained by writing and enclosing payment to:

Superintendent of Documents
U. S. Government Printing Office
Washington, DC 20402

Federal Procurement Regulations and *Defense Acquisition Regulations*

These two publications provide specifics on the regulations surrounding civilian and defense procurement. With each publication come updates and changes in regulations for an indeterminate time period. *Federal Procurement Regulations* is $50 and *Defense Acquisition Regulations* is $68.50.

Various subsets of regulations exist that aren't covered in those two publications, however. Searching out all the procurement regulations involves going through the multivolume *Code of Federal Regulations* and ordering the appropriate volume on procurement regulations. An index to the code can be ordered for $8.50; major libraries have the volumes of the code available for perusal. Specific volumes cost between $8 and $10 each.

U. S. Government Purchasing and Sales Directory, $5.50

Lists the products and services purchased by military and civilian agencies along with the appropriate purchasing offices to be contacted. Also lists types of surplus property sold, with contacts.

GSA Supply Catalog, $5.50

Lists items commonly purchased by GSA.

Doing Business with the Federal Government, free

Available from GSA, Washington, DC 20405, or from local GSA Business Service Centers.

Provides an overview in fairly understandable language on the federal procurement process. Not surprisingly, it stresses all the assistance potentially available from the GSA.

Selling to the Military, $4

Gives instructions on the procedures for selling to the armed forces and lists major buying offices within the military, along with descriptions of their purchasing activities.

Commerce Business Daily, $105 annually via first-class mail; $80 via second-class mail

Ostensibly lists all purchases being planned by all federal agencies, so that any company that feels qualified can seek to bid on the work. In reality, it lists only about 10 percent of intended purchases. Still, it's a good source for the newcomer to discover potential government markets, since it's the most complete single listing of what government agencies are planning to buy. Available for perusal at all SBA, Commerce Department, and GSA offices.

Contractor Paths to Grief with Some Solutions, free

This booklet, published by the SBA, describes some of the commonest problems small businesses encounter in doing business with the government. It's surprisingly frank for a government publication and, for this reason alone, is valuable. This and several other SBA publications on selling to the federal government are available from the SBA, 1441 L St., NW, Washington, DC 20416.

CHAPTER 11

Foreign Trade—Exporting

INTRODUCTION: POTENTIAL RICHES ABROAD

Small-company owners who read enough federal government pamphlets and small-business magazines could easily come to believe that selling goods and services overseas is a snap.

"You don't have to be big to be profitable in exporting," says one U. S. Commerce Department pamphlet. Another is entitled "The Small Business Market Is the World."

Magazines directed at small-business readers have picked up on the same theme. An article in the July–August 1979 issue of *In Business* magazine was headlined, "Exporting Is Easier than You Think." And the title of an article in the September–October 1979 *Harvard Business Review* promised small-business owners a "Systematic Approach to Finding Export Opportunities."

But if exporting is so easy, small-business owners might ask, Why are so relatively few doing it? According to U. S. Government estimates, small businesses account for no more than 10 percent of American exports. The remaining 90 percent or so are the domain of the country's largest corporations.

The tiny role of small businesses in exports is not easily explained. What is clear is that the absence of small businesses from significant involvement in exporting not only costs them important profit opportunities, but robs the American economy of vital foreign currency. In recent years, the United States has more often than not imported more than it exported; the trade deficits that have resulted have contributed to inflation and weakened the dollar in relation to other currencies.

Moreover, in comparison with other countries, American exporting activity has been weak and declining. In one recent year, exporting accounted for less than 7 percent of this country's gross national product, which was the lowest percentage of any industrialized nation. (In contrast, exporting accounted for 12 percent of Japan's GNP and 23 percent of Germany's.) And the American share of total world exports declined from about one fourth to about one sixth during the 1970s.

Increased small-business involvement appears necessary to offset the trade imbalances and reverse the declining role of the United States in foreign trade, but accomplishing that goal may not be as easy as the pamphlets and magazine articles suggest. According to a report on international trade prepared by organizers of the 1980 White House Conference on Small Business:

> Although there are many reasons for the U.S. trade imbalance, part of the deficit may be attributable to the inability of many potential small exporters to successfully identify, develop, and market their goods, products, and services to foreign markets.

IDENTIFYING THE PROBLEMS

Overseas markets can easily appear foreboding to American small-business owners contemplating exporting. How does one overcome the various language and cultural barriers, find reliable and trustworthy distributors, and understand foreign customs regulations? How does one ensure being paid by overseas customers whose credit history can't be easily determined? What kind of competition can be expected in different foreign countries?

The questions go on and on. Rather than attempt to answer them, many businesses opt for the familiarity of the American market, where one at least understands what customers are saying and who the competition is. Answering the questions just posed, though, isn't necessarily as difficult as it might seem. A wide variety of government and nongovernment sources exist which can provide answers and solutions to the common problems that arise for exporters.

Oftentimes American companies discover that doing business overseas is easier in important respects than doing business in the United States. For instance, letters of credit, which are commonly used in international trade, provide greater assurance of being paid for goods and services than most domestically available credit vehicles.

But as was suggested previously in this introduction, exporting isn't quite as simple as it's frequently portrayed to be. The reasons don't have as much to do with language and marketing barriers as they do with other more complex factors like history and policy decisions. Small-business owners considering exporting should be aware of these factors as they decide whether to attempt selling overseas.

HISTORICAL PERSPECTIVE

In the context of American history, the notion of large-scale exporting is a relatively recent phenomenon. "Exporting has never really been a high priority in this country," observed the report on international trade prepared for the White House Conference on Small Business.

> The domestic market was large enough to satisfy the expansionist desires of the numerous growing industries during the 19th century. Raw materials were plentiful and what surpluses were generated were absorbed by other countries. It was not until after World War II that the United States expanded its export sector for the primary purpose of utilizing the excess industrial capacity which was developed during the war.

As the American economy turned stagnant during the middle and late 1970s, many companies began considering exporting as a way of developing new markets. More often than not, though, they discovered that foreigners, like the Germans, Japanese, and Italians, were several steps ahead of them in terms of experience and penetration of markets.

A STACKED DECK?

If tough competition was the only obstacle faced by potential American exporters, the situation might not be so bad. After all, most American companies are used to tough competition in this country.

But American companies are by and large up against competition that has some extremely important additional advantages. "Compared with Japan and other strong competitors in world markets, the U.S. has been underinvesting, and we are now using a lot of obsolescent plant and equipment," noted an article in the July 14, 1980, issue of *Fortune* magazine. "High energy costs have made matters much worse—plants, machinery, and processes were often designed on the assumption that cheap energy was here to stay," the article added.

In addition, foreign competitors frequently have backing from their governments and private networks that Americans are unable to obtain. Some foreign governments, for instance, help defray the considerable expenses associated with displaying products at international trade shows, at which substantial orders may be obtained. In addition, European and Asian countries typically have large export trading companies, which maintain networks of contacts with domestic banks and foreign distributors; the trading companies aid small companies both in obtaining special financing for exporting and locating potential customers.

Small American companies could benefit greatly from such assistance, but don't have it, many small-business executives and trade group leaders argue. Thus, even if American small companies can compete with foreigners on the basis of such factors as price and quality, they can't be expected to compete against government subsidies and giant export trading companies, it is argued.

OR A LACK OF COMMITMENT?

Many government officials and international trade experts contend that instead of complaining, American small companies should be taking greater advantage of the resources available and doing more to help themselves. According to a Commerce Department brochure:

> Ninety-two percent of all American firms sell only in this country. Ridiculous! For most, the cost of constantly changing product lines, with all the attendant start-up and marketing expenses, is greater than learning to export existing products . . . Take advantage of all the services available to you from the U.S. Department of Commerce. The department and its 43 district offices can help you pinpoint the likeliest markets by providing you with the research, marketing data, and trade statistics you need.

American small businesses also come under criticism for trying exporting but failing to stick with it. An article in the September–October 1979 issue of *Harvard Business Review* by an Iranian-American writer noted:

> . . . a serious shortcoming of many American small businesses that have become involved in exporting: a lack of commitment. Small business owners frequently consider exporting only when they are burdened with excess production capacity. Their goal is to make a quick buck or simply obtain extra business to cover overhead. As demand rises at home to consume the surplus production, foreign sales efforts are reduced or stopped.

In these views, the trick for small businesses contemplating exporting is exploiting all the resources at their disposal and being persistent. Exporting proponents note that thousands of American small businesses have successfully overcome the various obstacles and derive substantial profits from exporting. Moreover, they contend, federal agencies have become increasingly sensitive to the importance of encouraging small businesses to become more active exporters. According to the White House Conference report on international trade: "In March 1978 four federal agencies launched a concerted attempt to educate small business on the programs, services, and opportunities available in international trade."

SOME CHANGES AFOOT

It seems clear that government officials at all levels along with small-business owners have become increasingly aware of the importance of small-business exporting. Efforts have begun in the U. S. Congress to encourage development of private export trading companies modeled after successful European and Japanese trading companies. At least one port authority, the Massachusetts Port Authority, has undertaken an extensive program to train and assist small New England companies in developing foreign markets. And as noted in the descriptions of state programs to assist small businesses in Chapter 4, several states offer guidance to small businesses contemplating exporting.

The rest of this chapter describes various sources of assistance for exporters, including federal agencies, world trade clubs, chambers of commerce, port authorities, export management companies, courses, and relevant publications. In addition, this chapter considers a frequently neglected area of foreign trade—sources of assistance for small companies that wish to investigate importing goods and services from overseas.

FEDERAL GOVERNMENT AND RELATED PROGRAMS

On paper, the federal government provides a wealth of services for small businesses considering exporting. The services include information on overseas markets, advice on how to sell in foreign countries, introductions to potential customers, financing, and insurance.

But simply sorting out which agencies do what is not easy. According to the report on international trade prepared for the White House Conference on Small Business, "Responsibility for administering foreign trade programs is thoroughly scattered throughout the federal bureaucracy."

Moreover, the relevance of many of the programs to small businesses appears questionable. "These export promotion programs have often been criticized for lack of attention to the needs of the small, inexperienced firms," the White House Conference report noted.

> While some of these agencies have recently adapted their programs to focus more strongly on small business needs, there are many additional changes that are needed to truly promote small business into foreign commerce.

Whatever their faults, though, federal agencies remain a primary source of information about overseas markets and conditions. That is because the government has more people scattered around the globe than any other organization. And while the federal programs for providing foreign contacts and financing for exporting might be of questionable value for small businesses, these programs have substantial funding and should be explored first by small companies looking to export.

The federal programs are as follows:

Bureau of Export Development
Industry and Trade Administration
U. S. Department of Commerce
Washington, DC 20230
(202) 377-5261; (202) 377-4811

Assistance is also provided through forty-three district offices around the country.

The Commerce Department's Bureau of Export Development provides the bulk of the federal government's exporting services and is thus the logical starting point for small businesses investigating exporting. Each of the department's forty-three district offices employs international trade specialists who can provide guidance on steps to take for getting started in exporting, overseas markets that might provide the best opportunities for specific companies, and making use of the department's services.

Services of the department's Bureau of Export Development include the following:

• The Worldwide Information and Trade System (WITS), a relatively new computerized system that provides various foreign trade information. WITS provides names of potential business contacts in the U.S. and abroad, information on specific overseas markets, schedules of international and domestic trade conferences at which products can be promoted, and the names of thousands of potential overseas customers. Small businesses can make use of the system by calling Commerce Department offices in Washington, Boston, Chicago, Dallas, Los Angeles, or Seattle. Charges vary depending on the services used, but are nominal.

• An agent-distributor service, under which international trade specialists help individual businesses locate up to six potential overseas agents or distributors. It is up to the individual businesses to contact the agents and distributors to determine if they are appropriate liaisons.

• A foreign buyer program lists all American companies that wish to be visited by foreign companies on trade missions to the U.S.

• The Trade Opportunities Program is a computerized matching of American businesses with overseas trade leads generated by American embassies and consulates.

• World Traders Data Reports provide trading information, credit sources, and financial data on individual overseas companies. The reports are prepared by the U. S. Foreign Service and are available from the Commerce Department for $15 each; they take about two weeks to produce.

• Trade and seminar missions, which involve small numbers of American executives in overseas trade shows and seminars at which the executives can promote their products. The Americans are expected to pay all costs for such gatherings, which can run to several thousand dollars per participant.

• Trade center marketing services and exhibitions. Eleven overseas U. S. Trade Centers provide offices for up to five days and help businesses set up appointments and locate interpreters while selling in the areas. The centers also sponsor six to eight exhibitions by American companies each year.

• The New Product Information Service enables American companies which have developed new products to get them publicized via publications distributed by American embassies and consulates as well as by "Voice of America" radio broadcasts.

• The Foreign Traders Index, a computerized file of more than 140,000 foreign importers and some exporters. The index is the source from which the Commerce Department provides several services, including names of specific companies for various geographic areas and mailing lists of overseas companies.

• Dozens of publications on exporting and on specific countries. Some of the publications of widest interest to small businesses are listed at the end of this chapter.

Export-Import Bank of the United States
811 Vermont Ave., NW
Washington, DC 20571
(202) 566-8990—general information about agency programs
(800) 424-5201—information about exporting and referrals to appropriate federal agencies for assistance

The Export-Import Bank of the United States (Eximbank) is a rarity in the federal bureaucracy—an independent, financially self-sustaining agency. Its primary purpose is to finance overseas projects and to provide credit insurance for American businesses.

The Eximbank readily acknowledges in a brochure, however, that its lending program "is designed to provide long-term financing for large industrial projects or multimillion-dollar product sales." In other words, small businesses need not apply.

But the agency contends that its various credit insurance programs "can directly benefit small business exporters . . . More than 50% of the authorizations under these programs support export sales of $200,000 or less."

Credit insurance can be extremely important for American companies attempting to sell products overseas. In competing with companies from other countries for various foreign business, American firms usually discover that the credit terms they make available to potential foreign customers can make the difference between success and failure in completing sales. But uncertainty about foreign buyers and their countries can make the American companies and their bankers understandably jittery about extending credit. Credit insurance protects American exporters against the failure of foreign buyers to pay their obligations for either commercial or political reasons; the coverage ranges from 90 percent up to 100 percent of the risk, depending on the program.

The credit insurance is issued in cooperation with the Foreign Credit Insurance Association (FCIA), a group of fifty private American insurance companies, described later in this chapter. The policies cover varying terms ranging from a short term of up to 180 days to longer terms of up to five years.

The Eximbank also helps make credit available to small- and medium-sized foreign buyers of American products through banks in the foreign countries. In addition, the agency has started a program to involve minority and other small banks in its direct financing programs, which take place through commercial banks.

Information on Eximbank credit insurance programs is available through national insurance brokers, commercial banks, the FCIA, and the Eximbank.

Foreign Credit Insurance Association
One World Trade Center
New York, NY 10048
(212) 432-6311

Local offices in Washington, DC, Atlanta, Milwaukee, Chicago, Cleveland, Los Angeles, and Houston.

Although the Foreign Credit Insurance Association (FCIA) is not a government agency, it works closely with the Eximbank (discussed immediately preceding) to insure exporters against losses when overseas customers fail to pay their bills. The FCIA is an association of fifty private American insurance companies, which administers the policies.

Among the FCIA's various policies is a special Small Business Policy for companies with a net worth of under $2 million and less than $350,000 in annual export sales; the companies must not have previously used FCIA or Eximbank programs. The policy covers 95 percent of the commercial risk and 100 percent of the political risk on companies' credit to foreign businesses.

Small businesses can obtain the special policy for two years, after which time they must buy the standard FCIA-Eximbank policies covering either 90 percent or 95 percent of risk for terms starting at 180 days or as long as five years. The average cost of both the small-business and regular policies is about 22 cents per $100 coverage.

Policies can be obtained through the FCIA or commercial banks, trading companies, and commercial credit agencies.

Overseas Private Investment Corporation
1129 20th St., NW
Washington, DC 20527
(202) 632-1854
(800) 424-6742

The Overseas Private Investment Corporation (OPIC) is a federal agency that encourages American business investment in about 100 underdeveloped countries in Asia, Africa, Latin America, and the Caribbean. OPIC's encouragement takes the form of market evaluation assistance, support of feasibility studies, direct and guaranteed loans, and insurance protection. Since 1978, OPIC has been attempting to extend its services as much as possible to smaller businesses, which it defines as companies not ranked among the largest 1,000 corporations in the country.

Like Eximbank, OPIC is an independent and financially self-sustaining agency. Projects approved for its assistance "must offer potential benefit to the host country in such areas as job creation, skills training, import savings, export earnings, and tax revenues," says a government brochure. Projects "also are reviewed to assure that the United States gains net benefits in expanded trade, employment, access to needed materials, and investor earnings."

OPIC sponsors group visits by American business executives to underdeveloped countries, where the executives meet government and business officials. For projects it decides show sufficient promise, OPIC will pay up to $50,000, or 75 percent of the cost, whichever is less, of feasibility studies.

OPIC's most enticing form of assistance is its loan program, which provides funds directly and guarantees 90 percent to 100 percent of bank loans. The loans usually range from $100,000 to $4 million to be repaid in from five to twelve years at market interest rates. The loans generally cover 35 percent to 40 percent of a project's cost, and can't exceed half of the cost.

In addition, OPIC offers insurance protection to cover companies' initial investments and earnings against such problems as expropriation, war, and revolution. For smaller companies, OPIC will assume certain insurance registration, brokerage, legal, and consulting fees it wouldn't ordinarily pay.

330

OPIC makes available a number of brochures on its programs along with a newsletter on its investor missions.

U. S. Small Business Administration
1441 L St., NW
Washington, DC 20416
(202) 653-6881
(202) 653-6570

Information available through more than 100 offices in medium- and large-sized cities around the country. (For a list of SBA offices, see Appendix A.)

The Small Business Administration (SBA) provides counseling on exporting approaches through its various management assistance programs, including the Service Corp. of Retired Executives, Small Business Institute program, and Small Business Development Center program. These programs are described in Chapter 2, "Consultants and Management Assistance." The SBA also conducts periodic workshops around the country on exporting; information is available at local SBA offices.

The SBA in 1980 started its first financing program specifically for American small-business exporters. Under the program, qualified small companies receive up to $500,000 in bank loans that are 90 percent guaranteed by the SBA for working capital to support exporting activities. Initially the program was made available through banks in four states—California, Illinois, New York, and Texas—but it was expected to be gradually expanded into other areas. Criteria for obtaining the loans are the same as for other SBA loans; these criteria are discussed in Chapter 3, "Federal Government Financing Sources." One significant shortcoming of the program: the loans have been repayable in a year, which might be less time than small businesses need to develop and serve overseas markets.

Office of Commercial Affairs
Bureau of Economic and Business Affairs
U. S. Department of State
Washington, DC 20520
(202) 632-0355

The State Department provides little in the way of direct assistance to businesses of any size. It concentrates on the policy aspects of foreign trade, such as tariffs and trade agreements. The State Department through its network of embassies overseas collects a great deal of information about foreign markets, but it leaves dissemination of the material mostly to the Commerce Department.

Small businesses investigating specific foreign markets can try the State Department after they've exhausted the information supply of the

Commerce Department. The State Department publishes a series of issue papers on current events and policy questions for different countries. It also publishes a booklet on policy issues surrounding American trade, *The Trade Debate*.

> Export Trade Services Division
> Foreign Agricultural Service
> U. S. Department of Agriculture
> Washington, DC 20250
> (202) 447-6343

The Export Trade Services Division of the Agriculture Department promotes the sale of American agricultural products overseas. Its sixty-two foreign offices assist in collecting information on potential contacts and customers for American agricultural exporters. The division also offers advice on selling agricultural products overseas and various free publications on exporting.

If our experience is any indication, however, small-business owners shouldn't expect an enthusiastic reception from the division. A high-ranking official of the division was one of the few bureaucrats we dealt with in assembling this book who was genuinely uncooperative and uninterested in answering our questions.

OTHER PROGRAMS AND INFORMATION SOURCES

There are a variety of nongovernmental programs and sources concerned with small-business exporting. They are even more scattered than the government programs and differ widely in their quality. Thus, these nongovernmental resources require a great deal of patience and persistence in searching out and evaluating.

We attempted to identify the most relevant sources for small-business exporters. Among the resources we considered were foreign government officials stationed in the United States, port authorities, world trade clubs, commercial bank international departments, courses, and American exporting representatives known as export management companies.

The results of our investigation are as follows:

FOREIGN REPRESENTATIVES IN THE UNITED STATES

Consulates based in major cities around the U.S. can be good starting points for American business owners investigating potential foreign markets. The consulates can provide basic information on how to do business in their countries along with phone directories of major cities, and help in preparing shipping documentation and coping with visa requirements.

Many foreign governments also maintain commercial trade offices in the United States, the bulk of which are based in New York City. Though usually located in consulates, the trade offices tend to have their own staffs familiar with the nuances of doing business in their countries. The New York Chamber of Commerce and Industry has a list of more than eighty "foreign government trade promotion offices in New York" available free from:

International Affairs Group
New York Chamber of Commerce and Industry
65 Liberty St.
New York, NY 10005
(212) 766-1343

In addition, about forty binational chambers of commerce, which attempt to promote trade between a specific foreign country and the United States, are based in New York. They provide information on regulations and names of overseas contacts to potential investors in their countries. They have membership provisions and in some cases will provide services only to members. Information on the binational chambers of commerce is available from the International Affairs Group of the New York Chamber of Commerce and Industry as listed immediately preceding this paragraph.

PORT AUTHORITIES

The 165 or so deepwater ports along the country's Atlantic, Pacific, and Gulf coasts are each operated by a local port authority. It is usually concerned with expanding trade within its port in order to spur regional economic development. Port authority services typically include information on overseas trade contacts and guidance on the cheapest and quickest means of getting items to their foreign destinations.

Unfortunately, most of the port authorities do little on behalf of small-company exporters. Port authorities tend to be concerned primarily with encouraging large companies to use their facilities in the belief that large orders will make most efficient use of the port facilities and result most directly in economic development.

Port authority services, however, are available to businesses of all sizes. A trade group of the nation's port authorities can provide information on the services available from individual port authorities:

American Association of Port Authorities
1612 K St., NW
Washington, DC 20006
(202) 331-1263

Port authorities could change their attitudes toward small businesses in coming years if the Massachusetts Port Authority is any indication. With help from the Smaller Business Association of New England (SBANE, described in detail on pp. 358–59 of Chapter 12), Massport has developed the most extensive formal port authority program in the country for encouraging small-business exports.

New England manufacturers never before involved in exporting can apply to Massport to participate in the Small Business Export Program. Applications are sent to Massport's European office, and the New England companies judged to have the greatest potential for selling their products overseas are allowed to participate. Small-business participants receive research assistance in identifying which of their products are likeliest to sell where, guidance in understanding foreign trade rules, and the opportunity to go on specially designed overseas trade missions on which they meet potential foreign customers. The research and guidance are free to participating businesses, and Massport even extends interest-free loans to cover the overseas travel and expenses.

New England businesses that wish to explore the program should contact:

Director of Marketing and Development
Massachusetts Port Authority
99 High St.
Boston, MA 02110

WORLD TRADE CLUBS

World trade groups offer information on foreign trade opportunities and, probably most important, the chance to learn about the exporting experiences of other business owners. After all, the most significant business advice and information frequently comes from others who have learned the ropes firsthand.

World trade groups appear to vary widely in quality and activity. Of about ten that we attempted to contact, half either didn't answer their phones on any of several attempts or else weren't listed in local directories. The other half appear to offer a variety of programs, including seminars and newsletters on exporting.

The world trade groups are for the most part associated either with the U. S. Chamber of Commerce in Washington or the World Trade Centers Association in New York. Both organizations can provide the names of groups in specific areas and can be contacted as follows:

U. S. Chamber of Commerce
1615 H St., NW
Washington, DC 20062
(202) 659-6000

World Trade Centers Association
One World Trade Center
New York, NY 10048
(212) 466-3063

A sampling of sizable world trade groups and their services is as follows:

Foreign Trade Association of Southern California
Los Angeles World Trade Center
350 S Figueroa St.
Los Angeles, CA 90071
(213) 627-0634

The Foreign Trade Association of Southern California draws its approximately 1,000 members from around the State and even has a few from outside California. The association sponsors luncheons and seminars that include speakers on such subjects as exporting to specific countries and new customs regulations. The association also provides a weekly newsletter and monthly update bulletin on foreign trade issues. Annual dues are $100.

Sell Overseas America, Association of American Export
22041 Clarendon
Woodland Hills, CA 91367
(213) 883-5237

Although Sell Overseas America doesn't promote itself as a world trade club, it serves that function. Sell Overseas America was started in 1980 by Maureen Reagan, daughter of the President, as part of an effort on her part to assist small companies in obtaining overseas customers.

The organization has attracted substantial financial support from more than two dozen large corporations and has thus been able to hire over twenty staff members to service its more than 1,000 small-business members. Sell Overseas America researches potential foreign markets for members' products, sponsors seminars on marketing overseas, and advises companies on making use of government foreign trade programs. It also puts out two regular publications on selling overseas: *Showcase U.S.A.* and *Yankee Trader*.

Ms. Reagan in a New York *Times* article (January 5, 1981) described the organization as "a kind of automobile club of trade." She said it is intended for "companies that don't have export managers, that don't even know what a letter of credit is. What these American companies need is someone in the private sector who will hold their hands all the way to the wharf."

Annual membership in Sell Overseas America is $100.

Houston World Trade Association
World Trade Center
1520 Texas Ave.
Houston, TX 77002
(713) 225-0967

The Houston World Trade Association's 650 members include not only companies of all sizes, but representatives of exporting specialists such as shipping companies, freight forwarders, insurance companies, and the fifty area consulates. The association sponsors monthly luncheons with speakers who are expert on various aspects of foreign trade. Membership costs $250 for an initiation fee plus $31 monthly.

World Trade Association of Milwaukee, Inc.
756 N Milwaukee St.
Milwaukee, WI 53202
(414) 273-3000

The World Trade Association of Milwaukee is fifty years old and has 1,200 members. The association sponsors dinner meetings and seminars on various aspects of exporting; it also publishes a monthly newsletter on local and national exporting news and trends. Dues are $17.50 annually.

International Business Center of New England, Inc.
22 Batterymarch St.
Boston, MA 02109
(617) 542-0426

The International Business Center of New England has been in existence thirty years and has about 350 members. It holds frequent one- and two-day seminars on such topics as locating appropriate foreign markets and assembling proper export documentation. In addition, the Center introduces new members with little export experience to veteran members in similar businesses who can help the novices to avoid common exporting mistakes. Annual dues range from $150 to $250, depending on company size.

INTERNATIONAL DEPARTMENTS OF BANKS

Large commercial banks with international departments can be valuable sources of assistance to small businesses considering exporting or well involved in exporting. The international departments can offer the following services:

1. Advice and guidance. International department officials are usually expert enough to help business owners decide fairly quickly if their products or services are viable for exporting. The officials can also frequently offer suggestions as to specific countries to explore.

2. Essential banking services. International departments can arrange for letters of credit, transmittal of funds, foreign exchange transactions, and various forms of interim financing to allow fulfillment of orders. Such services can be essential for completing sales because the more attractive the terms and procedures exporters can offer to foreign customers, the more able the American exporters are to compete with sellers from other countries.

3. Special financing arrangements. For companies that get heavily involved in overseas sales, international department staff members will aid in trying to arrange substantial loans or loan guarantees from the Export-Import Bank of the United States. (For details on Eximbank, see pp. 327–28 of this chapter.) Such loans, though, are usually available only to relatively large companies.

How should small companies go about finding an appropriate and helpful international department of a commercial bank? Bankers suggest that small-business owners seek assistance first from the bank they regularly deal with for loans and other services. If it doesn't have an international department or international expertise, the bank can usually provide a referral to a nearby bank that does.

Another source of referrals can be the Federal Reserve Bank, which has branches in major cities around the country. If the nearest branch is no help, the Federal Reserve Bank in New York City, which handles the bulk of international transactions for American banks, can help in identifying banks in various areas that have international departments:

Federal Reserve Bank
33 Liberty St.
New York, NY 10005
(212) 791-5000

The Eximbank can also provide the names of banks with international departments in specific areas via its toll-free information number: (800) 424-5201.

COURSES AND SEMINARS

Various organizations sponsor classes on exporting for small-business owners. Among the organizations are the following:

World Trade Institute
World Trade Center
New York, NY 10048
(212) 466-4044

The World Trade Institute specializes in courses ranging from basic beginning instruction to sophisticated managerial and marketing aspects of exporting. It also offers language instruction. Prices vary widely.

The Wharton School
Executive Education
Dietrich Hall
Locust Walk
University of Pennsylvania
Philadelphia, PA 19104
(215) 243-7604

The Wharton School has sponsored a two-day traveling seminar entitled "Foreign Market Entry Strategies." In 1980 it was offered in Miami,
Boston, Dallas, and Atlanta at a cost of $650.

EXPORT MANAGEMENT COMPANIES

If domestic markets appear large and unwieldy, foreign markets can
seem positively awesome. Small companies that investigate exporting but
are uncertain about which markets to pursue and also feel they don't have
the internal capabilities to launch a foreign sales program might explore
export management companies (EMCs).

Export management companies are essentially manufacturers' representatives for overseas sales. Nearly 1,000 EMCs operate from this country, mostly based along the East and West coasts. They represent thousands of small American companies in foreign markets.

EMCs can assist small manufacturers in various ways—for example,
by researching foreign markets, locating distributors and other foreign
representatives, handling the routine but frequently complex customs and
insurance procedures, arranging appropriate foreign advertising, and negotiating credit terms. In some cases, EMCs buy products directly from
American manufacturers, paying cash, and then arrange for credit from
foreigners on their own. In other cases, EMCs work on a straight commission basis and do not extend credit themselves.

EMCs tend to handle specific categories of noncompetitive products,
such as construction or medical equipment. This approach enables the
EMCs to understand the world market for their category and establish a
network of contacts so that sales on one specific product can often lead to
sales of complementary products in that category.

Not surprisingly, EMCs vary widely in their quality and services.
Some EMCs are single-person operations while others are relatively substantial firms with several dozen people. The small firms are often new
and looking for clients, while the large firms may be well established and
highly selective in the small businesses they'll agree to represent.

Small companies that arrange for representation by EMCs are sometimes disappointed with the results. Sales often don't materialize for two
or three years, and when they do, they may seem quite small. The reasons
behind such disappointments can vary; finding the appropriate foreign

markets for new products is often a time-consuming and tedious process, as it is in this country; in some cases, EMCs pay most attention to products that are selling best and neglect those that don't seem to be catching on.

Foreign trade experts familiar with EMCs warn small manufacturers to be particularly careful in dealing with new EMCs, since most fail within five years of start-up. These experts also suggest trying to work out with the EMC that's chosen a specially tailored exporting plan to be used in selling the products involved.

EMCs that purchase products directly for sale overseas usually pay the domestic wholesale distributor price, less 10 percent to 20 percent to cover their own expenses. Those EMCs that act as exclusive sales representatives usually charge a sales commission of 7½ percent to 20 percent of the wholesale distributor price. Some EMCs also charge several thousand dollars for the initial developmental period when they are researching and exploring marketing opportunities; foreign trade experts feel that such an investment may be worthwhile to encourage a knowledgeable EMC to follow up on specific products.

Actually finding and choosing an EMC is a difficult task. Local U. S. Commerce Department officials can sometimes provide recommendations, as can state international representatives. Business owners in similar industries can also provide recommendations.

But no single trade group for EMCs exists; instead, there are several EMC groups, each representing a portion of the total number of EMCs. Small manufacturers can write to one or more of the trade groups, giving a brief description of their product line and asking to be contacted by interested member EMCs and also to be sent the names of appropriate EMCs. The trade groups are as follows:

National Association of Export Management Companies
65 Liberty St.
New York, NY 10005
(212) 766-1343
A national organization of about 130 member firms

Export Management Association of California
10919 Van Owens St.
North Hollywood, CA 91605
(213) 935-3500
A regional organization of about 100 member firms

Overseas Sales & Marketing Association of America
5715 N Lincoln Ave.
Chicago, IL 60659
(312) 334-1502
A regional organization

We also attempted to identify a cross section of EMCs to provide another possible starting point in locating appropriate firms and also to provide an indication of EMC approaches. The EMCs we investigated are as follows:

International Management Services, Inc.
134 S 13th St.
Lincoln, NE 68508
(402) 475-4002

International Management Services is a six-year-old EMC that represents companies within about a 650-mile radius of Lincoln. It has eight full-time staff members in Lincoln and one at a branch office in Holland, NE.

International Management handles four product categories: nonelectronic medical and dental equipment; construction-related equipment; automotive repair equipment; and specialty agricultural products. The firm attempts to make sales by setting up new channels of distribution as opposed to hard-nosed selling and trading.

International Management's fee structure varies somewhat depending on clients' stages in the exporting process. A typical company getting started can expect to spend $35,000 to $50,000 annually the first two or three years as International Management researches and develops markets. Thereafter, export sales levels are usually sufficient to warrant a commission system of 10 percent to 30 percent of net sales.

Walter M. McKim & Son
238 Main St.
Cambridge, MA 02142
(617) 876-4733

The McKim firm has twenty full-time staff members and has been in business since 1925. It works with about fifteen companies at a time, which manufacture small hand tools and maintenance and repair materials like epoxy.

An official says the firm differs from most other EMCs in that it functions as a client company's export department rather than simply as a manufacturer's representative. It uses client firms' stationery and has its phone answered, "Export department."

Client companies do their own invoicing and thus know who their customers are and how much their products are being sold for; that isn't always the case with EMCs, which buy products as brokers and then sell the products overseas. The McKim firm also seeks out as clients companies whose products complement those of clients it already represents; client products thus become part of a portfolio of related but noncompeting products.

The firm accepts clients from anywhere in the country, depending on its client load, which is usually heavy thanks to its low turnover; it still has clients dating from the 1930s. The McKim firm's commissions vary according to sales volume, but average about 20 percent of net sales.

OPICO Inc.
P.O. Box 849
Mobile, AL 36001
(205) 438-9881

OPICO was started in 1946 and now has twenty-six full-time staff members in Mobile plus twelve overseas sales managers. The firm represents makers of agricultural machinery whose overseas sales volumes range from $50,000 to $2 million annually. Clients include manufacturers of land-clearing equipment, plows, planting and fertilizing equipment, cultivation and harvesting equipment, and processing equipment.

OPICO represents about forty American companies and boasts distribution channels in eighty-three countries located on every continent. The firm sends orders obtained by its overseas sales representatives to its clients and takes title to goods when they're ready for shipment; OPICO then handles all documentation and actually finances some of the transactions itself.

The firm doesn't require any upfront payments before sales materialize. Once sales begin, OPICO collects an average of about 20 percent of net sales. The firm requests clients that eventually obtain substantial foreign sales to give a couple of years' notice before terminating their relationships with OPICO, but says it requires no written contracts and conducts business on handshakes.

Singer Products Co.
875 Merrick Ave.
Westbury, NY 11598
(516) 333-2000

Singer Products Co. was established in 1937 and is now one of the larger EMCs in the country. It has 105 full-time staff members in its Westbury office and also maintains fifty overseas branch offices. The firm handles anywhere from 150 to 200 companies at a time, distributing products in more than 120 countries.

Singer Products represents companies in two business areas: electronics and automotive products. Its electronics clients tend to be in the radio and stereo products area, and its automotive clients in the battery business.

This EMC buys its clients' products and then resells them to overseas customers. Thus, Singer Products usually assumes all marketing responsibilities and credit financing obligations. The firm sometimes asks clients to share the costs of trade show space rental and advertising.

Singer Products doesn't charge clients any advance fees; it assumes initial marketing and research costs until sales are made, which usually takes about a year. The firm requires clients to enter into a written agreement to retain Singer Products for three years, with the agreement being renewable on an annual basis. Its fees average about 20 percent of the manufacturer's lowest domestic price.

Wiesman & Co.
P.O. Box 1151
Tucson, AZ 85702
(602) 623-4373

Wiesman & Co. was started in 1970 and has eight full-time staff members. The firm works with about seventy clients at a time, representing them nearly exclusively in Central America and South America. Its clients specialize in machinery and machine parts—compressors, welders, and motors.

Because Wiesman's product line is so specialized, making potential customers easily identifiable, the firm contends it can frequently generate sales for appropriate new products in less than a year. It acts as a manufacturer's representative, selling companies' products on a commission basis that averages about 12 percent of net sales.

IMPORTING

This chapter, like most discussions of foreign trade, focuses on exporting. That isn't to say that importing isn't worthy of consideration, of course. The reason exporting usually gets priority in examinations of foreign trade is that exporting involves a direct inflow of cash to American businesses, while importing involves an outflow. Imports also frequently represent competition to domestically made products. Thus, the impact of exporting is considered much more beneficial to individual businesses and the American economy as a whole than importing.

Importing, of course, can result in increased sales for individual American businesses and thus deserves some attention. But American importers seeking government assistance of the sort described earlier in this chapter won't find much. The federal government's main source of information on importing is the U. S. Customs Service, which applies duties, tariffs, and other regulations on imported goods. The Customs Service distributes a number of booklets and brochures describing its rules and regulations. To obtain literature or ask questions about importing regulations, contact the Customs Service as follows:

Department of the Treasury
U. S. Customs Service
Washington, DC 20229
(202) 566-8195

Some of the nonfederal sources—particularly foreign consulates and commercial trade offices, port authorities, and world trade clubs—described on pp. 331–35, can also provide information and guidance on importing. The foreign consulates and commercial trade offices based in this country are often more eager to encourage imports into the United States from their countries rather than vice versa, for the same reasons as the United States is seeking to encourage exports.

Finally, American companies whose businesses are adversely affected by competition from imports can seek financial assistance from the Economic Development Administration, as noted on p. 94 of Chapter 3, "Federal Government Financing Sources."

ADDITIONAL INFORMATION SOURCES

World Trade Information Center
One World Trade Center
New York, NY 10048
(212) 466-3068

The World Trade Information Center does research for individual businesses to locate overseas contacts, statistics, and market reports. Its basic fee is $30 hourly for most services.

The federal government issues a variety of publications that track foreign economic and trading trends. The publications listed can all be obtained from:

Superintendent of Documents
U. S. Government Printing Office
Washington, DC 20402
(202) 783-3238

Among the publications are the following:

Foreign Economic Trends, a series of publications issued by the U. S. Foreign Service on business developments and economic indicators in more than 100 countries. $50 annually.

Overseas Business Reports, a publication issued irregularly during the year that provides current and detailed marketing information, trade outlooks, and market profiles. $40 annually.

Global Market Surveys, a series of publications providing detailed information on fifteen to twenty of the best foreign markets for the products of various American industries. Prices vary according to the survey.

Country Market Sectoral Surveys, a series of publications that pinpoint the best exporting opportunities in particular foreign countries. Prices vary.

International Economic Indicators, a quarterly publication that presents a wide variety of comparative economic statistics for the United States and seven major competitor countries for recent periods. Annual subscriptions $10.

Business International Corp.
One Dag Hammarskjold Plaza
New York, NY 10017
(212) 750-6300

Business International Corp. issues a variety of publications on foreign trade trends around the world. Its publications also offer guidance on financing foreign operations and on investing abroad. Prices vary.

Foreign Trade Marketplace (Detroit: Gale Research Co., 1977)
This directory lists organizations, government agencies, and companies along with providing export and import procedures, trading zones, and other information regarding foreign trade.

Committee for Small Business Exports
Box 6
Aspen, CO 81611
(303) 925-7567

The Committee for Small Business Exports is a lobbying organization formed in 1979 for the purpose of pressing federal legislators and bureaucrats to aid small-business exporting. It has members in thirty states. Members include small manufacturing, trading, export management, and consulting companies. Any company up to $100 million annual sales is eligible for membership. An internal newsletter keeps members informed of activities. Dues are $100 annually for companies with less than $3 million annual sales and $200 for larger companies.

Complete Export Guide Manual by Steve Murphy (Manhattan Beach, CA: SJM & Associates, 1980); $9.95
This book is concerned mostly with the documentation that must accompany exported products. It also offers exporting rules for over 150 different countries.

CHAPTER 12

Small-Business Lobbying and Service Organizations

INTRODUCTION: VALUABLE PERKS AND CAMARADERIE

Starting and operating a small business can be an awfully lonely undertaking. It's easy for an entrepreneur to feel that he or she alone is experiencing difficulties arising from such problems as government regulations, uneven cash flow, or exorbitant health insurance rates.

It's also easy for the entrepreneur to be cynical about small-business organizations, viewing them as overgrown bureaucracies that spend most of their time spinning their wheels. And besides, entrepreneurs aren't supposed to need help from outsiders—entrepreneurs are too independent for that.

While some small-business organizations may seem overly concerned with perpetuating their own existence, small-business owners shouldn't be above exploiting all the resources at their disposal. Small-business organizations can provide resources of assistance to small-business owners in two broad areas:

1. They can help small-business owners to cope with a wide variety of daily problems. This help can come in various forms; it includes lobbying against unnecessary regulation and providing information on coping with existing regulations, seminars explaining how to deal with common operating problems like uneven cash flow, and opportunities to purchase at group rates such things as health insurance.

2. Equally important, small-business organizations can help relieve the sense of isolation many entrepreneurs feel. Through their publications, meetings, seminars, and other functions, they bring small-business owners

into contact with each other. Entrepreneurs quickly learn through these contacts that they aren't alone with the myriad of problems they face. Hearing how other business owners have coped can in itself be an important learning experience.

Unfortunately, picking one or more business organizations to join is difficult. There are literally hundreds of national, regional, and local small-business organizations representing a variety of constituencies and offering a variety of membership benefits. Some represent small businesses of all industries and some represent small businesses of particular industries. Some represent certain types of small-business owners, such as owners of family businesses or owners of particularly successful small businesses. Some groups primarily lobby on behalf of small-business interests, while others combine lobbying with educational programs, and still others primarily offer seminars and special benefits like discounts on health insurance, car rentals, and other purchases.

The quality of small-business organizations also varies widely. Some promise more than they deliver, while others spend excessive amounts of time competing with each other for lobbying influence and members. The dubious quality of some organizations is evident partially in their high membership turnover. Complaints about the effectiveness of some established small-business organizations were also widely voiced by small-business owners who attended the 1980 White House Conference on Small Business.

GROWING INFLUENCE

Criticism about the effectiveness of small-business organizations, however, has stemmed partly from the traditional low priority accorded small business in general. Small-business lobbying groups weren't taken very seriously in Washington because small-business problems weren't taken very seriously. Often small-business problems were lumped together with those of big business, even though the two areas often have quite different priorities.

All that seems to have undergone some change in recent years, however. As the importance of small business has grown in the minds of policy-makers, educators, and the general public, so too have the influence and numbers of small-business organizations.

Small-business organizations in Washington have attracted to their cause respected and influential lobbyists.

Tough-minded, politically wily and backed up by the increasingly vocal little guys of the business world, these operatives have emerged as a force to be reckoned with on Capitol Hill, observed an article in the July 27, 1979, *Wall Street Journal* on small-business lobbyists.

The organizations these lobbyists represent have also found themselves with newly won respect. The same *Wall Street Journal* article quoted a Senate Small Business Committee official as saying that representatives of a coalition of small-business groups "never got in the front door a few years ago . . . Now they meet with Cabinet Secretaries."

NEW GROUPS SPROUT UP

The growing respect accorded old-line small-business organizations has encouraged the formation of various new groups. Ironically, many are being backed by some of the nation's largest institutions. For instance, Walter E. Heller International Corp., a worldwide banking and financial concern, recently announced formation of the Walter E. Heller International Corporation Institute for the Advancement of Small Business Enterprises. The Rockefeller Foundation not long ago gave financial backing to an organization known as the Support Services Alliance to promote small-business interests. And the U. S. Chamber of Commerce, long identified as a representative of big-business interests, formed a Center for Small Business. (All these organizations are described in more detail later in this chapter.)

Small-business organizations have blossomed on a regional and local basis as well. The number of local chambers of commerce with small-business programs has approximately quadrupled in recent years, according to a U. S. Chamber of Commerce publication. The 1980 publication noted:

> Three years ago there were only 200 small business councils in chambers; today the number is approaching 800. This great increase is an indication of the burgeoning interest in small business activity in America today.

The increase is also a reflection of the marketing potential that chambers of commerce and other organizations see in separate small-business programs. In describing the most significant contribution of its recently formed small-business program, one local chamber of commerce wrote in in a chamber publication that the program "brings in new members . . ." Nor is the marketing aspect of small-business organizations limited to local small-business groups; it helps explain the interest by large organizations like Walter E. Heller International Corp. in establishing small-business organizations.

The growing numbers of small-business organizations have heightened competition among the groups for members. The organizations often try to outdo each other in the relevance of the seminars or in the number of benefits they offer in such areas as car rental and health insurance discounts.

MAKING CHOICES

The new prominence and growing numbers of small-business organizations suggest that small-business owners have more to gain than ever before from belonging to one or several groups. But the trends also suggest that the process of choosing small-business organizations to join has become increasingly difficult.

One approach is to join three or four groups that have different objectives. One group might be a Washington-based lobbying organization that keeps its members informed about legislative issues affecting small business; another might be a regional or local group that keeps tabs on state and city regulations and offers special small-business seminars; and a third might be one that specializes in the problems of a particular industry or type of business.

Since most of the organizations depend heavily on the opinions and involvement of members to decide which issues to pursue and services to offer, small-business owners should avoid simply sitting back and waiting for benefits, organization officials advise. Those members who voice their opinions and get involved in running committees or participating in seminars are likeliest to benefit from organizations' actions and contacts with other members, the officials say.

The remainder of this chapter is devoted to describing the activities and goals of major national small-business organizations, along with a sampling of regional and local groups as well as industry groups. Additional specialized small-business groups are described in Chapter 7, "Assistance for Minority Businesses"; Chapter 8, "Assistance for Women"; and Chapter 9, "Franchising."

Readers interested in obtaining further information on specific organizations should write or call; most of the organizations gladly provide brochures and sample publications on their activities.

We obtained our information for this chapter from a combination of phone calls to the organizations and material from their brochures and publications.

NATIONAL SMALL-BUSINESS ORGANIZATIONS

National small-business organizations break down fairly neatly into Washington lobbying groups and other groups mostly outside Washington that attempt some lobbying but also offer members additional benefits. The Washington lobbying groups tend to support similar issues, but they seem to have varying amounts of influence and attract different kinds of members.

The non-Washington groups tend also to attract different kinds of members, usually intentionally. Some seek out owners of businesses with as few as one or two employees; others seek out owners of more substantial small businesses. Some are open to nearly any type of small business, while some expressly limit their memberships to certain types or sizes of businesses.

National Small-Business Organizations

	Primarily Lobbying	Some Lobbying	Group Insurance	Other* Benefits	Educational** Services
The Center for Small Business	X				
National Family Business Council	X				X
National Federation of Independent Business	X				
National Small Business Association	X		X	X	
American Association of Small Research Companies		X		X	
American Entrepreneurs Association				X	X
International Council for Small Business					X
Small Business League of America		X	X		X
Small Business Service Bureau		X	X	X	X
Support Services Alliance		X	X	X	X
Walter E. Heller International Corp. Institute for the Advancement of Small Business Enterprises		X			X
Young Presidents' Organization					X

* (Such as discounts, group purchasing, etc.)
** (Such as seminars, counseling, etc.)

NATIONAL LOBBYING ORGANIZATIONS

U. S. Chamber of Commerce
The Center for Small Business
U. S. Chamber of Commerce
1615 H St., NW
Washington, DC 20062
(202) 659-6181

The Center for Small Business (CSB) represents a relatively recent effort by the U. S. Chamber of Commerce to associate itself with small-business issues after years of being identified primarily as a big-business proponent. The CSB, organized in 1977, is really an arm of the Chamber, which has more than 100,000 member businesses, of which 85 percent have fewer than 100 employees.

The CSB concentrates mostly on lobbying the federal government on behalf of small businesses. Although it has attempted to concentrate on issues such as reducing regulation and promoting increased availability of financing, the CSB has been burdened to some extent by the Chamber's traditional association with big business. In the eyes of many small-business organizations, the interests of small and large businesses are frequently at odds; for instance, big businesses have generally opposed efforts to limit acquisitions of smaller companies, while small-business groups have supported such efforts.

Thus, the CSB still has a way to go before it becomes viewed as more of a lobbying "heavy" for small business, as the head of a small-business organization puts it.

The CSB has also been pressing local chamber of commerce affiliates to set up their own small-business groups; as noted in the introduction, the effort has been quite successful, as the number of local small-business groups formed as offshoots of local chambers of commerce has quadrupled over the last few years.

The CSB publishes a newsletter, *Opportunities,* every other month for Chamber members, which discusses legislative issues and activities of local chambers, and an annual "State of Small Business" statistical report.

Annual membership dues for the U. S. Chamber of Commerce range from $100 to more than $10,000, depending on companies' invested capital; self-employed professionals can join for $100 yearly.

National Family Business Council, Inc.
1000 Vermont Ave., NW
Washington, DC 20005
(202) 347-2048

The National Family Business Council (NFBC) is the successor organization to the old Sons of Bosses International (SOB). It has about 500 members in thirty-five local chapters but, according to an NFBC news release, "speaks for some 10 million family businesses in the U.S. with aggregate sales of $1 trillion." The organization says it is "dedicated to the survival and well-being of family-owned businesses."

The NFBC devotes itself mostly to lobbying; one of its major recent causes has been legislation that would ease estate taxes on family businesses passed on from one generation to another. It also publishes a newsletter, *Family Business Forum,* nine times a year, which reports on small-business legislative and other developments. It sponsors seminars on subjects of concern to family businesses and holds an annual convention.

Membership for companies is $250 annually, plus a $100 initiation fee; individuals can join for $100 annually, plus a $50 initiation fee.

National Federation of Independent Business
490 L'Enfant Plaza East, SW
Washington, DC 20024
(202) 554-9000

or

150 W 20th Ave.
San Mateo, CA 94403
(415) 341-7441

With more than 600,000 members, the National Federation of Independent Business (NFIB) has been described as "the General Motors of small business." Its members are mostly owners of small retail and service companies.

The organization expends considerable effort polling its members on various issues to guide lobbying efforts. Eight times yearly it sends out a newsletter, *NFIB Mandate,* which includes presentations on the pros and cons of pending federal legislation and asks members to vote for or against the issues raised. A recent poll sought input on such issues as reducing the workweek to thirty-five hours from forty hours, providing federal programs to assist failing businesses, and exempting family-owned businesses from estate taxes when the businesses are left to the spouse or children of the owners.

The NFIB says its lobbying positions are dictated entirely by the outcome of its polls. Officials of other small-business organizations contend that the NFIB doesn't always allow itself to be tied to set positions by such votes and is open to compromise.

However the NFIB actually arrives at its final lobbying positions, it has established a reputation for effectiveness. According to the September–October 1979 issue of *In Business* magazine, the NFIB "is particularly good at mobilizing campaigns to deluge Congress with letters." It maintains computerized membership lists, said the magazine,

> broken down by state, congressional district, type of business, and whether the member knows his Congressman personally. With that kind of information, the group can instantly generate pressure on a Congressman to take a particular stand.

That, combined with its huge membership role, "gives it clout in Washington," *In Business* observed.

The NFIB makes similar efforts to influence state legislation in each of the fifty states through a nationwide staff of more than 500 people scattered in regional offices around the country. It conducts surveys of members on legislation pending in their states and uses results to guide its positions.

The organization bills itself as nonpartisan, but its positions are generally viewed by legislators on both the national and state level as being conservative Republican.

The NFIB has an interesting dues structure; members pay an annual fee of between $35 and $500, depending on what they can afford and how valuable they believe the group has been. "The average new member enters the program for approximately $50 for the first full year's dues," a membership application says. The NFIB winds up with resources of more than $20 million annually.

Potential members should write the NFIB at its California address.

National Small Business Association
1604 K St., NW
Washington, DC 20006
(202) 296-7400

The National Small Business Association (NSBA) says its memberships are open "to anybody who thinks they're small." Its 50,000 members tend to be small businesses somewhat larger than those which belong to the National Federation of Independent Business; about half are manufacturers, with the remainder service, retailing, and wholesaling businesses.

The NSBA concentrates most of its efforts on attempting to influence federal legislation so as to benefit small businesses. Though smaller in membership size than the NFIB, the NSBA is considered relatively equal in influence and competence by legislators and other small-business groups. It may even have something of an advantage over NFIB in that it can react to issues without needing to poll its members, as NFIB does. That allows NSBA to move more quickly on legislation it favors or opposes.

The NSBA has also strengthened its legislative influence by organizing and overseeing a federation of eighty-two national and regional trade associations with substantial small-business memberships known as the Small Business Legislative Council. The Council, which includes organizations like the Retail Druggists Association and the National Association of Realtors, represents about 4 million small-business owners. The Council gives the various industry-specific trade groups greater lobbying strength than they would have individually.

Unlike the NFIB, the NSBA offers its members some services in addition to lobbying. It has a service known as a Bidders Early Alert Message that gives members quick notice of government procurement opportunities. It also offers members some group insurance programs along with a couple of newsletters on small-business issues. The NSBA holds no regular meetings for members, because of its feeling that small-business owners don't have time for meetings.

Membership dues range from $40 to $600 annually, depending on businesses' number of employees.

OTHER NATIONAL ORGANIZATIONS

American Association of Small Research Companies
8794 Westchester Pike
Upper Darby, PA 19082
(215) 449-2333

The American Association of Small Research Companies works to promote the interests of small research and development companies. Its primary effort on behalf of member companies has been to obtain more work for R&D companies from both federal government agencies and large corporations.

The Association says it has been successful in getting an increasing amount of consideration from government agencies, particularly for granting R&D contracts to small companies. The Association tries to get as much of the procurement work as possible directed to its members by making available to corporate and government procurement officials a directory of its members.

The Association also acts as what it calls a "discreet clearinghouse" for member companies seeking to make acquisitions of other companies or to be acquired by large corporations.

The Association holds an annual conference which includes a meeting with government procurement representatives.

Membership is $50 annually.

American Entrepreneurs Association
2311 Pontius Ave.
Los Angeles, CA 90064
(213) 478-0437

The American Entrepreneurs Association (AEA) attempts to keep members informed about new business opportunities, or "the latest hot businesses," as the organization puts it. Through its magazine *Entrepreneur* and dozens of manuals, the AEA offers advice on starting such businesses as computer stores, skateboard parks, and chocolate chip cookie outlets.

The AEA also offers members tips on obtaining government and bank loans and other start-up assistance.

Underlying the AEA's efforts is a philosophy with which many small-business experts would disagree: that starting and succeeding in small business is easy. Also underlying the AEA's efforts is a big emphasis on promoting membership in the organization. It runs newspaper and magazine ads that play on the get-rich-quick element of starting businesses; in this same vein, it sponsors seminars around the country that purport to teach budding entrepreneurs about starting businesses, but also serve as major membership recruiting drives.

Members have access to several "business opportunities counselors," who answer questions about starting new businesses, and a research department. Members also get a 25 percent discount on Avis car rentals. Membership is $55 a year.

International Council for Small Business
University of Wisconsin Extension
929 N Sixth St.
Milwaukee, WI 53203
(414) 224-1816

The International Council for Small Business (ICSB) is an academically oriented organization open to anyone with an interest in small-business management, including educators, government officials, trade association executives, professionals such as bankers and lawyers, and small-business owners.

The ICSB's two major undertakings—an annual conference and a quarterly *Journal of Small Business Management*—are dominated by small-business educators. Thus, the annual conference features academically oriented research papers on various aspects of entrepreneurship and small-business management. The *Journal of Small Business Management* contains formally written articles mostly by educators.

Though the ICSB is the only academically oriented national small-business organization, it has had some difficulty attracting the best-known and -respected small-business academics to active involvement. That appears to stem at least partly from a lack of cohesion among small-business educators.

The ICSB has about 1,000 members. Dues are $25 annually in the U.S. and $40 in Canada, which includes the quarterly journal. The journal is available to nonmembers for $10 yearly.

Small Business League of America
5050 Poplar Ave.
Memphis, TN 38157
(901) 682-7651

The Small Business League of America was formed in 1980 for the stated purpose of "representing the small business people who are never invited to the White House." According to literature sent out to prospective members, it is intended as a national organization with nine regional districts to provide members with group-rate health insurance, workshops and seminars, information about "specific business problems and their solutions," and a research department to evaluate new products and opportunities.

Because the organization is so new, it is difficult to evaluate. We did notice that their brochure was full of misspellings. We also were unable to reach officials of the organization to obtain more specific information about what kinds of small businesses it expects to represent and what specific services it expects to provide members.

Annual dues are $35.

Small Business Service Bureau, Inc.
544 Main St.
P.O. Box 1441
Worcester, MA 01601
(800) 225-7312
(800) 262-2981 (in Massachusetts)
(800) 225-7247 (in North Carolina and Ohio)

The Small Business Service Bureau is a kind of all-purpose organization that provides its 30,000 members with state and federal lobbying, group health insurance programs, and business consulting and information by phone. Most of its members are from a seventeen-state triangle from Ohio to Maine to North Carolina; a few members are from other parts of the U.S.

The Bureau requires that its small-business members have firms with fifty or fewer full-time employees. Most members own retail and service businesses with under ten employees.

The Bureau polls members on various state and federal issues and then lobbies on behalf of those issues that seem most important; the group has concentrated much of its effort on family-business issues such as estate and gift tax legislation. The Bureau acknowledges that one of the big attractions to potential members is the availability of health insurance at group rates, even to sole proprietorships; the coverage isn't available in every state, however. The organization also offers group disability, travel, and term life insurance coverage, along with motel/hotel and rental car discounts.

The Small Business Service Bureau also has consultants available to answer questions and offer advice to members on various operational difficulties small businesses encounter. It sponsors occasional informal seminars on subjects such as small-business-owner pension plans and the effects of electric rate changes on small businesses. And it publishes a monthly newsletter on small-business issues and its own programs.

The Bureau recently started an "Exchange" whereby members can advertise selling and buying needs to other members; the Small Business Service Bureau has also started making the listings available to big corporations and federal government agencies to stimulate more procurement from small businesses.

Membership is $50 annually.

Support Service Alliance, Inc.
Crossroads Building
Two Times Square
New York, NY 10036
(212) 398-7800

Founded in 1977 with an $800,000 Rockefeller Foundation grant, Support Service Alliance is concerned primarily with providing small businesses and the self-employed with "the same benefits and services that big business enjoys." It has 12,000 members around the country.

Among its member benefits are group medical, disability, and life insurance; purchasing discounts on business merchandise; copying equipment and auto rental discounts; a legal inquiry and referral service; and educational loan guarantees for members' children.

The SSA also promises members a developing lobbying effort. A brochure states:

> SSA is becoming a vigorous spokesman for small organizations and the self-employed wherever appropriate and will be appearing before and communicating with committees of the U. S. Congress, administrative agencies of national, state, and local governments and relevant private sector forums.

It promises conferences on subjects of concern to small businesses as well.

The SSA publishes a bulletin every other month with management tips and SSA news along with booklets on small-business management problems.

The SSA charges a onetime enrollment fee of $10 that provides access to its services; for an additional $6 yearly, members receive the bulletin.

Walter E. Heller International Corporation Institute
   for the Advancement of Small Business Enterprises
105 W Adams St.
Chicago, IL 60603
(312) 621-7000

The Walter E. Heller International Corporation Institute for the Advancement of Small Business Enterprises was formed in late 1979 with three general objectives, according to the Heller Corporation's 1979 annual report: "to help small business survive"; "to give the small business person a greater sense of self-esteem"; and "to make sure that small business and entrepreneurs do not disappear."

The huge corporation's motives weren't entirely altruistic. According to the annual report, small businesses

> particularly concern Heller because they represent a major source of our business. The institute therefore fulfills an obligation to our clientele and serves to strengthen our market.

The Institute plans to issue policy statements on small-business issues, poll a nationwide sample of 1,200 small-business owners ("small business" being defined as companies having 40 to 500 employees), and sponsor small-business seminars.

The Institute isn't open to membership. The seminars will "be attended upon invitation by owners of small businesses," according to the annual report. If small-business owners learn of a seminar that especially interests them, they can call Heller and attempt to wrangle an invitation; all invitees are charged $200 to cover costs.

Young Presidents' Organization
201 E 42nd St.
New York, NY 10017
(212) 867-1900

The Young Presidents' Organization (YPO) is an upper-crust organization for presidents of companies with at least $3 million annual sales and fifty employees (financial corporations must have at least $60 million in assets and fifty employees). YPO defines "young" as those under age forty-four, though they must have achieved their positions before age forty.

Those who meet the basic qualifications don't just join. Much like a fraternity or exclusive club, YPO requires "sponsorship" by two members of a local YPO chapter. "In selecting potential candidates for YPO membership, quality, not quantity, has always been the ruling principle," says a YPO brochure.

> Integrity in personal and business life, enthusiasm and willingness to participate, are among the chief qualitative factors, as is compatibility with present members and YPO's dedication to education and idea exchange.

YPO's air of exclusivity permeates even its approach to handing out information on the organization. Potential members must request information in writing on company stationery; no phone requests are honored.

The group has more than 3,500 members and serves them by sponsoring seminars and short courses on a variety of small-business subjects, such as acquiring and selling businesses and making use of outside directors. It also offers annual week-long gatherings that include courses and social functions at both an American university and an overseas university.

YPO is broken down into local chapters, which encourage extensive member involvement in planning and participating in the various seminars, conferences, and courses. Membership dues vary among the local chapters.

REGIONAL AND LOCAL SMALL-BUSINESS ORGANIZATIONS

Regional and local groups vary at least as widely as the national small-business organizations in their objectives and membership benefits. Some concentrate solely on lobbying, some concentrate solely on seminars, and some have a wide variety of benefits.

Not every region, state, or city has a small-business organization. Most of those that do exist, though, are affiliated with the local chamber of commerce and have been formed in the last few years.

The descriptions that follow cannot even come close to being all-inclusive. They are meant to give readers a feeling for the wide variety of programs available from such groups; the descriptions may stimulate suggestions for additional programs for certain groups. To find out about small-business groups in a particular area, readers will usually be well advised to inquire at the local chamber of commerce. Other area business owners can also provide suggestions and evaluations of groups with small-business members. Our sampling of regional and local small-business groups is as follows:

Index to Regional and Local Small-Business Organizations

Northeast

Smaller Business Association of New England
Smaller Manufacturers Council
Council of Smaller Enterprises

Midwest

Independent Business Association of Wisconsin
Small Business Group of Greater Des Moines Chamber of Commerce

West

Small Business Council of Seattle Chamber of Commerce
Small Business Council of Colorado Association of Commerce and Industry

Southeast

Small Business Council of Greater San Antonio
Georgia Business and Industry Association

Smaller Business Association of New England
69 Hickory Drive
Waltham, MA 02154
(617) 890-9070

The Smaller Business Association of New England (SBANE) is the oldest and apparently only truly regionally oriented small-business organization. Founded in 1938, SBANE has more than 1,600 members, including operators of small manufacturing, retail, service, and professional businesses.

The organization works hard to involve members in a variety of activities. Its members and staff meet frequently with federal legislators and various federal agency officials to present concerns of New England small businesses.

SBANE offers members twenty-two one-day seminars each year on various aspects of small-business management, such as acquiring computers and financial planning. It also offers an annual three-day course at Dartmouth's Amos Tuck Graduate Business School on improving small-business management skills.

The organization has been active in promoting exports by its members. It organized an export program for small businesses with the Massachusetts Port Authority and conducts special seminars in setting up company export programs.

In addition, SBANE sponsors what it calls an "Executive Dialog" program in which noncompeting business owners and managers who don't have boards of directors meet monthly to discuss common business problems.

Other membership benefits include group life and health insurance and overseas cargo insurance. SBANE publishes two newsletters, one on internal developments and another on legislative developments.

Annual membership dues range from $120 to $480, depending on businesses' number of employees. All employees of member businesses can participate in all SBANE programs.

Smaller Manufacturers Council
339 Boulevard of the Allies
Pittsburgh, PA 15222
(412) 391-1622

The Smaller Manufacturers Council dates from 1945 and has 1,100 Pennsylvania and New Jersey small manufacturers as members.

Its services include the following: various group insurance, car and truck leasing discounts, group retirement plans, and a purchasing referral service.

The Council sponsors annual one-day seminars with Allegheny Community College on small-business operations. It also sets up meetings for company owners and managers to discuss specific management problems with outside consultants. And it offers assistance to members interested in exporting their products.

The Council partakes of what it calls "a low-key lobbying effort" with state legislators on what it considers to be important small-business issues. It also provides an information and referral service for all area businesses and works with other business groups to help new businesses locating in the area. The Council publishes a monthly newsletter about its programs and a directory of members that it sends to area purchasing agents.

Annual membership dues range from $150 to $455, depending on businesses' number of employees. Nonmanufacturing businesses with fewer than 500 employees can join as associate members; they can't vote but are accorded other membership benefits.

Council of Smaller Enterprises
690 Union Commercial Building
Cleveland, OH 44115
(216) 621-3300

The Council of Smaller Enterprises is a division of the Greater Cleveland Growth Association, which is the area's chamber of commerce. The Council has 3,500 small-business members, which represent about 10 percent of the Greater Cleveland total; they include manufacturing, service, retailing, wholesaling, and construction companies.

Among member benefits are group health insurance, reduced rates on leased cars, credit checks without belonging to Dun & Bradstreet, and group purchasing programs. The Council also sponsors four business seminars and lectures monthly and has developed a course on long-range planning; the planning course is limited to twenty-five participants whose companies have fast-growth potential and who work one-to-one with twenty-five consultants for eight sessions over an eight-month period for a cost of $595.

The Council also lobbies on behalf of small-business owners at the city, state, and federal levels. To become involved with the Council, small-business owners must be members of the Greater Cleveland Growth Association.

Independent Business Association of Wisconsin
7635 W Bluemound Road
Milwaukee, WI 53213
(414) 258-7055

The Independent Business Association of Wisconsin was founded in 1970 and has 600 members. Membership is limited to businesses which have no publicly owned stock; the number of employees is irrelevant.

The Association sponsors monthly breakfast meetings that include seminars on small-business management and speeches by politicians. The Association also attempts to involve members in the political process; it sponsors an annual lunch for members with state legislators and encourages members to testify before state and federal legislative hearings.

The Association publishes a newsletter on its activities and occasional notices about important small-business legislative developments.

Membership fees range from $100 to $300 annually, depending on businesses' number of employees.

Small Business Group
Greater Des Moines Chamber of Commerce
800 High St.
Des Moines, IA 50307
(515) 283-2161

The Small Business Group is a division of the Greater Des Moines Chamber of Commerce and was formed in 1978. About 1,000 of the Chamber's 3,200 members belong to the Small Business Group.

The Group is open to any business owners in the Des Moines area who consider their businesses to be small. The Group sponsors monthly seminars and quarterly full-day workshops on business management; it also makes available individual management counseling through its Business Advisory Resource Bank.

The Group has also been active in working for and against various state legislation affecting small business. It publishes a monthly newsletter on group events and plans a directory of business resources.

Any Chamber of Commerce member can join the Small Business Group at no additional charge.

Small Business Council
Seattle Chamber of Commerce
215 Columbia St.
Seattle, WA 98104
(206) 447-7200

The Small Business Council has no members as such; instead, it maintains a mailing list of business owners and others interested in its monthly seminars, which are its primary activity. The two-and-a-half-hour seminars cover such subjects as financial planning, tax laws, marketing, advertising, personnel management, employee benefits, and inventory control.

The seminars cost $7.50 for Chamber of Commerce members and $12.50 for others.

Small Business Council
Colorado Association of Commerce and Industry
1390 Logan
Denver, CO 80203
(303) 831-7411

The Small Business Council of the Colorado Association of Commerce and Industry involves fifty members of the Association. The Council's primary activity is lobbying at the state and federal level on such issues as government regulation, taxation, inflation, and government attitudes toward small business.

The Council is open to all members of the Association without charge.

Small Business Council
Greater San Antonio Chamber of Commerce
Box 1628
San Antonio, TX 78296
(512) 227-8181

The Small Business Council was set up in 1979 as a division of the Greater San Antonio Chamber of Commerce and has 500 of the 3,500 Chamber of Commerce members affiliated with it. The Small Business Council limits involvement to locally owned or operated companies with 150 or fewer employees.

The Council sponsors monthly seminars on such subjects as financial analysis, contracting with the federal government, acquiring computer systems, and obtaining loans.

The Council has also begun polling members on local, state, and national issues as the start of an effort to become more involved in small-business legislative issues. It has started a small-business information service for start-up entrepreneurs in San Antonio. It also publishes a newsletter on Council events.

Membership is open to qualified members of the Greater San Antonio Chamber of Commerce.

Georgia Business & Industry Association
181 Washington St., SW
Atlanta, GA 30303
(404) 659-4444

The Georgia Business & Industry Association is primarily a lobbying organization that works at both the state and federal levels. It publishes various bulletins and newsletters designed to keep members informed about pending legislation and regulations. It also sponsors conferences on business problems such as energy and productivity, and administers the Georgia Waste Exchange Program, which makes available to members information on potentially useful production byproducts that companies can trade and sell.

While the bulk of the organization's more than 1,000 members are small companies, the Association also includes some of the State's largest employers. Dues for businesses with between one and twenty-five employees are $250 annually; for companies with twenty-six to fifty employees, $400.

INDUSTRY ORGANIZATIONS

Organizations that represent owners of businesses in specific industries are devoted primarily to keeping members updated about developments in their industries, via seminars, meetings, and publications. Such developments might include technological changes, competitive information, and regulatory developments. The organizations also lobby at the local and state level on behalf of their members and increasingly are banding together with other industry organizations in legislative and other sorts of councils to influence legislation that affects small business in general.

The following are organizations that represent industries with especially large concentrations of small businesses:

Associated General Contractors of America
1957 E St., NW
Washington, DC 20006
(202) 393-2040

Its 9,500 members are engaged in construction of factories, office buildings, warehouses, highways, bridges, and other projects.

Automotive Service Councils, Inc.
188 Industrial Drive
Elmhurst, IL 60126
(312) 530-2330

The 6,000 members are owners and operators of independent automotive repair shops involved in such areas as engine rebuilding, brake and wheel alignment, and transmission replacement.

National Restaurant Association
One IBM Plaza
Chicago, IL 60611
(312) 787-2525

Its 13,000 members operate restaurants, cafeterias, clubs, catering services, institutional food services, and drive-ins.

National Hardwood Lumber Association
332 S Michigan Ave.
Chicago, IL 60604
(312) 427-2810

Its 1,400 members are American and Canadian manufacturers, distributors, and sellers of hardwood lumber and veneer products.

National Association of Realtors
430 N Michigan Ave.
Chicago, IL 60611
(312) 440-8000

Its 705,000 members own and manage real estate firms.

National Retail Merchants Association
100 W 31st St.
New York, NY 10001
(212) 244-8780

Its 35,000 members own clothing and home furnishing stores.

National Retail Hardware Association
770 N High School Road
Indianapolis, IN 46224
(317) 248-1261

Its 18,000 members own independent hardware retail stores.

National Home Furnishings Association
405 Merchandise Mart Plaza
Chicago, IL 60654
(312) 527-3070

Its 13,500 members are retailers of furniture, carpeting, and related home furnishings.

OTHER SOURCES

United States House of Representatives
Committee on Small Business
U. S. House of Representatives
2361 Rayburn House Office Building
Washington, DC 20515
(202) 225-6020

and

United States Senate
Select Committee on Small Business
U. S. Senate
424 Russell Senate Office Building
Washington, DC 20510
(202) 224-5175

Small-business owners who wish to do some of their own lobbying or checking into the status of small-business legislation can contact either of the above congressional committees. Both have staff members who monitor opinions of the small-business community and keep track of the progress of legislation affecting small business.

The committees have responsibility for overseeing the Small Business Administration and its programs as well as investigating small-business issues such as restraint of trade and availability of financing opportunities to small business. They also investigate issues and problems of specific industries.

Just how effective the committees are is a matter of some debate. A column on small business in the July 28, 1980, *Wall Street Journal* labeled the two committees

> one of the legendary backwaters of Congress . . . Membership on the committees does offer an excellent opportunity for issuing election-year press releases about small business, but it provides little legislative responsibility. That's because major tax and regulatory issues affecting small business are assigned to other House and Senate committees. Thus, most Senators and Representatives treat their small-business duties as a minor sidelight.

Not surprisingly, staff members of both committees argue that such an assessment is untrue. They contend that just the opposite is true, that the two small-business committees are becoming more influential and attractive to senators and congressmen. To back up their assessment, they note, for instance, that the Senate Select Committee on Small Business was enlarged to seventeen members from nine members during a recent congressional session to accommodate a sudden rush of senatorial interest.

Whatever the real situation, the committees can be good information sources on small-business legislative issues.

Small Business Administration
Chief Counsel for Advocacy
Office of Advocacy
Small Business Administration
1441 L St., NW
Washington, DC 20416
(202) 653-6533; (202) 653-6579

Representatives of the Office of Advocacy are based in each of the SBA's ten regional offices—Boston, Philadelphia, New York, Atlanta, Chicago, Kansas City, Dallas, Denver, Seattle, and San Francisco.

The Chief Counsel for Advocacy of the SBA plays an ombudsman role within the federal bureaucracy, attempting to resolve complaints from individual small-business owners and make bureaucrats more aware of small-business concerns. Though the Chief Counsel's duties and powers are somewhat vague, the position is certainly a unique one in the bureaucracy's scheme of things. The Chief Counsel is a presidential appointee, subject to Senate approval; he or she works within the SBA but has wide latitude to voice complaints to all federal agencies, including the SBA, regardless of whether the SBA's top officials agree or approve.

Thus, small-business owners who encounter problems working with federal regulatory agencies like the Environmental Protection Agency or federal procurement officials should voice complaints to the Office of

Advocacy. Similarly, small-business owners who feel that specific regulations or laws are unfair to small businesses should make their displeasure known to the Office of Advocacy. The Chief Counsel position was only started in 1978, but complaints and recommendations from the Office of Advocacy seem to be taken seriously within the bureaucracy, the result being greater sensitivity to the needs of small business. In addition, the office has been able to work out compromises in some disagreements between small-business owners and federal regulatory officials.

BOOKS

Encyclopedia of Associations (Detroit: Gale Research Co.)

This three-volume annual publication lists and describes 14,000 associations in alphabetical order within broad categories. Besides providing addresses, phone numbers, and officials to contact, the publication also includes number of members, staff sizes, and member services.

National Trade & Professional Associations of the United States & Canada & Labor Unions (Washington, DC: Columbia Books, Inc.)

This single volume lists 6,300 national trade associations, labor unions, and professional and scientific societies. Listings are in alphabetical order, but not by category. It provides names, addresses, phone numbers, membership sizes, annual budget, staff sizes, and similar additional information along with one- or two-line descriptions.

Local Small Business Administration Offices

REGION		CITY	STATE	ZIP CODE
	RO	Boston	Mass.	02110
	DO	Boston	Mass.	02114
	POD	Holyoke	Mass.	01050
I	DO	Augusta	Maine	04330
	DO	Concord	N.H.	03301
	DO	Hartford	Conn.	06103
	DO	Montpelier	Vt.	05602
	DO	Providence	R.I.	02903
	RO	New York	N.Y.	10007
	DO	New York	N.Y.	10007
	POD	Melville	N.Y.	11747
	DO	Hato Rey	P.R.	00918
	POD	St. Thomas	V.I.	00801
II	DO	Newark	N.J.	07102
	POD	Camden	N.J.	08104
	DO	Syracuse	N.Y.	13260
	BO	Buffalo	N.Y.	14202
	BO	Elmira	N.Y.	14901
	POD	Albany	N.Y.	12210
	POD	Rochester	N.Y.	14614
	RO	Philadelphia	Bala Cynwyd, Pa.	19004
	DO	Philadelphia	Bala Cynwyd, Pa.	19004
	BO	Harrisburg	Pa.	17101
	BO	Wilkes-Barre	Pa.	18702
	BO	Wilmington	Del.	19801
III	DO	Baltimore	Towson, Md.	21204
	DO	Clarksburg	W.Va.	26301
	BO	Charleston	W.Va.	25301
	DO	Pittsburgh	Pa.	15222
	DO	Richmond	Va.	23240
	DO	Washington	D.C.	20417
	RO	Atlanta	Ga.	30309
	DO	Atlanta	Ga.	30309
	DO	Birmingham	Ala.	35205
	DO	Charlotte	N.C.	28202
	POD	Greenville	N.C.	27834
	DO	Columbia	S.C.	29201
	DO	Jackson	Miss.	39201
IV	BO	Biloxi	Miss.	39530
	DO	Jacksonville	Fla.	32202
	DO	Louisville	Ky.	40201
	DO	Miami	Coral Gables, Fla.	33134

ADDRESS	COMMERCIAL TELEPHONE NUMBERS FOR PUBLIC USE ONLY
60 Batterymarch Street, 10th Floor	(617) 223-2100
150 Causeway St., 10th Floor	(617) 223-2100
302 High Street, 4th Floor	(413) 536-8770
★ 40 Western Avenue, Room 512	(207) 622-6171
★ 55 Pleasant Street, Room 211	(603) 224-4041
One Financial Plaza	(203) 244-3600
★ 87 State Street, Room 204, P.O. Box 605	(802) 229-0538
57 Eddy Street, 7th Floor	(401) 528-4580
★ 26 Federal Plaza, Room 29-118	(212) 264-7772
★ 26 Federal Plaza, Room 3100	(212) 264-4355
401 Broad Hollow Road, Suite 322	(516) 752-1626
★ Chardon and Bolivia Streets, P.O. Box 1915	(809) 753-4572
★ Veterans Drive, Room 283	(809) 774-8530
★ 970 Broad St., Room 1635	(201) 645-2434
1800 East Davis Street	(609) 757-5183
★ 100 South Clinton Street, Room 1071	(315) 423-5383
★ 111 West Huron St., Room 1311	(716) 846-4301
180 State Street, Room 412	(607) 733-4686
99 Washington Ave., Room 301-Mezzanine	(518) 472-6300
★ 100 State Street, Room 601	(716) 263-6700
231 St. Asaphs Rd., Suite 646-West Lobby	(215) 597-3311
231 St. Asaphs Rd., Suite 400-East Lobby	(215) 597-3311
100 Chestnut Street, 3rd Floor	(717) 782-3840
20 North Pennsylvania Avenue	(717) 826-6497
★ 844 King Street, Room 5207	(302) 573-6294
8600 LaSalle Road, Room 630	(301) 962-4392
109 North 3rd St., Room 301	(304) 623-5631
Charleston National Plaza, Suite 628	(304) 343-6181
★ 1000 Liberty Ave., Room 1401	(412) 644-2780
★ 400 North 8th St., Room 3015, P.O. Box 10126	(804) 782-2617
1030 15th St., N.W., Suite 250	(202) 655-4000
1375 Peachtree St., N.E., 5th Floor	(404) 881-4943
1720 Peachtree Street, N.W., 6th Floor	(404) 881-4325
908 South 20th St., Room 202	(205) 254-1344
230 S. Tryon Street, Suite 700	(704) 371-6111
★ 215 South Evans Street, Room 206	(919) 752-3798
★ 1835 Assembly Street, 3rd Floor	(803) 765-5376
★ 100 West Capitol Street, Suite 322	(601) 969-4371
111 Fred Haise Blvd., 2nd Floor	(601) 435-3676
★ 400 West Bay St., Room 261, P.O. Box 35067	(904) 791-3782
★ 600 Federal Pl., Room 188, P.O. Box 3517	(502) 582-5971
2222 Ponce De Leon Boulevard, 5th Floor	(305) 350-5521

REGION		CITY	STATE	ZIP CODE
	POD	Tampa	Fla.	33602
	DO	Nashville	Tenn.	37219
	BO	Knoxville	Tenn.	37902
	POD	Memphis	Tenn.	38103
	POD	West Palm Beach	Fla.	33402
	RO	Chicago	Ill.	60604
	DO	Chicago	Ill.	60604
	BO	Springfield	Ill.	62701
	DO	Cleveland	Ohio	44199
	DO	Columbus	Ohio	43215
V	BO	Cincinnati	Ohio	45202
	DO	Detroit	Mich.	48226
	BO	Marquette	Mich.	49855
	DO	Indianapolis	Ind.	46204
	DO	Madison	Wisc.	53703
	BO	Milwaukee	Wisc.	53202
	POD	Eau Claire	Wisc.	54701
	DO	Minneapolis	Minn.	55402
	RO	Dallas	Tex.	75235
	DO	Dallas	Tex.	75242
	POD	Marshall	Tex.	75670
	DO	Albuquerque	N.M.	87110
	DO	Houston	Tex.	77002
	DO	Little Rock	Ark.	72201
	DO	Lubbock	Tex.	79401
	BO	El Paso	Tex.	79902
VI	DO	Lower Rio Grande Valley	Harlingen, Tex.	78550
	BO	Corpus Christi	Tex.	78408
	DO	New Orleans	La.	70113
	POD	Shreveport	La.	71101
	DO	Oklahoma City	Okla.	73102
	POD	Tulsa	Okla.	74119
	DO	San Antonio	Tex.	78206
	POD	Austin	Tex.	78701
	RO	Kansas City	Mo.	64106
	DO	Kansas City	Mo.	64106
VII	DO	Des Moines	Iowa	50309
	DO	Omaha	Neb.	68102
	DO	St. Louis	Mo.	63101
	DO	Wichita	Kans.	67202

ADDRESS	COMMERCIAL TELEPHONE NUMBERS FOR PUBLIC USE ONLY
700 Twiggs Street, Suite 607	(813) 228-2594
404 James Robertson Parkway, Suite 1012	(615) 251-5881
502 South Gay St., Room 307	(615) 637-9300
★ 167 North Main St., Room 211	(901) 521-3588
★ 701 Clematis St., Room 229	(305) 659-7533
★ 219 South Dearborn St., Room 838	(312) 353-0355
★ 219 South Dearborn St., Room 437	(312) 353-4528
One North, Old State Capital Plaza	(217) 525-4416
★ 1240 East 9th St., Room 317	(216) 522-4180
★ 85 Marconi Boulevard	(614) 469-6860
★ 550 Main St., Room 5028	(513) 684-2814
★ 477 Michigan Ave.	(313) 226-6075
540 W. Kaye Avenue	(906) 225-1108
★ 575 North Pennsylvania St., Room 552	(317) 269-7272
212 East Washington Ave., Room 213	(608) 264-5261
★ 517 East Wisconsin Avenue, Room 246	(414) 291-3941
★ 500 South Barstow St., Room B9AA	(715) 834-9012
12 South 6th St.	(612) 725-2362
1720 Regal Row, Room 230	(214) 767-7643
★ 1100 Commerce St., Room 3C36	(214) 767-0605
★ 100 South Washington Street, Room G-12	(214) 935-5257
5000 Marble Avenue, N.E., Room 320	(505) 766-3430
500 Dallas Street	(713) 226-4341
611 Gaines Street, Suite 900	(501) 378-5871
★ 1205 Texas Avenue, Room 712	(806) 762-7466
4100 Rio Bravo, Suite 300	(915) 543-7586
222 East Van Buren Street, P.O. Box 2567	(512) 423-4534
3105 Leopard Street, P.O. Box 9253	(512) 888-3331
1001 Howard Avenue, 17th Floor	(504) 589-6685
★ 500 Fannin Street, Room 5B06	(318) 226-5196
★ 200 N.W. 5th Street, Suite 670	(405) 231-4301
616 South Boston Street	(918) 581-7462
★ 727 East Durango Street, Room A-513	(512) 229-6250
★ 300 East 8th Street	(512) 397-5288
911 Walnut St., 23rd Floor	(816) 374-5288
1150 Grande Ave., 5th Floor	(816) 374-3416
★ 210 Walnut St., Room 749	(515) 284-4422
19th & Farnum Sts., 2nd Floor	(402) 221-4691
One Mercantile Center, Suite 2500	(314) 425-4191
110 East Waterman Street	(316) 267-6571

REGION		CITY	STATE	ZIP CODE
	RO	Denver	Colo.	80202
	DO	Denver	Colo.	80202
	DO	Casper	Wyo.	82602
VIII	DO	Fargo	N.D.	58108
	DO	Helena	Mont.	59601
	DO	Salt Lake City	Utah	84138
	DO	Sioux Falls	S.D.	57102
	BO	Rapid City	S.D.	57701
	RO	San Francisco	Calif.	94102
	DO	San Francisco	Calif.	94105
	POD	Oakland	Calif.	94612
	BO	Fresno	Calif.	93712
	POD	Sacramento	Calif.	95825
	DO	Las Vegas	Nev.	89101
IX	POD	Reno	Nev.	89505
	DO	Honolulu	Hawaii	96850
	BO	Agana	Guam	96910
	DO	Los Angeles	Calif.	90071
	DO	Phoenix	Ariz.	85012
	POD	Tucson	Ariz.	85715
	DO	San Diego	Calif.	92188
	RO	Seattle	Wash.	98104
	DO	Seattle	Wash.	98174
	DO	Anchorage	Alaska	99501
X	BO	Fairbanks	Alaska	99701
	DO	Boise	Idaho	83701
	DO	Portland	Oreg.	97204
	DO	Spokane	Wash.	99210

10 REGIONAL OFFICES [RO]
63 DISTRICT OFFICES [DO]

18 BRANCH OFFICES [BO]
19 POST-OF-DUTY [POD]

ADDRESS	COMMERCIAL TELEPHONE NUMBERS FOR PUBLIC USE ONLY
1405 Curtis Street, 22nd Floor	(303) 837-5763
721 19th Street	(303) 837-2607
★ 100 East B Street, Room 4001, P.O. Box 2839	(307) 265-5266
★ 657 2nd Ave., North, Room 218, P.O. Box 3086	(701) 237-5771
★ 301 South Park Avenue, Room 528, Drawer 10054	(406) 449-5381
★ 125 South State St., Room 2237	(314) 425-5800
101 South Main Ave., Suite 101	(605) 336-2980
★ 515 9th St., Room 246	(605) 343-5074
★ 450 Golden Gate Ave., P.O. Box 36044	(415) 556-7487
211 Main Street, 4th Floor	(415) 556-7490
★ 1515 Clay Street	(415) 273-7790
1229 "N" St., P.O. Box 828	(209) 487-5189
★ 2800 Cottage Way, Room 2535	(916) 484-4726
★ 301 E. Stewart, P.O. Box 7525, Downtown Station	(702) 385-6611
★ 50 South Virginia St., Room 308, P.O. Box 3216	(702) 784-5268
★ 300 Ala Moana, Room 2213, P.O. Box 50207	** (808) 546-8950
Pacific Daily News Bldg., Room 508	** (671) 477-8420
350 S. Figueroa St., 6th Floor	(213) 688-2956
3030 North Central Avenue, Suite 1201	(602) 261-3611
★ 301 West Congress Street, Room 3V	(602) 625-1063
★ 880 Front Street, Room 4-S-29	(714) 293-5440
710 2nd Ave., 5th Floor	(206) 442-5676
★ 915 Second Ave., Room 1744	(206) 442-5534
1016 West 6th Ave., Suite 200	** (907) 271-4022
★ 101 12th Avenue, Box 14	** (907) 452-1951
1005 Main St., 2nd Floor	(208) 384-1096
★ 1220 S.W. Third Avenue, Room 676	(503) 221-2682
★ West 920 Riverside Avenue, Room 651, P.O. Box 2167	(509) 456-5310

★ FEDERALLY-OWNED PROPERTIES (All Others—Federally Leased)
** Operator Assistance May Be Needed In Some Areas

APPENDIX B

Small-Business Information and Data Sources

PUBLICATIONS

Boardroom Reports
500 Fifth Ave.
New York, NY 10110
(212) 354-0005

Boardroom Reports presents a combination of practical advice and information to aid business managers and owners in running their businesses and their personal finances. It provides advice on cutting business costs, saving time, and keeping tabs on competitors, along with forecasts about business trends and the stock market. It also offers an assortment of personal tax advice. Written extremely concisely, with little emphasis on graphics. Published every other week; $44 annually.

The Business Owner
Thomar Publications, Inc.
383 S Broadway
Hicksville, NY 11801
(516) 681-2111

The Business Owner offers small-business owners advice on various aspects of business operations, such as cutting taxes, negotiating loans, and issuing stock. Its articles are concise and the advice appears to be helpful and fairly specific. No razzmatazz or fancy graphics in this publication—it doesn't even have any advertising. Published monthly; $48 annually.

Harvard Business Review
Soldiers Field
Boston, MA 02163
(617) 495-6800

Harvard Business Review publishes at least one or two articles each issue directed specifically at small-business management problems in its "Growing Concerns" feature. Articles have examined the problems of choosing an accountant, working with bankers, selling small companies, and controlling accounts receivable. Articles are written by academics, business owners, and consultants. Published every other month; $24 annually.

In Business
Box 323
18 S Seventh St.
Emmaus, PA 18049
(215) 967-4135

In Business, which was started in 1979, is directed to new, quite small businesses. Its articles emphasize the basics of business management with articles on measuring cash flow, choosing small-business computers, and the essentials of marketing. It also publishes profiles of specific small businesses to illustrate how business problems can be solved. *In Business* is also concerned with the effects of business ownership on communities and the lifestyles of owners and employees; as a consequence, it takes an interest in small businesses involved in such things as alternative energy and natural foods. Published every other month; $14 annually.

INC.
United Marine Publishing, Inc.
38 Commercial Wharf
Boston, MA 02110
(617) 227-4700

INC. is another of the crop of small-business magazines started in 1979, only it's directed at well-established, existing businesses with more than $1 million annual sales. Its articles consider problems common to fast-growing small businesses, such as delegating authority and planning ahead. *INC.* usually contains a mix of small-business profiles to illustrate specific situations and how-to articles by consultants to aid in solving problems. It also updates readers on regulatory and legislative developments affecting small businesses. The magazine is well-written and boldly designed to capture the interest of readers. Published monthly; $18 annually.

Small Business Report
Small Business Monitoring & Research Co.
497 Lighthouse Ave.
Monterey, CA 93940
(408) 649-1691

Small Business Report is similar to *The Business Owner* in format and approach. It is devoid of advertising and fancy design, instead concentrating on offering guidance for solving small-business problems. Its articles deal with such matters as vendor relations, essentials of marketing, and minimizing various business taxes. The articles are concise, though not particularly colorful.

Venture, The Magazine for Entrepreneurs
35 W 45th St.
New York, NY 10036
(212) 840-5580

376

Venture is a relatively new publication, having started in 1979, and is aimed primarily at start-up entrepreneurs. It offers tips on obtaining government and private financing and assessments of the latest franchising trends. It also examines business areas that appear to be attracting large numbers of start-up entrepreneurs. It's a colorful magazine which manages to reflect the excitement of the venture creation process. Published monthly; $15 annually.

The Wall Street Journal
22 Cortlandt St.
New York, NY 10007
(212) 285-5000

The Wall Street Journal offers a wealth of information to business managers of all types as it follows specific corporate and government news. In 1980, it started offering a weekly column, published Mondays, addressed to small businesses. The column explores management problems of entrepreneurs as well as federal and state actions affecting small-business prospects.

DATA SERVICES

Association of Computer Users
P.O. Box 9003
Boulder, CO 80301
(303) 499-1722

Like a "Consumer Reports of Computers," the Association of Computer Users makes available reports on the quality of computers in the $15,000 to $50,000 price range. Reports examine individual machines and are written especially for business users. A dozen reports can vary in price from $150 to $450. Membership is $25.

Bottomline Management Association
10 E 40th St.
New York, NY 10016
(212) 683-5353

Bottomline Management Association sponsors a "dial-an-answer" service on payroll-related problems. Questions concerning payroll taxes, insurance, equal employment opportunity, employee benefits, and recruitment are answered as often as the need arises. The cost of the service is $150 per year. The fee includes regular bulletins which analyze common business problems.

Business Growth Services
General Electric Co.
120 Erie Blvd., Dept. 392
Schenectady, NY 12305
(518) 385-2577

Business Growth Services provides information on new businesses or products immediately available for acquisition or licensing. Its *"New Product/New Business Digest"* discloses over 500 unique new products and processes developed by both small and large companies; these new business ventures did not fit General Electric's product lines. The digest costs $45.

Bureau of the Census
Current Industrial Reports
Subscriber Services Section
Publications
Bureau of the Census
Washington, DC 20233
(301) 763-7472

Current Industrial Reports provides shipment and sales data for over 100 industries. Tables include data on imports, exports, and shipments, with breakdowns within industries.

Department of Commerce Publications

Superintendent of Documents
U. S. Government Printing Office
Washington, DC 20402
(202) 783-3238

The U. S. Department of Commerce publishes reports that can help small-business owners plan their marketing efforts. The reports are inexpensive and are often found at local libraries. Major Department of Commerce reports include:

- *The U. S. Industrial Outlook.* Contains reports on 200 industries. Important industry developments and patterns are discussed along with statistics on such things as the total value of shipments, number of establishments with more than 200 employees and less than 20 employees, exports, and annual rates of change. The 1980 *U. S. Industrial Outlook* contained a section on opportunities for small business in the 1980s.

- *County Business Patterns.* Contains statistics on the number of businesses, by type, in each county. Specific employment and payroll data is included. The number of establishments, broken into nine categories based on number of employees, is also given for each industry in each county.

Findex
Find/SVP
500 Fifth Ave.
New York, NY 10036
(212) 354-2424

Findex is a directory of market research reports, studies, and surveys, which is updated every six months. Findex contains descriptions of over 4,000 reports available from 200 publishers, including the publication date, price, and instructions for obtaining copies. These reports cover a wide range of industries and businesses. Findex can lessen a small business' outlay seeking published research on such things as developing technology trends as well as changes in foreign markets. Findex costs $115 annually.

The Information Bank and Advertising and Marketing Intelligence
Mount Pleasant Office Park
1719-A Route 10
Parsippany, NJ 07054
(201) 539-5850

The Information Bank, which is part of the New York Times Company, consists of a data base of sixty major worldwide publications, including business and financial journals. Advertising and Marketing Intelligence (AMI) consists of trade journals and public relations statements relating to the advertising and marketing areas. Information for both data bases is current within a few days. Any topic or combination of topics can be researched to yield abstracts of relevant newspaper and magazine articles. Applications of this service vary from marketing trend analysis to international finance. For example, topics such as trends in do-it-yourself home improvement and import-export activity could be quite important to certain small businesses. Other uses might be gathering information on prospective merger, acquisition, or takeover candidates.

Both data bases are available to small business on a fee-for-service basis. The Parsippany office can offer advice on what is available. Research can be performed and an abstract sent the same day. Full text copies of articles are also available.

The fee for basic research is $110 per hour. A typical run is usually 12 minutes, or $22.

Information Data Search, Inc.
1463 Beacon St.
Brookline, MA 02146
(617) 232-1393

Information Data Search (IDS) bills itself as "a modern, one-stop research and information center equipped to answer virtually any question you have on a wide variety of subjects, technical or general." IDS has access to more than 100 computer data bases nationwide and thus is in a position to choose those most likely to yield information customers request. Costs of the service vary according to the project, with quotes offered before research begins. IDS says a typical range for services is $14 to $500.

Lockheed DIALOG Information Retrieval Service
3460 Hillview Ave.
Palo Alto, CA 94304
(800) 227-1927; CA (800-982-5838)

The DIALOG service offers access to more than 30 million journal and newspaper articles, conference papers, and reports from over 100 data bases covering all areas of science, technology, business, medicine, social science, current affairs, and humanities. One example of its application might be for marketing a device for the handicapped. An entrepreneur could search a medical data base to ascertain product need and search a business data base to determine the present state of the market, including competition, dollar sales, and market share.

Nasa Industrial Application Centers

Several universities have information centers to provide technically oriented reports, studies, and literature searches. They provide access to over 150 data banks and National Aeronautics and Space Administration (NASA) research. A typical bibliography with 250 to 300 sources costs $100, but fees may range from $30 to thousands of dollars. Fees are discussed before research begins. The information centers are as follows:

Technology Use Studies Center
Southeastern Oklahoma State University
Durant, OK 74701

Technology Applications Center
University of New Mexico
Albuquerque, NM 87131

Western Research Application Center
University of Southern California
University Park, Los Angeles, CA 90007

New England Research Applications Center
Mansfield Professional Park
Storrs, CT 06268

North Carolina Science and Technology Research Center
P.O. Box 12235
Research Triangle Park, NC 27709

Knowledge Availability Systems Center
University of Pittsburgh
Pittsburgh, PA 15260

Aerospace Research Application Center
Administration Building
1201 E 38th St.
Indianapolis, IN 47401

Developing and Using a Business Plan

You are enthusiastic about an idea for a new business. You think the business has excellent market prospects and fits well with your skills, experience, personal values, and aspirations.

But what are the most significant risks and problems involved in launching the enterprise? What are its long-term profit prospects? What are its future financing and cash-flow requirements? What will be the demands of operating lead times, seasonality, and facility location? What is your marketing and pricing strategy?

Once you have convinced yourself and your partners that the answers to such questions are favorable, can you also convince prospective investors? If you seek out investment capital or loans, you will face much skepticism from venture-capital firms, banks, insurance companies, and other financing sources. For example, only 3 percent to 7 percent of proposals to venture-capital sources for start-up or ongoing financing are actually funded.

An effective business plan will convince the investor that you have identified a high-growth opportunity, that you have the entrepreneurial and management talent to effectively exploit that opportunity, and that you have a rational, coherent, and believable program for doing so.

The development of such a business plan is neither quick nor easy. Properly preparing a business plan can easily take 200 to 300 hours. Squeezing that amount of time into evenings and weekends can make the process stretch out to between six and twelve months. One might ask if such a time-consuming effort is really worth the trouble.

Wouldn't a more effective approach be to have an outside professional quickly prepare the business plan and then have the founders use their time to obtain financing and start the business?

REWARDS OF PREPARATION

Keep in mind that the careful preparation of a business plan represents a unique opportunity to think through all facets of a new venture. You can examine the consequences of different strategies and tactics and determine the human and financial requirements for launching and building the venture, all at no risk or cost.

One entrepreneur with whom I worked discovered while preparing a business plan that the major market for his biomedical product was in nursing homes rather than in hospital emergency rooms as he and his physician partner had previously assumed. This realization changed the focus of his marketing effort.

The business plan is thus an important way to evaluate the start-up venture.

For the investor, the business plan is the single most important screening device. Once the plan has passed initial screening, the investor may request the entrepreneur to make an oral presentation describing key features of the venture. If the investor is still interested, the plan will be given a more detailed evaluation and will become a prime measure of the founders' ability to define and analyze opportunities and problems and to identify and plan actions to deal with them.

A PLAN'S LONG-TERM VALUE

Most founders find the business plan to be even more helpful after start-up. As the founder-president of one venture that grew to sales of $14 million in seven years put it:

Once you are in the business, you realize that everyone, including the founders, is learning his or her job. If you have a thoughtful and complete business plan, you have a lot more confidence in your decisions. You have a reference already there to say, "Well, I have already run the numbers on inventory, or cost of goods, and this is what will happen."

If an outsider prepares the plan, you probably won't have the same sense of confidence and commitment.

The business plan can be especially valuable in the important area of product pricing. In one instance, the initial strategy of the founders of a rotary-drill venture was to price its products below the competition, even though the venture had a superior product innovation in a growing market. When the founders consulted outside experts, they were persuaded to price 10 percent over the competition.

By its second year, the new company enjoyed pre-tax profits of $850,000 based on about $9 million in sales. The revised pricing strategy made a significant difference. Without the detailed analysis of the industry and competition that is central to the marketing section of the business plan, it is unlikely that outsiders would have seen the basis for a different pricing strategy.

Feedback on your business plan by trusted and knowledgeable outsiders can help in refining strategy and making difficult decisions. A Nova Scotia entrepreneur who builds commercial fishing boats recently decided to raise his prices more than 40 percent based on an outside analysis and critique of his business plan. He knew he would lose two orders, but he also knew he would make more profit on the remaining three than all five at the old price. His delivery time would be cut in half as well. He's convinced that the shortened delivery time will lead to additional sales at the higher margins. And with up-front progress payments, he won't have to raise outside equity capital.

The process can also clarify the venture's financial requirements. Another entrepreneur with a three-year-old $1 million business erecting coal-loading sites believed he needed about $350,000 in expansion capital. After reflecting on a detailed critique of his business plan presentation, he concluded: "The worst thing I could do right now is put more money into the business. The first thing I should do is get my own backyard more in order. But I will be back in two or three years."

True to his prediction, he returned two and a half years later. His company was now approaching $3 million in sales and had a business plan for expansion that resulted in a $400,000 debt capital investment, without relinquishing any ownership.

COMMON MISCONCEPTIONS

Entrepreneurs tend to downgrade the business plan because of certain false notions they hold about it. Technical and scientific entrepreneurs share one misconception I call the "better mousetrap fallacy." They frequently place unwarranted faith in a product or invention, especially if it is patented. Indeed, technological ideas must be sound, but marketability and marketing know-how generally outweigh technical elegance in the success equation. The rotary-drill venture discussed earlier reached $40 million in sales last year, yet has no patents on its products.

To further illustrate, less than one half of 1 percent of the best ideas contained in the *Patent Gazette* five years ago have returned a dime to the inventors. In essence, the patent is usually a useful marketing tool, but not much else, and may be worth 15 percent or considerably less of the founding equity.

A second misconception new entrepreneurs often have is that the business plan is essentially a negotiating and selling tool for raising money. It isn't considered relevant or useful beyond that. Indeed, I have heard more than one entrepreneur comment that the plan is "destined for the circular file" once the funds are in the bank.

Such a view is dangerous for several reasons. To prospective partners, investors, or suppliers, it communicates a shallow understanding of the requirements for creating a successful business. It can also signal a promoting quality —a search for fast money and a hope for an early sellout—that creates mistrust of the entrepreneur. If the plan isn't a serious promise of what the team can deliver, should investors believe anything the founders assert?

A third misconception some entrepreneurs have is a belief that the primary and most important task in the start-up process is to determine if they can raise money as an indication that their idea is sound. This "cart before the horse" approach usually results in a hastily prepared business plan and exuberant shopping around among prospective investors.

Because most venture-capital firms are quite small—often no more than two or three partners—they generally cannot take the time needed to get to know each entrepreneur and to explain the details for rejection. They use the business plan for initial screening as well as for making investment decisions. I have met many entrepreneurs who, as much as two years later, still do not understand that they were unable to raise capital because their business plans were deficient.

A fourth misconception is a belief among some entrepreneurs that their particular plan has no fatal flaws. These entrepreneurs ignore the need to test the plan's soundness with knowledgeable outside sources. Entrepreneurs must search for flaws in the market analysis that would make further consideration of the venture unnecessary.

One potential flaw is excessive dependence on outside suppliers for important state-of-the-art components that materially affect product development and prices. Suppliers of Viatron, a computer leasing company that obtained substantial public and private financing in the late 1960s, helped drive the company into bankruptcy in large part because they were unable to produce several semiconductors at low enough prices to enable Viatron to meet its own heavily promoted inexpensive prices.

A final misconception among some start-up and early-stage entrepreneurs seeking venture capital is the belief that retaining a minimum 51 percent control of the company is essential. This view seems to assume that control depends on legal percentage ownership rather than on management's behavior. In short, 51 percent of nothing is nothing. Compare this with the 20 percent ownership retained by the four founders of Digital Equipment Corporation.

Sound investment partners do not want to run your company—they invest in you and your team. More than anything else in the early going, the founders' actions are the ultimate controlling influence on the venture.

PUTTING TOGETHER A BUSINESS PLAN

What format should the business plan take? The outline in the Exhibit on pp. 384–85 suggests one commonly used organizational approach. Entrepreneurs should also keep in mind some important general guidelines for preparing such plans:

1. Keep the business plan as short as possible without compromising the description of your venture and its potential. Cover the key issues that will interest an investor and leave secondary details for a meeting with the investor. Remember that venture-capital investors are not patient readers.

2. Don't overdiversify your venture. Focus your attention on one or two services or product lines and markets. A new or young business does not have the management depth to pursue too many opportunities.

3. Don't have unnamed, mysterious people on your management team, such as the Mr. G who will join you later as a financial vice president. The investor will want to know early on exactly who Mr. G is and what his commitment to your venture is.

4. Don't describe technical products or manufacturing processes in terms that only an expert can understand. Most venture capitalists do not like to invest in what they don't understand or think you don't understand.

5. Don't estimate your sales on the basis of plant capacity. Estimate your potential sales carefully on the basis of your marketing study, and from these estimates determine the production facility you need.

6. Don't make ambiguous, vague, or unsubstantiated statements. They make you look like a shallow and fuzzy thinker. For example, don't merely say

384

that your markets are growing rapidly. Analyze past, present, and projected future growth rates and market size, and be able to substantiate your data.

7. Disclose and discuss any current or potential problems in your venture. If you fail to do this and the venture capitalist discovers them, your credibility will be badly damaged.

8. Involve all of your management team, as well as any special legal, accounting, or financial help, in the preparation of the business plan.

9. Don't overstate or inflate revenue and accomplishments; be rigorously realistic and objective in making estimates and discussing risks.

The search for seed and expansion capital is usually time-consuming and exhausting. Failure under such circumstances can leave the founders illiquid and demoralized. A carefully prepared business plan can aid substantially in planning a new venture, screening would-be partners, evolving winning strategies, and joining with a sound investment source, before actually launching the venture. In other words, it can mean the difference between success and failure.

(This material on business plans was previously published as an article by Jeffry A. Timmons in the *Harvard Business Review* of March–April 1980.)

EXHIBIT

Outline for Preparing a Business Plan

Introduction

Summary of business plan and strategy

The company and its industry
The company
Discussion of industry
Strategy

Products or services
Description
Proprietary position
Potential
Technologies and skills

Market research and evaluation
Customers
Market size, trends, and segments
Competition—strengths and weaknesses
Estimated market share and sales
Ongoing market evaluation
Economics—margins, costs

Marketing plan
Overall marketing strategy
Pricing
Sales tactics and distribution
Service and warranty policies
Advertising and promotion
Profitability and break-even analysis

Design and development plans
Development status and tasks
Difficulties and risks
Product improvement and new products
Costs

Manufacturing and operations plan
Geographical location
Facilities and improvements
Strategy and plans
Labor force

Management team
Organization—roles and responsibilities
Key management personnel
Management compensation and ownership
Board of directors
Management assistant or training needs
Supporting outside professional services

Overall schedule (monthly)

Important risks, assumptions, and problems

Community impact
  Economic
  Human development
  Community development
  Environmental

*Financial plan (monthly for first
  year; quarterly for next two to
  three years)*
  Profit-and-loss forecast
  Pro forma cash-flow analysis
  Pro forma balance sheet
  Break-even charts

Proposed company offering
  Desired financing
  Securities offering
  Capitalization
  Use of funds

Source: Jeffry A. Timmons, Leonard E. Smollen, and Alexander L. M. Dingee, Jr., *New Venture Creation: A Guide to Small Business Development* (Homewood, IL: Richard D. Irwin, Inc., 1977), p. 426.

Outline of a Venture-Capital Investment Agreement*

What follows is a detailed outline of the contents of a venture-investment agreement. The main sections of a typical agreement are briefly described and many of the terms that might appear in each section are noted. However, not all of the terms listed will appear in an investment agreement. Venture-capital investors select terms from among those listed (and some not listed) to best serve their needs in a particular venture-investment situation. For more detail on investment agreements we recommend the papers by Gardner[1] and Stewart.[2]

1. Description of the Investment

This section of the agreement defines the basic terms of the investment. It includes descriptions of the:
a. Amount and type of investment.
b. Securities to be issued.
c. Guarantees, collateral subordination, and payment schedules associated with any notes.
d. Conditions of closing: time, place, method of payment.

When investment instruments are involved that carry warrants, or debt conversion privileges, the agreement will completely describe them. This description will include:
a. Time limits on the exercise of the warrant or conversion of the debt.

---

* Excerpted from Jeffry A. Timmons, Leonard E. Smollen, and L. M. Dingee, Jr., *New Venture Creation* (Homewood, IL: Richard D. Irwin, Inc., 1977), pp. 599–602, used with permission.

[1] W. E. Gardner, Jr., "Venture Capital Financing: A Lawyer's Checklist," *The Business Lawyer*, Vol. 26, No. 1 (January 1971), p. 997.

[2] M. D. Stewart, "Venture Capital: Semi-Industry," *Venture Capital* (New York: Practicing Law Institute, 1973, Publ. 44–1092), p. 29.

b. Price and any price changes that vary with the time of exercise.
c. Transferability of the instruments.
d. Registration rights on stock acquired by the investor.
e. Dilution resulting from exercise of warrants or debt conversion.
f. Rights and protections surviving after conversion, exercise, or redemption.

2. Preconditions to Closing

This section covers what the venture must do or what ancillary agreements and documents must be submitted to the investor before the investment can be closed. These agreements and documents may include:
a. Corporate documents: e.g., bylaws, articles of incorporation, resolutions authorizing sale of securities, tax status certificates, list of stockholders and directors.
b. Audited financial statements.
c. Any agreements for simultaneous additional financing from another source or for lines of credit.
d. Ancillary agreements: e.g., employment contracts, stock option agreements, key man insurance policies, stock repurchase agreements.
e. Copies of any leases or supply contracts.

3. Representations and Warranties by the Venture

This section contains legally binding statements made by the venture's officers that describe its condition on or before the closing date of the investment agreement. The venture's management will warrant:
a. That it is a duly organized corporation in good standing.
b. That its action in entering into an agreement is authorized by its directors, allowed by its bylaws and charter, legally binding upon the corporation and not in breach of any other agreements.
c. If a private placement, that the securities being issued are exempt from registration under the Securities Act of 1933 as amended, under state securities law, and that registration is not required under the Securities Exchange Act of 1934.
d. That the capitalization, shares, options, directors, and shareholders of the company are as described (either in the agreement or an exhibit).
e. That no trade secrets or patents will be used in the business that are not owned free and clear or if rights to use them have not been acquired.
f. That no conflicts of interest exist in their entering the agreement.
g. That all material facts and representations in the agreement and exhibits are true as of the date of closing (includes accuracy of business plan and financials).
h. That the venture will fulfill its part of the agreement so long as all conditions are met.
i. That any patents, trademarks, or copyrights owned and/or used by the company are as described.
j. That the principal assets and liabilities of the company are as described in attached exhibits.
k. That there are no undisclosed obligations, litigations, or agreements of the venture of a material nature not already known to all parties.
l. That any prior year income statements and balance sheets are accurate as

presented and have been audited. And that there have been no adverse changes since the last audited statements.

m. That the venture is current on all tax payments and returns.

4. Representations and Warranties by the Investor

This section contains any legally binding representations made by the investor. They are much smaller in number than those made by the company. The investor may warrant:

a. If a corporation, that it is duly organized and in good standing.
b. If a corporation, that its action in entering into an agreement with the venture is authorized by its directors, allowed by its bylaws and charter, legally binding upon the corporation, and not in breach of any existing agreements.
c. If a private placement, that the stock being acquired is for investment and not with a view to or for sale in connection with any distribution.
d. The performance of his or her part of the contract if all conditions are met.

5. Affirmative Covenants

In addition to the above representations and warranties, the company in which the investor invests usually has a list of affirmative covenants with which it must comply. These could include agreeing to:

a. Pay taxes, fees, duties, and other assessments promptly.
b. File all appropriate government or agency reports.
c. Pay debt principal and interest.
d. Maintain corporate existence.
e. Maintain appropriate books of accounts and keep a specified auditing firm on retainer.
f. Allow access to these records to all directors and representatives of the investor.
g. Provide the investor with periodic income statements and balance sheets.
h. Preserve and provide for the investor's stock registration rights as described in the agreement.
i. Maintain appropriate insurance, including key man life insurance with the company named as beneficiary.
j. Maintain minimum net worth, working capital, or net assets levels.
k. Maintain the number of investor board seats prescribed in the agreement.
l. Hold prescribed number of directors' meetings.
m. Comply with all applicable laws.
n. Maintain corporate properties in good condition.
o. Notify the investor of any events of default of the investment agreement within a prescribed period of time.
p. Use the investment proceeds substantially in accordance with a business plan that is an exhibit to the agreement.

6. Negative Covenants

These covenants define what a venture must not do, or must not do without prior investor approval; such approval not to be unreasonably withheld. A venture usually agrees not to do such things as:

a. Merge, consolidate with, acquire, or invest in any form of organization.
b. Amend or violate the venture's charter or bylaws.
c. Distribute, sell, redeem, or divide stock except as provided for in the agreement.
d. Sell, lease, or dispose of assets whose value exceeds a specified amount.
e. Purchase assets whose value exceeds specified amount.
f. Pay dividends.
g. Violate any working capital or net worth restrictions described in the investment agreement.
h. Advance to, loan to, or invest in individuals, organizations, or firms except as described in the investment agreement.
i. Create subsidiaries.
j. Liquidate the corporation.
k. Institute bankruptcy proceedings.
l. Pay compensation to its management other than as provided for in the agreement.
m. Change the basic nature of the business for which the firm was organized.
n. Borrow money except as provided for in the agreement.
o. Dilute the investors without giving them the right of first refusal on new issues of stock.

7. Conditions of Default

This section describes those events that constitute a breach of the investment agreement if not corrected within a specified time and under which an investor can exercise specific remedies. Events that constitute default may include:
a. Failure to comply with the affirmative or negative covenants of the agreement.
b. Falsification of representations and warranties made in the investment agreement.
c. Insolvency or reorganization of the venture.
d. Failure to pay interest or principal due on debentures.

8. Remedies

This section describes the actions available to an investor in the event a condition of default occurs. Remedies depend on the form an investment takes. For a common stock investment the remedies could be:
a. Forfeiture to the investor of any stock of the venture's principals that was held in escrow.
b. The investor receiving voting control through a right to vote some or all of the stock of the venture's principals.
c. The right of the investor to "put" his stock to the company at a predetermined price.
   For a debenture, the remedies might be:
a. The full amount of the note becoming due and payable on demand.
b. Forfeiture of any collateral used to secure the debt.
   In case of a preferred stock investment, the remedy can be special voting rights (e.g., the right to vote the entrepreneur's stock) to obtain control of the board of directors.

9. Other Conditions

A number of other clauses that cover a diverse group of issues often appear in investment agreements. Some of the more common issues covered are:

a. Who will bear the costs of closing the agreement; this is often borne by the company.
b. Who will bear the costs of registration of the investors' stock; again, the investors like this to be borne by the company for the first such registration.
c. Right of first refusal for the investor on subsequent company financings.

Glossary of Financial and Venture-Capital Terms

Acceleration Clause
In a commercial loan agreement, the outstanding loan balance becomes due immediately (at the lender's option) if the borrower is in default of the repayment schedule or other covenants and restrictions in the agreement.

Advance Rate
In accounts receivable financing, the percentage of the eligible accounts (usually those less than sixty to ninety days old) against which a loan is advanced.

Affirmative Covenants (in commercial loan or venture-capital agreements)
Those specific actions that the recipient of loan or investment funds must perform, such as maintaining a minimum net worth, to meet the requirements of the loan or investment agreement.

Amortization
The repayment of a loan through periodic, equal installments including both interest and principal.

Bailout Provision
An agreement that provides the investor with options for selling his ownership stake when a public market for the securities does not exist.

Balloon Payment
A lump-sum payment at the end of the amortization of a loan in order to fully retire the debt, while drastically improving cash flow over the life of the loan.

Bank Clearing Days
In factoring or receivables financings, the time between the customer's remittance of an account receivable and the date the lender credits the account to the borrower's loan balance.

Bond
A long-term promissory note, often ten to twenty years, that is generally secured by some assets of the borrower.

Buyback
An agreement between small-business founders and the venture capitalists to enable the founders to repurchase the stock acquired by the investor, at some predetermined terms.

Capitalization
Includes the total long-term capital in a venture-debt, preferred and common stock, capital surplus, and retained earnings.

Capital Surplus
The amount paid by an investor to the issuer of original stock that exceeds the par value; sometimes called paid-in surplus.

Cash Flow (positive)
When the sum of all cash receipts exceeds cash disbursements for a given period.

Chattel Mortgage
A mortgage on personal property other than real estate, such as furniture, machinery, or equipment, usually of an intermediate term; now called a security agreement.

Clean-up Provision
An agreement, usually part of a loan agreement, that requires the borrower to pay off short-term bank borrowings for a certain period each year, usually sixty days.

Collateral
Assets pledged to a bank, finance company, factor, or other lender to secure a loan, and which the lender can liquidate to recover the loan in the event of default.

Compensating Balance
An amount of money left on deposit by borrower. The bank usually keeps 10 percent to 20 percent of the loan, which is used as collateral against the loan, and which increases the effective interest rate on the loan.

Conditional Sales Contract
A method to finance new equipment by purchasing it in installments over a one- to five-year period, and in which the seller retains title until all payments have been made.

Contribution
Gross margin on the difference between the selling price and variable costs.

Convertible Debenture
An unsecured loan that, at the lender's or investor's option, may be converted into common stock at a predetermined price and number of shares.

Convertible Preferred Stock
Same as a convertible debenture except the preferred stock has the conversion option.

Covenants and Restrictions

Specific terms and conditions in a loan or investment agreement which define what the small-business recipient can and can't do insofar as paying dividends, accumulating additional debt, and making other financial decisions; also can specify financial ratios that must be maintained to prevent the loan from being called or foreclosed on.

Current Ratio

Current assets divided by current liabilities, which defines liquidity; 2 to 1 or better is normal.

Debenture

An unsecured long-term loan obligation.

Debt-to-Equity Ratio

Total liabilities divided by total stockholder equity, which indicates the degree of the firm's leverage; normally 1½ to 2.

Dilution Clauses

Provisions which govern the extent to which an investor's percentage of stock ownership will be maintained or altered if stock or warrants are sold at a price less than the investor paid.

Equity Kicker

A provision in a debt or preferred stock investment that enables the investor or lender to participate in the capital gains if a company performs well; usually in the form of warrants, conversion rights, or stock privileges.

First-state Investment

A venture-capital investment in a firm with one to a few years of operating history, beyond start-up, where the risks are still high but much lower than start-ups.

Float

A temporary overstatement of a bank balance to the extent deposits exceed the amount actually cleared on checks written.

Gross Margin

See *Contribution.*

Inventory Lien

A lender's right to sell inventory designated as collateral for a loan in the event of default.

Leverage

The extent to which debt, rather than equity, is used to fund a business. Increasing leverage can increase return on equity, but also increases the need for cash flow to cover debt amortization.

Leveraged Buyout

An arrangement whereby investors or entrepreneurs use debt and the underleveraged assets of a business to finance the purchase of the business.

Lien

A lender's security interest in collateral (see *Collateral, Inventory Lien*).

Line of Credit
An agreement with a bank to provide short-term credit on an as-needed basis, up to an agreed-upon limit, by transferring funds to the firm's checking account.

Liquidity
The extent cash and near cash assets meet or exceed maturing loan and credit obligations.

Loan Agreement
The legal document that specifies the terms and conditions of the loan between the lender and borrower.

Maturity
The date on which a loan or debt obligation becomes due and payable; short-, intermediate-, and long-term.

Mortgage Note
A long-term debt instrument which secures a specific piece of real property, such as land, building, or house.

Note Payable
A written promise to pay unconditionally a specific sum of money on demand or at a particular time.

Net Worth
A firm's or individual's total assets less total liabilities.

Personal Guarantee
A personal pledge by a borrower of all, or part, of one's net worth as collateral for the firm's loan.

Prepayment Option
The specific right in a loan agreement to repay part or all of the debt prior to its maturity date.

Prepayment Penalty
A specific clause in a long-term loan agreement which imposes a charge for early repayment of a loan; used to discourage refinancing when interest rates decline.

Preferred Stock
An equity instrument that has no voting rights, but carries a dividend requirement and has preference ahead of common shares, but behind creditors, in the event of liquidation.

Private Placement
The sale of stock or debt directly to individual investors, such as high-tax-bracket person or institutions; usually exempt from federal and state regulations common to public stock offerings.

Regulation A
A private placement of stock by which a small firm can raise up to $2 million, with assistance of an underwriter, without the stringent and costly federal requirements of an ordinary public offering.

Revolvers
Lines of credit which are rolled over continually after the initial maturity has been reached.

Rollovers
The constant renewal of short-term debt.

Second-stage Financing
A venture-capital investment in a young firm, usually during years three to six, when the firm has several million dollars in profitable sales.

Secured Loan
A loan with personal or business assets pledged as collateral.

Seed Capital
Start-up funds, usually from personal resources and other informal sources, used to launch a venture before revenue and cash are generated.

Subordinated Debt
A note or debenture whose claim on the firm's assets is secondary or junior to some or all lenders.

Term Loan
Normally, a debt commitment by a lender to a firm for three to five years, with quarterly repayments.

Third-stage Financing
A venture-capital investment in a rapidly growing firm, often five to ten years old or more, with sales of $5 million to $10 million or more and substantial profit and growth prospects.

Two-tier Rate
A lower interest for small firms, offered by over 100 banks in the U.S.

Unsecured Loan
A note or loan that has no collateral pledged to cover it.

Venture Capital
Investments in start-up or early-stage technology, manufacturing, and other growth-oriented ventures usually shunned by commercial and governmental finance sources as too risky.

Warehouse Receipt Loan
A specialized secured loan used to finance inventory stored in a public warehouse or in a designated area on the borrower's premises.

Warrant
A specific clause in an investment agreement that provides an option to the investor to purchase a certain number of shares at a specific price for an agreed time period. It enables an investor to participate in a substantial upside capital gain, should the market stock price exceed the warrant price.

Index